THE ATHENIAN WOMAN

Ceramics are an unparalleled resource of evidence about women's lives in ancient Greece, since they show a huge number of female types and activities. Yet it can be difficult to interpret the meanings of these images, especially when they seem to conflict with literary sources. This much-needed study shows that it is vital to see the vases as archaeology as well as art, because context is the key to understanding which of the images can stand as evidence for the real lives of women and which should be reassessed.

Sian Lewis considers the full gamut of female existence in classical Greece – childhood and old age, unfree and foreign status, as well as the ageless woman characteristic of Athenian red-figure painting. Specific topics investigated include domestic labour, women's work outside the household, seclusion, status and relationships with men. Dr Lewis explores the reasons for the artistic focus on some areas of women's lives and the neglect of others. The text also engages with deeper issues of methodology and explores current debates about the portrayal of women in classical art.

Accessible, informative and lavishly illustrated with more than 150 photographs and line drawings, *The Athenian Woman: an iconographic handbook* is indispensable as a guide for students and a resource for academics in the disciplines of ancient gender, ancient history and classical art and archaeology.

Sian Lewis is Lecturer in Ancient History at the University of Wales, Cardiff. She is also the author of *News and Society in the Greek Polis* (1996).

THE ATHENIAN WOMAN

An iconographic handbook

Sian Lewis

London and New York

First published 2002
by Routledge
11 New Fetter Lane, London EC4P 4EE

Simultaneously published in the USA and Canada
by Routledge
29 West 35th Street, New York, NY 10001

Routledge is an imprint of the Taylor & Francis Group

© 2002 Sian Lewis

Typeset in Garamond by
Keystroke, Jacaranda Lodge, Wolverhampton

British Library Cataloguing in Publication Data
A catalogue record for this book is available from the British Library

Library of Congress Cataloging in Publication Data
Lewis, Sian.
The Athenian woman: an iconographic handbook/Sian Lewis.
p. cm.
Includes bibliographical references and index.
ISBN 0–415–23234–1—ISBN 0–415–23235–X (pbk.)
1. Woman—Greece—History—Sources.
2. Woman—History—To 500—Sources. 3. Women in art.
4. Pottery, Greek—Themes, motives. I. Title.

HQ1134 .L49 2002   2001058922
305.4'09495—dc21

ISBN 0–415–23234–1 (hbk)
ISBN 0–415–23235–X (pbk)

CONTENTS

ILLUSTRATIONS

Note on illustrations

One can never provide as many illustrations as one would wish: I have therefore tried to illustrate representatively, and, where a pot is not illustrated, to make reference in the notes to other recent works or collections of images where an illustration can most easily be found.

In the interests of clarity, I have included in references to pots as much information as possible: current collection, Beazley catalogue number(s), attributed artist (if useful) and provenance. Where no provenance exists for a pot (the majority of cases), this is indicated by 'n.p.'. The use of names of attributed painters is intended as a convenience, and should not be taken as a statement of belief in artists as individuals.

All line drawings (except figs. 1.2, 2.1, 2.25) are by Zadia Green, © Z.A. Green 2001.

ACKNOWLEDGEMENTS

The writing of this book has been a long process, and I am pleased to be able to thank so many people who have assisted in different ways. I am grateful to the Arts and Humanities Research Board and to my own institution, the University of Wales Cardiff, for their support of the sabbatical which enabled me to complete the project. Many colleagues and students at Cardiff and elsewhere have contributed discussion and practical advice, particularly Nick Fisher, James Whitley, Robin Osborne, Stephen Mitchell, Paul Nicholson, Doug Peksa, Lloyd Llewellyn-Jones, Fiona Hobden and Esther Cox. My thanks are also due to Richard Stoneman, to Liz O'Donnell as production editor, and to the anonymous reader for Routledge for comments on part of the manuscript. My greatest debt is to Catherine Bousfield, without whose patience and assistance such a complex project could not have been completed, and to Alan Fidler who, as copyeditor, saved me from more errors than I care to imagine.

Thomas Mannack of the Beazley Archive, Oxford, offered invaluable advice and assistance; the importance of the Beazley Archive in the researching of this book is hard to overestimate. I am also grateful to the many curators of museum collections all over the world who assisted with photographs and permissions, and in particular George Ziombakis (Museum of Fine Arts, Houston), Christopher Atkins (Museum of Fine Arts, Boston), Karin Sowada (Nicholson Museum, Sydney), Amy Smith (University of Reading), Simon Bean (Liverpool Museum), Mette Catharina Hermannsen (National Museum of Denmark), Nicole G. Finzer (Art Institute of Chicago), Margaret Evangelista (Accademia dei Lincei, Rome), Giorgia Masone (DAI Roma), Michael Vickers (Ashmolean Museum, Oxford), and Dr H.A. Cahn. Professor François Lissarrague very kindly gave permission to reproduce several of his drawings. All other line drawings were prepared by Zadia Green, whose enthusiasm was as important to me as her artistic skill.

The support of family and friends has been invaluable to me throughout the project; most of all, no one could have been more patient and encouraging than my partner Robin MacKenzie. I said many times that this book would never be finished, but now it is.

Sian Lewis

INTRODUCTION

Fountains and fictions

The black-figure hydria illustrated in fig. 0.1 was made and painted in Athens *c*.520 BC. A hydria is a type of container designed for carrying water, having two horizontal handles for lifting, and one vertical at the back for pouring. This example is now in the British Museum; its painter is identified as the A.D. Painter, to whom some ten other pots have been attributed.[1] The illustration on the pot depicts women fetching water at a fountain-house. Four women, their flesh shown in added white paint, stand filling their water jars at animal-head and equestrian spouts, among the columns of the fountain. Two of them reach up to place garlands on the spouts, which are also decorated with branches. Three of the jars shown are the same type as the hydria itself, and two are more rounded shapes. The interpretation of this scene is usually presented as perfectly straightforward: it is a scene of 'everyday life', drawn from the painter's own experience in Athens. The illustration of a fountain, and women fetching water from it, is an appropriate decoration for a water jar: the hydria illustrates its own function, and because hydriai were regularly used by women, a scene of women is doubly appropriate. The status of the women depicted offers a subject for debate based on their appearance and activity: are they slaves or free women?

I have chosen this pot as an example with which to begin because it demonstrates very well some of the pitfalls of the desire to find direct illustration of Athenian women's lives in vase-painting. A photograph, especially of a hydria, can be very deceptive. Until the mid-fifth century, hydriai were divided by painters into two zones for decoration – the body and the shoulder – with a 90 degree angle between them. A photograph of the body scene thus tends to obscure the shoulder scene, and vice versa. The cropping of photographs also obscures the frieze which runs under the main field. On London 329 (fig. 0.1), the shoulder scene depicts Herakles fighting the giant Kyknos, and under the fountain-house scene runs a predella of opposed lions and boars. It is easy to say that water jars carry water scenes, and that this represents suitable subject matter for women's pots, but what is Herakles doing here, and the beasts appropriate to the Homeric hunt? These are not scenes of 'real life': how can the iconography be coherent?

Many hydriai follow this pattern, combining a fountain-house scene on the body with an exploit of Herakles on the shoulder (e.g. fig. 2.15, p. 73); one example in Boulogne (fig. 0.2, p. 3) brings these elements together in the most surprising way.[2] The body of the pot shows a fountain-house at the right, with a woman filling a hydria. Herakles is depicted in the centre of the scene attacking a snake and a small lion which emerge from the fountain. To the left stands Athena with her chariot. This suggests that distant though

1

Figure 0.1 Attic black-figure hydria, London, British Museum B329, *c*.520 BC. Courtesy British Museum. © The British Museum.

Figure 0.2 Attic black-figure hydria, Boulogne, Musée Communale 406, *c*.510 BC.
Photo: B. Devos, courtesy Château-Musée, Boulogne-sur-Mer.

the individual motifs may appear, they are indeed connected – that the scenario of the fountain is not 'real' in any easy sense. Suggestions for the interpretation of this image are various: some see a version of Herakles' labour in the Garden of the Hesperides, while Boardman interprets it as a figurative labour of Herakles taking place in a fictionalised Athens, possibly depicting an actual ceremony at a real fountain-house.[3] He suggests that the woman can be thought of as figurative as well, 'an attribute of the fountain'. Such an argument, however, must be open to question: if we think women on hydriai in general are real, can we decide that this female figure is not real because she appears in the same scene as Herakles? A fountain-house scene on another black-figure hydria in the British Museum, on which the deities Dionysus and Hermes stand at each side of a fountain-house, further indicates the interpenetration of the mythical and the realistic.[4] Other images current on black-figure hydriai, such as bridal processions and warriors arming, also tread the boundary between myth and reality, so why should women be different?

Second, in what sense was this hydria 'used for fetching water'? The hydriai carried by the women in the painting are not miniature representations of our pot: they are plain and undecorated. The A.D. Painter's hydria was found not in Athens, nor in the remains of a house, but in the tomb of a wealthy Etruscan in Vulci in Northern Italy, placed there as a grave offering by the relatives of the dead person. There is no indication that the hydria was ever used for its ostensible purpose: most Athenian black-figure pots were made, decorated, and immediately exported for sale in Italy.

Finally, the relationship between form and function. The A.D. Painter has credited to him (or her) eleven hydriai, of which eight depict women at the fountain, with martial scenes on the shoulder: one shows women picking fruit in an orchard, one Athena and Herakles, and one mythical creatures (sirens). The shoulder scenes depict Dionysus and his attendants.[5] The identified output of just one painter, then, shows considerable variation of subject. The hydriai are not always decorated with water scenes: chariots, gods, the labours of Herakles and warriors arming are all equally numerous. Nor, for that matter, are water scenes confined to hydriai: they appear on amphorae and lekythoi (oil-flasks) as well. In fact the production of hydriai with fountain scenes is a speciality of one group (workshop) of painters, centred around the Priam Painter. The popularity of fountain-house themes lasts from 530 to 500 BC, after which the theme dies out and hydriai are decorated primarily with scenes of myth. One cannot argue a necessary connection between form and decoration, independent of other influences. The fountain-house scene thus serves to show that images on pottery cannot be extracted from their context and interpreted uncritically. The relation of one scene to the decoration of the whole pot; the provenance of the pot and its actual use; the relation of the scene to those on similar pots, all serve to qualify and question a single interpretation.

Pottery: the nature of the evidence

Athenian figure-decorated pots have been preserved in very large numbers. In museums and collections across the world, tens of thousands of pots and fragments are displayed or stored. The scenes they show are usually unique: there are very few true repetitions of designs from one pot to another. Most of those we possess are repetitive genre scenes, often poorly executed: there are hundreds of unimaginative scenes of athletes, women conversing, warriors arming or leaving home. Any attempt to comment on so large a field inevitably becomes an exercise in filtering: it is impossible to know and present every example, so scholars concentrate on the best examples of themes, the most striking, the clearest or the most aesthetically appealing. The rushed, the indistinct and the bad receive very little attention. Most concentrate on one particular artist or one particular theme, or offer an overview of development, one example at a time. This leads to the creation of a 'canon' of pots on specific themes: whenever that theme is discussed, a few high-quality examples are reproduced. The black-figure amphora in New York with scenes of weaving by the Amasis Painter is a case in point: it is in fact one of the very few examples of wool-work in black-figure, yet its detail and skill of execution make it very hard to resist, and it is always reproduced in discussions of female life.[6] This illustrates one of the difficulties of research on pottery: how can coverage of the pots be made representative? If there are a thousand examples of a particular scene, one can illustrate it a few times and say 'there are many more'; if there are only two examples of a scene, one can illustrate both, and the reader will be left with the impression that both scenes are equally representative. What if there are a thousand examples of one type, and only one counter-example? How can a sense of balance be maintained? And finally, if there are no scenes of a particular type, how can one illustrate a meaningful absence?

This is part of a larger question: how do we know when an absence is meaningful? Recently attempts have been made to calculate the proportion of total Athenian pottery output which survives today. How representative is the sample which we have? Calculations have been made based on one type of pot, the Panathenaic amphora.[7] These were produced for the festival of the Great Panathenaia in Athens, held every four years in the period 560 to 310 BC, at which prizes were awarded in the form of specially decorated pots of high-quality Athenian olive oil. Each pot carries on one side a picture of Athena, in whose honour the games were held, and on the other the event in which the prize was won. More importantly, each pot carries the name of the magistrate presiding in the year it was made. This allows an accurate assessment to be made: if we know how many pots were made each year (one per event in the games), we can judge how many were made in total through the period in which these prizes were awarded. The conclusion is perhaps surprising: we possess between 0.5 and 1 per cent of the total Panathenaic amphorae made. This may be high compared to less special pots: there is some evidence that Panathenaic amphorae were valued as heirlooms, and so may have survived in larger numbers than ordinary pots. Relating this to pottery overall, the sample that we have of total output, although quite large in absolute numbers, is in fact a vanishingly small proportion of the whole. Can we be sure that it is representative, that scenes which appear to be uncommon are not just under-represented through accidents of survival, or that scenes which appear to be frequent are simply fortuitously better preserved? In general terms, it is possible to be fairly confident that our sample is not too badly skewed: one can trace the development of Athenian painting through time in a way which seems fairly smooth, and the proportions of genre scenes which we have (and their quality) indicate that we have preserved a lot of the mass market. But the caveat is worth bearing in mind when considering some under-represented topics.

The question of the circumstances of preservation of Greek pottery is also of great relevance. Pottery has survived in such quantities because of its innate qualities (resistance to decay), but also because, by and large, the Greeks did not use their pots as we use ceramics today, that is, for domestic or decorative purposes. Enormous numbers of pots were placed in tombs as offerings to the dead, and it is from these tombs that they have emerged in such large numbers. Excavations in cities and sanctuaries have found some evidence of figure-decorated pottery deposited as votive offerings or used in public and domestic contexts, it is true, but still more than 80 per cent of the total has been recovered from tombs.[8] Ongoing excavation makes it unlikely that areas of other significant use will be found, so this statistic must be borne in mind. It relates to the vexed question of provenance, or rather the lack of it, which is the besetting problem of pot studies. Most pots, as I have said, were excavated from tombs, primarily in Italy but also in Greece, in the eighteenth and nineteenth centuries.[9] Only about half of recovered pots have a recorded provenance today; the rest have no recorded origin, either because they were the product of unsystematic and unpublished excavation, or because they were stolen or looted from tombs and sold on to unquestioning collectors. The provenance of a pot sold long ago and now in a museum simply cannot be traced. Modern excavations have produced some well-documented groups of pots from tombs in Greece, but an enormous amount of information has vanished for good. This means that any statistical analysis of the origins of pottery is necessarily based on weak foundations; in many cases we will never know where a pot came from, or what it was used for.

In recent years new technologies have taken their place in the investigation of theme and iconography. There has been a development from book-based to computer-based catalogues, making search tools much more flexible and powerful. Any system, however, is only as good as the information and structure with which it is set up; statistical analysis is much more easily done, but this does not make it any more sound.[10] Computers can search a catalogue very widely and rapidly, but they have paradoxically made scholars more dependent on someone else's listing and interpretation of imagery. More seriously, there remains a heavy bias, rooted ultimately in the aesthetic standards of earlier scholars, in favour of Attic pots. Fabrics other than Attic – Corinthian, Boiotian, Ionian, Italian and Etruscan – were regarded as 'minor', and were therefore not listed and catalogued in the same systematic way; nor are the catalogues which do exist properly integrated into the current system.[11] This makes it very difficult to trace a theme across different fabrics, and leads to even greater concentration on Attic painting.

The state of the subject

Such a diverse body of material, and such difficulties in its handling, has produced a variety of different responses among modern scholars. There is a current debate among archaeologists about the value of rival approaches to ceramic imagery. Traditionally the 'connoisseurship' approach has concentrated on the identification of artists and groups, and the detailed description and elucidation of individual scenes and decoration. Clearly, without the bedrock of this approach the study of imagery would be impossible; no one can deny the value of Beazley's initial cataloguing of Attic pots, which created the study of ceramic iconography.[12] Nevertheless, the study of individual pots or groups often all but ignores meaning in the search for style and relative date, and ends up isolating pots because of a concentration on artificial constructs like painters and potters. The habit of naming painters encourages us to think of them as individuals, artists expressing personal style and preferences in their work, but this is fallacious. Painters of Athenian pots are not real individuals: peculiarities of style and execution in a pot's decoration are used to assign it to a particular hand, and each group of pots is given a name. The assignment of pot to painter is subject to constant revision and dispute: the work of 'the A.D. Painter', for instance, was later thought by Beazley to be the work of 'the Priam Painter' instead.[13] 'The A.D. Painter' is thus a twentieth-century invention, who enjoyed a brief existence but has now been subsumed into a different invented personality. It is easy to start crediting painters with personalities and ideas, but the arguments are inevitably circular.[14]

More recently this approach has been challenged by 'iconology', a method which seeks to evaluate imagery across the whole range of available pottery, concentrating on the ideology which underlies painting as a thought system. While this has provided some very valuable studies, there is a tendency to treat all scenes as the same, all born from the collective consciousness of the polis, and hence to draw completely generalising conclusions.[15] Considerations such as economics, use, findspots and the differing circum-stances of potential viewers are sidelined as one discovers the ideals of the polis laid bare. In its most extreme form, iconology sees a codified system of meanings across all images, as though the production and decoration of pottery were controlled by a single entity, expressing an unvarying set of ideas.

In fact the extreme forms of both these views have attracted criticism: few accept that pots are documenting life, just because they are lifelike, nor do many sink individual differences into a 'polis' interpretation. But the central question is whether pots can be considered more alike by similarity of shape, of theme, or of attributed artist. Is a pelike with a picture of Theseus on it more like another pelike with a different picture, or more like a pyxis with a theme of Theseus? Or is it more like an oinochoe with a picture of Medea attributed to the same hand? Different scholars privilege different links in their work: some concentrate on particular shapes (e.g. Philippaki, *The Attic Stamnos*, or Kurtz, *Athenian White Lekythoi*), others on specific artists (e.g. Buitron-Oliver, *Douris*, Lezzi-Hafter, *Der Eretria-Maler*), and yet others on particular themes (e.g. Kilmer, *Greek Erotica*, or Pfisterer-Haas, *Darstellungen alter Frauen*).[16] Clearly none of these has a monopoly on correctness. My own aim in this study is to bring together iconology and archaeology: to bring attention to the archaeological background of the pottery to bear on the interpretation of the imagery. Such an approach, for the reasons outlined above, is not easy to apply but, where knowledge of provenance and use can be combined with iconological 'reading', it can open up new understanding of our evidence.

Pots and literature

Do we need illustrations on Greek pottery to tell us that Athenian women visited fountains in order to fetch water? Essentially, no: literary sources would make us quite well aware that they did, even if not a single representation of the activity had been found. Herodotus tells us that the tyrants in Athens constructed fountains for the benefit of their subjects, and comedy indicates that women fetched water from them, and that this was a public arena where men and women met.[17] What, in that case, can vase-painting add, apart from a purely illustrative role? Scenes by the Priam and A.D. Painters were certainly used in 1930 to provide evidence for the construction and appearance of fountain-houses.[18] But the relationship of visual evidence to literature needs careful analysis. The tradition of using pots to illustrate ideas derived from literature is long-standing, as is the use of literary sources to elucidate the imagery. And in its simplest sense, vase-painting can provide knowledge of objects and processes too mundane or too trivial to find their way into the literature – clothes, for instance, household equipment or armaments. Aspects of female life too mundane to be recorded in literary sources can also be recovered through visual evidence, such as the mother shown with her baby sitting in a high-chair (fig. 0.3).[19]

All too often, however, pottery and literature are contradictory. To return to the fountain-house scenes, so far as the mechanics of the job are concerned the historians and artists are in agreement: that women in Athens regularly fetched water from public fountains. But the quotation from Herodotus illustrates the problems of further interpretation. Initially, he says, Athenian citizen women carried out this task; only after the Persian Wars was it deputised to slaves. This comment has caused continuing problems for analysts of the pottery; the women depicted at the fountain-house do not appear (from their dress or hairstyle) to be slaves. Extensive analysis has been applied to fountain scenes, with the intent of determining the status of the women involved; the task has proved intractable, status being one of the most vexed questions of female iconography on pottery.

This demonstrates that pots and literature cannot be read in tandem for mutual confirmation. Statements about the role and preoccupations of women are not congruent in the two media: they emphasise different roles. For example, there is a huge emphasis

Figure 0.3 Attic red-figure cup, Brussels, Musées Royaux A 890, *c.*460 BC (drawing of detail). Reproduced by permission of Prof. F. Lissarrague.

in written sources on the importance of status within Athenian society – on the gulf which separated slave and free, citizen and non-citizen, wives and other women. Scholars operating with these distinctions, explicitly or implicitly, encounter difficulty with iconography, since status is one of a set of aspects which are very hard to discern in Attic (and other) imagery; in most cases it is impossible to identify clear expressions of citizen, non-citizen or slave status, direct or symbolic. The point has often been made that one cannot ask of an image questions which it is not able to answer, and this is precisely where the investigation of status leads. We expect to bring presuppositions from literature to bear on pots, and are disappointed when the images cannot be made to accord clearly with the evidence. In their reluctance to lose what we 'know' from literature, scholars have advanced evermore complex arguments: because pots fail to illustrate the stereotypes familiar from oratory, they are taken to be a sophisticated commentary on these stereotypes, subverting and commenting on them, and probably only explicable if the customer has read his Apollodorus.[20] In a similar way, literature establishes our expectations about the importance of certain occupations. Comedy, for instance, presents the self-sufficient farmer as the quintessential Athenian hero (Trygaeus in *Peace*, Dikaiopolis in *Acharnians*, Strepsiades in *Clouds*), yet representations of agricultural life are very scarce on pottery: we see much more commercial activity than we do farming. Legal activity is central to Athenian self-perception in literature, yet there is not one painted scene of a law court. The record of pottery is therefore often seen as skewed, fragmentary, incomplete as compared to literature, when the truth is that neither tells us the whole story. The purpose of this study is therefore to examine literary and iconographic evidence side by side: to expose both where they agree, and where they disagree, using each to comment on the other.

Female iconography

It is not new to observe that Athenian (and other Greek) pots cannot be treated as a homogeneous group. Some pots were made and sold in Athens itself, to be used in domestic contexts, or as votive offerings. Others were created for a specific purpose within a particular community and were used only for that purpose, such as the white-ground lekythoi, which are extremely common as burial deposits in Athens and Eretria and rare outside these places. Yet others were created solely for an export market, and were exported en masse to Etruria, where they were placed in tombs.

When considering the topic of women, both chronological and geographic distribution of scenes are important. Images of women change through time, with themes becoming fashionable and then fading in popularity. Scenes of mourning and the fetching of water are common in black-figure, whereas slaves, sex and domestic work appear in archaic red-figure. The repertoire of female scenes becomes much more standardised and limited after 440 BC; many of the topics common in early red-figure, such as symposia, sex, courtship and domestic work, disappear, to be replaced by scenes set in domestic interiors, preparations for weddings, and funerary scenes. The most striking feature of any study of female iconography is this huge increase in thematic types which takes place in the later period; at about the time of the Peloponnesian War, images of women at home or engaged in ritual come to dominate decorated pottery. There is at the end of red-figure a tendency to abstraction, with the female head emerging as a decorative theme, and more stylised versions of familiar themes. This change in emphasis is mirrored by a change in distribution: black-figure pottery was primarily an export product, giving Athens dominance in the markets of the West, and this trade continued with the invention of the red-figure technique. After the middle of the fourth century, however, more decorated pottery began to be used in Attica, and the increase in female scenes after 440 BC happens largely on pots which stay in Attica – pyxides, lekythoi and hydriai. Rather than using all images of women indiscriminately, we have to be alive to these changes, and to ask why fashions should come and go.

The stance of those using pottery as a medium for the study of social life is that theme is the most significant factor: that one can draw together a range of pots of different shapes, by different hands, and from different periods, and gain useful information by analysing them. Pursuing a history of women in this way, however, will not work. Defining themes is an entirely subjective process – we can gather images under a heading, but there is no ancient source which can indicate whether contemporary ideas about pictures on pots would agree with the categorisation. Images are grouped into themes such as 'domestic', 'sympotic', 'erotic', which are mapped by modern cultural perspectives. The category of erotica is a case in point: for red-figure pots it was defined by Kilmer in his study *Greek Erotica*, but his selection of images is not self-defining. Really his group of images is defined as those which seem erotic to a modern viewer, which break our taboos or concentrate on activities we define as sexual.[21] To this extent we create the study as we investigate – by deciding what to investigate one predetermines some of one's interpretations. Clearly there is a danger that a study of 'women on pots' will do exactly this, bringing together widely varying images and presenting them as a unitary theme. What I aim to do as an antidote is to restore the archaeology to the approach, asking where and why pots were made, and how this affects our reading of the imagery.

This also allows questions of reception to be applied. A primary consideration must be what use women themselves made of decorated pottery. It has become a truism that women in Greece did not buy pots themselves, but had them chosen and bought by male relatives, and that certain types of pot such as pyxides and lekanides were created and decorated for exclusively female use. But what do we know about female use of pots? There is evidence for women as 'users' of pots, in the widest sense. Women dedicated pots to deities in sanctuaries across Greece, as inscriptions attest: a black-figure lekythos with a Dionysiac scene was dedicated to Hera at Delos by a woman named Phanyllis; pots were dedicated by women to Artemis at Brauron. Many fragments of pots from the Athenian Agora carry 'owner's marks', among which are nineteen with female names, on pots as varied as bowls, skyphoi, cups and stands. The names vary from slave-type ethnics through to citizen names.[22] Other inscriptions reveal an eye-cup decorated with warriors, awarded as a prize to a woman named Melosa in a carding contest at Taranto, and a present of a black-glaze kantharos to a woman from her husband in Boiotia, 'that she may drink her fill'.[23] Both of these run against the grain of our expectations, in that the Taranto cup, illustrated with hoplites in battle, would not seem an appropriate subject for a female contest, and the kantharos shows a wife drinking (in a festival context) with the approval of her husband. The Taranto cup might make us reconsider some ideas about 'appropriate' subject matter, especially given the cup's status as imported object in the Greek colony of Taranto; it may be that we expect too close a match between decoration and purpose. On pots themselves women are depicted using pots in ritual: sacrifice, weddings and tomb offerings, in cooking, in the gynaikeon (lekythoi and pyxides), in symposia, both with men and alone (kylikes and skyphoi). Women used pots to earn a living – one example (a hydria in Milan) shows us a woman painting a pot – and they used them in death: fig. 0.4, a detail of a krater in New York, shows a dead woman, newly arrived in Hades. Her chin is still tied with the binding used in the laying out of the dead, and she holds the alabastron which has accompanied her to the grave.[24]

Figure 0.4 Attic red-figure krater, New York, Metropolitan Museum of Art 08.258.21, 440–430 BC (drawing of detail). After Richter/Hall fig. 135.

These examples indicate that one need not always assume a male viewer in order to interpret the imagery, and this is a further problem of iconological approach. There is frequently a rather glib labelling of pots as 'symposium shapes' or 'women's pots', which draws the commentator into interpreting them only from the point of view of the assumed viewer. The discussion of black-figure hydriai above has already exposed the folly of this, as has the eye-cup presented to Melosa. It should not be so surprising to suggest that an image would reach a range of potential viewers, Greek, Phoenician, Etruscan, female, slave, male, and might offer a different interpretation to each. It is more difficult to be alive to these alternative interpretations, and to use the archaeological evidence wherever possible to provide a real situation for particular images, but a number of recent articles have demonstrated the value of such an approach.[25]

Setting the agenda

The traditional tendency to use Athenian vase-painting solely to illustrate conclusions drawn from literary sources has, thanks to modern methodological awareness, all but vanished, but in its place lurks the opposite danger. Any student of Greek pottery cannot fail to be impressed by the variety of themes chosen by the painters, the wealth of roles in which women and men are shown. It is possible to adopt a diametric opposite of the traditional approach, and draw an account of female experience only from the pottery. One can reconstruct a female life from vase-painting: childhood, marriage, participation in ritual, work in the household, and death, with a brief detour for sex and slavery. If an activity such as music is illustrated by the pot-painters, it is evaluated and given its place in the reconstruction. The danger is that silences and omissions will be ignored. Painters preferred to illustrate certain activities, very often those of the elite, but others, either because they were not depicted, or because their depictions have not been found, are absent. Also, fashion in pot-painting itself plays a part: the pioneers of red-figure show interest in a huge range of novel themes, particularly trade, and the depiction of variant human types, both of which fade away after 450 BC. Similarly, themes from the theatre are very prominent in Italian red-figure painting, while domestic and athletic scenes become much more generic. We must remain aware of the twists and turns of our evidence; if one is led to discuss only what one can show on a pot, the version of female experience resulting will reflect the potter's choice and the accidents of preservation, rather than creating a balanced and comprehensive account. Silence and absence, then, will play some part in my analysis.

My aim in this book is thus to approach iconography not with expectations derived from literature, nor as a symbolic system complete within itself, but purposely to expose and explain the divergences between the images of Athenian women offered by competing sources. I hope to present a rounded picture, taking images in their context, indicating where our evidence fails or is lacking, and examining the nature and purpose of female representations. Rather than focusing solely on women as objects of the gaze, I will try to bring to the fore woman as subject, as reader, and to consider the multiple readings available in the imagery of vase-painting. The conclusions thus drawn about women's experiences will not be simple, nor easily reached, but they will be founded on a contextualised reading of all branches of the evidence. In structure the study is organised into five thematic chapters, taking their lead from the iconography (although themes such as status and reception are pursued across the whole). In the first chapter, I consider

11

representations of the female life cycle, noting the painters' emphasis on maturity and the moment of marriage, but examining too how painters treat (or do not treat) stages such as infancy, childhood and old age. Chapter 2 considers women's labour and the representation of domestic work, focusing on the nature and purpose of such imagery. Chapter 3 turns to images of female labour outside the house, concentrating particularly on the figure of the 'hetaira' in vase-painting, a topic on which the disparities with literary evidence become acute; I examine the problematic representation of female sexuality, and the relationship between the ideologies of painting and those expressed elsewhere. Chapter 4 treats representations of women at leisure within the house, examining the symbolism of pastimes, pets and furniture, and the responses of female users. The final chapter treats relationships between men and women, where the evidence is again at odds with literature: pots allow one to investigate ideas about courtship and intergenerational relationships.

1

BECOMING VISIBLE

Many of the processes of a Greek woman's life are mysterious to us. Comparative studies suggest that the central concerns of female life in the ancient Mediterranean were the family, including childbirth and child-rearing, events such as marriages and funerals, illness and death, and domestic chores.[1] Yet in the case of classical Greece we know little of women's early childhood, of female friendships, of training for married life, or of the experience of motherhood, probably the most significant emotional relationship in any woman's life. In part this is due to the lack of literary sources written from a female perspective, but it is also a result of the agenda of Greek artists. A lekythos in Oxford attributed to the Providence Painter (fig. 1.1) illustrates very effectively the image of Greek women transmitted by pottery: an ageless and serene figure stands alone on a pot, lifting a chest in a vague domestic task; she is well-dressed, carefully depicted with clothes and jewellery as an object to be admired.[2] Both image and activity are abstract, and the agelessness of the figure removes it from any consideration of the roles played by women throughout their lives – as daughters, sisters, wives, mothers and grandmothers. Can such an image offer any comment on the reality of female life at Athens?

Ceramic evidence, just like literature, is partial. It is possible to construct a cradle-to-grave story of female life using pots as illustrations, but only at the price of a very broad-brush use of evidence, taking scenes from disparate periods and regions to create an apparent whole.[3] The lekythos in fig. 1.1 is a case in point: it appears to encapsulate the image of the ideal Athenian woman, yet it comes from Greek Sicily, from Gela, as do most of the lekythoi attributed to the Providence Painter (and indeed most red-figure lekythoi in absolute terms). The image was exported (possibly in a batch if the attributions to an individual artist are correct), and placed by an Italian Greek in a tomb. It was not painted for a specifically Athenian audience, nor was it a photographic representation of real life. A closer examination of the evidence is needed to determine the ways in which women became visible, both to Greek artists and to the citizens themselves. The woman of the Athenian potter appears in certain roles (as wife, as mourner, as worshipper), but is very infrequently shown in others (as young girl, as grandmother, as widow). Some aspects of female life such as ritual are richly illustrated; others, such as pregnancy, are never depicted. This arises at least in part from the use of the objects themselves; where pots were used in ceremonies or in practice, they tend to illustrate the occasion of their use, and hence evidence is plentiful, but where pots were not used, evidence is often lacking. This chapter will consider female life in the polis through the prism of ceramic iconography, to examine the ages of woman, and how they are (or are not) depicted on pottery.

From the cradle . . .

Let us begin at the beginning, with the birth of a girl. This immediately illustrates the nature of our evidence, since there are no scenes of childbirth on extant Greek pottery. The reason for this is complex, since childbirth was not a taboo subject: in other media, images of pregnancy, labour and birth are all found. On Athenian grave stelai, for instance, scenes of women in labour are frequent, relating either to mothers who died in childbirth, or to midwives as illustration of their profession. Although scenes of actual birth are rare, pregnancy is sometimes depicted.[4] Birth is shown more fully on votive plaques and terracottas portraying pregnant women, or birth itself, which were dedicated in shrines across Greece, undoubtedly as offerings to pray (or give thanks) for successful delivery (fig. 1.2).[5] Certainly birth is a topic more appropriate to some media than others, yet given the funerary use of so much pottery it is surprising that painters should avoid a theme so close to reality. From a comparison of the frequency of their depiction on pots, one would conclude that childbirth had a negligible importance, and that marriage was the most important event of female life. Pots illustrating weddings or preparation for marriage are extremely numerous, yet simply counting numbers of scenes does not expose the underlying meaning of the representations. Circumstances of survival play a part, since pots, especially loutrophoroi and lebetes gamikoi, were used in marriage ritual, and regularly carry images of their own function.[6] The vessels used in marriage ceremonies were subsequently dedicated at the sanctuary of the Nymph on the Acropolis, and those who died unmarried often had them placed in their tombs, so they have tended to survive in the archaeological record. In contrast, pottery does not appear to have figured in rituals of birth: we are perhaps influenced by thoughts of our own customs in seeing birth as a moment for commemoration – in the ancient world, most babies would die, so their existence was less assured at the time of birth. But just because childbirth does not appear on pottery does not mean that it was not important to women: the birth of a child was a moment of

Figure 1.1 Attic red-figure lekythos, Oxford, Ashmolean Museum 1925.68, 470–460 BC. Photo courtesy The Ashmolean Museum, Oxford.

Figure 1.2 Cypriot terracotta, Cyprus Museum, seventh century BC. After P. Dikaios, *A Guide to the Cyprus Museum* (Nicosia, Cyprus Government Printing Office, 1947), pl. 25.2.

enormous social significance. A marriage was completed not by the ceremony but by the birth of the first child, and the mother thereby completed the transition from parthenos to wife.[7] Perhaps because of this, labour and birth formed, from the indications of both images and texts, an intensely private and female occasion. We have hints in Attic comedy that it was an occasion on which women gathered, with men excluded, and births were largely overseen by midwives.[8] It was an occasion of great danger for the mother, and hence one in which the favour of the gods was essential. The arenas in which women celebrated successful birth were also private – by dedications of plaques, terracottas or personal belongings at the shrine of female deities – and were not rituals in which pottery played a part. As a personal and private event, childbirth never became a theme of pottery, which celebrated the public aspects of Greek life.

That birth was considered a private female domain can be seen by comparing those scenes of birth which do appear on Greek pottery: mythological births. Scenes of the birth of gods and heroes are frequent: we see Athena and Dionysus emerging from Zeus' head and thigh, Helen emerging from the egg, or Erichthonios being born from the soil of Attica itself.[9] What these births have in common is of course their unnatural nature: the divine child emerges fully formed, either from the ground or from some part of a male deity. Only those births completely outside the regular pattern are depicted, the supernatural elements completely divorcing them from the pain and danger of normal birth. The only exception to this rule is Leto, mother of Artemis and Apollo: although representations of Leto actually giving birth appear only on non-Greek reliefs, pyxides found at Brauron depict her labour, or Leto with her infants.[10] This is not coincidental: Artemis was the protector of women in labour, and Brauron the most important centre of her worship in Attica. The appearance of the scene illustrates the difference between male and female worlds; as we shall see, the creation of special shapes or scenes for women's rituals is particularly linked with the rites of Brauron.

But if we see no female baby at birth, what about infancy? With childcare, as with other themes, reproducing a few well-known images can give a distorted view of ancient attitudes; it is easy to put together a set of images of mothers and children, both mythical and non-mythical, but context is of great importance. The representation of children on pottery was slow to develop, clearly because early artists found it difficult to depict babies and older children accurately. Babies are not shown in black-figure at all (one example on a pinax by Exekias demonstrates the struggle to define an iconography of the child), and children appear only in genre scenes such as mourning families, the departure of warriors, or with women at the fountain-house.[11] In red-figure an iconography distinguishing infant, toddler and child gradually develops, and the range of scenes in which children are depicted becomes wider. Babies appear most often in the hands of a mother or nurse, as on the hydria in Harvard on which a nurse in a sleeved garment reaches out to take a baby from its mother (fig. 1.3), or another in London, on which a nurse hands a baby to its mother.[12] The intention behind representations of children, however, is of a distinctive

Figure 1.3 Attic red-figure hydria, Harvard University, Sackler Art Museum 1960.342, *c.*430 BC. Photo: Michael Nedzweski. Courtesy of the Arthur M. Sackler Museum, Harvard University Art Museums, Bequest of David M. Robinson.

kind. The fact which needs emphasising is the funerary meaning of most of these images – rather than pictures of 'everyday life' they are pots illustrating death. The most obvious examples are those found on white-ground lekythoi, which were used in Attica and Euboia only, as funerary dedications, and on these the child of either sex is often shown in death: on a lekythos in private hands, a little girl stands at a tomb and holds out a doll (fig. 1.8); on another in Athens a child seated on the shoulders of a slave girl reaches out to his mother (fig. 1.4); a famous example in New York shows a male child gesturing to his mother as Charon's boat approaches to take him to the Underworld.[13] The lekythoi share the iconography of tomb monuments, and girls are depicted in death in this way, although boys are more commonly shown.

It is from white-ground painting that some of the more moving examples of mother–child relationships come, such as the white-ground cup found in a tomb at Athens (fig. 0.3), which shows a mother holding out her hand to a young child seated in a high-chair. The expression of this kind of emotion was a private matter, rather than an aspect of Athenian life for public display and export, and the same is often true of child representations on red-figure pots: the Harvard hydria (fig. 1.3) is regularly used to illustrate female life, but it is one of several pots from the same source, a tomb in Vari (Attica); it forms a pair with another hydria, also in Harvard, which depicts three women preparing for a visit to the tomb.[14] In the light of both context and decoration it seems reasonable to read the mother and child scene as funerary in meaning too, reflecting the iconography of both white-ground lekythoi and grave monuments.

Figure 1.4 Attic white-ground lekythos, Athens, National Museum 12771, *c.*450 BC. Photo courtesy National Archaeological Museum, Athens.

This fact has implications for the representation of children. One factor which has received much discussion in recent years is the idea that all of the infants depicted on pottery are male, and that a canonical twisting pose is given to babies by painters, designed to present the male genitals to clear view. This practice is presumed to be in the service of an ideology: the production of a male heir was one of a wife's main roles, and so the depiction of a woman with boy child is a scene of a job well done. To illustrate a girl child would be second best.[15] This assumes that the role of the imagery is to endorse fundamental social attitudes, but in fact the evidence is more complicated than this view implies. Several pots, it is true, present mother and baby in a domestic setting, babies which are shown to be male. Others, however, depict infants of indeterminate gender: the white-ground lekythos in Athens (fig. 1.4) shows a child sitting on the shoulders of a slave, and a red-figure example in Oxford a child whose sex is obscured by the arms of its mother. We have already seen the white-ground cup (fig. 0.3) with a child in a high-chair.[16] In mythological scenes, the baby Erichthonios is sometimes shown in the twisting pose that emphasises his masculinity, but on other pots attention is not focused on the gender of the baby. What is really significant, though, is that babies on pots provide us with a clear example of the unrealistic nature of artistic representation, since the swaddling of babies was the norm in Greece. This can be hard to remember, as in the images of mothers and babies most commonly reproduced swaddling is absent; but there is clear evidence that it was considered essential to the well-being of the infant. Literary sources are explicit that infants in classical Greece were swaddled, at least for the first months of life; it was considered necessary for the correct formation of the child's limbs, and methods and duration are discussed in the medical texts.[17] The depiction of the swaddled child is uncommon on pots – babies are depicted in 'heroic' nakedness, with swaddling bands sometimes present (as on a scene of the birth of Erichthonios on a kalpis in London), but never used. There is an obvious contrast between pottery and other media over such depictions: among terracottas, for instance, images of the swaddled child are found as dedications (fig. 1.5), and in the arms of nurses, and the same is true of grave stelai – for example, a stele in Paris on which a woman and servant hold twin swaddled babies.[18] Not all babies on stelai are swaddled, but nor are all the naked ones male: on the grave stele of Ampharete, for example, the deceased woman is shown holding her grandchild, which is wrapped in her own mantle, leaving only its head unobscured. The sex of the infant cannot be determined, and the accompanying inscription also avoids defining the child's gender:

τέκνον ἐμῆς θυγατρὸς τόδ᾽ ἔχω φίλον, ὅμπερ ὅτε αὐγὰς ὄμμασιν ἠελίο
ζῶντες, ἐδερκόμεθα, ἔχον ἐμοῖς γόνασιν καὶ νῦν φθίμενον φθιμένη ᾽χω.

[I hold the dear child of my daughter, whom I held on my knees while we were both alive and beheld the light of the sun; and now that we are both dead I hold (the child) still.][19]

Similarly, on the stele of Phylonoe an infant is shown with a cloth wrapped around its waist. There is greater realism in the iconography of sculpture and terracotta than on pottery, and the indeterminacy of the gender of infants may therefore be deliberate, since

Figure 1.5 Italian terracotta, London, British Museum 68.1–10.725, *c.*450 BC. Photo courtesy British Museum. © The British Museum.

stelai were required to suit a variety of customers. In most of these cases, however, the artist's focus is on the dead mother, and we may be wrong to assume that the child is the focus of the image; they are as likely to be commenting on the parent as the child, and it is worth remembering that the Sotades white-ground cup was found in a woman's grave. If this is the case there is no need to screen out female children in favour of male. The typical scene emphasises interaction between mother and child, with the child often making very adult gestures to reach out to the mother, something which swaddling would simply obscure, reducing the personality of the infant. The few instances of swaddling depicted on a pot provide an interesting counterpoint: a scene of a warrior departing on a red-figure lekythos includes a woman holding a swaddled child, and in this instance neither the gender of the child, nor its interaction with its parents, are important; it serves solely as an indicator of the marriage relationship.[20] If pots illustrating children are funerary, then the interaction of mother and child is most important, not the gender of the child or the mother's achievement – especially if the child has died. While it may be true, therefore, that baby girls were more visible in death than in life, it is not true to say that they were totally devalued in art.

If female babies are infrequently visible in Greek art, the same is not true for girls past the age of infancy. Greek potters are interested in small girls in a number of specific roles, each of which provides valuable illustration of aspects of child life. Athens offers a particularly good resource for the depictions of young children, through the group of pots known as choes, miniature jugs associated with the festival of the Choes, part of the Anthesteria. Choes are abundant because both in Athens and Eretria they were buried with children who had died young. The age of celebrating the Choes festival was around three, so a child reaching this stage had a good chance of growing up, while a child dying before this age was buried with a chous as a memorial to lost childhood.[21] Participation in the festival was an early rite of passage, and while choes carry a range of scenes, associated more or less closely with the festival, the greatest number depict children, singly or in groups, in a range of ages from late infancy to older childhood. Most depict boys, but a significant proportion carry images of girls. Modern conceptions of gender in the analysis of choes imagery are interesting: in his extensive examination of the iconographic pattern of choes, Hamilton refers to 'the virtual absence of females from the paintings on the small choes', a view echoed by Demand, who suggests that girls played no part in the Choes festival.[22] Such a view, however, is pessimistic: van Hoorn's catalogue includes thirty-nine choes illustrating girls, and Hamilton himself notes forty-three. This should suggest that choes were given as presents to girls too, and that the disparity in numbers simply reflects the proportion of child deaths.[23]

Given the range of images, we can draw several conclusions about the depictions of girls as children. They are shown as babies with choes and cakes, playing with balls and roller carts; as toddlers and older children they appear with pets, especially Maltese dogs, carrying trays, driving carts, interacting with younger children, and playing in mixed-sex groups. On fig. 1.6 from Athens a girl balances a stick on one finger; she is attended by her pet dog, and a bunch of grapes (a reference to the festival) hangs in the background.[24] Surprisingly little distinction is made between male and female pastimes: both girls and boys play with balls, carts and animals. The choes are engaging as a celebration of the energy and playfulness of childhood, and artists' attitudes towards girls are just as positive as towards boys. Children are not shown segregated by gender, but play together in mixed

Figure 1.6 Attic red-figure chous, Athens, National Museum 1322, *c.*420 BC. Photo courtesy National Archaeological Museum, Athens.

groups, as on a chous in London, on which a boy and a girl hold a hoop for a dog to jump through, or another in Munich on which a girl and two boys play together.[25] Even in depictions of older children with babies there is no sign of different roles for girls: both sexes hold out toys or rattles to entertain younger children. The only significant difference in the treatment of choic girls and boys lies in their costume: boys appear naked more often than not, but girls are usually clothed, and appear as miniature adults (fig. 1.7). This is no doubt because the representation of female infants and children presented an artistic difficulty: if a girl is too young to be provided with female characteristics in physical form, how else can she be marked as female except by dress? A female infant needs to be given adult clothing, jewellery and an elaborate hairstyle to mark her gender.[26] It is an interesting question as to why we should see groups of boys playing, but not groups of girls; they appear in mixed groups, or with one boy, but never in pairs or more. It has been suggested that sister relationships were comparatively rare except among the very wealthy, and perhaps we are meant to envisage the children of choes as family groups.[27] Images on choes, then, suggest that in early childhood girls were valued, and that they shared the same roles as boys both at the festival and in death. Choes depict girls as part of the life of the family and city, well-fed, well-dressed and important to their family.

Youth

Choes, nevertheless, are the only major group of pots which exhibit an interest in girls as children. Once past this rite of passage, girls offered far less interest as a topic for painters than boys. One has to ask whether this represented reality or convention, since it is the red-figure painters who introduce new themes of child life into their art at the beginning of the fifth century, and while we can find newly popular themes of boys at school, playing games, with their fathers in public, or in the women's quarters, depictions of young girls do not begin to match them in frequency.[28] In fact girls fall out of the picture just as boys enter it with scenes of masculine childhood. This possibly reflects a distinction between public and private, with boys a part of the visible public world in the Greek city, while girls took part in fewer activities beyond the household. But it also reflects a contrast between forms of art for private and public consumption: pottery which is exported displays a view of Greek life in which girls are of limited importance, but within the city the visibility of girls is far greater. For example, contemporary grave stelai offer a very full depiction of female childhood: a separate iconographic category exists for young girls,

Figure 1.7 Attic red-figure chous, St Petersburg, The State Hermitage Museum P1867.89 (ST 2259A), *c.*350 BC. Photo courtesy the State Hermitage Museum, St Petersburg.

who are shown wearing high-waisted dresses emphasising their undeveloped figures, and like the girls on choes they are shown with pets, especially dogs, with birds such as doves, and with playthings associated with childhood such as balls.[29] It is not coincidental that the objects held by girls on stelai were those dedicated later on to mark the end of childhood: they are a clear reference to the preoccupations of childhood. Little of this spills over onto pottery, and where there are parallels they are to be found on white-ground lekythoi, again indicating the importance of the child in death: one white-ground lekythos in New Orleans depicts a woman and a girl on either side of a tomb, the little girl holding up a doll (fig. 1.8), and another in Harvard shows a woman and little girl at a tomb.[30] Girls might have had little or no role to play in public, but were clearly valued by their families and became visible in death.

At this point it is interesting to compare the literary evidence for this part of female life. Texts produced by men tend to focus on marriage as the central event of a girl's life, and girls rarely have a part to play if too young to be marriageable: they become relevant to male concerns only in their early teens. Texts produced by women, however, offer a different perspective, describing friendships between young girls, childhood games, and the training of girls in the domestic skills they will need in marriage.[31] There is some difficulty in adopting this evidence wholesale for Athens, since the poets who write about female friendships are from either the archaic period (Sappho) or the Hellenistic (Erinna), and neither is Athenian. Similarly texts from early Greece (Sparta and Lesbos) offer evidence of groups of young women trained as choirs, to sing and dance at weddings and festivals, and we might assume that similar kinds of training took place in Athens, although our sources do not say so. How far girls socialised among themselves we simply cannot know – in images of childhood Athenian pots very rarely show more than one or two girls together. There is, however, a thread common to both female poets and to Athenian tragedians, which depicts female childhood as a period of calm and happiness, before the alienation and loss of family brought about by marriage. If this is a traditional literary motif, it may reflect popular beliefs:

αἳ νέαι μὲν ἐν πατρὸς
ἥδιστον, οἶμαι, ζῶμεν ἀνθρώπων βίον·
τερπνῶς γὰρ ἀεὶ παῖδας ἄνοια τρέφει.
ὅταν δ᾽ ἐς ἥβην ἐξικώμεθ᾽ ἔμφρονες,
ὠθούμεθ᾽ ἔξω καὶ διεμπολώμεθα

Figure 1.8 Attic white-ground lekythos, New Orleans (private collection) 460–450 BC (drawing).

θεῶν πατρῴων τῶν τε φυσάντων ἄπο,
αἱ μὲν ξένους πρὸς ἄνδρας, αἱ δὲ βαρβάρους,
αἱ δ᾽ εἰς ἀγηθῆ δώμαθ᾽, αἱ δ᾽ ἐπίρροθα.

[As young girls, I think, we lead the sweetest life of all mortals in our father's house; for innocence always keeps children in happiness. But when we reach the age of marriage, we are thrust out and sold away from our ancestral gods and our parents, some to strangers, some to barbarians, some to a good house and some to a hostile one.][32]

It remains, however, that there are no depictions on extant pots of girls' friendships, or of the process of training for marriage, beyond the odd image of girls with groups of women (see Chapter 2). A cup in New York is sometimes reproduced as a scene of a girl being educated, but it is not compelling as evidence: in the interior of the cup, a woman holding writing tablets is led by another woman, and has been described as a 'reluctant schoolgirl', but she is adult, not a child, and the scenes on the exterior of the cup show similar women with no educational setting.[33] This aspect of female life is simply closed to us, because vase-painters (or rather their customers) were not interested in these activities.

There are, nevertheless, two domains in which young girls are of interest to pot-painters because of the significance of their presence: mourning and ritual – and girls are in fact more visible in these areas than boys because of their particular status within the family and city. Black-figure painters produced both plaques and pots with scenes of prothesis, where the dead person is laid out, surrounded by mourners. These were buried with the dead, or dedicated on the Acropolis, and hence offer good evidence for mourning practices. In these scenes of family mourning, small girls are unusually prominent, as can be seen on the well-known plaque on which a small girl sits with hand to head in mourning on a stool at the right of the prothesis scene.[34] Boardman, in a study of black-figure funerary plaques, notes the frequency with which a girl is depicted standing at the end of, or beneath, the bier; on ten of his thirty-nine examples, a small girl mourner is among the women. A plaque from Dresden (fig. 1.9) depicts a little girl among the mourners at the bier, tearing her hair in adult fashion.[35] The relationship of these small figures within the family is made clear on a plaque by the Sappho Painter in the Louvre, which labels each participant in the scene with their role (MHTHP, ΘHΘH), the girl standing at the head of the bier is ΑΔΕΛΦΗ, sister to the deceased, not child.[36] While boys are occasionally present too, the girl is more frequently depicted, presumably to represent the completeness of the family's grief, down the generations. Women had the primary role in mourning, because of their capacity to bear the pollution of death, and pots emphasise that this responsibility began for women in early childhood. It is interesting that girls are so commonly shown as part of the extended family; the large numbers of mourning women in funerary scenes suggests that the prejudice against raising female children cannot have been as great as is sometimes suggested. An extension to the ritual role of girls in mourning is found on a loutrophoros in Karlsruhe (fig. 1.10) depicting a wedding procession, in which one of the women leads a small girl by the hand, and also on a volute-krater in Ferrara, which has a scene of Dionysiac worship where women dance and handle snakes, two small girls among them. Both of these suggest that from an early age girls were required to fulfil the female role in family ceremonies together with the older women.[37]

Figure 1.9 Attic black-figure plaque, Dresden, Antikensammlung 814, *c*.520 BC. Photo: H.-P. Klut, courtesy Staatliche Kunstsammlungen, Dresden.

Figure 1.10 Attic red-figure loutrophoros, Karlsruhe, Badisches Landesmuseum 69/78, *c.*440 BC. Photo courtesy Badisches Landesmuseum, Karlsruhe.

The other area where iconography becomes interested in the young girl is public ritual, specifically the pottery produced in relation to female rites of passage. This relates mainly to the pottery finds from Brauron; large numbers of miniature kraters have been found, at Brauron and at other shrines of Artemis in Attica, used in, and illustrating, the ritual of 'playing the bear' for Artemis Brauronia. These have been extensively documented by Kahil, and like the choes are a category of evidence used and found solely in Athens.[38] Some show girls in procession to an altar, others girls' races, clothed and naked. As well as the young girls who play the 'bear', racing or dancing, we find older women helping the girls to prepare for the rite (fig. 1.11), and the priestess herself playing the role of the bear.[39] Dedications of all kinds by women were common at Brauron, from textiles to valuable metal vases, because it was a site of particular importance for women. Our evidence, however, demonstrates a three-way split between pots, archaeology and literature, each of which emphasises different aspects of the ritual. Krateriskoi show girls running naked, some of the bear symbolism, and the involvement of mothers in the rite. Aristophanes' *Lysistrata* (644–645 BC) refers to the wearing and shedding of the krokotos, a yellow tunic, as the central act of the ritual; but this act is not depicted by painters, nor indeed is any identifiable krokotos. Archaeology reveals the dedication of both textiles and pots, including small versions of the epinetra used in textile work.[40] The discovery of large numbers of figure-painted pots at Brauron, with images of the rites, has caused concern that the images cannot easily be squared with the play or its scholia, but this is undoubtedly because different aspects of the rites are reflected in the different objects associated with them. This in turn has led to some more interesting features of the Brauron material being overlooked. Given that the rare appearances of Artemis as a child with her mother Leto appear on pyxides from Brauron, we might see in the depictions an aspect of female bonding and solidarity; Artemis was not only a god of maturation but protected children as kourotrophos, as well as helping women in childbirth and menarche. A series of terracottas from Brauron shows the goddess with a young girl, and the evidence from

Figure 1.11 Attic red-figure krater fragment, Basel, Collection H. Cahn, inv. HC501, 430–420 BC (drawing).

Brauron offers us a very specific view of a women's rite, in which mothers prepare daughters for their maturation and marriage, in an all-female milieu.[41] It suggests a dimension to relations within the family not reflected in the texts, reinforcing bonds down the female generations, and one which may also be paralleled in sources from other states, such as the pottery from Corinth depicting all-female festivals (fig. 1.30). On some of the Corinthian examples young girls appear alongside the women, and it may be that there is a rich vein of female experience here which is only hinted at in our sources.[42] An epigram of Nossis from the third century records a dedication made to Hera by Nossis and her mother, in which the women draw attention to the continuity of matrilineal descent:

'Ηρα τιμήεσσα, Λακίνιον ἁ τὸ θυῶδες
πολλάκις οὐρανόθεν νεισομένα καθορῇς,
δέξαι βύσσινον εἷμα, τό τοι μετὰ παιδὸς ἀγαυὰ
Νοσσίδος ὕφανεν Θευφιλὶς ἁ Κλεόχας.

[Queen Hera, you who from heaven often look down upon your fragrant Lacinian shrine, accept this linen garment which Theuphilis daughter of Kleodoche wove for you, with her noble daughter Nossis.][43]

Other rituals placed young girls in a position of importance to the city, and these too can be documented from a combination of art and literature. The festival of the Anthesteria, for instance, involved swinging as a ritual activity, and this is shown on nine black- and red-figure pots. Young girls are prominent in the black-figure swinging scenes, sometimes with other children, and although the theme later expands into an erotic motif (see Chapter 3), the pots place girls at the centre of the ritual.[44] Second, there are many scenes in both black- and red-figure of women engaged in ritual fruit-picking in orchards, and a hydria in Pregny has a scene of this with a little girl at its centre (fig. 1.12).[45] Third, and best documented, are the festivals of Athena. The well-known (and much-debated) passage in *Lysistrata* (638–647 BC) detailing female participation in civic religion lists the rites in which aristocratic young women would take part – as arrêphoros, aletris, arktos and kanêphoros. These are presented as canonical stages through which girls would pass, yet the passage names two roles which we can barely illustrate from extant pottery, namely the aletris, or grinder of corn for Athena, and the arrêphoros, who took part in the rites of Athena at the Panathenaia. A lekythos from Paestum (fig. 1.13) depicts a girl walking, holding sprigs in her hands, followed by a woman who shades her with a parasol, and it has been suggested that we should see here an arrêphoros taking part in the festival of the Panathenaia.[46] Other literary sources tell us that ritual ball-games played a part in the duties of the arrêphoroi, and one fragment of a red-figure cup seems to illustrate this.[47]

Figure 1.12 Attic red-figure hydria, Pregny, Collection Rothschild, *c*.460 BC (drawing).

26

Figure 1.13 Attic red-figure lekythos, Paestum, Museo Nazionale Archeologico, *c.*480 BC (drawing).

All of these roles are specific to a particular period of female life, between puberty and marriage, when a girl became a parthenos. The idea of the parthenos, marriageable but not yet married, was very important in ritual terms, and in their depictions of parthenoi pot-painters seem to reflect the same ideology as Athenian writers, who made the parthenos central to their preoccupations because the role was so significant. Dramatists represented the parthenos as the self-sacrificing heroine of plays like *Antigone, Herakleidai* and *Iphigeneia at Aulis*, maidens choosing death for the sake of family or city instead of marriage; pottery too seems to recognise and identify the role, making it more easily distinguished than other ages of female life.[48] Studies of both pottery and grave reliefs suggest that in general depictions of children and young women are aimed not at depicting a specific age, but at defining females into age categories. So, for instance, the children on choes are either babies, at the stage before learning to walk, or old enough to run and play: the iconography depicts them either as 'baby' or 'child'. Grave reliefs, according to Stears, depict three stages of childhood: the baby, the small girl and the parthenos.[49] Little girls are denoted by dresses with a high girdle and lack of breasts, and are shown holding toys and pets, while parthenoi tend to hold more adult objects like jewellery and mirrors, and to have small-breasted figures. On pottery, as a rule, age distinctions are less strong, but an interesting indicator of status is to be found in the depiction of hair; some red-figure painters appear to have distinguished the unmarried girl from the married by hairstyle. Although female hairstyles are not used consistently by painters to denote status, they do sometimes have particular associations: little girls tend to be shown with loose hair or a topknot, matrons with hair in a bun, held up with a kekryphalos, or in a sakkos.[50] Some styles can be quite elaborate, with the hair emerging from the bun and fanning out at the end. Peculiar to the parthenos, however, is a style in which the hair is plaited down the back, and the ends tied up in a small bag wrapped round with thread. It can be seen on the girl in the orchard in fig. 1.12, and on fig. 2.2, a hydria on which three women put wool into a basket: all three have the same style.

The appearance of a specific hairstyle was first noted as a historical feature of vase-painting, and it is true that the style is a fashion of early red-figure painters, dying out in the later period; it may therefore represent a real fashion of contemporary Athens.[51] But an examination of those scenes in which women wear it shows that its use is not indiscriminate: in mythological scenes the style is shown most commonly on Artemis and Athena, as well as Nike and the Nereids. It also appears on Medea in a scene with the Peliades, and Amymone.[52] Not all representations of these figures use the style, but deities like Hera and Aphrodite never wear it, and we can identify it as a style of virgin goddesses and attendants, and of human parthenoi, indicating youth (before a woman wore her hair up) and pre-marital status. Representations of parthenoi in ritual, as we have seen, give girls the style, and it also allows us to expand the meaning of some of the non-mythical scenes where it appears – for example, a privately owned skyphos which shows two women picking fruit.[53] The women stand on either side of a fruit tree, one holding a situla, and both with fruit in their hands; both wear crowns and have the ends of their hair tied. Just as on the Pregny hydria, the scene is placed firmly in the area of ritual by their depiction as parthenoi. A similar scene is found on a stamnos once in Copenhagen which shows two girls folding cloth under the supervision of a woman; the girls holding the cloth both have plaited and bundled hair, which has strengthened interpretations of the scene as ritual, depicting the peplos presented to Athena every four years at the festival of the Panathenaia.[54] The style is also found on some white-ground lekythoi which carry scenes of two women, and in these cases it comments usefully on the status of the individual figures. Scenes on which two women place lekythoi and hold baskets and fillets (fig. 4.22), or dress, are often characterised as 'mistress and maid', but it is unlikely that a slave would be presented as a parthenos, and hence one should see preparation for a visit to the tomb by two women of the family.[55] This interpretation, however, is complicated by two cups attributed to Douris: one, in Christchurch (fig. 3.23) has an exterior scene of a symposium, matched by an interior of a young man and woman together in a bedchamber. The woman embraces the youth, yet she has a hairstyle apparently appropriate to a parthenos. On the other cup in New York two naked women are depicted placing their clothes on a chair, and one of these also has the parthenos style.[56] Do two contradictory examples indicate that the style is no more than a fashion which could be given to any female? In the first place, the images do not contradict the idea that it is a style appropriate only to unmarried women, since mothers never wear it. But should a connection with sex make it impossible to identify a woman as a parthenos? The idea of partheneia (maidenhood) is in fact created by opposition to sexual maturity – a parthenos is so by virtue of being as yet unmarried, so it should not be unduly surprising to find some connection of the imagery in art. Clearly the parthenos representation does not appear solely in scenes of ritual, but it does serve to mark out a particular status for the young woman. The existence of that status, and of methods for its representation in the imagery, demonstrates that in early adulthood girls were far more important in ritual roles than boys.

Child workers and child slaves

The discussion of status markers on white-ground lekythoi above leads to the question of whether distinction can be made between slave and free children. The experiences described so far are obviously those of the lives of the privileged: the daughters of citizens who took their place in ritual and had no need to work. Can we compare the experience of the child slave, or of the working child of the impoverished craftsman, through the evidence of pottery? Child slaves at first seem numerous on pots, but they can be difficult to distinguish, since realistic depiction was not the aim of the painters; slaves were so much part of the everyday in Greece that few pots make explicit comment on the status of slavery. There is great scope for confusion given that the indicators of youth – small size and unsophisticated dress – are also used to denote slave status when necessary, and hence it is not always possible to be certain whether we should see a slave or a child. This attitude is of a piece with recorded behaviour towards slaves: they were denied full adult status, male slaves were addressed as 'pais' whatever their age, and they were permanently under the power of another. Nevertheless, we can recognise some child figures where slave status may be intended to be shown: two lekythoi in Athens and Brussels depict women attended by young girls dressed in black; the first carries a child on her shoulders (fig. 1.4), while the second holds a box (fig. 1.14). The dark dress often marks lower status, as on the Orchard Painter's fruit-picking krater in New York: a figure stooping to carry baskets in the foreground is set apart from her companions by a dark dress and short hair.[58] On another lekythos in Berlin, a woman visiting a tomb is accompanied by a girl with apparently African features, who carries a stool on her head.[59] Small stature also marks a difference on an interesting alabastron in Glasgow (fig. 1.15) which depicts a mistress and two maids, both of whom are dressed in the same way, but one, holding a fan, is clearly smaller and younger than the other.[60] This would fit well with the idea that menial tasks were reserved for the young. Other images, however, are more ambiguous: a figure may appear young for reasons of contrast rather than realism, and on the alabastron in Paris (fig. 1.16) depicting a young woman and her bridegroom, the childlike figure standing behind the bride has no features which we would recognise as slavish: her hair is long and loose, and her full-length chiton pale in colour.[61] It is therefore not always possible to identify a child figure securely as a slave, largely because of the limited range of available signifiers for age and status. The scenes which we have discussed also show the kinds of work in which girl slaves are depicted – mostly fetching and carrying, and occasionally looking after children. All these slaves appear with adult women, not in any scene suggesting that they are the centre of interest themselves: this is in contrast to depictions of boy slaves, who were a topic of considerable erotic interest to painters, especially the Pioneers, and it bears out the idea suggested by Rühfel that the female slave is an attribute of the citizen woman rather than a figure with a real and separate existence.[62]

Depictions of child slaves, then, have little to offer as evidence for the lives of the underprivileged; although they are often simply dressed there is a margin of poverty below which painters will not go in their depictions. But what about children's work outside the household? The literary evidence which we have for the training of girl slave children in professions begins (and ends) with prostitution, most famously the seven small girls bought as infants by Nikarete who were raised to be prostitutes and sold to customers as soon as they were old enough ([Dem.] *Against Neaira* 18–19). In Aristophanes' *Thesmophoriazusai*, the slave girl who fools the Scythian policeman is brought on by a 'madam' proposing that she practise her dance. She is then sold to the Scythian for sex for a drachma, but the dance here may be more than a smokescreen for prostitution – dance constituted a profession in itself, and Xenophon's *Symposium* describes skilled slave dancers and acrobats.[63] Instruction in dance (rather than the performance itself) is a surprisingly frequent theme on Attic pottery, and opinion is divided about the interpretation of the motif: whether we should see an aspect of general female education, or the training of young prostitutes. Rühfel includes in her study of child life a section on the education of girls, focusing her attention on dance, and she relates training of this kind to girls' participation in choruses and the education offered by teachers like Sappho. She interprets

Figure 1.14 Attic white-ground lekythos, Brussels, Musées Royaux d'Art et d'Histoire A1019, 470–460 BC. Photo: RMAH, courtesy Musées Royaux d'Art et d'Histoire, Brussels.

Figure 1.15 Attic red-figure alabastron, Glasgow, Burrell Collection 19.9, *c.*450 BC (drawing).

the girls as Athenian citizens and the dances they learn as part of civic festivals. Delavaud-Roux, on the other hand, suggests that all female practitioners of dances like the pyrrhic were professional entertainers, and characterises them as slaves and prostitutes too.[64] The blanket attribution of prostitution to dancers seems unjustified, given Xenophon's depiction of a dancer as a skilled professional, but it is worth asking how we can tell whether those learning to dance are slave or free. Dance was a part of every woman's life in classical times, performed in ritual and on occasions like weddings, but it is not clear whether formal training at dance schools was the province solely of working women. One example of a 'dance school' appears on a phiale in Boston (attributed to the Phiale Painter), found near Sunium (fig. 1.17): under the gaze of male and female instructors two girls learn to dance, one with castanets, and the other 'muffled' in a cloak, while another plays the aulos. Given the primary use of the phiale in cult, and the cult scenes often depicted on them (such as the festival in honour of Artemis, fig. 1.30), it seems difficult to interpret the scene as training for prostitutes – one of the women holds an oinochoe and phiale in the scene.[65] On the other hand, a hydria by Polygnotos in Naples (fig. 1.18) with a similar dance-school scene introduces elements which belong far more strongly to the field of entertainment: one girl performs acrobatics on a low table, while another dances among swords on the ground.[66] Learning to dance, however, is the only kind of obvious training for girls that we find depicted: it is unreasonable to seize on it as denoting training in prostitution, since other 'accomplishments' of hetairai are not depicted. Examining the use of the pots can shed light on the problem: both the phiale, with its ritual use, and pots,

31

Figure 1.16 Attic red-figure alabastron, Paris, Bibliothèque Nationale 508, c.470 BC. Photo: Bibliothèque nationale de France, Paris.

Figure 1.17 Attic red-figure phiale, Boston, Museum of Fine Arts 97.371, *c*.430 BC. Photo courtesy Museum of Fine Arts, Boston.

such as an Apulian bell-krater with a scene of a girl dancing and her teacher, show that images of dance were used in ritual and as funerary ware, not as entertainment for party-goers. Terracottas of dancers were also dedicated at shrines with great frequency.[67] Dance was an activity in which every woman would take part, and while it is possible that some scenes may represent training of girls for a career in entertainment, others must have a wider application, given the importance of dance to civic life.

As the comments above would suggest, there are few other scenes of children or young women being trained for work that we can document: unlike Rome, Greece offers few recorded instances of specialised training. Xenophon refers to the training of female slaves in domestic tasks, thereby increasing their value, but there are no references to slaves trained in anything other than wool-work.[68] Perhaps because training in work of most

Figure 1.18 Attic red-figure hydria, Naples 3232, 440–430 BC. Photo courtesy Soprintendenza Archeologica di Napoli e Caserta.

kinds was not formalised it is difficult to show. There are one or two inscriptions recording the emancipation of freedwomen, which show daughters following mothers in the same profession – Rhodia and her daughter Cordype, wool-workers; Lampris and Eupeithe her child, wet-nurses, although one would not be able to become a wet-nurse unless of child-bearing age.[69] Examples of non-slave child labour, however, are very hard to distinguish, undoubtedly because there was little distinction between free working poor and slaves outside a household. It is not surprising if images of working children are absent, since childhood for Greek painters was expressed through ideas of play and amusement; childhood may not have been a relevant concern for those outside the wealthy classes, except in so far as it made children objects of erotic desire.

Female relationships

So far the images we have been examining have been on groups of pots which can be localised mainly to Athens – on choes (never found outside Attica and Euboia), on white-ground lekythoi (also localised to Attica and Euboia), on ritual pots from specific sites such as the krateriskoi of Brauron, and on funeral plaques from the Acropolis. The imagery of childhood thus seems to be a private concern, internal to the polis, and indeed to the family. A clear divide appears when we consider the adult woman, the parthenos and the wife. Images involving these figures are much more widely distributed, because they found their way onto pots which were exported. In this sense they become the public face of the polis, and we therefore need to examine not only how women are presented, but why – why should scenes of the adult family be far more frequent on pots in Magna Graecia than in Athens itself?

When it comes to representations of the family in Greek art, it is immediately apparent that our sources, artistic and literary, are idealising or simplifying. Scenes tend to be generic: the wedding procession or the departure of the warrior concentrate on a few figures (warrior, woman, old man, servant, sometimes child). The depiction of real families is extremely rare, and the triad of husband/wife/child uncommon.[70] Comedy, in contrast, tends to invoke the nuclear family very much as an ideal, and comic characters tend to reflect the family type of father, mother, son or daughter or both, like Dikaiopolis with his wife and daughter in *Acharnians*, or Strepsiades with wife and son in *Clouds*.[71] This in turn contrasts with the extended and fractured families of real life known through the law courts; in speeches describing real family affairs from the fourth century, we encounter families composed of children and partners from several different marriages, wives and children living alone, a husband who has abandoned his home to live with his freedwoman and illegitimate children, and freedwomen living as members of the family.[72] Should we therefore expect to interpret pot scenes in a 'realistic' way when reality is so complex? Where more than one or two figures are present there is often nothing to distinguish them, and in a scene such as that on the kalpis in Heidelberg which depicts a man with three women, one standing, one seated, and one carrying a jar on her head and gesturing (fig. 1.19), the relationships between the figures are simply impenetrable to us – it is not an attempt to depict a family in any sense that we understand.[73] Speculative explanations of some scenes have been offered – older women might be aunts, grandmothers or nurses, younger women sisters or cousins – but these have little foundation. It is equally likely that a painter thought that he was depicting slaves, or an aspirational wealthy household where even girls could be raised. This should make us all the more aware that what we

Figure 1.19 Attic red-figure hydria, Heidelberg University, Archaeological Institute 64.5, 440–430 BC. Photo courtesy Archäologisches Institut der Universität Heidelberg.

encounter on pottery is not a photographic representation, and cannot be reduced to the attribution of roles.

An area where pots may be particularly prone to mislead us is the significance accorded to particular rites of passage in female life. For instance, our texts all emphasise the centrality of marriage in women's preoccupations, because they were written from a male perspective; women were important in so far as they married and bore children. Pottery seems to back this up, as there is an enormous number of illustrations of wedding ceremony and preparation.[74] But the pots with marriage scenes have survived largely because of their role in the ritual: they were used in ceremonies and then dedicated at a shrine, or placed in the tomb of those women who died before marriage. They may be telling us a lot about ideology, but the idea that marriage was the most significant thing to happen to a woman may well be wrong from the woman's point of view. Elements invisible on pottery, such as childbirth, the raising of children, or female friendship could be personally much more significant. This last topic, female friendship, has attracted comment in recent years: there are one or two passages in literature which signal that friendship between women outside their oikos was expected and normal:

τῆς γὰρ μητρὸς τῆς ἐμῆς χρωμένης τῇ τούτων μητρὶ πρὶν τούτους
ἐπιχειρῆσαί με συκοφαντεῖν, καὶ πρὸς ἀλλήλας ἀφικνουμένων, οἷον εἰκὸς
ἅμα μὲν ἀμφοτέρων οἰκουσῶν ἐν ἀγρῷ καὶ γειτνιωσῶν, ἅμα δὲ τῶν
ἀνδρῶν χρωμένων ἀλλήλοις ἕως ἔζων.

36

[For before they tried to bring this case against me, my mother and their mother were friends, and they visited each other, as you would expect, since they lived as neighbours in the country, and their husbands too had been friends while they were alive.]

(Dem 55.23–4)

The above passage, though, very much conforms to the idea of female interests as subordinate to the needs of their family. Athenian comedy represents women visiting each others' houses on small errands, or to attend a birth, and an inscription of the late fifth century makes an interesting reference to a deceased woman as 'hetaira' of another, apparently the term for a friend.[75] Yet the evidence is rather poor, contrasting as it does with the regularly expressed norm of women who stayed securely at home, avoiding gossip and the company of other women. Attempts have been made to use the images of pottery to expand our knowledge of this aspect of female life: it has been suggested, for instance, that a pyxis in Sydney (fig. 1.20) which shows a number of women in an interior, some wrapped in their himatia, is a representation of a visit by one woman to another household, with the seated and veiled women as the visitors, but I know of no explicit representation of the idea of visiting – the interpretation is again speculative.[76] Petersen has made the more radical suggestion that women might find alternative readings in apparently traditional imagery, and could understand scenes of women engaged in work or leisure as a reference to female solidarity and friendship.[77] While some of the examples she uses as illustration are problematic (there is no reason, for instance, to think that the black-figure amphora with a scene of women bathing would have been viewed by women of any kind in Athens, as it was placed in a tomb in Cervetri), or come from outside Athens, it is entirely possible that scenes depicting women at work could be interpreted in this positive way. It is important to remember, however, that scenes of domestic

Figure 1.20 Attic red-figure pyxis, Sydney, Nicholson Museum 53.06, 460–450 BC. Photo courtesy The Nicholson Museum, The University of Sydney.

work are actually quite rarely found in Athens, as the next chapter will show, and many of the female scenes which are found there relate to specific events such as marriage. There are certainly no explicit attempts to depict female friendship except in the form of all-female gatherings in religion, which again reflects the prevailing ideology that festivals and funerals were the only opportunities for women to meet in public.

One also has to wonder how realistic a scene involving a room full of women might really be: how many households chose to raise large numbers of sisters? The oikoi we encounter in the speeches of the orators such as Isaeus tend to be the very wealthy and often have several daughters, but there are indications that few poorer families would raise more than one girl.[78] Obviously we should expect to find members of the extended family among the women of the house, as in Lysias' speech *Against Simon*, where the speaker's sister and nieces lived with him, but stories such as that of Aristarchos in Xenophon's *Memorabilia*, who after the Peloponnesian War found himself responsible for a household of fourteen dependent women, and sought Sokrates' advice on providing for them, occurred under the extreme circumstances of a catastrophic military defeat.[79] The importance of the sister relationship has been examined by Golden, who sees some indications of a continued close relationship between sisters in adulthood, although the requirements of marriage would have tended to disrupt women's relationships with their sisters more than with brothers. Nevertheless, if these were aspects of life important to women, we are left guessing. There are no clear signs of relationships or age differences on pots with scenes of work or leisure; the painters were not aiming to depict sisters, aunts or cousins, and hence our interpretations of relationships between the figures in all-female scenes are merely speculative.

A related theme which has occupied scholars recently is the idea of emotional or sexual relationships between women: it has been suggested that women denied emotional warmth within marriage would seek it in relationships with other women, and although the idea is absent from sources such as comedy, which dwell on penis substitutes like the olisbos as the key to women's satisfaction, some have tried to detect this in the imagery of pottery.[80] Although erotic relationships between women are recorded for archaic Greece by Sappho, the idea that Athenian pot-painters would illustrate private female friendships is unlikely, and those seeking evidence for it can ultimately produce few relevant images. Most often cited are a plate from Thera from the archaic period, on which one woman touches the chin of another in a gesture of courtship, and an Apulian pelike from almost 300 years later, on which a well-dressed woman touches another's breast. Neither of these relates to mainland Greece in the classical period, and only two fifth-century cups have a tangential relevance to the theme: on a cup in Tarquinia a naked woman perfumes another, an image with erotic overtones, but not one which depicts any relationship between the women, while a fragmentary cup in Leipzig shows a woman offering another an egg and a flower.[81] Although some are keen to bring these together into a set of images relating to lesbian relationships, it is not clear that there is any more than the occasional evocation of friendship at Athens – just as with matters such as pregnancy and birth, it would be surprising to find female erotic friendships celebrated by painters.

Motherhood

The imagery of pottery, then, cannot tell us which relationships were significant to women, nor about their connections with sisters or friends. The role which pots do privilege in the most consistent way is that of mother: we have discussed childhood from the point of view of the girl, but many suggest that, as in other traditional societies, the role of mother was the most meaningful of a woman's life. The idea of the mother in classical Greek thought is heavily freighted with expectations about maternal devotion and self-sacrifice. Greek writers express this in a way which we can recognise – according to Aristotle καὶ [φιλοῦσι δὴ μᾶλλον] αἱ μητέρες τῶν πατέρων, ὅτι μᾶλλον οἴονται αὐτῶν εἶναι ἔργου τὰ τέκνα [mothers (love their children more) than fathers, because they think that children are particularly their concern] – but the evidence of pottery indicates some attitudes which are more surprising to the modern eye.[82] As indicated above, the focus on childhood in vase-painting is almost exclusively on the child alone; depictions of mothers with children are less common and, as we have seen, mainly funerary. In the funerary sphere the bond between mother and child is shown very strongly, even when the child is quite old – the small boy who stands at a tomb with his toy cart, waving to his mother, is best known, but we have seen a mother with a young girl at a tomb (fig. 1.8), and a white-ground lekythos in Athens has another scene at a tomb in which a woman on one side kneels and gestures in sorrow, while a young woman stands on the other side of the tomb holding a hare.[83] The funerary, however, is the only domain in which such emotion is shown – there are few examples of the mother surrounded by her family in pottery, although the theme is strong on grave reliefs. One very striking exception is a hydria in Berlin with a scene of Alkmaeon being suckled: this is a very rare depiction of breastfeeding on Greek pottery, and appears in a family scene, with the infant Alkmaeon being nursed by his mother Eriphyle, watched by Amphiareus. The harmonious scene is overshadowed by the knowledge that Eriphyle will send her husband to his death, and Alkmaeon, now a baby, will kill her in revenge.[84] Certainly the mother's sentimental relationship with her child is not celebrated in red-figure as it is on tomb reliefs; only in death is emotion found.

Motherhood plays a much more significant part in the iconography of adulthood: as mothers of adults, one of women's most important functions in the iconography of the polis was to mourn their sons. The relationship between mother and adult son on ceramics is one of the paradigmatic relationships for the state. From black-figure onward, the scene of the departing warrior was very frequently depicted, and takes a canonical form (fig. 1.21): at the centre of the scene a young man stands, either holding or receiving his weapons; he is surrounded by members of his family, and various points in the ritual of departure are shown, such as the offering of libations, the extispicy (examination of omens), the receiving of armour. Several figures make up the typical scene: the aged father, bald or white-haired, and beyond the age of bearing arms; the servant boy who brings the entrails for examination, other warriors, and one or more women. The women bring arms and armour to the men, hold phialai or pour libations, or stand in attendance at the extispicy.[85] Their importance in this role is emphasised by the numerous lekythoi which show women alone, carrying armour or oinochoe and phiale – these scenes excerpt the woman in her role in the departure as suitable for funerary use. Arming is also adapted as a theme on white-ground lekythoi, where a man and woman sit or stand with arms. On the well-known example by the Achilles Painter, a woman holds out a helmet to a man with shield and spear; the notion of departure to death is very clear.[86]

The role of the women in such scenes is interesting, as there is a change in the type of representation from black-figure to red. In black-figure departure scenes, arming, the departure in a chariot and the extispicy are the most common thematic variants, and the interactions between the figures are few and formal. Women in scenes of extispicy hold a

Figure 1.21 Attic red-figure amphora, Munich, Antikensammlungen J411, 500–490 BC (drawing). After Pfuhl, fig. 373.

muffled hand to their face as a gesture of awe.[87] In early red-figure the emphasis changes, and libation becomes a much more common action; red-figure departure scenes are on a more human level, focusing on the relationships of the individuals. Modern writers tend to assume that the emotion of departure is shown primarily between husband and wife, and there are some instances in which this is the case – for example, a stamnos in St Petersburg, which shows a warrior and woman confronting each other, the woman with a lowered gaze, and an older couple flanking them. Although there is no gesture between husband and wife, the emotion between them clearly dominates the scene.[88] But the role of the woman in the canonical departure is far more frequently indeterminate, meaning that it is unclear whether we should see husband and wife, or mother and son. Age distinctions are sometimes made where two women are present, as on the stamnos discussed above, or on the neck-amphora in Oxford (fig. 1.22), where the mother is heavier and more elaborately dressed, with a different hairstyle; but when one woman alone appears, as happens most often, she is ageless.[89] Men in departure scenes are clearly depicted as aged, either balding or white-haired, making the distinction between non-combatant father and warrior son, and the fact that the child is not a frequent component of the scene suggests that the emotions between parents and child are what is being

40

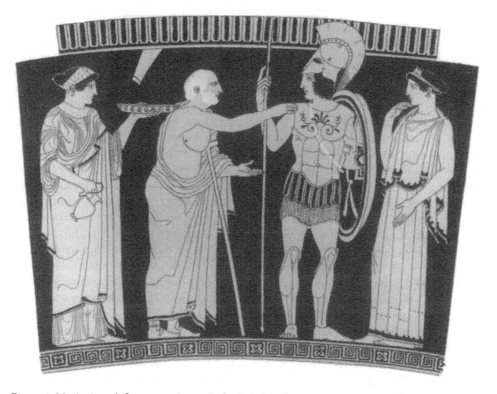

Figure 1.22 Attic red-figure amphora, Oxford, Ashmolean Museum 280, *c.*460 BC (drawing). Photo courtesy The Ashmolean Museum, Oxford (after P. Gardner, *Catalogue of the Greek Vases in the Ashmolean Museum*, Oxford, Clarendon Press, 1893, pl. 12).

dramatised. This is supported by the named characters in mythological scenes of departure: we find Hektor bidding farewell to Priam and Hekuba more often than to Andromache.[90] It seems that we are meant to understand the choice of characters as the warrior with father and mother, and that it is the warrior's mother who expresses her emotion in seeing her son set off to possible destruction (fig. 1.21). This reflects reality; many men of fighting age would be as yet unmarried, and the loss of a child in warfare is irreparable in the way that the loss of a husband is not. Literature illustrates very directly the sorrow of the relationship: the women of Aristophanes' *Lysistrata* claim the right to speak on warfare because, as mothers, they contribute to the city sons who they will see die in battle, while a Spartan woman gives voice to the clearest expression of the sacrifice in Plutarch's *Moralia*:

> Θάπτουσά τις τὸν υἱόν, ὡς γραΐδιον εὐτελὲς προσελθὸν αὐτῇ "ὦ γύναι, τὰς τύχας" εἶπε, "νὴ τὼ σιώ, ἀλλὰ τᾶς καλᾶς γ'" ἔφη· "οὐ γὰρ αὐτὸν ἕνεκεν ἔτεκον, ἵν' ὑπὲρ τᾶς Σπάρτας ἀποθάνῃ, τοῦτό μοι συνέβη."

> [A mother was burying her son, when a worthless old woman approached and said to her, 'Woman, what bad luck!', but she replied, 'No, by the gods, it is good luck, for I bore him so that he might die for Sparta, and that is just what has happened.']

> (*Mor.* 241D)[91]

In part, departure scenes evolve from mythical prototypes in black-figure: the mytho-logical locus for arming, for instance, is Thetis bringing armour to Achilles. This underlying narrative reveals an interesting feature of scenes of departure: one prototype is clearly the Homeric departure of Hektor, who is depicted with mother (Hekuba) or wife (Andromache), and Hektor later develops into the figure of the idealised hoplite, who can represent any citizen. But a myth of equal prominence in black-figure is the departure of Amphiareos, found as a theme on Corinthian pots, and on significant black-figure examples such as the François Vase. Ill-omened though the departure of Hektor might be, the episode of Amphiareos is far worse, since in every example of the theme Eriphyle bids goodbye to her husband holding the necklace with which she has been bribed to send him to his death.[92] The idea of the treacherous wife is thus present in the scene from its beginning, and it is striking that in later red-figure, when traditional departure scenes become much less popular, the myth of Eriphyle mutates into a different form more suitable to the painters' preoccupations, concentrating on the moment of bribery (fig. 4.25) instead of the departure; but the story never disappears. The relationship between wife and husband carries the potential for danger: it is the mother to whom one looks for devotion. The mirror-image scene to the departure of the warrior is the return of the body of the defeated, and here too mothers have a major part to play in the iconography of the scene. The warrior needs the mother to show the city's sacrifice, in the same way that a mother needs a child to show her devotion.[93] The sense of impending doom over the departure, or indeed the outright grief of the return, is ideally suited to a funerary context, accounting for the export of this type of scene.

The public nature of female roles in the military life of the polis does, however, overshadow a large omission – mothers with adult daughters. As a son was sent away as a warrior to battle, so a daughter was sent away in marriage, but while there are some scenes of weddings on which the mother appears (though positive identification as the *bride's* mother is hard), and they are of course shown on krateriskoi, there is nothing like the same concentration on the mother–daughter relationship as on that of mother and son.[94] Demand is pessimistic about the possibility of close relationships being formed between mothers and daughters, suggesting that early marriage gave women little opportunity to form a friendship as adults, and that instead a woman's primary relationship was with her mother-in-law, who would be the most influential female in the family into which she married.[95] But I do not think one should dismiss the possibility of friend-ship between mothers and daughters so readily: there are hints of a continuing close relationship in the anecdote of Herodotus about the unhappy marriage of Megakles' daughter to Peisistratos, in which the bride is shown confiding in her mother, and possibly also in the scandalous episode of Kallias' liaison with wife and mother-in-law in the fourth century.[96] We can remember too the dedication made by Nossis and her mother jointly to Hera in the third century. Whatever weight one gives to the literary evidence, though, there is no doubt that pot-painters considered such relationships irrelevant to their agenda. Neither mothers nor mothers-in-law are recognisable on pots, and even when a group of women within a household is depicted, age differentiation is minimal, leaving the question of relationships unanswerable. The few scraps of evidence which we have suggest a view of the female family which is completely absent from the stylised world of pots.

Ritual

For those who find ancient attitudes towards women depressing, the field of ritual is always a saving grace. [Ritual, we are told, is the one domain where women were put at the centre of the polis, and although they might have had no importance in public or political life, their roles in the festivals of the city gave them status and significance.] As Sourvinou-Inwood has demonstrated, one should not belittle the importance of the religious sphere, seeing involvement as a kind of consolation prize for women: it is impossible to exaggerate the importance of religion as the central part of public life in the state.[97] Priestesses, arrêphoroi and women celebrating festivals like the Thesmophoria were equal in importance to male priests and worshippers, and essential to the well-being of the polis: every citizen of the polis was vitally involved. This very positive view is apparently upheld by the evidence of pottery – depictions of women participating in ritual are numerous and diverse, on a range of different shapes, and also through time. The ritual act is a moment at which women become visible on pottery, in a great variety of roles, and pottery also allows us to be precise about how and why women were involved in ritual. There is much cross-cultural evidence, relating to festivals involving women in different Greek states because, in contrast to the private and inwardly focused groups of pots which we have seen so far, religion was a theme very popular on pots for export, and therefore its imagery was not something internal to the polis.

This requires an initial consideration of the purpose for which pots were made. Some, such as the krateriskoi, were made for use at a specific site and depict the ceremonies performed in honour of that deity. Others were made for the export market, and hence their depictions are of a different quality. One cannot, for instance, treat the many representations of the worship of Dionysus as reflecting solely Athenian interest: many scenes of Dionysiac ritual are found on pots used as grave-goods in Etruria, and reasons for the popularity of the theme in pots used as tomb furniture have been advanced: as a god whose initiates were promised an afterlife, Dionysus and his rituals were appropriate as images for funerary use, and also (in his role as deity of wine and poetic inspiration) for vessels used to evoke the Etruscan banquet for the dead.[98] So we have to be aware that our explanations of ritual scenes should not be bound to Athens, and that the city is projecting itself on these pots through images for export.

This fact is acutely relevant to the simplest category of women in ritual: women as individual worshippers. The theme of a woman (or man) making an offering at an altar, of wine, incense or branches, is extremely common on lekythoi, such as that in Tübingen showing a woman with phialai at an altar (fig. 1.23), and also very frequently depicted on cups.[99] The theme of the female worshipper at the altar occurs on the inside of more than thirty kylikes, women shown with torches, sceptres, making libations or praying. Often there is an indicator of setting, either outside the house or within, and several larger cups depict goddesses in the same role; for example, the white-ground cup depicting Kore making a libation at an altar.[100] The occurrence of scenes of women worshipping on cups highlights in an interesting way the use of the cup as a cult object: cups were not made solely for use at symposia, but were used in religious practice too. A cup in Tarquinia shows a man at an altar making a libation from a kylix, and cups are also found as dedications in sanctuaries.[101] The ritual nature of the cup is demonstrated by the regularity with which a religious scene is the only decoration; the outside is undecorated, and the cup therefore removed from the realm of the everyday to that of ritual. This factor is

Figure 1.23 Attic red-figure lekythos, Tübingen 7319 (O.Z.119), 470–460 BC. Photo courtesy Institüt für Klassische Archäologie, Eberhard-Karls-Universität, Tübingen (neg. no. CV109c).

one which needs emphasis: cups can tell us about the importance of the woman as worshipper, emphasising female engagement with the divine on their own account, not through the family. In most cases the worship is the only scene, but sometimes it turns up in concert with other themes which apparently form a unity, such as domestic scenes, where the ritual can be placed as part of female life, or pursuit scenes, where there is a strong funerary theme.[102] Other juxtapositions of themes, however, seem more difficult to explain: athletes, a school scene or symposia.[103] Lissarrague discusses a cup in Berlin with a similar juxtaposition of scenes in the masculine world – a youth sacrificing in the interior, and a symposium of youths on the exterior – and suggests that it exploits the ambiguity of the space of the altar, which can be household or sympotic.[104]

The situation for female figures is more difficult, since the ritual world of the household is not supposed to overlap with the masculine space of the symposium. The most problematic combination of themes is said to be those on the cups which carry sympotic or courting scenes on the outside and female sacrificers on the inside, such as the cup in London with a symposium outside and a woman with phiale at an altar in the interior, or another sold in Basel which has men and youths outside and a woman pouring a libation in the interior.[105] One of this type, a cup in Toledo, has excited more comment than any other – the exterior shows men holding purses in conversation with women, and the interior a richly dressed young woman sacrificing at an altar with a ritual basket, the kanoun.[106] Unfortunately the cup has no known provenance, and we cannot state definitely where or why it was used. Beard has made this cup central to her argument about the use of vase-painting to inculcate female stereotypes, arguing that the woman in the interior is to be understood as an untouchable citizen wife or daughter, intended to contrast with the 'available' hetairai on the outside of the cup. Others have followed this interpretation, Reeder commenting that 'Makron's juxtaposition of the scenes was clearly intended as an ironic social comment'.[107] The difficulty with this kind of argument is that it assumes (because of the commentator's interest) that the woman is the salient feature of both scenes: that we should not contrast the religious theme with the sympotic, but rather wives with whores. Readings of this kind interpret cups from a masculine perspective (perhaps because of the presumed connection between cups and symposia), and therefore see women solely as sex objects, whereas in ritual they are actors. As shown by the example discussed above, we can be too ready to see a divide between the sacred and the secular: libations were part of the symposium, just as banqueting was part of ritual. Given the importance of the woman

pouring a libation in departure scenes, they can be seen as safeguarding the religious well-being of the household, as well as experiencing their own relationship with the divine. The woman as keeper of the ritual may be a powerful figure, not an object of thwarted sexuality. There is no sign that scenes were juxtaposed for 'ironic effect', nor that an Etruscan customer would have found the union of religion and symposium so odd.

Libations at altars are not the only aspect of female worship depicted: lekythoi carry scenes of sacrifice, with women bringing baskets of offerings or animals to sacrifice – fig. 1.24 is a scene from an alabastron in Copenhagen on which two women appear, one with a hen and the other with a wreath.[108] Nor is the theme limited to Athens; an early Argive krater shows a woman making a libation at an amphora, probably to be interpreted as an offering to the dead (fig. 1.25).[109] As well as images of women as individual worshippers, pots also carry scenes of family sacrifice, such as those on the column-krater in Naples with a family in procession to an altar, or the man and woman sacrificing at twin herms on a krater in Bologna.[110] Other media, too, represent the role of women in sacrifice: terracotta figurines of women carrying pigs for sacrifice became popular between 450 and 350 BC across the Greek world, probably relating to the worship of Demeter; votive tablets, dedicated as a record of a sacrifice, also show women as worshippers, again in scenes of family sacrifice – in some cases they were the dedicants of the votives.[111] The prominence of woman as worshipper across all media is a testament to the role of religion in female life.

Figure 1.24 Attic white-ground alabastron, Copenhagen, Nationalmuseet 3830, 460–450 BC. Photo courtesy Department of Classical and Near Eastern Antiquities, National Museum of Denmark.

Figure 1.25 Argive Geometric krater, Argos Museum C26611, early seventh century BC (drawing of detail).

Beyond personal religious activity, even the very earliest pottery across Greece depicts women in public religious roles, at funerals and festivals. Religion is actually one of the primary and original themes for pot-painting, from its origins both at Athens and elsewhere: the first pots were funerary in use, and so carried scenes of funeral rites. We have already seen images of women taking part in mourning rites, either standing around the body on the bier, or in the funerary procession; religious roles outside the family are represented in even greater numbers, with depictions of state sacrifice and festivals, including all-female festivals like the Lenaia and the Adonia. Very early pots tend to focus on dance as the chief female ritual activity, with depictions of female choruses and dances, the participants holding branches or wreaths. Fig. 1.26 is a detail of a sixth-century Klazomenian amphora in Berlin, showing a chain of dancers led by an aulos player. We can parallel this area in literature: in the poetry of sixth-century Alcman and Sappho we encounter choirs of unmarried women participating in both weddings and festivals of Aphrodite.[112] Once the black-figure period begins, painters produce a wider range of cult activity, including scenes of sacrifice at altars, other kinds of offering, and the consumption of the victim. From archaic times to the end of the red-figure period, women play a large part in all these depictions in both mixed

Figure 1.26 Klazomenian amphora, Berlin, Staatliche Museen 4530, *c.*540 BC (drawing). After Pfuhl, fig. 143.

Figure 1.27 Attic black-figure amphora, Berlin, Staatliche Museen 1686, *c.*540 BC. Photo: Antikensammlung, Staatliche Museen zu Berlin – Preussischer Kulturbesitz.

and all-female rites. In Attic and Boiotian black-figure an interest develops in scenes of animal sacrifice, with creatures brought in procession to an altar or cult image. Women very often figure as priestesses: in fig. 1.27, an amphora in Berlin, the priestess leads the sacrificial procession to the altar, and confronts the image of Athena as the men and ox lower their gaze; fig. 1.28 shows the link between deity and priestess even more clearly, as the priestess stands at the altar holding branches, next to Athena with her snake.[11] In the imagery of sacrifice, women form part of the religious hierarchy, and their participation was on a basis of equality with men. The role of priestess was hereditary, held for life, and bestowed personal status – without a priestess, the cult could not function. Priestesses represented both female and male deities in all states of Greece, in the worship of Athena, Aphrodite, Artemis, Hera, Dionysus and Demeter; they were widely known within their city, and we have preserved the names of some influential priestesses of Athena Polias in the fifth and fourth centuries – Lysimache and Phanostrate. Some, like the priestess of Hera at Argos, were eponymous, lending their name to the date: Thucydides

Figure 1.28 Attic black-figure hydria, once Rome Market, *c*.510 BC (drawing). After Pfuhl, fig. 297.

Figure 1.29 Attic red-figure pelike, Newcastle, Shefton Museum, *c*.470 BC. Photo courtesy Shefton Museum of Greek Art and Archaeology, University of Newcastle upon Tyne.

refers to Chrysis and her successor Phaenis.[114] In Attica it is the priestesses of Demeter (in the Mysteries at Eleusis) and Athena Polias who are most often depicted: many scenes take as their inspiration the Panathenaic festival, and so we see the priestess receiving the procession, overseeing the gift of a peplos to Athena, or, in one case, overseeing the filling of the prize amphorae with oil.[115]

In the scenes of sacrifice, the other constant figure is that of kanêphoros, the young girl who carried the basket for the priest or priestess with the sacrificial grain and knife (fig. 1.29).[116] The cup by Makron in Toledo discussed above is often said to depict a kanêphoros, but true depiction of this role is to be found in images of sacrifice. In most cults (though not all, that of Hermes being one exception) the role of kanêphoros was reserved for a woman: consider the tiny celebration of the Rural Dionysia by Dikaiopolis in *Acharnians*, where Dikaiopolis officiates as priest and assigns the role of kanêphoros to his daughter:

’Αγ’, ὦ θύγατερ, ὅπως τὸ κανοῦν καλὴ καλῶς
οἴσεις βλέπουσα θυμβροφάγον.

[Come, daughter, make sure you carry the basket with a graceful step, and a serious savory-eating expression.]

(Ach. 253–4)

At Corinth an interesting series of pots from the archaic period depicts women in all-female festivals: some simply show processions or dances in an inexplicit way, but on others seated women hold children on their knees, while others dance or carry offerings in baskets (fig. 1.30). It has been suggested that these are festivals in honour of Artemis, relating as at Brauron in Attica to her role as kourotrophos, protector of young children.[117] It is notable that female festivals are one of the few religious themes found in Corinthian art: Attic painting covers a much wider range, but the all-female festival still occupies a significant place in the production.[118] Along with the large production of pots for the rites of Artemis at Brauron, we find many other women-only festivals depicted: the Lenaia, the Adonia, the Thesmophoria. It is perhaps surprising that all-female rites appear on pots, given that male artists could not participate in them, but, unlike those of the Mysteries the rites were not secret. All-female festivals were significant to the state, not just to women. The numbers of representations on pots do not necessarily reflect the importance of the festival: as we have seen, the rites of Artemis are very frequently depicted, not only at Brauron: one of the best illustrations is the white-ground phiale by the Phiale Painter (fig. 1.31), which shows seven women holding hands around an altar, on which a flame burns; the presence of a kalathos refers to female concerns.[119] In contrast, the Thesmophoria is very ill-served by painters: only two examples seem to relate to this important festival. The first is a lekythos in Athens showing a female

Figure 1.30 Corinthian flask, London, British Museum 1865.7–20.20, 625–600 BC. Photo courtesy British Museum. © The British Museum.

Figure 1.31 Attic white-ground phiale, Boston, Museum of Fine Arts 65.908, *c*.440 BC. Photo courtesy Museum of Fine Arts, Boston.

worshipper holding a dog for sacrifice and a basket (although this may be intended as an image of sacrifice to Hekate). The second is a black-figure cup, one side of which depicts a dance of five women and a boy, with a priestess at an altar and a seated female figure, probably the goddess Demeter; the other side shows a man ploughing with two oxen while a figure sows seed behind him.[120] The linking of agriculture and festival on the two sides, and the clear reference to seed reflects the purpose of the Thesmophoria, which was to ensure the fertility of the fields. One can also compare the wealth of scenes of the worship of Artemis with the infrequency of depiction of festivals in honour of Hera; Hera was celebrated at Argos, but not Athens, and hence few Athenian rites in honour of Hera are depicted. The newer festival of the Adonia also attracts illustration (fig. 1.32), and it is an interesting iconographical case, since although the festival was long-established in Athens it did not become an iconographic theme until the fourth century.[121] Its popularity is part

Figure 1.32 Attic red-figure squat lekythos, Berlin, Staatliche Museen 3248, *c.*350 BC. Photo courtesy Antikensammlung, Staatliche Museen zu Berlin – Preussischer Kulturbesitz.

of the sparking of interest in female themes after the Peloponnesian War; as a domestic women's festival it lent itself to interior depictions.

The interest in women's religious rites forms a major part of what is by far the most frequent depiction of ritual on Athenian pottery: Dionysiac cult. Its popularity is, as noted above, in no doubt because of its applicability to both funerary and ritual uses. The cult is, of course, an area where myth and reality tend to shade into one another: images of polis sacrifice stand beside those of nymphs and maenads, mythical attendants of Dionysus himself. City festivals, such as the Lenaia, are very frequently depicted: a series of stamnoi carry very formal scenes of women worshipping at a mask of Dionysus with

51

Figure 1.33 Attic red-figure stamnos, Oxford, Ashmolean Museum V523, *c.*460 BC (drawing). After Pfuhl, fig. 516.

wine and dance, as on fig. 1.33, a stamnos in Oxford, where women wearing ivy wreaths ladle out wine from a large stamnos on a table draped with ivy, as a third woman plays the aulos.[122] Other Lenaia scenes, such as that on a cup in Berlin, depict more lively aspects of the festival – the women dance around an altar and statue with loosened hair and wild gestures.[123] Although the occasion is more ecstatic, we are still in the world of the city, and the women are real citizen women. It becomes more difficult to judge between myth and reality in scenes of individuals: if women are depicted in Dionysiac regalia, with animal skins and thyrsoi, are we seeing maenads or women playing the role of maenads? Keuls suggests that some images of maenads and satyrs should be understood as husband and wife playing out Dionysiac roles, but surely the point is that there is no hard distinction to be made.[124] Women were essential to the worship of Dionysus, and the nature of the rites required a lifting of inhibitions and a celebration of the ecstatic, but depictions obviously show Dionysus the god and his satyr and maenad attendants, to which worshippers were assimilated. A good example of the lack of determination between myth and reality is the image on a skyphos in Berlin (fig. 1.34) on which a well-dressed woman is attended by a satyr who holds a parasol above her head – it is suggested that she is the basilinna, wife of the archôn basileus, who became 'wife' of Dionysus in a ceremony of holy marriage at the Anthesteria, a real woman attended by a mythical

Figure 1.34 Attic red-figure skyphos, Berlin, Staatliche Museen 2589, *c.*440 BC. Photo courtesy Antikensammlung, Staatliche Museen zu Berlin – Preussischer Kulturbesitz.

representative of the god.[125] The image of the maenad in Attic pottery is more restrained than the idea in literature, where maenads are true madwomen, possessed by the god, handling snakes and tearing their prey apart, embodying the terrifying result of loss of female control.[126] On pottery, however, there is a difference between the maenad and the satyr: while the satyr represents the bestial side of man, engaging in acts of self-indulgence or loss of control which a citizen cannot, such as drunkenness, sexual over-exuberance, and play, the relation between the maenad and the woman is more subtle. Where maenads and satyrs interact, maenads are often the victims of satyr advances; they do not demonstrate free female sexuality in the same way.[127] Most of the maenads one encounters in the imagery are 'domesticated', not creatures to terrify men.

The repertoire of ritual activity depicted thus varied over time – dance and funerals in the Geometric period, sacrifice in black-figure, and festivals in red-figure – and different aspects of female life come to the fore according to painters' overall interests. What is most interesting is the prominence of female ritual activity in the export market: pots did not carry religious themes only because they were used in ceremonial, but because this was an aspect of polis life offered as a public face to the Mediterranean world. Women appear in ritual not because 'women's pots' reflect 'women's themes' but because they were primary actors in the religious life of the city. For this reason, the images cannot be read as a simple commentary on Athenian life; for example, of the twelve pots with recognisable Adonia scenes, ten have known provenances, and of these two are from Thrace, two from North Africa, one from Italy, four from Attica and one from Greece.[128] The scenes were directed at an external market, and the prevalence of religious themes on shapes like cups or kraters shows that pots cannot be defined in a meaningful way as 'drinking vessels' or 'symposion ware': kylikes can be used to pour libations, stamnoi contain wine for the festival of Dionysus, and a krater appears in a scene of the Adonia; and women are at the heart of all of these scenes.

Old age

At the opposite end of the female life cycle, images on Athenian pots demonstrate what it is to a woman to be old. An iconography of female age exists from early in the red-figure period: the most obvious signs of old age are white hair and a stooped posture, but details such as a wrinkled face and arms and downturned mouths are included too. Aged women

are not frequently illustrated on pots, and unless in mythological scenes are most often found as servants or slaves. In scenes of mourning the aged nurse is sometimes shown, as on a loutrophoros in Athens.[129] Here the wrinkled face of the nurse as she bends over the bier contrasts with the smooth and youthful face of the dead woman, lending poignancy to the idea of the untimely death. A few other aged women can be found: an old woman feeds a pig on a lekythos in Naples (fig. 1.35), and a hydria fragment in Athens depicts an old woman at an altar (fig. 1.36). The kanêphoros in fig. 1.29 is accompanied by an old woman, and in a komos scene on a lekythos in London we find an older woman with wineskin and oinochoe.[130] Most examples of old age, however, are found in scenes of myth, primarily the figures of Hekuba and Aithra in the Trojan cycle, or the scene on a unique kalpis in Hamburg which depicts a youthful warrior (Theseus) standing before a kalathos as an old woman (Hekale) offers a phiale to him. Otherwise the old in myth also tend to be slaves, from Geropso, the nurse of Herakles, who appears as an aged tattooed Thracian slave on a skyphos in Schwerin, to Eurykleia, the servant of Odysseus (a skyphos in Chiusi shows the episode from the *Odyssey* where Eurykleia washes Odysseus, and clearly represents her as an old woman).[131] On pottery, the associations of old age are with slavery and mourning, and its use in myth, to accentuate suffering and weakness, reinforces the idea that to be old implies sorrow and hardship. This is the nature of the role of the old woman in myth: both Aithra and Hekuba are mothers who suffer. Aithra, captured by the Dioskouroi, taken to Troy and rescued by her grandsons Demophon and Akamas, is shown being led from the scene of her captivity,

Figure 1.35 Attic red-figure lekythos, Naples H3353, *c.*460 BC. Photo courtesy Soprintendenza Archeologica di Napoli e Caserta.

Figure 1.36 Attic red-figure hydria fragment, Athens, Acropolis Museum 2.1009, *c.*480 BC. Photo courtesy National Archaeological Museum, Athens.

while Hekuba sees her children killed around her after the fall of Troy, and is enslaved. The painters' emphasis is on the women's weakness and dependence on their children.

As we have seen, in family groups – whether the departure of a warrior or domestic scenes – women are rarely given signs of age to differentiate between them. This differs strongly from depictions of men, for whom a far greater range of age depictions is possible. They can be slender or muscular, hairy, bearded, balding or white-haired, and a variety of ages are often shown in a single scene. In the departure of the warrior on an amphora in Paris, for instance, a youthful and muscular soldier contrasts both with his ageing father and his immature slave.[132] The women in such scenes have far more homogeneous characteristics; mothers and wives are rarely differentiated by age. It is worth remembering that the normal age-gap between husband and wife in an Athenian marriage was about fifteen years, so a mother would be considerably younger than her husband, but this does not take into account the effects of continuous childbearing, nor does it explain the similarity between mothers and wives in departure scenes. It is true that fewer symbols of ageing in women were available to the artists (women do not go bald), but even those developed by the Pioneers are avoided in family scenes – mothers are not depicted with wrinkles or white hair. Pfisterer-Haas, in her study of representations of old women, comments that mothers are distinguished by their style of clothing; generally, though, dress and hairstyle are the same for all women in a scene.[133] What we find on pottery is the depiction of roles; a woman is either immature, sexually mature (as bride or mother), or beyond reproductive age (an old woman). Just as with young girls, fine distinctions of age are less relevant: an old woman is simply old. That this is conventional is confirmed by depictions on grave stelai, which regularly show women as young, even when the inscription indicates a greater age. A case in point is the famous stele of Ampharete, on which a grandmother, indistinguishable from a mother, is depicted with a grandchild.[134] Even those figures from myth stated in literature to be old, such as the Graiai, are not noticeably old when they appear on pottery; the Fates themselves are young in a black-figure scene of the wedding of Peleus and Thetis.[135] Age is therefore used not in the service of realism but to symbolise weakness or pathos.

Yet age is one of those rare topics on which the evidence of literature can offer a more positive view than the iconography. Depictions in oratory and comedy suggest that passing the age of reproductive ability offered an experience of liberation to citizen women. [The period of life after child-rearing had certain roles and privileges attached to it] older women had greater freedom of movement, since the threat to their sexual integrity was less, and they were subject to fewer taboos once they had reached the menopause. The speaker of Demosthenes' *Against Kallippos* records a friendship between his mother and her neighbour as they aged, and we also see the favoured role within the family accorded to a now-aged nurse:

ὡς δὲ οὗτος ἀπέθανεν καὶ αὐτὴ γραῦς ἦν καὶ οὐκ ἦν αὐτὴν ὁ θρέψων, ἐπανῆκεν ὡς ἐμέ. ἀναγκαῖον οὖν ἦν μὴ περιιδεῖν ἐνδεεῖς ὄντας μήτε τιτθὴν γενομένην μήτε παιδαγωγόν.

[When her husband died, and she was an old woman without anyone to support her, she came back to live with me. For one cannot ignore it when one's nurse or tutor is left in poverty.][136]

Older women frequently acted as midwife or healer for their community, and could gain considerable status if holding a religious post. Priestesses mostly served for life, and so could become venerable and authoritative figures in the state.[137] These roles do not find their way onto pottery; images even of old men are often pathetic, and old women doubly so. On the other hand, comic writers reveal another strand of Athenian attitudes: contempt for aged women, who represent excessive sexual appetite combined with physical repellence – the final scene of Aristophanes' *Ekklesiazusai* is constructed on the joke of three grotesque old women demanding the sexual attention of a young man. Many literary references to age in women fall into this category, such as Perikles' comment to Elpinike that she was too old to use her attractions to persuade him to moderate his prosecution of her brother Kimon.[138] This attitude does find iconographic expression in one of Theseus' labours, the killing of the Sow of Krommyon (a parallel to the contest of Herakles with the Erymanthian boar). The killing of the sow has sexual overtones, supported by the development of the motif, as the cycle of the deeds of Theseus became canonical, in which an old woman appears with the sow as its protector. On one pot she is given the name Krommyo, eponymous from the region, and she seems a manifestation of femininity as threat: female sexuality, made manifest in the form of both the sow and the old woman, is defeated by the warrior.[139] It is possible that the Naples lekythos showing an old woman feeding a pig is also a reference to this myth.

The idea of the old woman as grotesque dominates more thoroughly the main source of depictions of female age, which is in fact neither pottery, literature nor grave stelai: by far the most representations of old women are to be found among terracottas made outside Athens (fig. 1.37). These terracottas have been very effectively studied by Pfisterer-Haas, who documents the roles in which old women are depicted, dividing them into

Figure 1.37 Boiotian terracotta, Paris, Musée du Louvre MNB 1003, *c*.320 BC. Photo courtesy Musée du Louvre, Paris.

nurses, usually holding babies, 'hetairai' and women in cult.[140] The increasing number of statuettes depicting old women comes about mainly through the growth in popularity of themes from comedy – the terracotta nurses and fat naked women who become much more common in the fourth century are characters from New Comedy. Most of these figures, however positive the essential role, are grotesque: old age is associated with fatness, ugliness and lack of modesty. One has to ask the reason for the manufacture of terracottas of this kind: they were not purely decorative, although small groups of figurines have occasionally been found in domestic contexts. Although (as ever) the provenance of most is not known, of those that are, half come from graves and the rest from sanctuaries (the sanctuary of Athena Kranaia at Elatea in particular). The presence of grotesque statuettes in graves is explicable in terms of apotropaic decoration, and Pfisterer-Haas also suggests that the figures of nurses with babies might be intended to accompany children into the afterlife. This would imply that unflattering though the figures are in their portrayal of age, the nurse is intended to be a figure of comfort and security, reflecting the experience brought by ageing. The dedication of grotesque terracottas in sanctuaries can be paralleled by the imagery of the pots found at sites like the Boiotian Kabeirion; these too show the same link between comic grotesques and the divine.[141] What the terracottas do indicate, however, is that the invisibility of older women in non-Athenian cultures was less marked, even if opinions of the old were similarly low.

All this suggests that Bremmer is right to refer to the 'functionalist' view adopted by men in classical times – that women were seen to be useful in so far as they were sexual and fertile beings, and, once past the age of fertility, they were considered insignificant by men.[142] Even those priestesses for whom age or widowhood was a prerequisite of the position were chosen not for their wisdom and experience but because their age offered a protection against sexual threat, or fulfilled a requirement of chastity: electing an aged woman meant that a younger woman did not have to reduce her fertile years, nor a man lose access to his wife. Once again, our evidence for the views which women themselves held about age is slight, although there are signs that they could take a wider view of the opportunities offered by old age. Greater personal freedom is obviously a part of this – in the speeches of the Athenian orators it is old women who are able to go about in the city and converse with men. There are also interesting hints of the status of the older women within the household – some domestic images represent a seated female figure presiding over younger and lesser figures, and some of the families depicted in oratorical speeches included the mother of the husband as well as wife and children.[143] The implication is that the mother-in-law would become a powerful figure as she aged, as in modern societies where the extended family is the norm. An interesting suggestion has been made by Stears, that since women regularly outlived men in Greek families they might become the lasting centre of the family, and repository of knowledge, playing a vital role in the continuity of the oikos.[144] That this aspect is ignored in the iconography, and that aged female roles are so very negative, is a clear indication of the painters' agenda.

Conclusion

Evidently the painters of Athenian pots presented women according to the dominant ideology of feminine behaviour – women become visible in art only in certain roles, as brides, mothers, celebrants of religion, or the grotesquely aged. Although the imagery shows images of women throughout their life cycle, the vision we have is patchy; there are very limited views of some stages of female life, such as childhood and widowhood, and other areas of experience private to women are not pictured at all. There are significant disparities between both art and literature, on the one hand, and art and the actuality of Athenian society on the other; art and literature frequently offer contradictory evidence because they focus on different aspects of a topic, and, equally, both (for example on the subject of slaves) represent ideal rather than reality. Ceramic art can tell us a great deal about the ways in which women were valued and felt to be relevant to their society, but there remains a further question: if women are visible on Athenian pottery only in specific roles, are these the roles in which they would recognise themselves? For some of the objects considered, women certainly had an input into what was depicted and an investment in the ideology, as with the depictions of motherhood in funerary art. But the images of female life created for use within Athens tie women very closely to particular roles, from that of mourner to participant in ritual, and are difficult to find 'alternative readings' for. Those points on which female existence varies from the civic agenda – the importance of childbirth, the power of old age, and the closeness of female family members – are unlikely to find expression in art at all, and archaeology indicates that it was through other media that expression of these ideas was made. The argument that all images of women were open to recuperation by female viewers as positive images of female solidarity and friendship does not seem satisfactory from an archaeological perspective: the imagery of most pottery was created with export in mind, and the view of women offered is that of the public face of the polis – the centrality of the female in religion, the role of women as mourners, and the relationship between the mother and the warrior – which is hard to escape.

2

DOMESTIC LABOUR

Of all themes on pottery, that of domestic work is most often invoked as evidence of everyday life in classical Greece. It is a familiar topic in discussions of women's life: authors duly present a series of images illustrating different household tasks, and the illustrations are taken to be photographic reproductions of Athenian housewives at typical daily jobs. As is often the case with iconography, a deceptively small number of pots are frequently reproduced to illustrate women's tasks within the household. But domestic work, like every other iconographic theme, has its own conventions of representation, is subject to change over time, and is unevenly patterned over the Greek world. This chapter will illustrate and comment on women's tasks, as shown on pottery, but with an appreciation of the fragmentary and partial nature of the evidence. It will also focus on the relative frequency of scenes, since simply illustrating each task which is depicted can conceal significant variations in the actual numbers of pots representing individual themes. For example, the process of carding wool before it is spun is always included in a list of female occupations known from scenes on pots, yet very few examples of the theme are found in comparison to spinning with the distaff.[1]

It is easy to be drawn into the expectation that 'everyday life' will naturally be documented on pottery; in fact, what is remarkable is not that some scenes should be absent but that any are present: why should painters at different periods develop an interest in certain domestic tasks? To echo the comments of Boardman, it is only by exploring the limitations of the iconography that we can gain an understanding of what is present.[2] Any discussion must also take account of the circumstances in which scenes of domestic work were painted and viewed, since a striking feature is that most are not found on those shapes of pottery for distinctly 'female use'. Shapes such as pyxides, lekythoi or lebetes tend to carry images of marriage and leisure; work proper appears far more often on cups, kraters or pelikai. This has implications for our interpretation of these scenes, since it indicates that the purpose of domestic imagery cannot be, as has been suggested, to reinforce the stereotypes which guided the lives of Athenian women. Pots found within Athens show that female buyers were subscribing to an ideology of the desirability of leisure, while domestic work is found more often on pots intended for export. Images of women at work were sent to Italy and Magna Graecia, where they were placed in tombs by their purchasers; the reasons for their marketing and use require explanation.

The nature of women's work

As I said in the Introduction, to define a topic is essentially to create it. Can one treat domestic work as a theme the parameters of which are self-evident? Some Greek sources discuss the duties of a wife, and these reflect a common conception of the female domestic role. Xenophon in the *Oikonomikos* describes through his speaker Ischomoachos the role that the wife of a 'καλὸς κἀγαθός' [gentleman] should fulfil (although this is at an elite level), and similar ideas can be found in comic and legal sources. Xenophon's depiction of the female role relies on a sharp distinction between indoor and outdoor work: Ischomachos prefaces his account with a discussion of how men are formed physically and mentally for outdoor work, and women suited to indoor work (7.22–8). It is not surprising that his definition of the female role should involve his wife remaining indoors, with the organisation of the house as her chief occupation:

> Δεήσει μέντοι σε, ἔφην ἐγώ, ἔνδον τε μένειν καὶ οἷς μὲν ἂν ἔξω τὸ ἔργον ἦ τῶν οἰκετῶν, τούτους συνεκπέμπειν, οἷς δ' ἂν ἔνδον ἔργον ἐργαστέον, τούτων σοι ἐπιστατητέον, καὶ τά τε εἰσφερόμενα ἀποδεκτέον καὶ ἃ μὲν ἂν αὐτῶν δέη δαπανᾶν σοὶ διανεμητέον, ἃ δ' ἂν περιττεύειν δέη, προνοητέον καὶ φυλακτέον ὅπως μὴ ἡ εἰς τὸν ἐνιαυτὸν κειμένη δαπάνη εἰς τὸν μῆνα δαπανᾶται. καὶ ὅταν ἔρια εἰσενεχθῆ σοι, ἐπιμελητέον ὅπως οἷς δεῖ ἱμάτια γίγνηται. καὶ ὅ γε ξηρὸς σῖτος ὅπως καλῶς ἐδώδιμος γίγνηται ἐπιμελητέον.

> ['Your role, however', I said, 'is to remain indoors, and to send out whichever of the slaves has work to do outside, and to take charge of those whose work is indoors. You should receive whatever is brought in, and you must distribute that part of it which needs to be spent, and that part which should be kept in store you must take good care to keep, so that the money laid aside for the year's expenses is not spent in a month. When wool is brought to you, you should see to it that cloaks are made for those who need them, and you should see to it too that the dry corn doesn't spoil.']

> (*Oik.* 7.35–6)

Xenophon's speaker Ischomachos thus envisages a household with many slaves, in which the role of the wife is mainly supervisory, sending the outdoor workers out and observing the indoor workers. Nevertheless domestic work is defined in certain activities: overseeing wool-work, breadmaking, looking after stores, and keeping the house in order. The care of children is mentioned, although only in passing, as is the care of the sick.[3] The same view of domestic roles is reflected in sources like Lysias 1.7, in which the speaker praises his wife as 'οἰκονόμος δεινὴ καὶ φειδωλός' [a clever and thrifty housekeeper], and the comment in Euripides' *Melanippe*:

> νέμουσι δ' οἴκους καὶ τὰ ναυστολούμενα
> ἔσω δόμων σώιζουσιν, οὐδ' ἐρημίαι
> γυναικὸς οἶκος εὐπινὴς οὐδ' ὄλβιος.

> [women manage homes and preserve the goods which are brought from abroad. Houses where there is no wife are neither orderly nor prosperous.]

> (fr. 499 N)

In this view the role of the husband is that of production, and that of the wife the preservation and processing of what is produced. It is an idealising view, and as we shall see there are some contrasting views of female work detectable in genres such as comedy. But should we expect pottery to tell the same story?

Female domestic work has specific characteristics which influence any artistic representation, as well as being a topic which carries strong cultural expectations, as a comparative example will show. In modern Western culture, images of women at domestic tasks are very limited. Even supposedly lifelike genres such as television soap operas ignore everyday chores – repetitive drudgery hardly makes compelling television. In Victorian times, however, when female self-image depended to a large extent on domestic competence, guides on domestic management, such as *Mrs Beeton's Book of Household Management* (1861), were commonplace, and publications for women up until the Second World War, such as *Every Woman's Enquire Within*, published in the 1940s, included instruction on particular aspects of household work.[4] As the female domestic role has diminished in social importance, however, the instructive mode has been replaced in women's publications by features on tasks seen to be more creative, such as decoration, craft and cookery. The genre of household advice is nevertheless still with us, having been taken over principally by advertisements. Producers of cleaning agents and appliances illustrate the efficacy of their product, while simultaneously offering advice or instruction: use product X to add freshness to your wash; simply spray your bathroom with product Y and wipe; clean and disinfect your kitchen with product Z. Within this genre the nature of representation is obviously influenced by the character of the work. Some aspects of household work are more popular and more frequently shown: for example, hoovering, folding clean clothes, washing dishes (or unloading a dishwasher). Other aspects are less popular: personified cleaning agents, rather than humans, are shown cleaning bathrooms and sinks, while bedmaking and tidying are also less common because fewer products exist to assist with them, and because they are dull and repetitive.

Furthermore, advertising as a medium is subject to particular strain because it is required to both form and follow public opinion: adverts must be novel in order to interest and persuade, yet however novel its content an advert which is not consonant with expectations will not succeed.[5] Ideology has come to underlie the presentation of domestic work very strongly, making it a public arena for gender hostility – while domestic work is still mainly the province of women, since the 1990s it has become much more common in advertising for cleaning agents to show men engaged in domestic tasks extolling the virtues of a product which enables tasks to be done more quickly and efficiently than traditional (female) methods. This approach both embraces feminist ideology (men must do housework too) and at the same time recuperates it (women make too much fuss about housework when it can be performed so easily with product X).

In what ways does this shed light on ancient representation of domestic tasks? Greek domestic work was of far greater importance than modern, since it involved the processing of raw materials into usable forms – milling grain, baking bread, spinning and weaving – as well as caring for domestic plants and animals. Although vital to the household it was not seen as inherently interesting or important work and was considered to be very much inferior to male work. Plato, discussing female competence in the *Republic*, admits that women are more skilful than men at household tasks, but dismisses this as an inappropriate arena for competition:

ἢ μακρολογῶμεν τήν τε ὑφαντικὴν λέγοντες καὶ τὴν τῶν ποπάνων τε καὶ
ἑψημάτων θεραπείαν, ἐν οἷς δή τι δοκεῖ τὸ γυναικεῖον γένος εἶναι, οὗ καὶ
καταγελαστότατόν ἐστι πάντων ἡττώμενον;

[Need I waste time in speaking of the art of weaving, and the management of
pancakes and preserves, in which womankind does indeed appear to excel,
and in which for her to be outdone by a man is of all things the most absurd?]

(Rep. 455c–d)

Xenophon's *Oikonomikos* is unusual as an example of the philosophy which defined female
work as 'different but equal' to men's work; most other sources assume female work to
be simple and unimportant. This means that in art the nature of domestic tasks as
unrelenting, hard and messy is played down; physicality – the strength required to carry
water or grind corn – is rarely portrayed, since women's work must by definition be easy.
The repetitive nature of female work is also significant: even more than today, tasks such
as fetching water and grinding grain for bread needed to be done constantly in order for
the household to function. In myth domestic tasks tend to serve as a metaphor for endless
or unproductive toil; for example, the Danaidai, depicted on pottery as filling a water jar
with leaking sieves, or the Moirai (Fates), whose endless spinning represents the lives of
men. And of course there is Penelope, weaving in the day and unpicking her work by night
for three years.[6] The metaphoric form through which the torment of unending work is
expressed is primarily domestic.

Wool-work

We should thus expect to find the representation of domestic work influenced by these
attitudes. What emerges most strongly from literary sources is a conceptual division in
the category of household work: in the Greek sources it falls into two groups. Wool-work,
the canonical expression of female domestic labour, childcare and household management
are highly rated tasks, while other activities are more often dismissed or omitted from
consideration. There can be no doubt that wool-work is the most significant aspect
of female work for the painters. This is because wool-work functions so much as
an ideological marker across all media: literature, epitaphs and art. Spinning and weaving
are the tasks which mark women as both female and virtuous, and hence items used in
cloth production, such as spindle-whorls, distaffs and loom-weights (used to hold down
the ends of the warp on the loom) are found as votive offerings and grave-goods, parallel
to the weapons deposited in male graves. Wool-work functions in epitaphs as a shorthand
for female work in general, and wool-working implements, or the activity itself, feature
in many scenes on pottery. Because of this an initial distinction needs to be made between
scenes of actual work, of production, where the activity is the focus of the scene, and scenes
of leisure or family life where wool-work is functioning as a marker. For instance, in many
wedding scenes a bride holds a distaff, but this is not a scene of work as such.

As well as indicating domestic virtue, working in wool constituted an important
contribution to the economy of the oikos. Women on marriage would bring with them
woven goods, as a store of wealth as much as to wear, and as early as the lawcode of Gortyn
it was specified that in the event of a divorce a woman of Gortyn had the right to half the
woven goods she had produced during her marriage.[7] We should think of the production

Figure 2.1 Attic red-figure pyxis, Paris, Musée du Louvre CA 587, *c*.450 BC (drawing). Reproduced by permission of Prof. F. Lissarrague.

of clothes as being more than just for immediate wear; clothes were also a means of storing up wealth which could be liquidated in a crisis, or (in the case of the poor) for immediate sale. Perhaps scenes involving the folding of finished cloth, such as that on a stamnos by the Copenhagen Painter depicting two young women folding a cloth ready to store it in an open chest, while an older woman looks on, refer to this idea of created wealth as much as pure domestic activity; one may also compare the pyxis in the Louvre (fig. 2.1) showing a wedding scene, on which one woman holds out a cloth for the bride to inspect.[8]

Naturally enough, the painters' interest focuses on certain aspects of wool-work: it is not possible to trace the whole process in exact stages. For instance, we do not see the preliminary stage of preparing raw fleeces, although these figure in literary women's complaints: in *Lysistrata* (728–32; cf. 574–8) one of the women tries to leave the Acropolis on the pretext that she has fleeces to prepare, while in Theocritus 15.19–20 Praxinoe criticises her husband for the shoddy fleeces he has bought for her to spin. On several pots we see lumps of wool put into or taken out of the wool basket (kalathos), as on a kalpis in Rhodes; on a hydria in Houston (fig. 2.2) a woman in a patterned dress places wool in a kalathos as another holds out two alabastra, and a heron-like bird looks on.[9] The wool here is shown as an undifferentiated lump, presumably indicating an early stage before spinning. One of the tasks of the wife described in *Oikonomikos* is to weigh out the wool for the slaves to work, an overseer's role mentioned in the *Distaff* of Erinna as well.[10] This activity appears on the well-known black-figure lekythos by the Amasis Painter with a frieze of wool-work, where two women weigh lumps of wool in a balance; in this example the weighing is not the high-status role suggested by the literature, since it is performed by two women while the seated mistress looks on. Carding wool, to remove burrs and dirt before spinning, is a theme which makes a brief appearance in red-figure (fig. 2.3), possibly because of the opportunity it offered to show women with legs uncovered (although it is worth remembering that a black-figure eye-cup was presented as a prize in a carding contest in the Spartan colony of Tarentum, so the correspondence between cups and carding may be closer than we think).[11] The representation of carding is clearly not realistic, since the women on these cups dispose of the usual aid to smoothing wool, the epinetron or shinguard, and draw the fibres across their shins instead – something which would be both uncomfortable and ineffective. It is also worth noting that form is not following function here – these images appear on cups, while epinetra, which were used in the carding process, were either undecorated or carried scenes of marriage or myth.[12] Scenes of carding were therefore not intended for the workers themselves.

Spinning with a distaff is a theme which becomes popular early on, and remains the principal way of denoting female wool-work; the distaff often hangs in the background

Figure 2.2 Attic red-figure hydria, Houston, Museum of Fine Arts 80.95, 470–460 BC. Photo courtesy The Museum of Fine Arts, Houston: Museum purchase with funds provided by General and Mrs Maurice Hirsch.

to a scene if not in use. On the other hand the process of threading a loom is not shown (although loom-weights are very common grave deposits for women), and depictions of weaving on a large loom are rare, although a full-size loom appears on a hydria in Harvard, empty of weaving, to denote activity in a symbolic way (fig. 1.3). Also, on the well-known skyphos by the Penelope Painter, Penelope sits in front of a full-size loom with an elaborate piece of weaving on it (though she does not work at it).[13] We have only one scene of a large loom in use, on the Amasis Painter's lekythos, where two small figures stand working at a loom which reaches the top of the field. Finally, there are no depictions of the process of finishing cloth or taking it from the loom, although the folding of finished cloth features,

Figure 2.3 Attic red-figure pyxis, New York, Metropolitan Museum of Art 06.1117, *c.*460 BC (drawing). After Richter/Hall pl. 96.

as noted above. The making of actual clothes, in so far as clothes were manufactured (rather than just pieces of cloth for draping over the body), is completely absent.

The choice of scenes to represent suggests that wool-work is fulfilling the same ideological function on pots as in other media. Obviously iconographic concerns dictate the processes shown: the distaff offers a convenient, small and easily represented symbol for wool-working, as does the kalathos or wool-basket which itself becomes metonymic for weaving, rather than the accurate but cumbersome loom. Wool-work can be shown on a very small scale, within the gynaikonitis, and is (comparatively) pleasant work, without dirt or undue exertion. The 'Lucretia' idea (wool-work as symbolic of both female virtue and sexual appeal, as in Livy's story of the rape of Lucretia) is very powerful: painters show women engaged in the dainty aspects of the work, rather than the physically demanding.[14] Weaving on a full-size loom, standing up, is very tiring. One factor worth noting is the extent of idealisation in such themes; small-scale cloth production is the norm on pottery, when in practice all cloth for the household had to be produced on the large loom. The object in which painters are most interested is the handloom, surely too small to be of practical use, yet easily depicted, and with a useful overlap in shape with an instrument of leisure, the lyre.[15]

Figure 2.4 Attic red-figure skyphos, Malibu, J.P. Getty Museum 85.AE.304, *c.*460 BC (drawing).

Food preparation

In the case of cloth production, then, the preoccupations of writers and painters are very close. In other areas of domestic work, however, there is a clear discrepancy between Attic painting and other media. The image of the wife keeping order in the house, storing provisions and managing foodstuffs, is, as we have seen, a central idea in literature, yet only one representation seems to reflect this role – a skyphos from Malibu (fig. 2.4).[16] On one side it has a unique depiction of a storeroom, in which amphorae and a chest are stacked, with a barred window in the wall. On the other a fat woman walks away, drinking from an outsize skyphos, followed by a small girl carrying a bundle on her head, possibly a wineskin. This woman is clearly not the οἰκονόμος δεινὴ [clever housekeeper] of Lysias 1.7; instead she is part of the alternative view of women and store-cupboards found in Aristophanes:

> ἃ δ' ἦν ἡμῖν πρὸ τοῦ
> αὐταῖς ταμιεῦσαι καὶ προαιρούσαις λαβεῖν
> ἄλφιτον, ἔλαιον, οἶνον, οὐδὲ ταῦτ' ἔτι
> ἔξεστιν. Οἱ γὰρ ἄνδρες ἤδη κλειδία
> αὐτοὶ φοροῦσι κρυπτά, κακοηθέστατα,
> Λακωνίκ' ἄττα, τρεῖς ἔχοντα γομφίους.

[But the way we used to be able to be our own storekeepers, and take out barley-meal, oil, wine undetected – even that isn't possible any more, because the men now carry around keys themselves, wicked secret Laconian affairs with three teeth.]

(Thesm. 418–23)

In comedy it is husbands who hold the keys to the stores, and women who steal secretly from them, especially wine. This comic theme which belittles women's role in housekeeping goes all the way back to Hesiod's and Semonides' depictions of women as parasites on hard-working men.[17] No other images, positive or negative, of women as storekeepers exist on Athenian pottery.

A second area where discrepancy between different media is strong is the preparation of food. Food as a theme in Greek literature is very prominent, from comedy to sympotic literature. Bread-making is definitely the province of women in literature: Thucydides famously relates that at the siege of Plataia all the non-combatants were evacuated from the polis, with the exception of 110 women retained as σιτοποιοί [baking women] (2.78.3). Aristophanes brings on stage an ἀρτοπῶλις [female bread-seller] in *Wasps* 1388ff., and his breadsellers are all female, as are his vegetable women (*Wasps* 497; *Lys.* 562–4).[18] Baking was an essential task, since grain had to be milled into flour and baked for every day's bread; it was also, as Sparkes points out, very time consuming, since fires had to be fed and, because of the irregular heat, food needed to be constantly watched while it cooked.[19] Grinding or milling of grain could take on a religious significance too: the women's chorus in *Lysistrata* name the role of ἀλετρίς [holy grinding-maid] to Athena as one of the duties to the city which they have performed, and the Scholia comment that 'ἱεροὶ μυλῶνες' [sacred millers] existed for other cults too.[20] Bread and cakes were frequent offerings in ritual, and women with loaves appear on two pots: a cup by Makron in Laon and a white-ground lekythos in Athens. Both show women carrying a plate or basket of loaves; the lack of other elements in the scene, and the funerary purpose of the lekythos, suggests that they represent ritual offerings rather than the act of cooking.[21]

On this topic it is important to be precise about the origin of cooking scenes, since images of food preparation are few on Athenian pottery and often indeterminate. For instance, evidence from the excavation of urban sites in Greece demonstrates that the milling of grain was commonly done on a domestic level, and grinding-stones have been found in domestic contexts such as Olynthus.[22] The commonest form was the simple but physically taxing saddle quern, where an ellipsoid stone is used to grind the grain in a

Figure 2.5 Attic red-figure cup, Berlin, Staatliche Museen 1966.21, *c.*500 BC (drawing).

shallow concave basin. Only one image seems to depict this activity: a red-figure cup in Berlin (fig. 2.5) shows two women standing at waist-level trays, their hands holding lumpy objects.[23] This has been interpreted in the past as women kneading dough, but this was more usually done in a basin. It is odd that so everyday a task is so little documented on pottery, since it is shown much more often in terracottas: a Boiotian example in Lausanne is of a woman kneeling at a grinding-stone, and another from Rhodes in London represents a woman standing as she grinds. Another terracotta from Rhodes depicts a woman grinding, and the arms of the figure are jointed at the shoulder to allow her to appear to rub the stone back and forth (fig. 2.6). If this is, as Sparkes suggests, a child's toy then it is one designed to produce early socialisation![24] More frequently depicted on pots than grinding (though only comparatively) is pounding with pestle and mortar, used both for hulling grain, as a preliminary to grinding, or for pounding pulses or fish. The pestle and mortar were typically made of wood (Hesiod, *Works and Days* 423), so were not likely to be used for daily milling. Pestle-and-mortar scenes are found on a few Athenian black-figure pots (an amphora in St Petersburg by the Swing Painter shows two women using pestles in a mortar (fig. 2.7), and a fragment from Eleusis similarly shows women at a mortar), but there is only one red-figure example known – on a fragmentary cup by Onesimos, showing on the outside a youth and girl pounding corn in a vessel, and inside another woman with a pestle standing behind her.[25] Athenian painters are interested in the pestle, but not as an implement of daily work; it appears far more

Figure 2.6 Rhodian terracotta, London, British Museum 233, *c.*450 BC. Photo courtesy British Museum. © The British Museum.

frequently on red-figure pots as a woman's weapon, wielded by the Thracian women in scenes of the death of Orpheus, and by Andromache at the sack of Troy (and in one case, an attack on Herakles). The use of a domestic implement as a weapon emphasises violence in a context of gender hostility. Andromache invariably uses a pestle to defend herself and her son against Neoptolemos in scenes of the sack of Troy; she has been presented in the myth as the perfect wife, so her vain defence against the rapacious Greek with a symbol of domestic labour is all the more poignant. The Thracian women, in contrast, are uncivilised, and attack Orpheus with female tools, pestles and sickles, as a reversal of the heroic scenario; these women are powerful, usurping the privilege of the male, not through the appropriation of masculine weapons such as spears or swords but through their own domestic tools turned to murderous ends.[26] The pestle, then, has more to communicate in myth than in simple scenes of reality.

Figure 2.7 Attic black-figure amphora, St Petersburg, The State Hermitage Museum 2065, *c.*540 BC (drawing).

The infrequency of scenes showing women milling or grinding is part of a general attitude towards food preparation in Attic pot-painting. Scenes of non-ritual cooking are not common: on a squat lekythos from Sicily a woman sitting in a well-equipped kitchen cooks cakes on an eschara, a type of oven (fig. 2.8); a cup by the Brygos Painter depicts a woman leaning over a cauldron, although the scene is too fragmented for the activity to be entirely clear; a woman leans over a smoking oven with a piece of dough in her hand on a fragmentary cup in the Louvre; and on a lekanis in St Petersburg with a wedding scene two women work at a table, moulding sesame cakes for use in the wedding feast, while another smaller figure by their side apparently kneads the dough in a small laver. One might also include a lekythos in Haverford College by the Pan Painter showing two women in a kitchen, one ladling liquid from a psykter into a skyphos (fig. 2.9).[27] These examples are few, and various in setting, yet in other fabrics and media representations of cookery are detailed and common. In Boiotian art, for instance, a lekythos in the Serpieri collection provides a good illustration of what Attic painters avoid (fig. 2.10): it depicts a busy kitchen scene, with little male figures fanning the fire, while women pound grain and cook loaves.[28] On another

Figure 2.8 Attic red-figure squat lekythos, Vienna, Kunsthistorisches Museum 4.1921, *c.*430 BC. Photo courtesy Kunsthistorisches Museum, Vienna (neg. no. 13535).

Figure 2.9 Attic red-figure lekythos, Haverford College, 480–470 BC (drawing).

Figure 2.10 Boiotian black-figure lekythos, Athens, National Museum Serpieri Collection 121, *c.*550 BC. Photo courtesy National Archaeological Museum, Athens.

black-figure skyphos in the Canellopoulos collection (fig. 2.11) two women named Kodoma and Euarchia pound in a mortar, while Eupharia looks on and spins.[29] An early Corinthian pot shows a woman taking food to two prisoners in the stocks, while an Ionian black-figure dinos shows a man and a woman pounding to the music of a flute player, with a dinos over a fire behind them.[30] Cooking as a female activity is even more strongly denoted in Boiotian terracottas, where scenes of women cooking, often with younger girls in attendance, abound. These figurines were found in large numbers in graves at Tanagra and Rhitsona, and at the start of the fourth century a whole series appeared depicting men and women cooking, as well as at other crafts. Female figures grind or pound grain, mix and knead dough in a basin, cook in a pot over a fire, carry cakes and loaves to the oven (fig. 2.12), and watch them while they cook. There are also two larger sixth-century bakery scenes from Argos, quite reminiscent of the Serpieri lekythos scene.[31] Higgins originally suggested that these figures were intended to supply the needs of the dead in the afterlife, or on their journey, but more recently has turned away from this explanation and suggests instead that they are children's toys.[32] Whatever their purpose, terracottas illustrate the mundane, in contrast to pottery, while Greek fabrics other than Athenian offer more 'realistic' views – especially Boiotia. Why should this be? It is true that Boiotian painting is often more rustic and comic in inspiration than Athenian, but the question may have more to do with gender: cookery may be found only once or twice on Attic pots as women's work, but it appears more often as men's work, specifically as part of sacrificial ritual. A cup in Paris, for instance, illustrates the stages of cutting up and roasting meat on the outside, and in the centre a man oversees a boiling cauldron.[33] The male responsibility for festal cooking is echoed in comedy, in which men are shown cooking more often than women: Dikaiopolis cooks his celebratory dinner in *Acharnians* (1003ff.), and Strepsiades refers to cooking a black pudding for the Diasia in *Clouds* (408–9). The contrast is most clearly marked in *Peace*, where Trygaeus cooks a sacrifice himself

Figure 2.11 Boiotian black-figure skyphos, Athens, Canellopoulos Museum 384, 525–500 BC (side A). Photo courtesy Canellopoulos Museum, Athens.

Figure 2.12 Boiotian terracotta, Boston, Museum of Fine Arts 01.7788, early fifth century BC. Photo courtesy Museum of Fine Arts, Boston.

(1040ff.), but later refers to his wife cooking in a domestic context (1146). On pottery the public face of cookery is definitely male; men are shown in exterior scenes, around an altar, while women who cook are very firmly in an interior, as on the Vienna and Haverford College lekythoi (figs. 2.8, 2.9). Only one pot shows men and women cooking together: a black-figure stand in Toledo.[34] It has been suggested that the exclusion of women from the ritual of sacrifice is a result of menstrual taboos on women handling meat in general; this can be traced from Homer onwards, and seems to be manifested in the types of food women prepared and sold in public (bread and vegetables). *Lysistrata* 457–8 identifies women as sellers of bread, garlic and vegetables, while throughout Aristophanes' plays the sellers of fish and meat are male (*Wasps* 494–7).[35] Certainly on the pottery we have, women do not cook meat; legs of meat sometimes feature as erotic gifts, and women do sometimes receive these, or appear with meat, as on a lekythos in Rome with a woman feeding a pet dog (fig. 2.13), but although

women handle meat, and sometimes take it to be cooked, it is only men who are shown cooking it.[36]

Just as the pestle featured in the arena of gender hostility, it is also possible that women's cooking carried the same suggestion of threat: an alternative aspect to cookery and women is the idea of magic, of women cooking up poisons and potions. It is no coincidence that we encounter on pottery the daughters of Pelias together with Medea, promising to rejuvenate their father Pelias by boiling him in a cauldron (fig. 2.14), and Circe bewitching Odysseus' companions, always shown with cup and wand for mixing the potion which turned them into animals.[37] Andokides' speech *Against the Stepmother for Poisoning* illustrates that such fantasy could have parallels in real life: a concubine is accused of poisoning her husband and his friend, having intended to administer a love potion to restore his waning affection for her. The undercurrent of threat, that domestic labour could always be turned to murderous ends, is psychologically very interesting.

Water

In contrast to cooking, water and washing scenes are much more enthusiastically shown by Athenian painters, and are more uncomplicatedly feminine.[38] The earliest 'domestic' task depicted on pottery is the fetching of water at the fountain-house, and, as we have seen, this demonstrates some of the difficulties of interpretation. It is the only female chore which is represented in black-figure, and is part of a suite of scenes chosen for the hydria and amphora by black-figure painters; some workshops, principally those of the

Figure 2.13 Attic red-figure lekythos, Rome, Accademia dei Lincei 2478, 470–460 BC. Photo: Foto Introne, courtesy Accademia Nazionale dei Lincei, Rome.

Antimenes Painter, the Priam Painter and the Leagros Group, use it as a motif on many hydriai. They depict groups of women at an architecturally sophisticated fountain-house, bringing empty hydriai and carrying away full ones (figs. 0.1, 2.15). Sometimes boys or men appear in the scenes too, and on one or two pots gods are present as onlookers.[39] One

Figure 2.14 Attic black-figure lekythos, Erlangen 1429, *c*.490 BC. Photo courtesy Institut für Klassische Archäologie und Antikensammlung, Universität Erlangen-Nürnberg.

reason for the popularity of the scene can be derived from comparison with other black-figure hydria scenes: the architectural aspect. On hydriai, there is a clear interest in images which fill the panel – the frontal chariot, for instance, or the centrally symmetrical battle scene. The fountain-house provides an exceptionally clear framework for the scene, and the women (or men) involved are shown in procession, one per panel or spout. Once the theme is invented, painters play with its representation – fountain from the front, with architrave, from the side, at one end of the panel, or absent altogether, but the balanced composition is always the same. So we find pots on which alternate women approach the water with an unfilled (horizontal) hydria on their head, and return with a filled, vertical pot; this culminates in the scene on a hydria in Florence (fig. 2.16), on which the fountain is absent, and we see only a procession of women carrying hydriai on their heads, with one figure at the left holding up an unfilled jar.[40]

But there is no simple correlation between water pots and fountain scenes. Fountains are frequent on hydriai, but not as frequent as certain other themes: the labours of

Figure 2.15 Attic black-figure hydria, Würzburg, M. von Wagner Museum L304, *c*.530 BC. Photo courtesy M. von Wagner Museum, Würzburg (neg. no. PF 9/7).

Herakles, warriors arming, departing or fighting, and chariots racing or being harnessed. In fact, the majority of scenes on black-figure hydriai are martial, fountains comprising only a small fraction of the whole. The placing of the scene is also noteworthy: most other scenes occur in different formats, on the body or the shoulder of the pot, whereas fountains appear only as body panels. This means that when the hydria was picked up, or viewed from above, the fountain scene was never the first scene that one encountered. Only by holding the pot up, or displaying it at a height, would the body scene be appreciated. Furthermore, the fountain scene is never the sole decoration of any black-figure hydria. All carry two scenes (shoulder and body), and some a further predella, and the scenes are drawn from the standard range of hydria decoration – heroes fighting monsters, chariots racing, warriors, hunting. When so few hydriai carry scenes of water-drawing, and those which do also carry other scenes such as Herakles and Kyknos on the shoulder and a boar-hunt below, we cannot claim that only the fountain scene defines the pot.

The question of how one makes sense of such a variety of images has been discussed by Manfrini-Aragno, who has tried to isolate thematic elements within the scenes in order to identify a coherent ideology.[11] She argues that the women at the fountain are to be seen as occupying an intermediate stage between adolescence and adulthood, similar to the ephebes whose hunting activities are depicted alongside. They are not part of a depiction addressed to women, but are designed for the symposium, to be read by men as part of male discourse about women. On this reading, the scenes of battle and of heroic exploits

73

Figure 2.16 Attic black-figure hydria, Florence 3792, *c*.530 BC. Photo courtesy Soprintendenza Archeologica di Firenze.

are designed for sympotic viewers, and the fountain scenes are a commentary on women designed for the same purpose. Other attempts have been made to connect the development of the fountain theme with the building of the Enneakrounoi fountain under the Pisistratids, and hence to see a motive of Athenian (or pro-tyrannical) propaganda in the representation; some see a ritual act depicted, either the festival of the Hydrophoria, at which a libation of water was made to Hermes, or the fetching of water from the spring Kallirhoe for the bridal bath in wedding ritual.[42] There are, however, two central problems with reading the fountain-house scenes. First, it is a scene which becomes fashionable in a particular ware, but dies out with the advent of red-figure after about 500 BC. Fountain scenes become both less common and more varied in type in earlier red-figure; in later red-figure they are absent. Hannestad has suggested that this is because slaves took over what had been a citizen's task, and so the scene became lower in status, but this will not explain why it dies out just at the time that domestic scenes in general, and those showing slaves, are becoming more common. Second, most black-figure hydriai with fountain (and other) scenes are found not in Greece, but in Italy – they come from a period of very high export of large pots to the Etruscan centres of Vulci and Cervetri, where they were used as tomb furniture rather than for domestic purposes. The workshops most fond of fountain themes are those whose works derive predominantly from Vulci, and who therefore realised that they were painting for the tastes of an export market. This forces a reinterpretation of the meaning of the imagery: for instance, the whole 'Pisistratan propaganda' argument would be irrelevant to an Etruscan market. One might suggest instead a need for a female scene to balance the martial imagery, if these pots were being chosen for male and female

Figure 2.17 Attic red-figure cup, Florence 76103, *c*.490 BC (drawing).

Figure 2.18 Attic red-figure pelike, St Petersburg, The State Hermitage Museum, *c*.470 BC (drawing).

graves, an idea supported by the range of other scenes depicted: we see married couples in chariots, and many scenes of Dionysus and his followers, as well as mythic and real warriors, all scenes assimilable to funerary themes in Etruscan culture.[43] The fountain-house, then, may be part of a gender-specific range of themes for the afterlife.

Water scenes of more varied types become much more popular in red-figure. Several iconographic themes depicting aspects of washing have been described – for instance, woman drawing water from wells. The cup in Milan by the Brygos Painter is the best-known example of this type – a woman stands beside a well (a giant pithos sunk into the ground) holding a bucket in one hand and a rope in the other.[44] The wall and roof in the background indicate a space inside the courtyard of a house. Several other examples repeat the theme: a cup in Florence (fig. 2.17) depicting a woman lowering a rope into a similar well, and another in Vienna on which a woman holds a bucket over a well with a tree in the background. A pelike in St Petersburg depicts a woman holding two water jars (fig. 2.18).[45] Then there are scenes of women washing clothes. The Pan Painter has two of the best examples: a pelike in Madrid (fig. 3.3) has a woman standing at a large krater from which an end of cloth hangs out, holding blocks in her hands, while another pelike in the Louvre (fig. 2.19) depicts two women standing at a krater, one holding up a piece of cloth and the other a block. Related to this theme is the cup in the Vatican with a scene of a woman standing in front of a krater holding up an alabastron.[46] Interpretation of the exact task shown is difficult, but the scene is set in a domestic context by the doorway behind the figure. Finally there is a series of cup tondi depicting women standing and working at a laver on a stand: these are quite numerous, and are found in the work of many early red-figure painters. For instance, a fragmentary cup in Leipzig (fig. 2.20) shows a woman bending over a basin close to the ground, either

Figure 2.19 Attic red-figure pelike, Paris, Musée du Louvre G547, *c.*470 BC. Photo: M. et P. Chuzéville, courtesy Musée du Louvre, Paris.

drawing water from a well or washing. The form of the laver and the kados behind suggest the latter. Also indeterminate is a cup in Paris, on which a woman leans over a very deep laver on a stand. A pestle stands against the wall behind her, but the depth of the krater, and her clothes, imply work in water.[47] Douris has three cups depicting women working at a laver, each presented with different objects in the background, basins or buckets at the foot of the laver, baskets, tables, and in two cases what seem to be aulos cases, hanging up to signal an interior (figs. 2.21 and 4.3). Further examples in Frankfurt, London and Copenhagen all repeat the theme, with objects such as oinochoai and pithoi in the scenes.[48]

The appearance of kraters and skyphoi in scenes of work at the laver has led some to interpret them as images of preparation for the symposion, but this seems an overinterpretation: objects such as klinai in the background signal 'interior' rather than simply 'banquet', and there is little reason to look for a link with sympotic scenes, especially as most of these cups are undecorated outside.[49] The aulos cases may perhaps be an exception, since the aulos is not a feature of domestic life, but the design of laver scenes tends to a 'port-hole' effect, suggesting an interest in the interior for its own sake. The exact type of work being done on these pots is indeterminate, but a cup in Munich, on which a woman stands at a laver holding a skyphos (fig. 2.22), perhaps

Figure 2.20 Attic red-figure cup, Leipzig T530, 490–480 BC (drawing).

indicates the nature of the activity most clearly.[50] The woman is unlikely to be pouring water into the laver using a skyphos, as has been suggested, for there is no bucket or basin from which to take water, nor is a skyphos the most sensible vessel to use. Pouring water is clearly shown on a similar cup in Boston, on which a youth pours water into a laver from an oinochoe – water which he has taken from a basin at his feet.[51] The woman in this example, if not adding water to her laver, may be doing something as mundane as washing up; other women working at lavers have been labelled as grinding or cooking, but water-based activities are much more likely from the objects which surround

Figure 2.21 Attic red-figure cup, Tarquinia RC 1116, *c*.480 BC (drawing).

them. The lack of very accurate depiction of the type of work is probably deliberate, either because the painters did not have an iconography to represent the task accurately or, more likely, because accuracy was not important. The painters are not necessarily interested in precisely what is being washed, but in the activity itself.

There is a significant contrast between the representation of washing in earlier and later red-figure. These scenes form a clear group among early red-figure artists, but disappear after the 450s, and later scenes of washing are entirely mythical in setting. Nausicaa and her maids washing clothes at the river are depicted on two pots, a pyxis in Boston and a neck-amphora in Munich.[52] On the latter, the women hold or wring out clothes, while more are hung up to dry in a convenient tree. One might suspect that washing of clothes would be most effectively done at the river or fountain, but in fact these scenes are less realistic. The non-mythical scenes of washing are extremely enclosed; the well is shown

Figure 2.22 Attic red-figure cup, Munich, Antikensammlungen 2679, *c.*480 BC. Photo: Renate Kühling, courtesy Staatliche Antikensammlungen und Glyptothek, München.

inside a courtyard, or a krater at the door of the house – never in more public spaces. The concern for the demarcation of space in such scenes may derive from the desire for the containment of women; if they are outdoors, it must be a controlled and domesticated exterior (as shown, for instance, by the tree on the Florence cup in fig. 2.17).

Well and laver scenes, then, are a novelty in their time, as red-figure painters developed a new interest in domestic themes, and generated a specific iconography of female work. Several iconographic types stand out: the woman framed, either forward-facing or side-on to the laver. There is a repetition of the working figure, bending forward with hands in a laver or krater to wash or knead. This pose signals active work, and is found both on washing cups and on some illustrating kneading or grinding too. Some red-figure Boiotian vases depict women in a similar pose, bent forward over a laver with hands outstretched (fig. 2.23).[53] The scene is very much reduced, with no articles other than the laver. Earlier scholarship was unsure whether to interpret them as scenes of washing or of hydromancy, but the very similar poses of the women in the Douris cups, and the fact that one has her himation tied around her waist in working style, locate them firmly in the domestic arena.

Figure 2.23 Boiotian red-figure hydria, Paris, Musée du Louvre CA 1341, *c*.470 BC (drawing).

Single figures of this type are most often found in cup tondi, shown full length, and often with their arms spread wide, exhibiting the body to the viewer, as on the cups in Milan and Vienna and on the St Petersburg pelike. These are generally depictions of drawing water, and the emphasis is not on the work of drawing up or carrying water but on the pose of the woman 'frozen' in mid-task. The composition of the Milan cup is echoed on a contemporary cup in Brussels with a scene of a nude woman preparing to wash (fig. 4.13): we are looking at the figure, not the work.[51] Common to most of these images is an iconography of work, in which a woman is shown with himation knotted around her hips to leave the arms free without it slipping off. Note too that work is done standing up, whether leaning over a laver or krater, or drawing water. The contrast between work and the leisured life within the house is very strong. Scenes with two women naturally fall into a balanced composition, as each leans forward over a krater or laver. An example is the Pan Painter's pelike in the Louvre, on which two women holding a cloth and a block respectively lean over a krater, a pose which is mirrored in the kitchen scene by the same painter at Haverford College, apparently depicting the same figures.[55] A similar composition is used in pestle-and-mortar scenes: two figures are much more frequent than one.

If women working together are a motif on some of these pots, it raises questions of status demarcation, a point on which expectations fired by literature tend to colour our understanding of iconography. Oratory and comedy depict a city in which all but the poorest Athenians owned slaves, and in which citizens sought to avoid manual work through the exploitation of slave labour. Female work, as I have shown, does not often attract comment, but Xenophon's *Oikonomikos* is premised on the idea that the wife will supervise a household of slaves rather than doing all the work herself, and Demosthenes' *Against Euergos* refers to a group of female slaves on the speaker's farm; Lysias' speech *On the Murder of Eratosthenes* depicts a household with one female slave, which seems to be the norm in comedy too.[56] We thus bring from literature the expectation that domestic work is servile work, and that slaves must be easily distinguished from the free in order to avoid ambiguity; but iconography offers a different pattern of representation.[57] In the scenes I have described there is a surprising lack of connection between domestic work and slaves. Most often we see only one woman, or a pair of similar figures, in 'working' dress and pose. One would expect, if pots were reflecting reality, to see slaves carrying out the heavy work at least, but this does not seem to be the case. In most working scenes there is no clear indicator of status at all, from clothes, length of hair or facial appearance. There is perhaps an iconography for some activities of woman and assistant, shown as smaller or younger, but these could equally well mean mother and daughter as mistress and slave. The Pan Painter's pelike in the Louvre (fig. 2.19) which depicts a larger and a smaller figure washing clothes does indicate a status difference between the two figures: the smaller woman on the left has short hair and wears only a chiton, while the right-hand woman is taller, with her hair in a sakkos and wears a knotted himation as well. However Ashmead comments that the distinction is hard to maintain, since the Haverford College lekythos (fig. 2.9) shows extremely similar figures, but with dress type reversed: the short-haired woman in this scene wears an apron, and the woman in the sakkos wears her himation normally.[58] The Boiotian cup with the scene of pounding on one side shows a similar confusion: the women are named, and on one side two women named Kodoma and Euarchia work at the mortar, while Eupharia stands with distaff in hand and watches (fig. 2.11). This might be thought to indicate a difference in status, but on the other side (fig. 2.24) Euarchia washes her hair while Euphrosyne pours water from a hydria, the more servile role. Others are more difficult to interpret, such as the St Petersburg pounding fragment, or the Florence well cup. Why show free women doing domestic tasks? Slaves perhaps function as a status symbol, rather than a representation of reality – they are common in interior scenes, where they make a statement about leisure and affluence, but painters are insufficiently interested in depicting domestic labour by slaves. An exception is the hydria depicting three Thracian slaves at a fountain; they are shown to be Thracians by the inclusion of tattoos on their arms and legs, demonstrating that status can be indicated quite clearly if the painter is interested enough, and also that attempts to define different social groups are subject to fashion.[59] Again, the fact that when two women are shown both engage equally in the tasks, rather than the larger figure watching, suggests that the work and not the status is the point of the scene. This may in fact reflect reality more closely than the literary sources lead us to suppose: it has been suggested that because women worked alongside one another at the same tasks, they may have developed close

Figure 2.24 Boiotian black-figure skyphos, Athens, Canellopoulos Museum 384, 525–500 BC (side B). Photo courtesy Canellopoulos Museum, Athens.

relationships across the slave/citizen boundary, and thus for women themselves the difference in status may not have been very meaningful in day-to-day activities.[60]

Childcare

The other aspect of a wife's role recognised universally by ancient writers is the care and upbringing of children. On this topic it is important not to be drawn by twentieth-century expectations: in classical times the mother–child bond was by no means as all-encompassing as it is today, nor was the mother considered to be the centre of the family – the father and his heirs were the central element of the oikos. Debate exists over the extent to which parents made emotional investment in their children, particularly infants whose survival could not be assured. Golden has traced attitudes through the literature, and finds a sometimes contradictory set of beliefs; he supports the idea that parents' affection for children was great, although fathers in particular often placed little value on daughters.[61] With childcare, as with the other themes we have examined, reproducing a few well-known images can give a distorted view of ancient attitudes; it is easy to put together a set of images of mothers and children, both mythical and non-mythical, but context is of great importance. The toddler or crawling child is a theme peculiar to the choes, a group of pots used exclusively within Attica for coming-of-age ritual, and on these children are most often shown without adult company. One or two examples of this motif do transfer to other red-figure pots – for example, the pyxis in Athens (fig. 2.25) where one child crawls and another is carried on the shoulders of a young woman, among women working wool in the house, or the pyxis in Manchester on which a woman holds a baby boy on her knee (fig. 2.26).[62] Older children too are sometimes shown with women in red-figure: almost without exception these are male children, as on a hydria in Munich showing a boy holding a hoop and stick standing among adults, or the cup with a woman and boy conversing.[63] There is little interaction between adults and child, and certainly nothing that could be called entertainment.

It is notable that few black- or red-figure pots illustrate an affectionate or senti-mentalised relationship between mother and baby. Instead, pottery is mainly interested in children as evidence of productivity: scenes of women with children in the household or in a landscape are not uncommon, but scenes of mothers actually looking after children are rare. Few babies do anything but stand or crawl, demonstrating their masculinity. This ideology is most clear on pyxides like those illustrated: women are shown with wool and babies, the two forms of virtuous production. As noted previously, it is only funerary pots

Figure 2.25 Attic red-figure pyxis, Athens, National Museum TE 1623, *c*.470 BC (drawing). Reproduced by permission of Prof. F. Lissarrague.

Figure 2.26 Attic red-figure pyxis, Manchester Museum 40096, 470–460 BC. Photo courtesy The Manchester Museum, The University of Manchester.

and monuments which offer a contrast to this: babies and children are shown with both parents, and in poses denoting affection. Mothers and grandmothers hold infants, or reach out to younger children – interaction is much more direct.[64] Toddlers and older children are mostly depicted without adults, chiefly on choes, which regularly show children playing singly or together.[65] In the main, children play with and teach each other; there are very few indications of women's educative role. On one cup in Amsterdam a woman reads a scroll and listens to a boy recite, a parallel to the more common school scenes.[66] Several pots pursue the theme of girls being instructed in dance, but this is for ritual purposes, and outside the household. In fact mothers and older daughters are the major omission of pottery: our evidence suggests that girls were taught domestic skills within the house, but no pottery shows a girl and mother obviously learning together. The wife of Ischomachos, in *Oikonomikos*, has learnt wool-work before her marriage, and the existence of a child-size epinetron among the dedications at Brauron demonstrates that such education did take place. On pottery few scenes even hint at this: the only daughter who appears is on a black-figure hydria in Naples, where a girl plays ball among the women at the fountain; but this scene should not be overinterpreted – there is no sign of teaching here.[67] Terracottas, in contrast, illustrate the teaching relationship well – one Boiotian example shows a woman cooking at a pot over a fire, with a girl standing at her side, holding onto her arm, perhaps mother and daughter cooking (fig. 2.12) – and there is also a black-figure plaque from the Athenian Acropolis, a dedication to Athena Ergane, which depicts a girl sitting on the floor behind a woman weaving.[68] One could perhaps include the Pan Painter pelikai here too, as showing mother and daughter or aunt and niece rather than mistress and slave.

It is an interesting point that the status of free child and slave should be difficult to distinguish in images of domestic work. Slavery was analogous to a state of permanent childhood (male slaves were addressed as παῖς [boy] all their lives), and when a slave iconography develops it involves small size and youth as marks of lower status. Evidence from literature indicates that uncertainty over status could be the case in reality as well: the speaker of Demosthenes' *Against Euergos* (61) claims that his enemies attacked his farm, and tried to take away his son, mistaking him for a slave, while Demosthenes' *Against Nikostratos* (16) describes an episode in which another group of enemies sent a free boy to pick flowers from the speaker's garden, in the hope that the owner would mistake him for a slave and so commit the crime of beating a citizen. This could be a reason for the painters' reluctance to portray children working alongside adults, since it would render their status ambiguous, and markers to distinguish between free and slave children are virtually impossible to find; the speculation about the status of the workers on the Amasis weaving lekythos illustrates the problem clearly.

Agriculture

A final theme to consider is agriculture. This aspect of the wife's work is not freely acknowledged in our sources; Xenophon's depiction of the female role, as already discussed, relies on a sharp distinction between indoor and outdoor work, where outdoor work is solely the province of the husband. He produces the raw materials for the oikos (wool, grain, wine) and his wife's responsibilities are within the house. But this depiction is ideologically driven and we should be suspicious of the limited range of activities it portrays, even for an elite household. It has been estimated by anthropologists that in traditional Mediterranean subsistence farming, women perform more than half of all labour, and we have no reason to believe that Greece was any different.[69] Du Boulay, in her study of Greek village life, recognised that while female work was centred on the house, it could include feeding and milking goats, feeding hens, making cheese, collecting fodder and firewood, as well as the more regular cleaning, baking, cooking and childcare.[70] It is easy to believe that the female contribution to farming was deemed unimportant or inappropriate to depict; studies of subsistence economies have demonstrated the often paramount need for individuals to maintain the ideology of women working only indoors, despite the necessity of their working in the fields alongside the men.

Such an ideology seems to dominate depictions of agriculture on Athenian pottery. Where agricultural themes are shown, they are entirely the province of men, and the scenes themselves are limited to a few specific types. By far the most common are vintage scenes, often showing satyrs rather than real farmers. There is a small group of ploughing scenes, all done by men, and one or two of men herding animals.[71] On the face of it the only scenes which may connect women directly with agriculture are those in which women feed domesticated animals; a lekythos in Naples depicts an older woman feeding a pig (fig. 1.35), and a cup in Berlin by Douris a woman feeding geese (fig. 2.27). We can compare with these a chous in Athens on which boys feed chickens.[72] The geese and chickens are sometimes interpreted as pets, but it is much more likely that we see here the acceptable face of female agriculture. The only kind of non-ritual horticulture we find is the joke of women raising phalloi – on a pelike by the Hasselmann Painter (fig. 2.28) a woman in a knotted himation sprinkles some phalloi sprouting from the ground with liquid from

Figure 2.27 Attic red-figure cup, Berlin, Staatliche Museen F2306, *c.*480 BC. Photo: Antikensammlung, Staatliche Museen zu Berlin – Preussischer Kulturbesitz.

a bowl.[7] Apart from these, there is one other large group of pots within the theme of agriculture which concerns women: the motif of fruit-picking. Many pots, mainly black-figure lekythoi and cup-skyphoi (though the theme does appear in red-figure too), carry scenes of groups of women in what appear to be orchards; in some scenes the women pick fruit and put it in baskets, while in others they simply sit around the tree (figs. 2.29 and 1.12).[75] Can this be counted as female agricultural work? A recent study of women in classical Greece includes one such scene under the heading 'Work outside the house', and describes it as 'agricultural work on the family property', commenting that this example may not seem very strenuous, but citing another example in which a woman sits in a tree. Others interpret the scene as ritual, but in a realistic setting; that is, that women really did work in groups in orchards.[76]

On closer examination, however, orchard scenes are not only a closely defined thematic group but exhibit some interesting concentrations of shape and period. The scene is more common in black-figure than red, and much more prevalent on small pots than large. There is a scatter of scenes on kraters, but most are lekythoi, cup-skyphoi or mastoid cups, all from around the same period and centring on particular workshops (the Haimon and the Kalinderu Groups). A close analysis of the distribution of Haimon Group pots offers

Figure 2.28 Attic red-figure pelike,
London, British Museum E819,
440–430 BC (drawing).

precise figures: 43 per cent (433) have a provenance, of which 159 (36.7 per cent) come from Athens, and 171 (39.5 per cent) from Greece. Only twenty-five come from Etruria.[77] Scheffer concludes that most of the Haimon Group vases 'never left the city. At least 60 have been found at Delphi, and most of the others were also found at a relatively short distance from Athens in Attica, Boiotia, the Cyclades and the northern Peloponnese.' This pattern of distribution indicates that black-figure lekythoi of the Haimon and associated groups were consumed within Attica and its immediate surroundings; the purpose of black-figure lekythoi was funerary, for offerings in the grave and libations to the dead. This provides a secure context within which to read the imagery: it was designed for the tomb. The other themes popular with the Haimon Group include mainly chariots with gods, Herakles or Dionysiac scenes, but also representations of women dancing and in orchard scenes.

Can we then take these as depictions of agricultural activity? The speaker of Demosthenes' *Against Euboulides* (45) comments that under pressure of poverty caused by war, women might work as grape-pickers, τρυγητρίαι, but vintage is not depicted in these scenes, and scenes of harvesting other fruits, such as olives, depict only male workers. Can it be a scene of active harvest or production? It lacks the large scale of activities like vintage: the women are well-dressed (some exhibiting a variety of fashionable hairstyles), not in the 'working' style, and there is never an element of stacks of fruit already picked. In many representations the women merely sit or stand around a tree bearing fruit: the collecting is not shown, suggesting that the work is not the central point of the theme. We should also wonder about the realism of the scenario in which we suppose fruit-picking to happen: orchards were familiar from Homeric times, and we may imagine that land in Attica was used to produce fruit such as apples, peaches and figs, but how many farms had a full orchard?[78]

In fact I suspect that what we see relates more strongly to the poetic motif of the apple, as found most famously in Sappho:

οἶον τὸ γλυκύμαλον ἐρεύθεται ἄκρωι ἐπ' ὕσδωι, ἄκρον ἐπ' ἀκροτάτωι,
λελάθοντο δὲ μαλοδρόπηες, οὐ μὰν ἐκλελάθοντ', ἀλλ' οὐκ ἐδύναντ'
ἐπίκεσθαι.

[Just like the sweet apple blushing on the very topmost branch of the tree, overlooked by the apple-pickers – no, not overlooked, but beyond their reach.]

(fr. 105)

The ripe apple stands as a metaphor for the marriageable girl, and this accords with the presence of fruit in baskets in marriage scenes and also its use as a gift from lover to beloved (figs. 5.12, 5.13). The motif of the fruit tree often transfers to the background of other female scenes, as on the Florence well cup (fig. 2.17) or a fragment in Boston on which two young women play see-saw.[79] The women in these orchard scenes thus inhabit an idealised pastoral rather than reality, and the exclusion of women from representations of agriculture is total: we cannot read these images to confirm reality. Agricultural work carried out by women is the 'great unspoken' in Athenian culture; writers and artists have succeeded in eliminating any suggestion of it from our sources.[80] To some extent this is true of all agricultural depictions, since even the work done by men is presented in a very stylised way. The nature of the agricultural themes we find in fact suggests that the choice of aspect for illustration was dominated by religious symbolism. Vintage is a Dionysian event, often with Dionysus or his followers present, and celebrates the creation of the wine that is to be drunk, and the gift of conviviality, as well as the general Dionysian mode of decoration on pottery. Ploughing has been seen as an expression of fertility ritual, and the cup which links a scene of ploughing on one side with a female festival on the other seems to bear this out.[81] The role of women in picking fruit certainly follows this pattern: what we see on the orchard scenes may be ritual, a celebration of harvest (like the Aiora, perhaps), in which women symbolically gathered fruit. Scenes of women gathering pomegranates figure among the dedicatory plaques to Persephone at Locri too, and this moves the scene even further into the realm of the mythical.[82] It is also likely (given the presence of the scene on so many lekythoi, and the link with Persephone) that it has a funerary symbolism, expressing ideas about marriage and unfulfilled ripeness.

Figure 2.29 Attic black-figure lekythos, Braunschweig, Herzog Anton Ulrichs-Museum AT 700, 480–470 BC. Photo: Museumsfoto B.P. Keiser, courtesy Herzog-Anton-Ulrich-Museums, Braunschweig.

The meaning of domestic labour

Although domestic work scenes have rarely been considered as a group, the interpretation of individual motifs tends in two opposing directions. Some scenes are interpreted as representations of ritual: the Amasis Painter's black-figure lekythos, for instance, which shows weaving on the body and a dance on the shoulder is interpreted as the weaving of textiles for presentation to the gods – in this case the peplos for Athena at the Panathenaia. By the same argument, other scenes of weaving are related to dedications to Brauronian Artemis, and scenes of cooking

Figure 2.30 Attic black-figure amphora (Tyrrhenian amphora), St Petersburg, The State Hermitage Museum B1403, *c*.560 BC (drawing of detail). After Pfuhl, fig. 205.

are related to the mixing and baking of the cakes used in the rituals of the Thesmophoria or Anthesteria. In certain contexts this seems quite appropriate; the only depiction of bed-making, for example, is found in a scene of marriage ritual on a Tyrrhenian amphora (fig. 2.30): as the wedding procession approaches the house, a woman inside prepares the marital bed.[83] As noted above, another scene of wedding preparations includes the cooking of sesame cakes, and fruit-picking scenes too fit well with a ritual interpretation. A pot frequently presented in this context is the later red-figure hydria in New York which depicts two women with clothes suspended on a swing above a fire (fig. 2.31).[84] One woman bends down to pour oil on the fire from a lekythos, and a small boy wearing a crown stands behind. The clothes piled on the swing are being perfumed by the smoke from the fire, but a ritual meaning is clearly signalled by the use of the swing (familiar in scenes representing the festival of the Aiora), the crowned boy, and the ornate dress of the two women. This is not a scene of ordinary domestic work, but preparation for a festival, and a similar explanation has been advanced for the black-figure image of two women pounding corn in a mortar (fig. 2.7) as a 'cult ceremony for Demeter'.[85]

Other scenes, however, are much harder to encompass in this framework. As we have seen, there exists an iconography of hard work, removed from a festive context. Women in working clothes, aprons or knotted himatia, work alone or in pairs in courtyard or house, without crowns or branches. It is plausible to associate the fetching of water with wedding ritual or the Hydrophoria, especially if the participants carry branches, or branches are present in the field, but drawing water from the household well, in the company only of household utensils, has few religious overtones. In these cases, an alternative explanation related to sexuality is dominant: the pots depicting women at the well are grouped with scenes of spinning and carding, also common on cups and given a sexual meaning. Scenes of domestic work, according to this theory, are juxtaposed with courting or symposion scenes, in cups in particular, to send a message to drinkers about domestic work and its attractiveness. Keuls has argued that depictions of 'respectable' women on kylikes must have an erotic meaning because kylikes were designed for use by men at symposia, where wives did not go. Indeed, the fact that a female figure appears on

Figure 2.31 Attic red-figure hydria, New York, Metropolitan Museum of Art GR 1243, *c.*420 BC (drawing). After Richter/Hall, fig. 159.

a cup is taken to render that image salacious: she says of the Brygan cups depicting women at the well that their 'frivolous' nature is underscored by the shape, and of the carding scene by the Stieglitz Painter that its 'lascivious aspect . . . is suggested mainly by its occurrence on a kylix'.[86] Since the women engaged in domestic tasks are invariably fully dressed, with long hair and alone, it has proved hard for scholars to declare them confidently to be hetairai. The interpretation offered has therefore been that the images show either 'hetairai pretending to be housewives', exploiting the erotic attraction of female work, or that the cups are designed as a kind of joke for the symposiast – he drains a cup with a picture of hetairai on the outside and discovers in the tondo an image of the chaste wife.[87]

Such an interpretation, however, relies implicitly on the concept of a male Athenian viewer; yet this is not the context of use of these cups. Although they may be 'symposium shapes' in origin there is no sign that they ever went near a symposium. As I have emphasised already, factors such as shape, period and provenance are all relevant, and an analysis of these reveals some interesting correlations. The *floruit* of work scenes is in early red-figure, a time of great expansion in the themes chosen by painters; there is a surge of interest in such scenes in the period 500–480 BC, followed by a shift to leisure scenes after 450 BC. Rather than see these scenes as 'specialisms' of particular painters, we should see instead a demand in the export market. Work scenes are not regular on pots where form reflects function; that is, pots used in domestic work are usually large coarse wares, not decorated, so the object is not painted with scenes of its use, nor on dedications for women, though men dedicate scenes of their own work.[88] Instead depictions of domestic work are common on pots with an Etruscan provenance, since most of the examples we have seen were exported, sold to Etruscan buyers, and chosen for burial in tombs. The group of Brygos Painter cups are an obvious example: they are decorated only with scenes of work, and have provenances all over Etruria.[89] Images of women in scenes of domestic leisure were rarely exported, possibly because the range of female activities depicted on Greek pottery was so limited; mirrors and other media produced in Etruria itself reflected the broader range of women's lives.[90] But if scenes of female leisure and seclusion were unpopular outside the Greek areas of Italy, there are still a surprising number of images of women engaged in domestic labour. Clearly Etruscan customers were interested in buying vases decorated with such scenes.[91]

We should thus seek the meaning of domestic scenes not in Athens but in Etruria. What relevance could these scenes have to the people who deposited them in graves, especially if the practice of deposition of imported pots was the preserve of the leisured rich? The male genre scenes, athletes, symposiasts and hoplites, have been persuasively interpreted as reflecting the roles of Etruscan aristocrats in death, as participants in funerary games or banquets, or as encapsulating the ideas of a class.[92] How can women engaged in household tasks, especially if their status is undefined, operate in the same way? The ideology of leisure had no appeal to Etruscan women, probably because it did not reflect the wider range of their experience, but domestic work as a specific theme was popular in graves. Could these images represent work for the dead, just like the ushabti figures which accompanied Egyptians to the grave (or indeed the Boiotian terracotta figurines)? This idea is supported by the wall paintings found in Etruscan tombs, which depict not only the Totenmahl, funerary banquet, but also scenes of cooking and preparation for the banquet, such as the 'Kitchen of the Underworld' in the Tomba Golini I, or the kylikeia in the Tomba di Vasi Dipinti.[93] In this context the status of the working figures is unimportant, as I have suggested, and it would also explain why specific kinds of domestic work are included (washing, cooking, water) and others excluded (cleaning, domestic animals).

A primarily funerary intention for such scenes also illuminates the appearance of phallic images in some domestic scenes, such as the cup in Berlin which shows two women working at raised trays (fig. 2.5). Above them, at the top of the field, is a phallos-bird. Boardman has proposed an erotic interpretation for the symbol, as 'a disembodied expression of female sexuality', signalling that the image is to be read as an erotic one.[94] Since the women are fully dressed, and there is no other indication of erotic interest, this seems unlikely. Kilmer suggests instead that the phallos-bird be understood as an apotropaic symbol, citing as parallels the kitchen scene in the Tomba Golini where a phallic image appears on a bread oven, and examples on pottery kilns in Greece.[95] A number of other Etruscan images link very well with the apotropaic themes; for instance, a winged phallos appears on the wall of the Tomba del Topolino.[96] If we interpret the cup as a funerary object, depicting the realm of female work for the tomb, then the appearance of an apotropaic image is unsurprising.

Conclusion

We have travelled a long way from photographic depictions of Athenian life, and demonstrated that it is not logical to assume that all pots were used by Athenian women, that they reflect the use to which they were put, or that they tried to impose cultural stereotypes on their users. Pottery can, it is true, give us a clearer understanding of female domestic work: pots show us women, both free or slave, washing, cooking and working in a way that literature does not. They can illustrate the mundane objects, such as lavers, buckets and wells, which supplied the Athenian household, and give us glimpses into the interiors where women worked. But this examination has revealed a complex pattern of distribution and use. Painters did not create the images we have discussed as part of a coherent theme of 'domestic work', however useful a category we may find it; instead particular tasks played different roles and signified different things in a broader iconographic scheme. As in modern times, a strong ideological element underlies the representation of work: while we can rely on pots to fill some of the gaps in literature, and vice versa, there are some tasks which are simply ignored – very menial tasks such as housecleaning, sweeping and bed-making, the care of domestic animals, and the education of daughters. Xenophon specifically mentions care of the sick as one of his wife's responsibilities, yet this is nowhere depicted. The hard grind of the Athenian woman, slave or free, remains uncelebrated in any medium. Wool-work is by far the most frequently depicted activity because of its place in the dominant ideology of gender roles; cooking, despite its status as a female task, is relatively little shown, and agricultural work not at all. Active scenes of domestic work at the laver are an iconography of hard work created for export, and designed for Etruscan customers for a funerary purpose. Despite their appearance on cups these scenes cannot be read from the point of view of a male citizen at a symposium, nor for that matter of an Athenian woman. These conclusions, as we will see in the next chapter, have important repercussions for images of female work outside the house too.

3

WORKING WOMEN

So far we have examined women's roles within the polis and within the oikos, but now need to turn to women's involvement in economic activity outside the household; that is, to commercial activity. There are two themes of female work to be considered here, one, production and trade (very under-represented on pottery), and the other, prostitution (apparently over-represented). The reasons for this are interesting and complex.

Commercial interests

At first sight our first category does not appear to be a very promising field for investigation, as commercial activity by women in Athens is an area where pottery does not offer us what we wish to know. Other sources of evidence – drama, inscriptions, dedications – indicate that many women (citizen, slave and freedwomen) worked in trade, producing and selling goods and services. This has been exhaustively documented elsewhere, but we encounter Aristophanes' wreath-, bread- and vegetable-sellers, the spinners, washerwomen and grocers of the inscriptions, not to mention cloak-sellers, reed-sellers, trumpet players and grooms.[1] Yet there seems to be little reflection of any female commercial role in the imagery. In part this is due to the relative lack of commercial scenes in general, but not completely: there are images of men engaged in both craft (smithing, potting, painting, sculpting) and commerce (shoemakers, amphora-sellers, vendors of oil and wine). This topic is in fact one of the type highlighted in the Introduction: there is one known scene of a female artisan, and a small group of female traders (comprising four images in total). Rather than presenting such a small number of representations to illustrate literature, the evidence needs contextualising and interrogating. Why should certain occupations appear in such small numbers and others not at all?

The female artisan is to be found on a hydria in Milan, which depicts a scene in the workshop of a vase producer.[2] Several workers decorate pots, and are crowned by Athena and a Nike; at the right of the scene a woman sits on a shallow platform, decorating the handles of a volute-krater. This unique representation can be paralleled from a fourth-century BC inscription which calls down a curse upon 'Dionysius the helmet-maker and his wife Artemeis', who is described as a χρυσωτρίαν, a gilder; their joint workshop is also cursed, hence it has been suggested that the woman should be taken as part of a family business, the potter or metalsmith's wife.[3] Such a realist interpretation, however, overlooks the fact that the gods appear in the scene: the point of the illustration is praise of the worker, raising him from artisan to honoured craftsman. It is tempting to see a self-referential joke, with a female painter putting herself in the frame, but why this

Figure 3.1 Attic red-figure pelike, Berne 12227, 470–460 BC (drawing).

should be our only example is harder to say. Beyond this single illustration, woman's work on pottery is always either retail or domestic; the scene of woman as producer is a one-off.

Scenes of vending, however, are more common. A valuable study of the Attic pelike has documented a tendency for pelikai to be decorated with scenes from commercial life (among other themes), especially with scenes of their own use. These include eleven scenes depicting the sale of liquids from amphorae, either perfumed oil or wine (and one the sale of pots themselves). Four of these pelikai, two black-figure and two red-figure, depict women selling oil or wine. On a well-known pot in Berne, for instance, a woman herself does the trading, sitting in front of an amphora as her customer proffers an alabastron to be filled (fig. 3.1). On another in Paris the woman is not directly selling, but sits on a stool measuring oil from a pelike while a man bargains with the customer behind her (fig. 3.2). It is significant that in these scenes the artist's interest focuses not on the customer but on the trader; despite the idea that trade was demeaning, on the pelikai we encounter the banausos as hero. Even when female, the vendors are not subordinate: on the Berne pelike the oil-seller has short hair, which ought to indicate servile status, yet her other indications of status are high: she is shown as much larger than her customer, and sits while the other stands. On this example the customer is also female, which makes one think of the 'women's market' mentioned in Pollux and Theophrastus; but female vendors are also shown with male customers. Certainly the sharp-tongued vegetable- and bread-sellers of Aristophanes are unafraid to challenge their male customers and passers-by, offering a hint of the freedom enjoyed by women of the trading class.[7]

The number of scenes of female labour, then, does seem very limited: although painters are quite keen to depict their own craft on cups and amphorae there is nothing like the situation in Italy, where we find elaborate tomb reliefs depicting the trade of the deceased, through which women, even those who were not well-to-do, reveal considerable pride in their occupation. These depict mainly vendors

Figure 3.2 Attic black-figure pelike, Paris, Musée du Louvre F376, c.510 BC. Photo: M. et P. Chuzéville, courtesy Musée du Louvre, Paris.

(of vegetables and poultry) too, but also include nurses, a bookkeeper, a shoemaker and midwives.[8] But in fact the apparent lack of working women on Greek pots may be perceived rather than actual, more to do with modern preconceptions about female roles than ancient choices. The oil-selling pelikai illustrate the standard iconography for trade: the vendor sits with the tools of the trade, and the customer observes or tests the product. The customer who carries a money pouch, indicating his ability or willingness to pay for the goods, is an integral part of the scene. The purse, however, has proved a very problematic symbol in scenes where men and women are involved, tending to derail the interpretation: when a man and woman are shown together, a purse is read as an incontrovertible sign of the purchase of sexual favours. But the purse, as shown by its appearance with the oil-sellers, does not necessarily refer to sexual trade, a factor which opens the possibility of reinterpreting some well-known pots. A pelike in Madrid by the Pan Painter (fig. 3.3), for instance, juxtaposes images of the domestic and the commercial in an interesting way: it has on one side a woman apparently washing clothes – she stands in front of a large laver, from which a piece of cloth hangs, holding a block in each hand. On the reverse is a youth holding a bag of money, a finger at his lips. Interpretations of the scene vary: Boardman suggests that the figures are husband and wife, while Sutton describes the woman as a hetaira, and sees a youth about to approach a woman in order to buy sex.[9] Nothing about either the figure or the scene suggests 'hetaira', nor is the woman attentive to the youth; she concentrates on her work. This is, furthermore, a pelike, a shape which, as noted above, tended to carry scenes of commercial activity. Interpreting the scene simply from the elements present, we see a woman carrying out a task (washing

Figure 3.3 Attic red-figure pelike, Madrid, Museo Arqueologico Nacional L157, *c.*470 BC. Photo courtesy Archivo Fotografico, Museo Arqueologico Nacional, Madrid.

Figure 3.4 (this page and facing) Attic red-figure cup, London, British Museum E61, *c*.480 BC. Photo courtesy British Museum. © The British Museum.

clothes) and a man approaching with money, suggesting payment for that service. Should this be understood as commercial rather than domestic or sexual work – a customer paying to have his washing done? It would accord with evidence from other media: we have inscriptions indicating that washing was practised commercially by women: one from the sixth century BC was put up by Smikythe, a πλύντρια [washerwoman], when she offered a tithe, and another from the fourth century is a dedication to the nymphs made by a group of washers [πλυνής], including two women, Leuke and Myrrhine.[10] The scene can also be paralleled by a fragmentary black-figure skyphos from the Acropolis (and therefore a dedication) depicting youths and men washing clothes and drying clothes: washing was a serious occupation, and one in which an individual might take pride.[11] There is no prima facie reason to accept an exclusively domestic context for all female work.

A cup by Makron in the British Museum (fig. 3.4) raises another possibility in the depiction of female trade: the sale of wreaths.[12] We know from literary sources that wreath-selling was a recognisably female occupation – Aristophanes' *Thesmophoriazusai* presents a widow with five children who supported her family by selling wreaths – and this passage in fact suggests that the purchase of wreaths was a regular preliminary to the symposion, thus making the theme particularly appropriate to pottery.[13] On the cup a seated woman holds up a wreath, a man stands behind her with a money-pouch, and a partially draped young man gestures, while an aulos player holds up her pipes and a third man looks on. Why should we not identify the wreath held by the woman as the object for sale? There is no interaction between the men and women, only the pouch as symbol of some

transaction, and the general conjunction of purchasing power with the production of wreaths suggests preparations for the symposion rather than negotiations for sex. The connection with the symposion leads us to one of the areas in which huge numbers of women worked in Athens: entertainment, from music, dance and acrobatics to outright prostitution. The other side of Makron's cup represents a scene similar to the first: another male figure with purse stands at one side, but this time there are two women playing the aulos. Again it makes more sense to read the image as the purchase of commodities for the symposion, in this case the hiring of musicians; the decoration in the tondo (a woman playing the aulos as a girl dances) lends weight to the interpretation. Once the possibility has been raised that a woman may be selling more than herself, it is possible to identify a group of illustrations of transactions between musicians and patrons, such as a pelike in Rhodes by the Hephaistos Painter which depicts a woman seated on a chair playing the lyre, while in front of her a youth leans on his stick holding a purse.[14] The scene has some similarities with that on the Berne oil-selling pelike: it too appears on a pelike, and shows a seated vendor approached by a potential customer. The female lyre-player is again larger in stature (though seated) than the man. A second pot, a column-krater by the Pig Painter in Taranto (fig. 3.5), follows the same theme, this time with an aulos player.[15] The musician is seated at the centre of the scene, and plays; a female attendant stands before her with a case for the pipes, while a man stands behind, leaning on a stick and holding a purse. A lyre and box hang in the background, symbolic of music as on the interior vases. I believe we have here a hidden crop of commercial transactions within the scenario of 'preparations for the symposion'.

Of course much of this goes against what is written about images of women, because of the perceived associations of music, and especially of the aulos. It is taken as axiomatic that aulos players in classical Athens were prostitutes; that they formed the lowest class

Figure 3.5 Attic red-figure column-krater, Taranto, Museo Nazionale Archeologico 0.6436, *c.*470 BC (drawing).

of prostitutes, that they would play music early in the evening, then later have sex with the symposiasts, and that all auletrides were expected to offer oral sex to their patrons at the end of an evening.[16] But how much of a foundation do these claims have? The main pieces of evidence are from Menander's *Perikeiromene*, a passage which equates auletrides with prostitutes (or at least available women), and Aristophanes' *Wasps*, in which the speaker claims to have rescued an aulos player before the sexual act was required of her:

ὁρᾷς ἐγώ σ' ὡς δεξιῶς ὑφειλόμην
μέλλουσαν ἤδη λεσβιεῖν τοὺς ξυμπότας·

[You see how deftly I sneaked you away, before you had to give blow-jobs to the diners.][17]

This is not decisive evidence – first, because Menander is very late in comparison to the pots discussed; second, because several other pieces of evidence argue in the opposite direction. Plato, for instance, speaks of women as potentially having a gift for music, and depicts an aulos player sent to entertain the women of the family. Although he is disparaging about their accomplishments in comparison to men, nothing indicates that these women are considered to be no more than prostitutes, the lowest of the low. Similarly Xenophon's *Symposium* depicts entertainers hired from a Syracusan slave-owner; these are musicians, dancers and acrobats, and their role is purely as skilled practitioners of their arts, not as sexual partners for the symposiasts.[18] I wonder if the Aristophanes reference has not been taken out of context: is the joke about oral sex actually based on the nature of the aulos player's musical specialism, arising not because all aulos players had to give oral sex but because, given the nature of their instrument, the parallel was too tempting to ignore?

In fact the aulos was an instrument used in all areas of Athenian life: in ritual, to accompany sacrifice or song; in work, to give rhythm for activities from marching to pounding grain; and for entertainment. Female aulos players abound in scenes of sacrifice (figs. 1.26, 1.31, 1.33), wedding processions, and dance (figs. 1.17, 1.18), as well as symposia. Xenophon recounts that when the Athenians were called on to demolish their walls after the defeat in 404 BC, they did so to the music of auloi: καὶ τὰ τείχη κατέσκαπτον ὑπ' αὐλητρίδων πολλῇ προθυμίᾳ [and they pulled down the walls to the accompaniment of girl pipers, with great enthusiasm] (Xen. *Hell.* 2.2.23). Davidson takes this as evidence that prostitute aulos players lived in Piraeus, but the context of the passage is of public action, not of a demi-monde.[19] A useful comparison can be made with Victorian attitudes towards actresses; the profession was seen as having low connections, and many actresses were strippers or prostitutes, but equally, many were respected professionals.[20] To equate auletrides with prostitutes *tout court* is an overgeneralisation, which in turn impacts on the reading of the imagery.

The very complexity of the literary evidence should make the viewer more receptive to the variety of imagery on the pots. Many images of auletrides at symposia represent what we might call a 'Sokratic' symposium, where a female aulos player accompanies a singing symposiast, and the scene is sober in the extreme: there is no crossover between performer and sexual partner. A fragment of a dinos by the Kleophrades Painter shows a veiled aulos player, while on several cups by the Brygos Painter (e.g. fig. 3.6) a riotous komos scene includes a female aulos player standing still and composed at the centre of the action, a sober figure in contrast to the revellers around her.[21] Of course other auletrides do take part in the interactions of the symposium or komos – sometimes they are naked, or are molested by the revellers, but the variety is wide, just as with the symposium in literature.[22] One should also recognise a difference between active playing of the aulos and the presence of an aulos or case in a scene: painters use this element to symbolise the symposium, and, as it was played by men too, it cannot be construed as an indicator of the profession of the women shown in the scene. In order to support the idea that all auletrides provided sexual services, it is necessary to read scenes as though they are stills from a moving picture, something which is clearly unsatisfactory: a pot does not tell us what is going to happen, only what it shows, and that is a piper at a symposium accompanying a singer. Painters were not at pains to make auletrides the lowest of the low: as we shall see, there are scenes in which women are attacked or degraded, but there is no connection made between this and the aulos. Just as male aulos players can be competitors in musical competitions or accompanists to armies as well as revellers, so female aulos players on pots can be professional musicians.

Thus if we move beyond eroticised readings of male–female interactions, we can identify a larger group of pots with scenes of female workers and traders. The celebration of female

Figure 3.6 Attic red-figure cup, Würzburg, M. von Wagner Museum 479, *c.*490 BC (drawing). After Pfuhl, fig. 423a.

work is not on the same scale as that of men's, but the scenes can be compared with the more numerous examples depicting male workers, including carpenters, helmet-makers, sculptors, painters and pot-sellers, which also figure mostly on cups or pelikai. In these it is the occupation rather than the status of the individual which is at stake: although some male workers have citizens' staffs beside them, there is no sense that the work in itself is degrading. As Shapiro suggests, we should understand praise of the banausos as well as of the aristocrat.[23] Crafts were not highly regarded in social terms, yet the workers are depicted with some care, and the female side too takes its place. Most of the female workers are connected with the symposion, and the pots offer the vendor or worker status: the women are not simply 'furniture' in scenes of masculine enjoyment but workers with a skill or object needed for the occasion. It is hardly a complete representation of female work: some professions, such as wet nurses and midwives, were too female to attract the painters' attention; others, such as market vendors, too mundane. Nevertheless the oil- and perfume-sellers, as well as musicians and wreath-makers, receive the same kind of attention as their male counterparts.

Prostitution and pottery

This discussion of commercial activities, and the status of the women who appear in the scenes, brings us to a topic which has assumed an undue prominence in ceramic studies: prostitution. This subject bears some exposition because, according to one view, prostitution is one of the most commonly represented female activities on Athenian pottery – pots are, literally, pornography, pictures of whores. This may seem a peculiar claim, but it turns on the question of female status: traditionally scholars have asked themselves, on seeing a depiction of a woman in classical art, what her social status must be. Initially it was assumed that any women on pots shown in the company of men must be prostitutes, because literary sources state so clearly that wives were secluded. Even women playing music in interior scenes could not by definition be interpreted as wives, since they displayed the accomplishments of the prostitute.[24] Scholars sometimes wondered why pictures of prostitutes were dedicated in sanctuaries or placed in tombs, but the symbolism was taken as incontrovertible. In its most extreme form, this view can produce serious misinterpretation of the evidence: one recent study discusses a white-ground lekythos (fig. 3.7) which depicts a standing woman holding a pillow which she is stuffing with balls of wool.[25] The lekythos carries on it the inscription ἡ παῖς καλή, a common formula commenting on the image. This inscription is interpreted as an indication that the woman is a prostitute, and the writer then reads the image as expressing this identity in a variety of different ways – the woman's body is visible through her clothes, suggesting brazenness, and her activity (stuffing a cushion) is an unskilled one, as opposed to the respectable women's task of weaving. All this flows from a fundamental mistaken assumption; the white-ground lekythos was a funerary item, used by Athenians in funerary ritual and nowhere else. There is no sign that the women on white-ground lekythoi are ever shown in contexts external to the family. The καλή inscription is a common feature on white-ground lekythoi of all kinds; the transparency of the clothing is partly a consequence of the fugitive colours used in white-ground, and we may compare the lekythos by the Achilles Painter in London depicting husband and wife (fig. 4.23), where the wife's clothes also reveal the contours of the body underneath.[26] A determination to establish female status can thus be very damaging to our understanding of an image; it

demonstrates how easy it is to 'read' features of an image in a way consonant with modern expectations. So what we need to investigate are some fundamental questions about the presentation of women on pottery, the use of the pots and the idea of prostitution itself.

Prostitution, of course, was not absent from the ancient world: in fact it was common in classical times. It is well documented that as societies became more prosperous they attracted service personnel of all kinds, and some cities with large transient populations, such as Corinth and Abydos, became known for the number of prostitutes who worked there.[27] Prostitution is an area where the ancient texts have the fewest useful comments to make, since we have few texts written by women, and none by women who worked as prostitutes themselves. Ancient male attitudes on this topic are peculiarly unhelpful, tending to be either moralistic or straightforwardly celebratory of the commoditised woman. Comparative evidence is most promising here, as it can indicate what motivates women from a variety of societies to come to work as (not to 'be') prostitutes.[28] The primary reasons are economic necessity (often in order to support children), coercion by pimps or partners, and the attraction to good money, earned in a job which requires few specific skills and no initial capital, and hence is open to all. Some women are still brought up with few other options, and the existence of slavery in Athens parallels this lack of choice: we hear of the seven girls bought by the freedwoman Nikarete to be put to work as prostitutes ([Dem.] *Against Neaira* 18). Most women working as prostitutes see little alternative to their occupation, although most in traditional societies would prefer to find one man as either husband or lover to protect and support them.

This emphasises an extremely important point: that prostitution is a trade, not an identity. Women can work as prostitutes at various times in their lives, and equally can leave the trade to marry or enter it as a result of changing circumstances. The woman who becomes a prostitute in childhood and works in that profession until old age is a rarity.

These provisos are particularly relevant to classical Greece, where there is a huge *décalage* between the claims made by writers about women's sexual roles and

Figure 3.7 Attic white-ground lekythos, Harvard University, Sackler Museum, Schimmel coll. 1991.28, *c.*470 BC. Photo: Michael Nedzweski. Courtesy of the Arthur M. Sackler Museum, Harvard University Art Museums, Gift of Schimmel Foundation, Inc.

what we see on the pottery. Just as with slaves, writers exploit the possibilities of literature to make unrealistic (and idealising) claims about women and sexual activity. Speakers in Athenian court cases, for instance, consistently suggest that it is easy to tell different kinds of women apart, to distinguish the faithful wife from the adulterous, or the foreign prostitute from the citizen's daughter; the cases, however, are testimony to the opposite. Apollodorus' rather glib categorisation of the three groups of women controlled by men as wives, whores and concubines was made in a speech intended to raise the perceived status of wives, and has been taken far too literally.[29] The case of Neaira, in which the statement was made, far from emphasising the huge gulf between wife and hetaira, demonstrates the very fuzzy boundary between the two. Neaira had passed as the wife of Stephanos for many years, and confusion obviously reigned over which of her children were also his. Her daughter Phano was given in marriage as though she were Stephanos' daughter from a previous marriage, and it is notable that when Phano's non-citizen birth was the cause of a divorce, on each occasion the result was not a straightforward prosecution on the grounds that she was not an Athenian, but a legal fudge. Similarly when she was (allegedly) prostituted to Epainetos, an agreement was made with him both for a contribution to her dowry *and* his continued use of her.[30] Isaeus' speech *On the Estate of Pyrrhus* concerns a similar dispute over status: did the wife of Xenokles, Phile, have a legal marriage or an irregular liaison? The speaker is forced to use the woman's activities as evidence for her status (attending dinners with her husband, and taking part in komoi) because this was not a situation in which there was a clear designator: there was no certificate which could settle the question.[31] Thus women could be wives and yet have their status called into question, or be prostitutes but also wives at the same time. The laws concerning adulterous wives in Athens offer an interesting parallel: the penalties imposed on wives known to have committed adultery seem concerned to mark their status visually – they were not to attend public festivals with the other women, nor to wear fine clothes and jewellery in public, and if they did, they could be stripped and beaten.[32] This has to be because the adulterous woman must be marked out artificially: 'being adulterous' cannot of itself be seen.

Many shifts between different statuses in one lifetime can also be documented: the two slaves whom we know to have been sold into prostitution, Phaedo and Neaira, both succeeded in finding patrons to buy their freedom, while in a reverse example the pallake of Antiphon's *Against the Stepmother* was about to be sold to a brothel, her owner having lost interest in her.[33] What all this should demonstrate is the folly of trying to impose strict categories: motherhood is not a role exclusive to the wife, nor is marriage incompatible with prostitution. Our cases indicate that motherhood, marriage and earning an income for one's husband could all be features of prostitute life; for many women, prostitution might be the most effective way to earn a living and to provide for a family, and it is important to understand it as a trade or an occupation rather than a moral state. If the example of Neaira is to teach us anything, it should be that prostitutes of sufficient beauty and character could find customers happy to establish permanent relationships, that men of the poorer classes might see in a partner's prostitution a source of income, and that issues of status and 'respectability' could be very difficult indeed for any inhabitant of the city to judge.[34] It is notable that the men who consorted with these women, though themselves citizens, saw nothing wrong with forming long-term relationships with non-citizen women.

The situation was thus far more complex than ancient (and modern) writers suggest: how can we use this knowledge to interpret the pottery? First, terminology: what does it mean to label female figures on pottery as 'hetairai', and what is the effect of the label?

Greek writers differentiate clearly between the idea of the 'hetaira' and of the 'porne'. 'Hetaira' was not a generic term for a prostitute: a hetaira was rather more than a woman who sold sex. The 'hetaira' in Greek society is easily recognised: a 'companion' was a free woman, educated, skilled in arts and music, who would provide conversation, company and (sometimes) sex for a man, at a (often considerable) price. The existence of educated and interesting female prostitutes is accounted for by the lack of education offered to Athenian citizen women: in order to find a female companion who could participate in their intellectual interests, men would turn to this class of woman. What can we know about these women? Those described in classical times, such as Aspasia and Theodote, took pride in themselves and their abilities: they project themselves as wealthy, beautiful, accomplished and influential.[35] It is easy to be over-optimistic about the quality of life enjoyed by 'courtesans', but clearly these women could choose their lovers and move in the most elite circles. 'Porne', we are told, was the term for a prostitute pure and simple; women of this status inhabit the plays of Aristophanes and vulgar jokes. But this distinction is one which was generated in the ancient world, and a recent study has argued convincingly that it is an artificial divide manufactured by ancient poets, and upheld by later writers.[36] According to this argument, the concept of the 'hetaira' emerged as part of a political discourse at the time of the introduction of democracy at Athens. The 'hetaira' is a category invented by sixth-century sympotic poets, such as Anacreon, as part of the elite and luxurious life of the symposium; hetairai are free and equal companions to the symposiasts, and are gained by gift-exchange, not commodification. Kurke then traces these ideas, and the conflicting ones of women as luxurious accoutrements like furniture, into the pottery. This idea has much to recommend it, since there is a danger of being deceived by ancient ideologies. It is not that there was really a clear divide between 'companions' and 'common prostitutes', just that it suited writers to say that there was; searching for signs of differentiated prostitute status in the imagery is pointless. Moreover, modern scholars tend to use the term 'hetaira' exclusively when discussing pots: it allows them both to soften the connotations of the word 'prostitute', and summon up the idea of a 'demi-monde' without there having to be explicit sexual contact. But indiscriminate use of the term to describe women on pottery creates more problems than it solves.

Recognising the 'hetaira'

A fundamental question is whether a hetaira is something a woman can 'be' on a pot: can there be a prostitute without a customer? Or to put it another way, if a woman is neither present at a symposium nor in the presence of a man, can she be characterised as a prostitute? The question is relevant because of the current trend in the treatment of pots: having decided that Athenians recognised two kinds of women, scholars have been quick to adopt the term 'hetaira' as a label for female figures in a wide range of scenes, using a variety of indicators to support the attribution. Is there then a set of signifiers which ancient painters used to denote a prostitute or 'hetaira' on pottery? From the claims of literature one would expect that there should be clear and simple features to ensure that female status be clearly shown, yet it is plain that on pottery no consistent indicator of sexual status can be found; in fact, all those indicators identified at different stages have proved to be used in an inconsistent and sometimes confusing way.

Nudity, for instance, seems initially an obvious sign: literature draws a clear contrast between wives, who were expected to cover and veil themselves, and prostitutes, whose

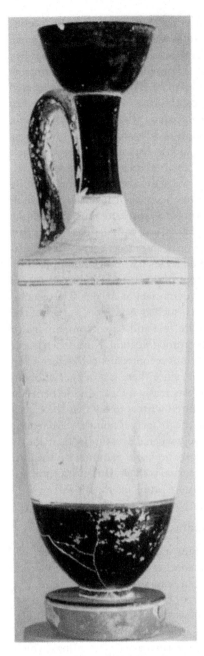

Figure 3.8 Attic white-ground lekythos, Baltimore, Johns Hopkins University 41.133, 440–420 BC. Photo: Aaron Levin, courtesy Johns Hopkins University Archaeological Collection.

profession called for the display of their body: ἑστᾶσι γυμναί, μὴ 'ξαπατηθῆς· πάνθ' ὅρα [they stand naked, lest you be deceived; you can see everything]. The position adopted by commentators at first was indeed that all naked women could be categorically stated to be prostitutes.[37] Gradually, however, this was demonstrated to be untenable: examples can be found of women shown naked who are emphatically not prostitutes. For instance, the image of a naked bride taking the ritual bath before marriage is found on more than one fifth-century pyxis: fig. 4.9 shows a nude woman at a laver within a domestic interior, in a scene of wedding preparations, and another well-known fifth-century example has a bride crouching as the water is poured over her in an attitude reminiscent of Praxiteles' Aphrodite. Mythical characters also appear naked, for example in scenes of the rape of Cassandra, where nudity is used to emphasise her vulnerability.[8] Nor is nudity for women in pottery confined to the private sphere – it can also be documented in religious contexts, as on the krateriskoi from Brauron, where girls run races naked. A very few white-ground lekythoi depict naked female mourners in scenes completely devoid of sexual content (fig. 3.8).[39]

Examples like this make it obvious that nudity for women in pot-painting cannot be read as having a single meaning in all scenes, nor can it be understood purely with reference to a set idea which equates clothing with 'respectability'. After all, although male nudity was regular in Greece in certain contexts such as athletics, men were not normally naked either; several anecdotes hinge on the disgrace of men who allow their clothes to become disarranged and display more than they should. Yet men are shown naked on pots – not only at exercise but in much less likely situations such as work or battle.[40] Pottery cannot be offering us a representation of reality, which highlights a serious problem in the depiction of women. If Athenian women, married or unmarried, were heavily muffled and veiled as a matter of course, why is veiling so rarely depicted on pottery? Most women on pots, whatever their actions, are unveiled, even in contexts where we would expect it, such as the visit to the tomb. Llewellyn-Jones has argued that the reason lies in the nature of Greek art – painters could have represented veiling if they wished, but rarely chose to do so.[41] If one accepts this argument (and it has some appealing implications), then it must mean that there was a huge gulf between what one saw in the city, where all women going about were veiled, and what was depicted on the pots. If there is such a gulf between life and imagery, how should we understand the images? It is not the case that all unmuffled women are automatically eroticised; in fact the converse is true since nudity was clearly not always sexualised, as in the case of ritual nudity. This has consequences for our understanding of certain images: for instance, the cup by the Agora Chaireas Painter (fig. 3.9), which was found in a well deposit in the Agora. It depicts a woman, naked except for a sakkos and

Figure 3.9 Attic red-figure cup, Athens, Agora Museum P24102, *c.*500 BC. Photo: American School of Classical Studies at Athens: Agora Excavations.

earring, holding a wreath before an altar on which a fire burns.[42] The cup carries no external decoration, and in this way is parallel to the theme of the woman at an altar examined in the first chapter. It also mirrors the pattern of another cup by the same painter, also found in Athens, similarly undecorated outside, which shows a dressed woman putting a sprig upon an altar. Yet how can we interpret the woman's nakedness? It depends how great an emphasis one puts on it: does the nudity override all other features of the scene, allowing one to say that it is a hetaira at an altar? Or is it a signal about the kind of worship taking place: some have suggested a sacrifice to Aphrodite, or possibly magical activity. What we need to realise is that the woman and her appearance cannot be extracted from the religious context – to ignore this is to lose sight of the purpose of the object. Nudity is obviously not incidental to a scene, but neither is it an overriding factor.

The same debate surrounds a hydria in Copenhagen by the Washing Painter, an extremely well-known image (fig. 3.10) – a naked woman stands and spins a distaff, wearing only an amulet around her thigh, her clothes piled on a chair behind her. Opposite a seated and clothed woman directs her actions.[43] This has been characterised as a particularly problematic scene, because of the woman's nudity; again it has been understood as an overriding signal indicating that the woman is a 'hetaira'. The fact that no man is present is immaterial: nudity must indicate a sexualised scene.[44] The image must, however, be placed in its context, both artistically and archaeologically. It is part of a series of small vases attributed to the Washing Painter, from c.440–30 BC, all of which depict women dressing or washing, often attended by Eros. Five examples, one pelike and four hydriai, show a naked woman washing at a laver, and one other a naked woman putting on a sandal. On four of these, Eros flies up to the washer with a rolled cloth or an alabastron; on one a kalathos stands, marking the space as an interior. Other images from the same series depict women playing games and swinging.[45] All those pots with a provenance were found at Nola, a Greek colony in Sicily, and a study by Sabetai has connected their imagery with marriage ritual, both washing and dressing, and game-playing.[46] To excerpt one scene and attempt to interpret it in isolation is a road to failure, since the nudity of the woman does not bear direct comparison with images of women at symposia on pots exported to Etruria a generation before. These pots are about the seductive appeal of women as part of marriage, not the world of brothels and commercial sex. To ask why the woman is naked is to look for a story which is not present: the hydria was used at Nola as a grave offering, and so served a purpose. To see a 'hetaira' is to assume that nudity alone can indicate setting, profession of the figures and implied activity. It is by no means the case that every naked woman is a prostitute; one cannot demonstrate consistency in the use of nudity as a symbol, nor is it easy to predict the ancient viewer's response.

More subtle symbols of prostitute status have been sought in elements such as hairstyle, on the grounds that slaves are distinguished in art by cropped hair, and hence prostitutes (most of whom would be slaves) will be shown with short hair. As we have seen, there are hairstyles appropriate to young girls or parthenoi, but among adult women on pots diversity is the rule: women at symposia wear their hair in a sakkos, tied up with a band, knotted or loose. Sometimes they have hair cropped short; more often they do not.[47] Even in similar scenes on the same pot, hairstyles can vary: a cup in Florence by the Antiphon Painter, for instance, shows on both sides a woman penetrated from the rear in a sympotic setting.[48] On one side the woman has her hair in a sakkos; on the other the woman's hair is short. The well-known pair of cups by the Triptolemos Painter (figs. 3.11, 3.12), show

Figure 3.10 Attic red-figure hydria, Copenhagen, Nationalmuseet Chr VIII 520, 440–430 BC.
Photo courtesy Department of Classical and Near Eastern Antiquities, National Museum of
Denmark.

scenes of copulation on a kline – one shows a bearded man and a woman with her hair in
a knot; the other shows a bald man and a short-haired woman.[49] Peschel made an extensive
study of hairstyles of hetairai on pots and found that although there are changes in the
hairstyles depicted, reflecting fashions among women (or painters) – the mitra and hair
worn in a knot becoming more common as the fourth century goes on – the balance
between long and short hair is never such as to produce solid conclusions about female
status.[50] A consideration of the claim also reveals the illogicality of trying to conflate

Figure 3.11 Attic red-figure cup, Tarquinia, Museo Nazionale Archeologico, *c.*480 BC (drawing).

Figure 3.12 Attic red-figure cup, Tarquinia, Museo Nazionale Archeologico, *c.*480 BC (drawing).

'slave' and 'prostitute' in the area of visual representations, since even if hetairai were slaves they would not be expected to look like it: would an owner crop a slave's hair if she were earning money as a high-class hetaira? Even the women who appear in some of the most demeaning scenes on pottery (discussed below) have long hair and are not characterised as slaves.

Garter amulets have been singled out as another possible indicator for hetairai. Amulets are worn by many children in depictions on choes and terracottas, a feature which presumably reflects reality: amulets were protective, intended to ward off sickness and bad luck.[51] Women also wear amulets when they are naked, most often around the thigh, in scenes of myth and life: they can be seen on many of our examples, such as the Washing Painter's naked spinner (fig. 3.10), and the dancers on the Polygnotan hydria (fig. 1.18). Possibly the garter amulet has attracted modern attention because its effect is to emphasise a woman's nakedness, but it cannot be shown to be connected to sexual status. An amulet is worn by a bride on a fifth-century BC pyxis, frequently by women shown in domestic settings, and even in scenes of myth, so it is impossible to draw clear rules about it. Although it is true that some later writers refer to amulets worn for their supposed contraceptive powers, most were directed at more general protection, and would be worn by women and children as being most at risk from malign influences.[52] Their use is illustrated by the anecdote in Plutarch's *Life of Perikles* that Perikles was very opposed to superstition throughout his life, but in his final illness was so demoralised as to consent to wear an amulet given to him by his womenfolk.

A more interesting debate centres on whether hetairai can be distinguished by name. Just as in mythological scenes, black-figure painters especially sometimes gave the figures in their scenes names, and the claim that names per se, or particular kinds of name, indicate that a figure is a hetaira has been made about both women at symposia and those depicted in other pursuits. Women are named by painters in scenes of water-gathering at the fountain – for example on a hydria in London, where Anthylla, Mnesilla and Rhodon visit a fountain; in scenes of fruit-picking, as on a black-figure hydria in Munich, where Philto, Rhode, Simyle, Tunnis and Korinno appear in an orchard; in domestic scenes, as on a lid from Athens on which women working wool are named as Kleimache, Aristomache and Hechyse [Hesyche]; and at some symposia: Smikros' stamnos in Brussels (fig. 3.13) depicts Choro, Helike and Rhode.[53] In its extreme form the very fact of naming a woman in public is seen as an indication of her prostitute status: any name on a pot must denote a woman of immoral status, since wives and daughters of citizens were not regularly referred to publicly by name.[54] The argument implicitly assumes that we are supposed to interpret the scene as reflecting reality, that the women in the scene really are called by the names they are given: a good example is the cup from Corinth (fig. 3.14) with two women shown in bust form. They are labelled Glyka and Nebris, 'Sweet' and 'Fawn', and predictably they have been taken as portraits of leading hetairai.[55] Another interesting case is the woman on the kalpis in fig. 1.18 playing the aulos for younger women to dance to: she is labelled Elpinike, and has been identified with Elpinike the sister of Kimon. Most have assumed both that the name must relate to the historical woman, and that it was an insulting joke at her expense.[56]

The concept of naming, however, is one where context is essential. The application of names to scenes on pottery begins as a fashion for letters, meaningful or not, on kraters and cups, and most notably on Tyrrhenian amphorae, some of which have every element of a scene named, including chairs and altars! This then evolved into labels in scenes of myth to identify the characters, and then to ordinary scenes too, in which athletes and symposiasts are named. Early examples seem to use regular Athenian personal names, although later we find more mythological or personifying names, as on the pots of the Eretria and Meidias Painters.[57] In earlier scenes, then, women are given names which appear to be everyday ones, and it is the status of these which has caused debate. The central question is whether

Figure 3.13 Attic red-figure stamnos, Brussels, Musées Royaux A717, c.510 BC. Photo: RMAH, courtesy Musées Royaux d'Art et d'Histoire, Brussels.

Figure 3.14 Corinthian cup, Athens, National Museum 992, *c.*580 BC (drawing). After Pfuhl fig. 191.

a certain name can be enough on its own to identify a woman in a scene as a prostitute. Athenaeus, writing much later, gives examples of prostitutes' names and nicknames (some of which seem very obvious, such as Didrachme), but these were often assumed and tend to relate to their origin or particular expertise.[58] A list of prostitutes' names drawn from literature and inscriptions in the fifth and fourth centuries was compiled by Schneider, and among these some names attributed to hetairai seem perfectly ordinary, such as Stratonike or Myrrhine.[59] In this list 303 names in total are attributed to hetairai, and of these 142 are recognised as being citizen wives' names too, suggesting that expectations of a real distinction between 'citizen' and 'hetaira' names may be misplaced. Some of the difficulty can lie in examining the meaning of a name too closely, since the suspicion that a woman is meant to be a hetaira may colour our view of the name. Ogden, for instance, in a study of Hellenistic prostitution, lists Callixeina (beautiful stranger), Oinanthe (flower of the wine) and Gethosyne (Joy) as appropriate names for courtesans, and Williams cites Rhodopis (the name of a famous Egyptian courtesan) and Aphrodisia as unmistakable hetaira names.[60] Yet all these are known from inscriptions to have been the names of citizen women as well. In part, of course, the distinction is a false one – a name could belong to a prostitute who was also a citizen and wife – but the concept of 'respectable' and 'unrespectable' names is clearly problematic. Did citizen parents never think their daughters pretty (Kallisto, Kallis) or loveable (Philo, Glyke)? Furthermore, most of the names found on pots are clearly Athenian: the idea that the women are marked as hetairai by foreign (and therefore slave) names is also impossible to demonstrate. Rhodon and its variants, for instance, are very frequent names on pots but are also found as names of wives; Lyda (Lydian) may possibly be an isolated example of a slave toponym (though it should colour our understanding of the potter Lydos!), and perhaps Iope, but this is unclear.[61] As with hairstyles, one must bear in mind the practicalities of the trade: would a slave prostitute retain an identifiable slave name, or seek higher status by adopting a free woman's name?

What is clear is that it is impossible for all named women to be prostitutes, given the range of scenes in which they are named. Apart from Amazons and maenads, women are named on white-ground lekythoi (a mistress and maid, Chryseis and Kallisto, appear on a lekythos in a private collection in Germany) and in scenes of mourning too (Myrrhine and Myrte appear on a black-figure phormiskos).[62] The naming of women in domestic scenes also seems far from any implication of sexualisation: it is useful to compare the Boiotian skyphos illustrated in the previous chapter (figs. 2.11, 2.24) on which named women (Euarchia, Kodoma and Eupharia) appear in a domestic setting. Among male figures, warriors and athletes are sometimes named, as are satyrs; sometimes the name is obviously relevant (for example a satyr named Kissos, Ivy), at other times not. The same seems to be broadly true of women: most are not named, and those who are may have names appropriate to their activity (like the aulos player Kleophonis) or appearance (a dancer, Kallisto), but names alone can tell us little because they do not seem to be particular to any one kind of figure.[63] Being named in itself cannot be a sign of prostitute status, nor are there any detectable hetaira name types.

The final, and most indisputable, determinant of prostitution is of course money. When we encounter images of men holding purses talking to women without an obvious product for sale, are these women selling the ultimate commodity, themselves? Originally this was believed to be the case: a purse in male hands was invariably held to signify the purchase of sex, therefore creating many scenes of 'negotiations with hetairai'. In fact, in Athenian pottery we find no representation of prostitution as such – of sex unequivocally exchanged for money. We do not even find the type of transaction seen in images of commerce, where the customer offers a purse and the vendor the object for sale. One or two images come close – for instance, a skyphos in St Petersburg (fig. 3.15) on which a man addresses a woman while holding a purse in one hand and a coin in the other, and a cup in Munich by the Wedding Painter which shows a couple having sex with what may be a purse hanging in the background – but there is no scene where a woman receives a purse and offers sex.[64] We do not find on pots women depicted doing the real work of prostitution. Instead, a group of pots has been identified as signifying the process of arranging sex, but, as we have seen, these could equally well imply the sale of other services, such as musicianship. Davidson usefully notes that a hetaira was hired for company and flirting,

Figure 3.15 Attic red-figure skyphos, St Petersburg, The State Hermitage Museum 4224, *c.* 460 BC (side A). Photo courtesy The State Hermitage Museum, St Petersburg.

not necessarily for sex ('paid for the evening' rather than 'paid for the deed'); a purse does not necessarily indicate that sex is the commodity under discussion.[65] The presence of a purse on one pot can also have an effect on the interpretation of similar scenes – there is often an unstated shift from scenes with money, which are interpreted as prostitution, to scenes without money which are then given the same meaning. Reeder, for instance, illustrates an oinochoe by the Berlin Painter which depicts a seated woman, and a man with purse and flower, and describes the woman as a hetaira; on the next page she illustrates an amphora by the Providence Painter on which a similar couple appear without a purse, and states that this is a repeat of the same theme of prostitute and customer.[66] This reveals the perils of pre-deciding painters' themes and preoccupations, then seeking to encompass all images under a few headings. Almost every prostitute on a pot is assumed to be so for reasons of preconception, because she is having sex, talking to a man, naked, receiving a gift, or stuffing a cushion.

This forces the conclusion that just as in reality there was no method of distinguishing a prostitute from any other woman simply by looking, so there is no immediate way of telling the status of a woman on pottery. Nothing on its own signals that a woman sells sex for a living. Even setting is an unreliable guide, since most scenes lack any identifiable setting. Such a conclusion may seem banal, but it runs against the grain of current interpretation, which asserts that because Athenian writers place so much emphasis on the social and civic status of the individual, this factor must be detectable in the imagery too.[67] Artists in the past have of course included elaborate codes in their paintings to indicate social status, or have unconsciously incorporated real indicators in costume or behaviour, and there is a view which insists that such codes must be present in Attic pot-painting too, even if undetectable to the modern eye. This view, however, is predicated on the idea of an Athenian viewer, and his or her need to establish the status of the figures seen; but there is no reason for us to presuppose an Athenian viewer, and in fact good reason to suppose that this was not the case (see pp. 8–11). The best illustration of the complete lack of status codes is the failure of modern scholars to find any image of the concubine. The role of pallake, lawful concubine, is one of the three possible statuses identified for free women in Apollodorus' speech, and we encounter in oratory several households where men had concubines, as well as laws relating to their formal relationships.[68] Yet any chapter written on the Athenian concubine goes unillustrated, because despite the claims of literature there is not one example of a securely identified concubine on a pot. So much of what we think about female status on pottery is inferred: how could the status of a concubine be shown? A concubine lived in the household and produced lawful children, like a wife; she might be kept for entertainment, as was the slave pallake in Antiphon's speech, in which case she would attend parties like a hetaira. Literature offers us no clues about how one recognised a concubine, and no modern scholar has succeeded in finding an image.[69] This raises a related question: if we accept that there is a lack of clear delineation of status for women on pottery, is the practice deliberate? A very influential article by Beard identifies the ambiguities about female status in several scenes, and argues that the ambiguity is deliberate on the part of the artists, who were trying to call attention to the stereotypical presentation of women and to question its validity.[70] This is based on fundamental assumptions about the painters' interest in depicting female status, which have become very detached from context: Beard herself makes the point that interpretation depends on the viewer, therefore what is needed is a more nuanced approach, taking into account scene type and provenance, rather than looking at pottery as an undifferentiated mass. It is an observation worth repeating that we can ask of pots only those questions which they are capable of answering.

Sex as work

So there are no hard and fast rules for recognising a prostitute: we need instead to look at what we actually see on pots about sexual work and women. More than any other theme, the sexual makes interpreters unwilling to accept scenes as they are, and too willing to create stories around them – about what will happen or has just happened in the scene: the woman playing the flute will later undress and sit on the kline; the youth talking to a woman has just paid for sex – in order to explain a scene, or make it fit a preconceived idea.[71] Comparison with representations of mythology demonstrates that this kind of invention is unnecessary; conventions for representing narrative did exist, and where a scene lacks narrative elements there is no need to import them. There is often also a desire to find continuity between the inside and outside of a cup, or two sides of a pot, which is not necessarily the case. Storytelling is often a consequence of trying to squeeze out answers to impossible questions about status or events.

The two arenas in which we can definitely seek representations of sexual work are the symposion and the brothel. The symposion is the only scenario in which identification of the hetaira is secure: by definition all women depicted at symposia would be hired entertainers – musicians, dancers and prostitutes – since the fact of attendance at symposia is one of the touchstones used by the orators to distinguish respectable women from hetairai. The symposion appears as a theme in pot-painting very early, crossing the boundary from myth (as in scenes of Herakles and Iole on a Corinthian krater, or the wedding of Peleus and Thetis) to human activity. It is frequent on Corinthian pots, and is adopted as a theme in Laconian and Athenian fabrics. Literary accounts of the symposion vary widely from the highbrow literary gatherings of Plato to that in the 'House of the Trireme' at Agrigentum, at which the symposiasts became so drunk that they believed themselves in a ship at sea, and threw all the furniture out of the windows to prevent themselves from sinking. Apollodorus claims that Phrynion had sex with Neaira in public at symposia, trying to cast such occasions in the worst possible light; we can contrast this with Xenophon's account of the guests at his symposion each going home to his wife.[72] Pottery too offers a spectrum of scenes, including decorous men-only symposia, those with dancers or entertainments, and those where the erotic is close to the surface. There is a clear development in the motif over time, and this reveals the danger of trying to read pots as a close reflection of society, since depictions of symposia become sexualised in early red-figure, then more decorous again in the fourth century, a change which cannot be reflecting reality in Athens since the fourth century was the age of the great courtesans; instead the demands of the market are being felt.[73] But what of the experience of women at symposia? A range of different depictions of women at symposia can be found: for instance, a cup by the Hegesiboulos Painter in New York (fig. 3.16) shows a very decorous sympotic scene: two men recline on a couch, waited on by a naked serving boy and a lyre player, while at either side of the scene two women wearing mantles sit in high-backed chairs.[74] There is segregation between the sexes, and the only licentiousness is between one of the diners and the slave-boy. These women's participation in the symposion is minor, but they are part of the symposiasts' experience: female company, like wine and song, was a necessary part of the occasion. A different form, however, can be seen on the

Figure 3.16 Attic red-figure cup, New York, The Metropolitan Museum of Art Rogers Fund 1907 (07.286.47), *c.*500 BC. Photo courtesy The Metropolitan Museum of Art, New York.

stamnos in Brussels by Smikros (fig. 3.13): an aulos player pipes for a singer at the centre of the scene, while two women are seated on klinai with the men: one couple embrace, while on the other kline the man touches the women's breast as she unbinds her hair.[75] In this scene the women are not simply passive objects in the experience of the men; although their role, as objects of desire, is primarily to provide sexual entertainment for the diners, there is evidence of reciprocal affection in the diners' actions. The idea becomes even more obvious on fig. 3.17, a cup from Basel which depicts eight symposiasts, four men and four women.[76] On each side two men and two women recline among cushions; all but one woman wear fillets (the other woman wears a band for her hair), and both women and men hold cups or branches. This is a vision of the symposion with songs and games in which all join together. The women here are like the hetairai of Athenaeus, who drink, tell jokes and play with their partners. The images bring home the fact that hetairai were not simply women paid as prostitutes; some images offer the idea of the hetaira as equal, her role in the entertainment as subject, not object.

The image of the active hetaira finds its most complete expression in those scenes which show women at symposia without men. Ten pots carry this kind of scene, depicting women as symposiasts with all the paraphernalia of the banquet, reclining, drinking toasts and playing games, but without any male partners.[77] Some show two women together, others parties of up to five: a psykter by Euphronios shows four women, naked but for a mitra or wreath, drinking toasts (fig. 3.18). These symposiasts interact without men, adopting masculine roles, such as the woman named Smikra who drinks a toast to Leagros. One of the most striking images is on a cup from Copenhagen (fig. 3.19), the tondo of which shows

Figure 3.17 Attic red-figure cup, Basel, Antikensammlungen Kä 415, 460–450 BC. Photo: C. Niggli, courtesy Antikenmuseum, Basel.

Figure 3.18 Attic red-figure psykter, St Petersburg, The State Hermitage Museum B644, *c.*510 BC (drawing). After Pfuhl, fig. 394.

a female symposiast reclining with a skyphos.[78] This elevates the woman from being part of the 'furniture' of a symposium to the central role: she reclines and drinks just as a man would, not in the service of a male purchaser. The response to images of women symposiasts has been divided: some scholars are convinced that the scenes cannot represent reality, that they must be fantasy, designed to appeal to male users of the cups; others accept the scenes as images of real women on real occasions, drinking toasts to their chosen partners.[79] Both these interpretations, however, are undermined by the provenances of the pots in question: all but one of those with a provenance were found in Italy, and this context makes the question of fantasy or reality rather beside the point. Whether or not it was possible in Athens for women to hold symposia of their own, and for painters to depict

Figure 3.19 Attic red-figure cup, Copenhagen, Thorvaldsen's Museum H616, *c*.490 BC (drawing).

the occasion, the question was not particularly meaningful in Etruria – from the point of view of the end-users the banquet was an occasion in which women could participate as equals, not one where their presence was degrading. The one image not from Etruria was found at Vari in Attica, in a grave, which suggests that the idea of fantasy for male drinkers has little substance. That pots should place women at the centre of the symposion, and as actors as well as objects, is surprising only in contrast to attitudes expressed in literature: the customers of potters had few difficulties in envisioning the female symposiast as equal, or indeed as the most important figure in a scene.

The image of women working at the symposion is thus very positive, possibly a result of the destination and use of the pots. But what about those women who worked as prostitutes outside the institution of the symposion? In literature the locus for sex outside the oikos is the brothel, which is made central to the masculine experience of paid sex – Solon is credited with the invention of the state brothel, and the comic poet Philemon writes in praise of the democratic sexual experience they offered. Writers are clear about what happened in a brothel – the women lined up, on display, for the customer to choose.[80] Surprisingly, given the emphasis on depictions of prostitutes in pottery, this is never shown: not one example has a 'line-up' of women and a customer's choice.[81] Nevertheless, commentators are certain that some pots illustrate brothels, although they tend to identify different examples. The difficulty in using money as an indicator of prostitution has already been highlighted – we do not find pimps or madams receiving money for their charges' services. Instead various aspects of individual scenes are taken to indicate the brothel context. A seated woman facing the viewer between conversing couples on a cup in Berlin is said by Davidson to show a 'madam' in a brothel; a woman seated in a sketchily outlined building on a hydria has been associated with the oikema mentioned by Aeschines, a booth or cubicle where individual prostitutes, female or male, worked; a cup by Makron showing six couples in various kinds of physical contact is said by Reinsburg to be unmistakably a brothel; and a cup by the Ambrosios Painter depicting six women with auloi and wreaths in the company of five men has been identified as a brothel by Williams because of the women's names.[82] In none of these scenes does money change hands, or even appear, nor is there any sexual contact: only the Makron cup shows affectionate contact between women and men. The question is why scholars are so convinced that brothels must be shown: 'there seems little doubt that this is a brothel and a cloth factory'; '[Louvre G143] admirably captures the atmosphere of a brothel'; 'a hetaira seated in the porch of what is surely a brothel, a familiar scene in any modern "red-light" district'.[83] The two underlying assumptions seem to be a conviction that all women shown in the company of men must be prostitutes, and that the pots will reflect the claims of literature about prostitution in a straightforward way. Additionally, once a motif has been identified with prostitution in one scene (e.g. the aulos case), the temptation is to apply it wherever it can be found. Only two pots seem to me to include an essential element suggesting a brothel, and these are two with onlookers to a sexual scene. On a hydria in Chicago a man and young woman embrace while two women and a man look on, and on a bell-krater in London two youths prepare to copulate with a man and woman looking on.[84] Even so, in neither of these scenes is money present, and the symbolism of both is quite odd: the male version has something of a stage set about it; the female version has some indeterminate symbolism, such as a lekythos on the wall, and the elegantly dressed woman with hand loom who stands at one side of the scene. Here, too, interpretations have varied from 'encounter of bride and groom' to 'scene in a brothel'. The conclusion is clear that the painters were not trying to illustrate the world of the prostitute as described in literature: images of sex are much more fluid in setting and meaning.

Defining the 'erotic'

Beyond these scenes of sex as work, there is to be found a much bigger hinterland of 'erotic' scenes, and the identification of the figure of the 'hetaira' has made our understanding of these much more difficult: the assumption that a woman is defined as a prostitute by her depiction in a scene with sexual overtones has led scholars to see sex scenes as 'real life' – as pictures of prostitutes. The often-repeated claim that because pot-painters lived in the Kerameikos in Athens they would see prostitutes around them, and paint what they saw, has thrown our interpretation of the images out of balance. As I said in the Introduction, a fundamental difficulty is the consideration of a category of art called 'erotica', because this implies material produced for a specific purpose. Books which examine sex in antiquity tend to group together any images on pots which contain nudity, those actions currently considered sexual, scenes of men and women washing, courtships, women with phalloi or phallos-birds, and scenes of excretion. This is the creation of a category – the images are assembled from many periods and places to imply a coherent body of work, produced with a single purpose in mind. But because an image such as an isolated scene of heterosexual intercourse seems similar to pornography in modern culture, this does not mean that an ancient viewer responded to it as obscene. It is worth remembering that attitudes towards sexual images were very different in classical Greece from the present day: a recent study of similar imagery in Rome has reminded us that images we would consider very explicit were part of everyday decoration in homes and businesses, and that those viewing them cannot have adopted an interpretation based solely on feelings of secret enjoyment and shame.[85] Our attitudes towards Greek images too are often inconsistent: we accept that the Herm (a pillar with a carved head and phallus) was not an obscene figure, that a model phallus could be the centre of ritual, and that sex itself could be part of a Dionysiac rite. Yet a picture of a couple engaged in erotic pursuits must, according to regular interpretations of vase-painting, be intended to titillate. There are thus two things to examine more closely: the meaning of an image – we must bear in mind the use of obscenity in religious rites, for instance – and an analysis of the archaeological background to apparently erotic images: where do these images come from, and what were they used for?

Scenes of sex on pottery exhibit an unusual pattern for two reasons: because they are found almost exclusively outside Athens, and because the theme makes several sudden shifts in presentation, then vanishes altogether in the mid-fifth century. The earliest

Figure 3.20 Attic black-figure cup, Rhodes, Archaeological Institute of the Dodecanese, 550–540 BC. Photo courtesy Archaeological Institute of the Dodecanese.

images of sex are found on Tyrrhenian amphorae, those pots made for a purely Etruscan market. Nine of these carry scenes of men and women copulating, as part of a general decorative scheme which includes animal friezes, battle scenes, komoi and scenes from myth. The figures are depicted in an ill-defined sympotic space, with kraters standing on the floor: some dance and hold kylikes, while others copulate in a variety of (impractical) positions.[86] The scenes are thus not realistic depictions of sex, or even erotica for titillation, but a representation of ritual. Similar themes appear on black-figure cups throughout the sixth century, and here too the most striking feature is the lack of context, as on the cup from a tomb deposit in Rhodes (fig. 3.20).[87] Men and women, highlighted in white paint, couple in a variety of positions; they are naked, and there is no setting. To label these figures 'hetairai' is pointless, just as it would be to label the men 'citizens' – there is no signification here.[88] On the latest black-figure the subject becomes less popular, while in red-figure the scenes become more varied, both more detailed and explicit, and also more decorous: we now find sex in sympotic scenarios, usually more clearly delineated, and a move from group sex to individual couples, though this is gradual. The red-figure painters illustrate furniture, mattresses and cushions (figs. 3.11, 3.12), sometimes with baskets and flute cases on the wall to indicate a sympotic setting. The high point of sex scenes comes in archaic red-figure, and after 450 BC they decline in numbers, fading from view by 420 BC.

This brief survey highlights one of the difficulties of treatment: the relatively small number of pots with explicitly sexual scenes. Even including peripheral scenes, Kilmer, in his study of red-figure erotica, finds about a hundred scenes of sexual activity in red-figure, with possibly thirty in black-figure – a very small proportion of the total of documented Athenian pots.[89] The shapes on which explicit scenes appear are primarily cups, and also psykters and kraters, and the dominant interpretation is therefore that the scenes were a form of erotica used in sympotic settings; that is, that they were designed to produce sexual arousal in the viewer. As such they are interpreted as having been used at symposia where wives would not be present, only prostitutes, and to have been (in some accounts) locked away within the andron (men's dining-room) where they could not be seen by women of the family.[90] Such an analysis is thoughtless on several counts. First

117

of all, to describe them as 'men's pots' is not useful when women (of whatever status) were present, and indeed are shown using cups, at the very same symposia. It seems very odd to treat these objects as the ancient equivalent of *Playboy* magazine, if they were utensils of domestic use, designed for mixing and serving wine. Second, if one concentrates on scenes of male–female erotic interaction, only fourteen examples come from Athens (including fragments), and of these, eight were found on the Acropolis.[91] Clearly, even though most are cup fragments they were not being used at symposia to encourage erotic activity; these objects were dedications to the gods, as the presence of an early red-figure plaque with scenes of copulation (bespoke for dedication) demonstrates. Of the other six examples, two were found in the potters' quarter itself, two in the Agora, and two have no specific findspot recorded. The total of six contrasts with the forty-one examples found in Italian graves. One of the houses in the Kerameikos ('House Z') has been identified as a brothel; whatever the value of this identification, it is notable that the pottery finds from the house are mostly plain ware, with the odd depiction of Aphrodite; there are no explicit sexual scenes found here.[92] By far the greater part of the pottery with known provenance comes from Etruria: more than 70 per cent of male–female erotica, and rather more of male–male. Despite their appearance on cups and kraters, 'erotic' scenes were therefore used primarily by Etruscan customers as gifts to bury with the dead; it is useful to those commenting on Athenian life to categorise sex scenes on cups as Athenian, but this does the evidence a disservice since the depictions were for an export market. Furthermore, since most of the cups with erotic scenes come from tombs, they cannot be taken as the choice of citizens to document either their lives or their fantasies.

The reception of these images in Etruria was obviously very different from their imagined use in Greece: they did not function as sex aids. A comparison with the use of erotic art within Etruscan society is illuminating, since in both Roman and Etruscan art, on mirrors and on pottery, we find a concentration on gentle and affectionate relations between men and women, rather than on the orgiastic: Etruscan mirrors depict mythical couples such as Turan and Atunis (Aphrodite and Adonis) or Thesan and Tinthun (Eos and Tithonos).[93] Tomb-painting from Etruria, however, does offer some explicit depictions of intercourse, both heterosexual and homosexual. These motifs occur in otherwise typical funerary contexts, combined with heroic or ritual themes. The best-known example is found in the Tomb of the Bulls in Tarquinia, where two erotic groups, one showing homosexual and one heterosexual intercourse, appear above a scene of Achilles ambushing Troilos (fig. 3.21).[94] Holloway has suggested that these groups are apotropaic in meaning, and that they can be read as part of a nexus of apotropaic elements in the tomb as a whole.[95] He associates with these as images whose function is primarily apotropaic a scatological image of a man defecating in the Tomb of the Jugglers; the use of erotic and scato-logical motifs for apotropaic purposes is well documented, and the tomb was certainly an appropriate place for such themes. Is it possible to see a link between the imagery of wall-painting and that of the goods found in the graves?

This idea has profound implications for our reading of 'erotic' scenes. Do they have any meaning within Athens, or were they created only for an export market? Did they (as the dedications might make us think) have different meanings in different cultures? Is it legitimate to use these scenes as documents of Athenian reality, or even Athenian mentality? This would affect, for example, the questions of female status which we have been examining: Etruscan users saw reflected in sympotic images their own banquets, where husbands and wives dined together, and therefore questions of the status of the

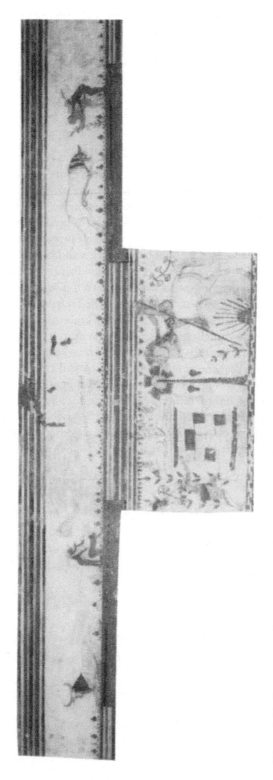

Figure 3.21 Etruscan tomb-painting, Tomb of the Bulls at Tarquinia, c.540 BC. Photo: Schwanke, D.A.I. Roma (neg. no. 81.4274).

women simply would not arise. I do not think this question can be sidestepped; clearly no image created in Athens could be free of Athenian cultural influence, but I think these are further from the literature than many of the scenes we have examined so far, because in most cases we can be certain that they were not used by Athenians in sympotic settings. We need to find a new road of interpretation which examines the images more critically and does not assume that an object of Athenian manufacture must necessarily be a valid cultural document.

Understanding 'erotica'

Bringing the idea of context to the fore helps to explain quite a lot about 'erotic' scenes. First, we should ask how useful it is to attempt to attribute social status to the participants in such images. For example, within scenes of copulation we can recognise two distinct types. The first comprises images of men and women engaged in sexual acts in vague or non-existent settings. These are found almost exclusively on cups, and are usually playful in tone: naked men and women roll about on wineskins and cushions, dance or copulate in sexualised play, as on fig. 3.22, a cup by the Antiphon Painter now in Malibu, on which a naked woman holding a skyphos sports with two men.[96] These scenes are found mainly in the work of the archaic pot-painters, and although their setting is clearly sympotic, with participants sometimes wearing wreaths, and with kraters, baskets and wineskins as 'furniture', there is not the same sense of organisation as in scenes where diners recline. Here we are in what Lissarrague calls 'l'espace du cratère' where dance and play, including sexualised play, are part of the scheme of things.[97] The playful aspects, including balancing acts with cups, and the lack of explicit setting should suggest that we are not meant to interpret these as scenes of reality: rather we are looking at a representation of the release of the symposium, a scenario in which inhibitions on behaviour are lifted. Again there is a difficulty in excerpting scenes with men and women together and labelling them scenes of prostitution: there are plenty of similar representations where youths or satyrs revel.

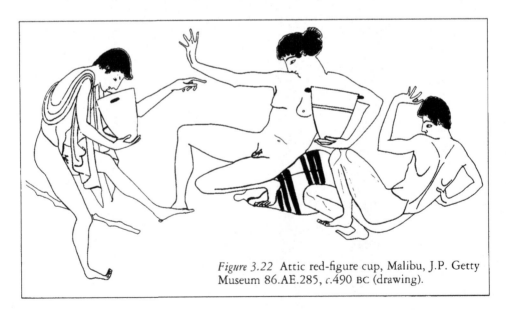

Figure 3.22 Attic red-figure cup, Malibu, J.P. Getty Museum 86.AE.285, *c.*490 BC (drawing).

120

In this way consideration of the status of the women (and the men) depicted is irrelevant – as we have seen, women in such scenes are represented in a variety of ways: some are short-haired, some have elaborate hairstyles and some wear wreaths. There is also a strong continuity between this and the sex which appears on black-figure pottery, which is both ritualised and detached from reality. Etruscan erotic scenes offer support for this more detached reading, as the erotic groups in the Tomb of the Bulls follow a similar pattern to that of black-figure iconography: the gender of the figure is indicated by colour (red for male flesh, white for female), but apart from this there is no 'scene' or context.

The second type of sex scene is distinguished by a more complex setting, including dress and furniture – klinai, mattresses, cushions and chairs. Objects depicted in the background, such as baskets and aulos cases sometimes make reference to sympotic settings, but other images show simple interiors, with stools and beds in the background. It is in these scenes that earlier comments about the distinctive features of the hetaira come into play: where we see a basket or aulos case in the field, this might signal a sympotic setting, and there is of course the one famous cup depicting sex with a purse in the background, but many other scenes have no explicitly sympotic setting and in these the status of the couple does not seem at stake. The two cups by the Triptolemos Painter (figs 3.11, 3.12) illustrate the idea well: both show a man and woman copulating on a kline with mattress and cushions; on one a staff stands in the background and on the other a bundle of clothes, but there is no reference to the symposion. One of the women, as noted above, has short hair, the other long hair caught up into a knot. Citizen and wife, freedman and hetaira, slave and owner: there is no way of telling. The act, not the status of the participants, is central, as one would expect if the scenes were aimed at customers outside Athens. An interesting cup in Canterbury, New Zealand, combines scenes of symposion on its outside with the image of a couple in the tondo (fig. 3.23): a door indicates that they are in an interior, and a chair and the end of a kline are visible in the background.[98] An alabastron hangs on the wall, and what is possibly a sandal, although damage to the cup makes it hard to see. The youth leans on his staff and gestures towards the kline; the woman, who is wearing a voluminous chiton, and has her hair in the bundled style, reaches up to embrace him as they gaze into each other's eyes. There is no basket or aulos case to signal a symposion: is the status of the woman of relevance here, or is the scene rather about the intimacy of the bedchamber? Some have suggested that husband and wife did not regularly share a bed, and that sexual pleasure was not expected in marriage, hence the scenes can only represent prostitution, but we have to contrast this idea of the unworldly and sexually uninterested wife with the riotous sexuality of wives at all-female festivals evoked in comedy.[99] Women were believed to want and enjoy sex, and it was an essential component of marriage: the law which stated that the husband of an epikleros (heiress) must sleep with her at least three times a month, was intended partly to ensure the birth of an heir, but also because a marriage without sex could not be considered a marriage at all. It is true that the imagery of marital ritual is very different to such explicitness – the groom leading a bride with downcast eyes, and only a hint of the marital bed in the background – but this was used in the rite of marriage itself; there is no need to see images of sex as the opposite pole of images of marriage. We can compare the scene in Aristophanes' *Lysistrata* between Myrrhine and her husband Kinesias, which hardly suggests a taboo on the enjoyment of sex by wives.[100] In fact, in the images of sexual activity there is a significant overlap with the imagery of courtship, taking them quite a long way from the idea of financial transactions and rapid departures.

Figure 3.23 Attic red-figure cup, University of Canterbury, New Zealand, James Logie Memorial Collection CML 6 (on loan), *c*.480 BC. Photo courtesy James Logie Memorial Collection, University of Canterbury.

The two scenes by the Triptolemos Painter are also interesting in their illustration of affectionate gestures between partners. While some images of sex seem fairly mechanical, such as the cup in Boston which includes a man's injunction to his partner to 'hold still', others indicate more contact and even affection between the participants. Men and women make eye-contact, holding one another's gaze, or reach out to cradle the other's head, a cross-cultural gesture of intimacy. Nor is the affection only female-to-male: on Makron's cup in Paris (Reinsburg's and Sutton's brothel) a man cradles the head of a woman with short hair.[101] Despite claims about male dominance both physical and metaphorical, there is a large element of affection and playfulness between partners: for instance, a cup in New Haven (fig. 3.24) has in the tondo a man and woman looking into each other's eyes

Figure 3.24 Attic red-figure cup, Yale University Art Gallery 1913.163, Gift of Rebecca Dartington Stoddard, 510–500 BC. Photo: Joseph Szaszfai, courtesy Yale University Art Gallery.

Figure 3.25 Attic red-figure cup, Berlin, Staatliche Museen 2269, *c.*500 BC (drawing).

in a clearly marked sympotic scene: the woman reaches up to touch his head in an intimate gesture, while he embraces her and makes eye-contact; the atmosphere is one of mutual affection, in spite of her short (possibly slavish) hairstyle.[102] Even in more explicit scenes of sex on a chair the partners still gaze at each other in an evocation of intimacy.[103] Kissing scenes are also found; there is in fact a Kiss Painter, who takes his name from a cup in Berlin (from Chiusi) in which a young man and smaller woman embrace each other, making eye-contact, and prepare to kiss (fig. 3.25). He wears a wreath, she a crown, and has long hair worn loose.[104] An enquiry regarding the status of the figures in such images is pointless – prostitution is not the point.

In counterpoint to these scenes of affection is another group of pots, which are usually seen as embodying Athenian male ideas about female exploitation and degradation. These have the same sympotic setting, but depict acts considered more degrading: women are shown performing fellatio, being beaten (fig. 3.26), or servicing two or more men simultaneously.[105] This group of images has been presented as an important part of the Athenian psyche: Kilmer sees them as realistic depictions of 'orgies', Keuls comments that 'many vase-paintings show the abuse and battering of women, as well as other forms of male supremacist behaviour', and Kurke that 'other contemporary vases take pains to rearticulate the differences and hierarchy within the sympotic world'. Closer analysis, however, reveals some crucial points. A very simple, but frequently overlooked fact is that pictures of this type are hardly numerous – there are at most five examples – yet they tend to be given an undue prominence in modern discussions of ancient attitudes towards women.[106] This is possibly because they feed modern suspicions about relations between men and women in Athens, but more likely because they reflect more accurately than most pots our idea of pornography. Statistically, however, they are not very significant, and again their findspots are not Athenian: two are without provenance, two from Vulci and one from Cervetri. What is noteworthy is that although their subject matter is different from the run of symposium cups, they were painted by the same painters, and exported to the same places. Explicit and non-explicit scenes form two sides of the same coin, but, more strikingly, they are often two sides of the same pot. The Pedeius Painter's cup in Paris has on the outside a gross orgy scene with forced entry, but in the interior a man embraces a lyre player in quite a delicate scene. Similarly the Brygos Painter's cup in Florence has inside a man with an aulos player, fairly friendly, together with an orgy scene with violence on the outside. Illustrations of the cups are often split in books, with violent scenes separated from the gentle, so the coexistence of scenes is not noted.[107]

It has become standard to comment that the women in these scenes are shown as old, fat or slavish, depicted as sympotic 'furniture' rather than participants, and reflecting Athenian male contempt for women. The argument is that whereas women on pots are usually uniformly young and pretty, where women are being objectified they are

Figure 3.26 Attic red-figure cup, Milan, Museo Archeologico A8037, *c*.490 BC. Photo: Foto Saporetti, courtesy Museo Archeologico, Milan.

deliberately made unattractive. This view, however, arises from treating images in isolation, rather than the scenes as a whole. There is no very strong division between degradation and violence on the one hand, and affection on the other; on the Brygos cup in Florence, for instance, among the images of beating and fellatio is a couple in 'athletic copulation', who make eye-contact as the woman touches the man's head. The women wear fillets and wreaths like the men. Similarly, the Louvre cup depicts a woman fellating a man who is not slavish; her hair is in a knot. Nor is it true to say that the women are characterised as fat; they do have folds of flesh indicated at their waists, but this is a result of their posture – they are bent over, and the folding is meant to be realistic, as are 'hanging breasts'. In the same scenes those women who are in upright postures have upstanding breasts and are not fat. Whatever is going on in these scenes, it is not the realistic depiction of ugly women.

This is not to say that we never encounter women who are shown to be fat or unattractive. On a cup by Phintias, for example, a craggy faced woman sits holding an outsize krater to drink from, with an ithyphallic youth opposite her, and in the tondo of a cup in Basel another fat older woman looks in a mirror at her toilette, described by Keuls as an 'aged hetaira primping'.[108] We have already seen the fat woman drinking in the cellar on the skyphos in Malibu (fig. 2.4). But obesity on pottery is not solely to do with the attractiveness of women. Obesity in men in particular was a cause for ridicule in an athletic and militaristic culture, as comedy demonstrates: Dionysius in *Frogs* mocks a fat athlete, while in *Clouds* the Right Argument promises that moral virtue (and vice) will be clear from the condition of a man's body.[109] Pot-painters take up the theme, with a tubby athlete among a group of slender youths on a cup by Pheidippos, and fat revellers on a black-figure oinochoe by Kleisophos.[110] Fatness in women attracts less literary comment, possibly because given social patterns of nutrition it was more rare, but we can find the same idea of ridicule of fat women in pottery. The tondo of the cup in Basel may be simply a joke about a fat woman making herself attractive, but on the Malibu skyphos it is an indication of excessive appetite, and I think this carries over into Phintias' scene too. To take up as little space as possible has always been a virtue in women, therefore fatness can equal female power and threat, especially in a poor community. These women are not to be despised so much as feared: like the monstrous women of *Ekklesiazusai*, they have big appetites for wine and, later, sex.

The violence demonstrated towards some of the women on the 'orgy' cups leads to another group of pots, included by Kilmer as 'erotica' but without an explicitly erotic content. A good example is the cup by the Foundry Painter in Milan, depicting a man attacking a woman with a sandal, and pulling her hair (fig. 3.26). There is no setting in the tondo, nor any decoration on the outside of the cup, and, despite the sandal, nothing to make it erotic but the presumed 'meaning' of the cup. These images raise very sharply the question of meaning within context: taken from an assumed sympotic context, what is there in violence to make us think of the erotic? Casual violence towards women and slaves comes through sources like comedy as completely normal at Athens, but there is no particular reason to localise it to attitudes towards hetairai in symposia: there is no reason to read the scenes as a group. For example, one of the least pleasant images of women in Athenian art depicts a fat woman tortured by satyrs: she is tied to a pillar and tortured with pincers and whip.[111] The scene has been interpreted as relating to a satyr play, but what is remarkable is its presence on a white-ground lekythos and its provenance in Eretria, implying that it is funerary, not sympotic. Depictions of violence can also be paralleled from Etruscan tomb-painting: the Tomba del Fustigazione in Tarquinia, for instance, is named for a scene in which two men beat a woman (fig. 3.27).[112] We may find

Figure 3.27 Etruscan tomb-painting, Tomba del Fustigazione at Tarquinia, 510–500 BC. Photo: Schwanke, D.A.I. Roma (neg. no. 81.4170).

such scenes repellent, yet their survival as grave-goods indicates that they were meaningful in more than an erotic way. One might also wonder whether certain scenes of myth should not also be considered as the same type: images such as the rape of Kassandra or the sacrifice of Polyxena can be fairly brutal, and in more than one scene of the Fall of Troy Kassandra is depicted nude. All writers agree that the nudity is meant to be pathetic, not titillating, but perhaps we should be looking at continuities in the violent nature of both mythical and non-mythical scenes, if they were all export material.

A similar outlook of the apotropaic rather than the erotic may underlie scenes of excretion. The depiction of excretion is a fairly common joke on pottery: revellers are shown vomiting or urinating in the bottom of a cup, so as to be revealed when the cup is drained, or are shown using the vessel itself as a chamber pot.[113] Although Kilmer includes examples of male and female excretion in his study of erotica, I am not sure that it is right to read these images as sexualised either. The idea of a taboo on the sight of bodily functions is very much a post-eighteenth-century phenomenon; Athenians went outside, not indoors, to perform bodily functions, as Blepyrus does in the opening scene of *Ekklesiazusai*, or the women of *Thesmophoriazusai*. Latrines, where they existed, were public: the idea that ancient viewers would find scenes of urination excitingly taboo is too modern.[114] In particular, Kilmer is replicating modern ideas by saying that female excretion is more erotic than male: there are only two pots which depict women urinating, though rather larger numbers exist of men, usually in a komos setting. On one cup a woman relieves herself in a large krater (again one of the type of painters' jokes), while on another a man plays the aulos while a woman urinates in a basin.[115] Two images are not many, and the scatological motif is one which also occurs in Etruscan tomb-painting with the defecating figure in the Tomb of the Jugglers.[116] Rather than searching for meaning in scenes on pots as representations of Greek reality or interests, it makes more sense to understand the images as apotropaic in function. A taboo does seem to exist concerning women and defecation; only dogs, satyrs and grotesques do this on pots, and it seems to run in parallel to the taboo in both art and literature in references to menstruation.

Finally we need to consider what are referred to as fantasy scenes, including those depicting creatures like phallos-birds or eyed phalloi, as well as women shown with olisboi, artificial phalloi. Obviously it is not always easy to establish where reality ends and fantasy begins: most commentators agree that fantasy plays a part in images of symposia and of explicit sexual scenes, but there is a distinction between images of what could happen, and those of horses with phallic heads, or satyrs copulating with sphinxes. Most unusual is the appearance of the phallos-bird (or phallos-horse), the disembodied male genitalia converted into a mythical creature.[117] Phallos-birds are common on pots, sometimes on their own or in the company of satyrs, but generally with women. They can assume a variety of shapes, from small birds to those with duck- and swan-like bodies, and there is one example of a very heron-like bird, which bends its neck to look at the woman who pets it (fig. 3.28). In contrast to assumptions about female fear of male sexuality, the imagery centres on affection for the phallos: women on pots sometimes cradle a phallos-bird on their arm.[118] A similar personifying idea appears in Aristophanes' *Acharnians*, when a bride asks Dikaiopolis for some of his private peace treaty:

Ὡς γέλοιον, ὦ θεοί,
τὸ δέημα τῆς νύμφης, ὃ δεῖταί μου σφόδρα,
ὅπως ἂν οἰκουρῇ τὸ πέος τοῦ νυμφίου.

127

Figure 3.28 Attic red-figure pelike fragment, Athens, Agora Museum P27396, *c*.480 BC (drawing).

[Ye gods, what a hilarious request from the bride, who asks me particularly {for some peace, so} that her husband's willy can stay at home!]

(*Ach.* 1058–66)

This may be male concentration on the importance of the phallos, but it does suggest an attitude of affectionate familiarity from women. Scenes where women appear with inanimate phalloi are harder to interpret, primarily because again they often attract an inappropriately sexualised interpretation. The comments above about cultural differences in the interpretation of images are relevant: phallic imagery played a part in several Athenian religious rites, and hence many scenes of women with phalloi are religious in nature, such as the pelike with a woman growing phalloi (fig. 2.28), or the women who hold baskets of phalloi (sometimes eyed). Even when the woman is naked it is a mistake to interpret the image as sexualised: we can compare the giant phallos carried by a nude woman on a column-krater in Berlin with the model phallos used in the worship of Dionysus.[119] These are connected with fertility, and the women who hold or nurture the phalloi are following their religious role. Obviously there is a shading of meaning from the ritual phallos to the olisbos or dildo, but we should note the presence of a fragment showing a woman dancing with olisboi on the Acropolis.[120] 'Nightclub acts' aside, their meaning in the Etruscan context is not hard to decipher: the winged phallos is found as a symbol in the Tomba del Topolino at Tarquinia, just as on the cup with women grinding in Berlin (fig. 2.5).[121] Again, this is a topic where nudity and the phallos need to be seen with ancient eyes.

Conclusion

Our discussion has moved a long way from the consideration of female work with which we began, and demonstrates how difficult it is to establish the meaning of scenes within their own culture. Women's work in classical Athens is too often assumed to be only sex work, and the interpretation of female figures on pottery has been made far more difficult by an insistence on establishing their status, and on the labelling of so many figures as 'hetairai'. While we do find some images of women involved in the sale of sex, they do not predominate; others present women in commercial roles, representing the reality of the poorer classes as well as that of the elite. Nor is the work of the 'hetaira' necessarily degrading – we should not expect pottery to replicate the attitudes expressed in literature. In more general terms, the difficulties with the interpretation of erotic scenes are a consequence of cultural difference: for instance, the mores of those who first excavated Greek pots in the nineteenth century led to many being shut away in private or closed collections because they were perceived to be obscene. This view may have moderated since the 1960s, but equally an insistence on reading the pots to reflect the contentious claims of literature has affected interpretations in a different way, since the desire to categorise every female as a 'wife' or a 'hetaira' has produced a set of forced readings of symbols, and a decontextualised view of the painters' aims. Considerations of provenance and use are essential in this field, and placing images in their Etruscan context offers a new understanding of their purpose, and of the apparent ambiguity of so many of the images. Pots do not offer us glimpses into the Attic bedroom, or even a complete exposition of Athenian ideas about men and women; 'erotica' are largely a creation of the export market, which used them as charms against the evil eye, constituting a small part of overall import. Such imagery appears to fall out of fashion in the later fifth century, at the same time as the representation of the symposion becomes more decorous, but this is because post-450 BC the export market changed, and scenes became more consonant with Greek ideas. The images which Athenians made for, and used, themselves are of a different quality, and it is this leisure imagery, the counterpoint to work scenes, that will form the topic of the next chapter.

4

THE WOMEN'S ROOM

The gynaikonitis, the women's quarters: how should we envisage this space? Was it 'dark, squalid and unsanitary', or a place of leisure and luxury?[1] Did it exist in reality, or was it merely a concept, a place within the house where the women should be? These questions become acute when one considers the change in themes depicting women in late fifth- and early fourth-century vase-painting. Classical artists show women in far greater numbers than their early counterparts, but depict a much narrower range of themes, and these themes become stereotyping and inexpressive. Women are depicted almost exclusively in interior settings, in large or small groups, playing music, working wool or adorning themselves; images of domestic labour, of children and of sacrifice all become far less common. Some religious scenes still appear, for example the domestic festival of the Adonia, but we see much less of women outside the house. The scenes become increasingly abstract from c.440 BC onward; interiors are far less clearly defined than in previous images of domestic work, and there is a gradual move towards the placing of women in indistinct exteriors: although landscapes are always limited in ceramic art, by the end of the fifth century we find women appearing in 'gardens', with trees and rocks (fig. 4.1).[2] At the same time the distinction between mortal and divine women becomes less sharp: female figures in apparently mundane contexts are often given the names of heroines or divine personifications. The figure of Eros, too, becomes a regular accompaniment to the women, fetching sashes and chests, holding up a mirror, or playing (fig. 4.2).[3]

Why should this change have taken place? Most commentators try to connect it with a change in Athenian social attitudes, reflected in art: Sutton speaks of a 'revaluation of female sexuality' under the influence of democratic ideas, and Boardman of a 'change in female status', while Burn associates the style of the 'gardens of women' depicted by the Meidias Painter and his followers with an escapist reaction to the deprivations of the Peloponnesian War (though the best examples of the Meidias Painter's work were found at Populonia in Etruria and at Ruvo).[4] But although the dating of Athenian pottery is notoriously subject to debate, it is difficult to associate this change with any distinct development in attitudes towards women; law-court speeches and philosophical texts of the 340s and 330s reveal the same attitudes of masculine condescension to, and desire for control of, women which are traceable in Old Comedy a century before. A development towards the concept of romantic love, and a greater equality between husband and wife may be detectable in Menander, but this dates to the end of the fourth century, far later than anyone would try to press classical vase-painting.[5] It is noteworthy too that the imagery of men on pots changes at just the same time in the fifth century; the scenes of manufacture and commerce from early red-figure disappear, there are fewer symposion

Figure 4.1 Attic red-figure hydria, New York, The Metropolitan Museum of Art 06.1021.185, *c.*440 BC (drawing). After Richter/Hall pl. 158.

Figure 4.2 Attic red-figure lekythos, New York, The Metropolitan Museum of Art 06.1021.90, 460–450 BC. After G. M. A. Richter, *Attic Red-Figured Vases: a survey* (New Haven, Yale University Press, 1958), fig. 56.

scenes, and there is a greater emphasis on athletics and leisure. Bažant has tried to explain the change in themes for both men and women as a consequence of democratic reform at the end of the sixth century, creating a movement away from the celebration of public roles and individual families in the art of the sixth century towards a concentration on the private and the experience of the individual.[6] Themes in pot-painting, however, do not become notably more democratic; in fact images of a leisured lifestyle replace depictions of work. It is better to seek reasons for change in artistic or economic concerns, and this necessitates a consideration of market and provenance.

Women's pots

There is a distinct change in the shapes of pots being produced in Attica after 470/460 BC, away from the cups and large kraters most frequent in the early red-figure period to smaller vessels – lekythoi, hydriai, lekanides and pyxides. Of the larger shapes, only bell-kraters and pelikai remain important. This change is not absolute, since small numbers of cups and kraters were still produced, but it reflects a detectable change in the export market: Etruria becomes much less important as a consumer of pottery, and the trade is taken up by other areas – Sicily, South Italy and North Africa.[7] Why this should happen is a difficult question (Boardman talks of the difficulties of Italians with Greeks), but clearly potters and painters found themselves working for a different market. Why, though, should subjects change? The usual answer is that the market had moved from demanding 'symposium ware' aimed at men, to 'women's pots', and therefore the favoured themes changed too: female customers preferred images of their own life and leisure, and sympotic images were no longer appropriate. This is, however, simplistic. Decorated cups and kraters were export pots, not by and large used in Greece outside religious contexts. Their imagery was dominated not by the concerns of the male citizen of Athens but by the demands of the Etruscan customer. The change in imagery is a consequence of the decline of this trade, but it is not a straightforward change from male to female customers. It has proved difficult to link developments in imagery to the new markets which Athenian exporters found: although new markets opened up in places like South Russia and Cyrenaica, attempts to discern changes in subject matter and myth to appeal to new customers have failed.[8] What is the case is that as the export market fragments, so the archaeology of the pottery becomes less coherent. Instead of being able to divide the pots into two groups – shapes such as cups which were exported to Etruria, and those such as black-figure lekythoi used as grave-goods in Athens – in the classical period one has to consider smaller groupings of pots and their provenances, based on particular shapes such as choes or lebetes gamikoi, or particular themes such as bathing or courtship. The purposes of pottery remain primarily either ritual or funerary – the new small hydriai and lekythoi were used in large numbers in graves in Sicily and South Italy – and it may be that the images of women, less interesting though they are in terms of inventiveness and variety, were closer to Athenian concerns: the export images with their wide variety of subjects may have been masking a much more limited repertoire for internal consumption. Certainly this seems to be the case with the truly localised pots, and it should make us wary of assumptions about customers and their demands.

The smaller vases described generically as 'women's pots' comprise several categories: those used in ritual (lebetes gamikoi, loutrophoroi), pots exported to Magna Graecia primarily for funerary use, and those which remained in Athens for domestic and funerary use. But even this last group is not transparent, as a consideration of one shape, the pyxis, will show. The pyxis, a small ceramic box with lid, probably modelled on a wooden original (figs. 1.20, 4.9, 5.2, 5.3 and 5.19), is seen as the 'women's pot' par excellence – Lissarrague defines them as 'boîtes à fards ou à bijoux', and Boardman as 'for the boudoir'.[9] The pyxis was used (it is supposed) for jewellery and cosmetics, and some have been found with traces of the cosmetics which they contained, cinnabar and psimythion (white lead).[10] That pyxides are often decorated with scenes of women in an interior is taken as a happy match of purpose and decoration. It is not, however, the case that most painted ceramic pyxides come from domestic contexts; far from it. They were frequently used as grave offerings: two examples found in the Athenian Kerameikos are a red-figure pyxis with the pursuit of Thetis among Nereids, and a group from an offering ditch which included a pyxis with interior scene among a large number of decorated and black-glaze pots.[11] More surprisingly, a pyxis was found in the public dining space of the Agora, along with bell-kraters and black-glaze cups: the pyxis shows two women, one holding an alabastron and one tying her girdle, perhaps indicating (as we shall see) nuptial preparations. Rotroff and Oakley find it difficult to account for the presence of a pyxis in a public and masculine context, commenting warily that 'The pyxis, a container normally connected with the women's toilet, could conceivably have had some function in a dining situation'.[12] As we have seen, many pyxides were offered as dedications in shrines such as that of Artemis at Brauron, and used in ritual: a lebes gamikos in St Petersburg shows a painted pyxis being carried in the nuptial procession of the Epaulia.[13] It is therefore unwarranted to assume that pyxides were designed solely for domestic use, or that they had invariably seen use in the household before burial as grave-goods. This should make us wary about generalisations about women's pots, which, as we saw with the hydria, usually derive from an incomplete view of the scenes and provenances. In fact pyxides on pots themselves are rarely shown in domestic and non-ritual contexts – women are shown using plemochoai and wooden chests very frequently, and alabastra for perfume, but not often pyxides. It is not enough, therefore, to interpret the imagery as designed solely for daily use in the toilette; as always, we need to consider wider questions of use and meaning.

The central questions relating to the imagery of pyxides and similar pots are why we should find an extensive depiction of female leisure, and what (if anything) such scenes can tell the historian. There is a detectable shift in attitudes towards leisure in literature – early on, writers like Hesiod and Semonides state the virtues of hard work for men and (especially) women – the perfect woman for both is hard-working and abstemious, and never spends time in idleness or gossip. In Semonides' list of female types, the mare-woman who sits and perfumes herself all day is a suitable consort only for a king or a tyrant. Yet by the fifth century the idea of leisure as a condition to which one might aspire had arrived: in Aristophanes' *Clouds* Strepsiades describes his wealthy wife's preoccupations:

ἡ δ' αὖ [ὄζων] μύρου, κρόκου, καταγλωττισμάτων,
δαπάνης, λαφυγμοῦ, Κωλιάδος, Γενετυλλίδος.

[And there she was, all scented of perfume and saffron and french kisses, of extravagance, self-indulgence and festivals of Aphrodite.]

(*Clouds* 51–2)

And by the time of Xenophon's *Memorabilia*, after the Peloponnesian War, the female relations of Aristarchus have to be encouraged to work, since they consider even wool-work for commercial purposes beneath them.[14] The images on pottery reflect this change – after 450 BC women on pots no longer work, instead they put on jewellery or perfume, dress, wash, sometimes play music or play with children, and take part in ritual. This shift in the imagery has significant implications for our understanding of the representation of women. First of all, it is not true to say, as many have, that the fifth century heralds an 'explosion of interest' in the lives of women. There are statistically more pots produced with images of women on, and there is development of certain types of scene (for instance, red-figure sees an expansion of types within wedding themes, from the procession of black-figure to arrival, preparations and so forth), but the range of thematic types overall becomes far narrower, and the image of female life much more predictable. This is because many of the types of scene we have already considered, such as sex or work, were export-driven, and when they die out we are left with an Athenian view of women which is predictably much more limited. It is paradoxical that this set of images is the closest we get to a concentration on female life by ancient artists, yet it offers very poor evidence for the historian, so narrow is its focus and so controlled its idealising. The pots have much less to offer as documents, since settings are abstract and indistinct, all women look very much the same, and the imagery is dominated by a single ideology of wealth and leisure. Nevertheless, despite this, the influence of classical imagery has been very powerful – discussions of female life often lean hard on this kind of pottery for illustration of dress, marriage, occupations and literacy, because the idea that we see true representations of female life is a tempting one. But how far is the imagery in the service of a particular ideology? Earlier chapters have asked how far the image corresponded to reality; this chapter has to ask how far reality corresponded to the image. Women are depicted in abstract or unreal environments, carrying out a limited range of symbolically significant activities; we can certainly explore aspects of this symbolic domain and attribute meaning to objects or creatures, but can so circumscribed a view tell us anything useful?

A case in point is the topic of marriage, which in modern opinion has come to dominate the interpretation of 'women's pots'; those scenes which do not illustrate the marriage itself are held to represent preparation for it, or to contain erotic motifs alluding to it. Oakley, for example, reads many minor features of mythological scenes, including veiling, wreaths and caskets, as references to marriage.[15] Implicit in this is the idea that marriage was the single event which dominated female life – a woman's own marriage, and then her daughter's, is seen to be the primary female preoccupation. But just because marriage is the main event of female life illustrated does not mean that it was the most important in the female view. If pots are used in a particular ritual and subsequently dedicated, or regularly placed in graves, they will survive in large numbers, but this need not imply that they were of overwhelming importance in an individual's life. The view offered by pottery that the wedding was focused on the bride may also be misleading: marriage at Athens was an agreement between two households, not a romantic union between husband and wife, and the face of marriage on pottery, celebrating the bride's role in proceedings, may be a minor aspect, exaggerating the centrality of the bride in images for female consumption.[16] There is always a danger in overenthusiastic adoption of any one interpretative approach: just as the tendency is to label women as 'hetairai' in archaic red-figure, so it has become habitual to see all women in classical red-figure as actual or potential brides. It is of course very difficult to establish whether classical painters did adopt an exceptionally narrow view of female experience, concentrating on marriage to the exclusion of all else, or whether the identification of 'nuptial nuances' is a modern preoccupation. But this question of interpretation exposes one of the issues central to the understanding of pots as evidence: is it possible to go beyond the identification and interpretation of 'symbols' in these scenes, and do they have any insight to offer into female experience, as opposed to aspiration? The chapter will show the need to question ideas imported into the imagery from literature, and to ask where realism ends and symbolism begins.

The women's room

Because so many classical pots illustrate groups of women in interior settings it has been assumed that classical art shows us the 'women's parlour' or gynaikonitis, the secluded interior space in which the women and children of the house spent their time and work such as textile preparation was carried out. Modern opinion has, however, been becoming increasingly sceptical about the existence of the gynaikonitis in recent years. At first, literary evidence was read as indicating the existence of separate quarters for women in the (wealthy) household, and both domestic architecture and the images on pottery were interpreted in the light of this: pots were assumed to show a secluded interior space to which women were confined, with the appearance of the closed door as a motif emphasising the enclosed nature of the room.[17] This interpretation has been losing ground in recent years, with historians arguing that the seclusion of women was not a reality but a 'social norm' to which all appealed, and archaeologists taking up more detailed studies of domestic architecture.[18] It has proved very difficult to find in domestic sites the kind of spatial organisation assumed from literature; in a meticulous study, Nevett rejects the idea of a distinct set of 'women's quarters' in the Greek house for lack of evidence:

> there is no obviously identifiable gynaikon . . . rather than being confined to
> a limited part of the house, artefacts associated with female activity are present

in a variety of spaces including the court and *andron* . . . It therefore seems likely that women were present throughout the house as their activities required.

She proposes instead an opposition between the andron, the public room of the house, to which visitors would regularly be admitted, and the rest of the house, where the female family members would live and work. Her conclusions are based to some extent on the finds of pottery in the domestic context, and her comments are interesting, suggesting that pot finds are rarely clear-cut in relation to rooms: ultimately she concludes that the diversity of finds in a room often suggests storage.[19]

This scepticism towards the existence of a gynaikonitis must undermine any approach to the imagery which assumes prima facie that this is what painters depict, and indeed by looking at what is actually present on the pots we find a more complex picture. Some domestic scenes, especially on lekythoi where decorative space is limited, have no explicit setting at all – the only thing in the frame is the woman. Others (like those of the Providence Painter) have the most minimal indicator of an interior setting – an object such as a mirror or sash hanging in the background, or a chair. In other scenes, architectural elements such as pillars appear, signalling an interior space (e.g. figs. 1.20, 2.25, 4.21),

Figure 4.3 Attic red-figure cup, New York, The Metropolitan Museum of Art 1986.322.1, *c.*480 BC (drawing).

but this is hardly confined to female scenes – pillars can mark the domestic courtyard, temples (fig. 1.28), gymnasia or workshops.[20] Some of the most elaborate interior settings are in fact found on scenes of women's work, like the rooms stuffed with objects where a woman works at a louterion (fig. 4.3, and figs. 2.21–2). There is often an interesting 'port-hole' effect in these cup interiors, giving us a sense of a room equipped with louterion, table or kline, chairs, buckets, jars and crockery. Two elements above all have been interpreted as indicating that a scene is set in a gynaikonitis: the door and the kalathos. The double door, which appears frequently in domestic scenes, is held to denote the separation in space of the figures in the scene; they are within a room, shut off from the rest of the household.[21] Where a door is depicted as shut, this may be the case, but not every door has a function this simple. The door indicates that a scene takes place within a house, but exactly where varies according to the illustration: a double door may represent the outer door of a house (as in many wedding-procession scenes), the door between house and courtyard (as in scenes of domestic work), or an internal door. In wedding scenes there is often a door shown half-open, revealing part of a bed (figs. 2.1, 2.30), and clearly this is a reference to the meaning of marriage, but what is significant is that the door leads to a space further interior to the scene, the bedroom; the women are indoors, but not yet in the private heart of the house. The door when ajar but not showing further space is harder to interpret: on an onos by the Eretria Painter depicting the preparation of wedding

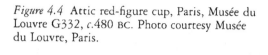

Figure 4.4 Attic red-figure cup, Paris, Musée du Louvre G332, *c.*480 BC. Photo courtesy Musée du Louvre, Paris.

vessels, the women are inside a room with a bed, and the door opens to (presumably) a less private space, though only a wall is visible.[22] In other cases the women appear in an undefined room with a half-open door, which does not suggest enforced seclusion; in some cases women enter or leave through a doorway. In the tondo of a cup in Paris (fig. 4.4), for example, a novel composition shows a woman reaching through a doorway to place a sakkos on a stool, while on a pyxis in London which shows marriage preparations among named nymphs, Iphigeneia stands in the doorway, putting a band around her hair.[23] There is a sense, reflecting Nevett's conclusions, in which the interior in general is 'female space' – men are infrequently depicted alone in a clearly defined indoor space – but there does not seem to be support for a systematic depiction of closed-off 'female quarters'.

The second symbol is the kalathos or wool-basket, which is often described as a kind of 'visual shorthand' for the gynaikonitis.[24] This is ironic, since the kalathos was made of wicker, and hence is never found in the archaeological record; we have only terracotta replicas from graves. The kalathos, from its use in textile production, is certainly very frequently shown with women, often more than one in a scene, and there is a case for interpreting it as a symbol of women's space, indicating a place where work goes on. The pyxis in fig. 2.25 twins the symbols of the child and the kalathos to suggest the virtuous productivity of the women in the scene. But the kalathos does not always signal work; it can serve as an indicator of function as well as space. The phiale in Boston depicting an all-female sacrifice scene (fig. 1.31) demonstrates this: a kalathos filled with wool stands next to the altar, signifying the nature of the rite. Its significance as a symbol is demonstrated by its use on tombstones: fig. 5.4 shows a grave stele topped by a kalathos to indicate the gender of the deceased.[25] The kalathos, then, can serve as a symbol of female work, but not necessarily that the woman is indoors: important though it is, the kalathos is not invariably present in domestic scenes.

It appears, then, that there is no definite symbolism for the gynaikonitis, and the variety of interior scenes should preclude establishing a set of features. Also to be emphasised is that interior scenes frequently include men, as we shall see in the next chapter, and assigning roles to them to explain their presence in the supposed women's quarters ('breadwinner', 'son') is no more than speculation. The depiction of groups of women perhaps reflects not so much an ideology of separation as a concentration on female affairs, such as adornment and marriage, where men are less likely to be present. We find scenes on pots of women all over the house: outside in the courtyard, at the door, in the andron, and the difference is not one of social habits, but one of artistic theme.

The idea of seclusion implicit in the concept of the gynaikonitis raises a related point about depictions in art. Literary sources insist on the secludedness of women, claiming that women themselves would be ashamed to be seen in public, and the impression they give is that to see a citizen woman was something unusual and special – comedy represents women peeking into the street from windows, with men eager to get a glimpse of them, and oratory suggests that men found opportunities to see women only at funerals or festivals.[26] Yet at the same time there emerges a whole genre of Athenian art which opens the interior of the household out for inspection. One might argue that comedy does the same, but the revelation in drama is false exposure, since the women of comedy were in fact male actors. This makes the development in vase-painting of the truly domestic scene with deliberately invoked interior settings rather odd. Scenes inside the women's quarters, according to literary sources, are clearly not expected to be public property, yet although the women in the pictures are properly secluded from the gaze of all but their relatives, at the same time they are on sale in the market. Women on vases are beheld by the male viewer in the very act of seclusion: what should the viewer's response to this be? Moreover, the woman in the pictorial gynaikonitis may be alone, but she is often preparing herself in some way for the male gaze, regarding herself in a mirror as she is regarded by the viewer. Whether the women in the picture are engaged in a sexual act or merely working wool, the intrusion on their privacy is the same. Probably the answer, as before, is that seclusion was an ideal, a norm, rather than a fact.[27] The idea that 'being seen' was a shocking idea for Athenian women is something invoked by orators trying to prove a case; what we see on pots is an idealising depiction of upper-class life, not a scene with which most men would be unfamiliar. Whatever the status of the individual who dedicated the pot, or in whose grave it was buried, the image represents the life they aspire to, just as the concentration on athletic scenes does with men. This is also a reason for the increasing abstraction of female imagery – as the private side of female life is more frequently depicted, the women become less real, as do the settings in which they appear. The woman working at a laver on an archaic cup is hard to see as anything other than an Athenian wife or slave, but the women in the 'gardens' and interiors of the Meidias Painter waver between nymphs, goddesses and ordinary women. This lack of realism also makes it harder to interpret pots as designed to inculcate ideas about desirable female behaviour, as is often argued. They perhaps mirror Athenian beliefs about women more closely in the limited range of activities that they offer in contrast to earlier export images – Athenian women in the classical period do not see themselves as vendors or entertainers or workers, but within the family, in a very circumscribed set of activities. Although the centrality of the female role in religion remains, there is no sign otherwise that women might take pride in roles other than those within the family, or aspire to anything except a life of wealth and leisure.

Status

Given the importance placed on the depiction of wealth, the relative status of the women depicted in domestic scenes has generated much debate. In some scenarios the social relations seem unproblematic – in a scene of preparation for a wedding, for instance, we see a gathering of female relations, sisters, cousins and aunts, for the ritual. In other cases there seems to be a clear division between women of the family and their slaves – in some marriage scenes slave figures attend a bride and her companions: while the bride may hold a lyre, and her companions bring vessels, fillets and torches, slaves carry boxes on their heads, or tie sandals.[28] On most pots, however, status is less clearly marked: fig. 2.3, a pyxis in New York, offers a good illustration of a domestic scene in which, despite their different

Figure 4.5 Attic red-figure pyxis lid, Toronto, Royal Ontario Museum 919.5.31, *c.*420 BC (drawing).

activities, the women are not distinguished by dress, size or menial task. This lack of distinction can give rise to some striking anomalies, and a pyxis lid by the Meidias Painter in Toronto (fig. 4.5) illustrates the problem of status thrown up by such depictions.[29] It carries a scene of a seated woman attended by others offering boxes and various other female accoutrements. They are, according to standard description, a mistress and her maids, and therefore the attendants can be considered slaves. Yet an identical lid in Mainz adds names to the figures, identifying them as Aphrodite and her nymphs. The lack of any obvious distinction between a nymph and a slave appears on the face of it disturbing: slaves can become nymphs or divine personifications with the addition of an inscription, just as a mortal bride can become Helen or Iphigeneia. There is no effort to make a realistic distinction between a slave and an immortal, and to understand this we need to examine attitudes towards slaves, and their depiction.

139

Literature rarely addresses the question of slavery directly, but is very informative in the assumptions that it makes about women and their households. In comedy women are regularly attended by female slaves – in Aristophanes' *Thesmophoriazusai* the kinsman, disguised as a woman, provides himself with an invisible female slave, 'Thratta' – and they also appear as maids-of-all-work.[30] The wife of Lysias' *Against Eratosthenes* had a maid to run her errands, while in his description of Neaira's affairs, Apollodorus refers to her maids as both possessions and status symbols:

ἃ δ᾽ ἐξῆλθεν ἔχουσα Νέαιρα παρὰ Φρυνίωνος χωρὶς ἱματίων καὶ χρυσίων καὶ θεραπαινῶν, ἃ αὐτῇ τῇ ἀνθρώπῳ ἠγοράσθη, ἀποδοῦναι Φρυνίωνι πάντα

[Neaira is to give back to Phrynion everything which she took from his house, except for the clothes, jewellery and maids, which were bought for her personal use.]

([Dem.] 59.46)

In later literature Simaetha has her maid Thestylis, as do the housewives of Theocritus' *Idyll* 15.[31] The idea of the lady's maid and attendant is thus fixed, and the slave is usually marked out by name as a foreigner. The representations on pottery, however, are by no means as well-defined as this. The slave iconography regularly used is far more distinct for male figures than for female, and although there are slave-markers specifically for women, they are not used consistently, leading to the kind of confusion we have seen. One of the most obvious markers is size, with the slave represented as smaller than the other figures. This is sometimes the case, but on white-ground lekythoi depicting two women ('mistress and maid'), there is equally often no distinction of size (fig. 4.22), or else, as on a pyxis by the Eretria Painter in London, a slave deliberately depicted as small may appear in addition to other slave figures which are larger, but indicated in other ways.[32] Posture is a second factor: if one woman sits in a chair while others stand, this may be taken to indicate that the seated woman is the mistress. However, there is no equivalent to the 'banausic' squatting posture associated with male slaves, and where all the figures are seated or standing the distinction is lost.[33] Dress is sometimes used – the long-sleeved tunic indicative of foreignness marks the nurse (fig. 1.3) – but other slave figures dress in the same way as the women with whom they appear. Short hair again is indeterminate as a symbol; mourners can have cropped hair as well as slaves, and some scenes combine the symbols in the form of mourning slaves, as on a loutrophoros in Athens which shows an aged nurse mourning a young woman.[34] Tattoos are the most obvious and indubitable symbol of slave status (or rather metaphor for slavery, since they represent foreignness, and therefore by implication slavery), but tattoos for slaves are a fashion of the Pioneer group of painters in early red-figure, and were never universally adopted.[35] Perhaps the importance of tattooing as a visual sign explains the choice of 'Thratta', 'Thracian', as a generic female slave name (in the same way as 'Xanthias', 'fair-haired' for men). As the iconography develops, female slave characteristics actually become progressively less distinct, and there is less to mark out the woman who brings an aryballos or jewellery chest to another as either a slave or a sister.

If pottery becomes less and less concerned to distinguish slave and free women, is this for artistic reasons or because there was an erosion in the importance of status? On the face of it, a lack of careful distinction between figures seems to run counter to the ideology of leisure: we would expect to see images of the wealthy household, where the mistress can sit at leisure while the slaves work. But perhaps instead viewers were being protected from the reality of slavery. Davies has suggested that we should see solidarity between women and their female slaves, based on the iconography of grave stelai, because as they worked side by side they shared preoccupations in a way that free men and male slaves did not.[36] This cosy friendship is unfortunately not clearly shown in literature – the housewives of Theocritus bully and abuse their slaves, and while some therapainai acted as go-betweens for mistress and lover, there is little sign that the desires of the slaves were ever considered. Aristophanes, in *Thesmophoriazusai*, casts slaves as the women's enemy, spying for their husbands:

ἢ δούλη τινὸς
προαγωγὸς οὖσ' ἐνετρύλισεν τῷ δεσπότῃ,
ἢ πεμπομένη τις ἀγγελίας ψευδεῖς φέρει

[(A curse upon) the slave who acts as go-between in an affair, and then whispers secrets to the master, or who brings back false messages when sent out on an errand.]

(*Thesm.* 340–2)

This is exactly what happened in the Eratosthenes case, when the slave was threatened with torture by her master and revealed the wife's infidelity. Wealthy women who mistreat their slaves are something of a topos in Roman poetry, especially those who injure their hairdressers out of spite, and there is in Greek literature too no real evidence for close relationships between free and slave women, except in the case of nurses.[37] So as the pottery moves away from realistic representation, the images begin to sidestep the reality of slavery, of the dirty ill-fed girls who waited on most women, and to depict instead graceful young women handing fans and jewellery to aristocratic mistresses. The ambiguity of these figures makes it difficult to use pottery as evidence for social life – we may be supposed to see relations, as on marriage and mourning pots, or we may be encouraged to see a rarefied environment of beautiful girls and wealthy women. The logical end of this process is the introduction of Eros in the role of servant, signalling the growing abstraction of the scenes.

The appearance of Eros indicates that in these images it is not important whether the attendant is a divinity, a sister or a slave: the painters were not trying to depict real life but to present an idealised image of domestic life. It is also worth remembering that such idealising would be for the benefit of a slave who might see or handle an object such as a pyxis. I have suggested elsewhere that the painters' own lowly status may have influenced their depiction of slaves: their representation, even when clearly marked, is rarely degrading, and the skyphos in Malibu (fig. 2.4) provides a clear example of a scene in which the mistress is caricatured, and not the slave.[38] A slave handling a pot with a domestic scene would be drawn into the abstract luxury of the depiction – it is aspirational for all kinds of user. One must therefore conclude that although status was as sharply defined as ever, its depiction changed in a move away from realism in domestic scenes; trying to read pots as clear representations of real households is bound to fail.

The body beautiful

The most popular of all female scenes are the countless depictions of women at their toilette, putting on jewellery, looking in mirrors, dressing their hair, or putting on sandals or sashes, waited on by maids, friends or erotes. The development of the motif is revealing of attitudes towards women: in black-figure the theme of female adornment is completely absent, as are private scenes of most kinds. Women dressing appear for the first time in early red-figure, when we find simple depictions such as lekythoi with women putting on or laying down clothes (e.g. fig. 4.6), or the cup by Douris in which a woman stands with a mirror next to a louterion.[39] As the theme becomes more common, especially on the growing number of pots for marriage ritual (loutrophoroi and lebetes gamikoi), the images take on a more regular form, in which a woman, seated or standing, receives objects such as a sash, necklace or chest from an attendant. Over time the imagery becomes more and more stylised, with less intrinsic meaning: the women are no longer individualised, or varying in their activity, and the seated woman waited on by Eros becomes almost an abstract pattern. Ultimately the theme becomes a repeating motif for use on lids and lekanides (fig. 4.7).[40] This development illustrates the narrowing of perspective in pot-painting: it reduces female activity to a completely secluded and self-centred pastime. Obviously in one sense the image of leisure was what women aspired to – not only the lack of the necessity of work but also the possession of jewellery, fine clothes and slaves – but the changing theme reduces women from family members (as in libation and departure scenes) or actors in the polis (religion) to passive self-adornment: rather than demonstrating a greater interest in women, in fact it suggests entirely the opposite.

Figure 4.6 Attic red-figure lekythos, Syracuse 21972, 470–460 BC. Photo courtesy Assessorato ai beni Culturali ed Ambientali e della P.I. della Regione Siciliana – Palermo.

Connected with the growing stylisation of female scenes is the appearance of Eros in otherwise mundane interior scenes. One or more erotes become regular figures, waiting on or fluttering around women, as on the hydria in fig. 4.8 on which an adolescent Eros offers sandals to a seated woman, or the pyxis in fig. 4.9, where an Eros

Figure 4.7 Attic red-figure pyxis lid, London, British Museum E778, *c.*350 BC (drawing).

Figure 4.8 Attic red-figure hydria, New York, The Metropolitan Museum of Art 17.230.15, 440–430 BC (drawing). After Richter/Hall, pl. 140.

pours water into a laver. On another pyxis in New York with a scene of marriage preparations one Eros pours water for the bride to wash, another holds a box, while a third sits in her lap. Not all appearances of Eros are in an explicitly marital context: on the lekythos in New York (fig. 4.2), for instance, Eros merely flies up to a seated woman.[11] What meaning should we attribute to Eros here? In early painting, Eros is the personification of desire, appearing in scenes of pursuit and of homosexual courting. Sometimes he is the pursuer, as a pure form of embodied desire, and sometimes he serves

Figure 4.9 Attic red-figure pyxis, Berlin, Staatliche Museen 3403, *c.*420 BC. Photo: Antikensammlung, Staatliche Museen zu Berlin – Preussischer Kulturbesitz.

as a kind of caption for the desire of others, as on the volute-krater in Oxford which shows the giving of Pandora to Epimetheus: a little Eros flutters between them to symbolise Epimetheus' desire for Pandora.[42] Yet in scenes with women, Eros is neither a mythological figure nor an allegory for an emotional reaction; he is an actor. He is present, naturally enough, in wedding scenes where a comment on the bride's desirability is relevant, crowning the bride or sitting in her lap, but also finds his way onto less obvious scenes such as the celebration of the Adonia, or images of generalised interiors. Here Eros symbolises not active desire, the desire of the women for something, but expresses the women's desirability in a passive sense.

Both the proliferation of toilette scenes in classical vase-painting, and the appearance of Eros, have led many to argue for a dominant emphasis on marriage in the depiction of female life: almost all domestic scenes are interpreted as part of nuptial ritual, illustrating the preparation of the bride for marriage. Sabetai, for instance, has argued that certain gestures, such as binding the hair or putting on a girdle, represent significant moments in marital ritual, and can be read across many different artistic contexts as references to marriage.[43] This view has been echoed in a different context by Reilly, who suggests that the women depicted on white-ground lekythoi, where they are engaged in dressing or gathering of fillets and wreaths, are also to be understood as brides preparing for marriage.[44] The central importance accorded to marriage by such theories is, however, the result of a concentration on imagery at the expense of context. White-ground lekythoi are funerary, and most of their decoration evokes the mourning process quite explicitly, with scenes of visits to the tomb or farewells to the dead. Elements of the scenes depicting two women, such as lekythoi, or the baskets with fillets, are components in mourning scenes too, and hence it is difficult to isolate one type of scene as having no relation to the funerary. Reilly's argument also implies that for the 'nuptial' imagery to be relevant on a funerary pot, large numbers of women must have died before or shortly after marriage, and the sheer numbers of such scenes argue against this. There is an established iconography of marriage preparation, which includes ritual objects such as lebetes gamikoi and the use of loutrophoroi in bathing, as well as acts such as putting on sandals or binding girdles. Most toilette scenes are far less elaborate, and the women depicted are all of an age and status, with no obvious bride figure. The fundamental misunderstanding is probably to assume that a theme must have one dominant meaning: adornment is too generalised a theme to mean only marriage.

A more specialised form of female toilette scene involves women bathing, another theme which comes to prominence in classical art. Scenes of washing, because washing requires nudity, have attracted much debate about the status of the women, and about the viewer's response to nudity. We saw in the previous chapter that nudity for women washing or dressing is frequent on precisely the kind of small pot which predominates after 450 BC, and no one denies that nudity is acceptable for women in classical vase-painting – the consensus is that women shown naked can be considered as citizens and brides. But the most widely credited view suggests that nudity in vase-painting begins as something suitable only for the hetaira, subsequently changing its meaning in later red-figure and becoming respectable: in art before the end of the fifth century women shown bathing should be understood as prostitutes, or the image as a pornographic one, but in the classical period we can recognise representations of brides bathing in preparation for marriage.[45] This theory is hard to fathom: why should a symbol like nudity suddenly alter its meaning for artists and audience alike? Sutton suggests that a shift towards acceptability for female nudity is part of a general development in classical art, parallel to the appearance of the nude goddess in sculpture. The two media clearly are related, since many bathers of classical vase-painting adopt the same crouching posture as the nude Aphrodite of Praxiteles in the 350s. Given the difference in period between them, however, it is not possible to argue for a general change in attitudes towards female nudity; pots seem to change c.420 BC, but the nude goddess does not appear until the middle of the next century.[46] The imagery on pottery requires instead an explanation based on the continuity of the motif, since the theme of women washing themselves goes back to black-figure. Is it correct to suppose that images produced after 450 BC were recognised to be different in nature from those which preceded them, and that audiences reacted in a manner different to their reception of 'pornographic' bathers twenty years before?

Washing, for both men and women, begins as a public act, performed outdoors. Early pots place female bathers in natural settings: a Laconian cup by the Hunt Painter depicts women washing in a river among trees and vines, and a Chalcidian cup with a Dionysiac scene includes three women washing among palm trees, stalked by satyrs (fig. 4.10).[47] The natural settings of these early pieces are echoed in Athenian black-figure, with the well-known amphora by the Priam Painter which depicts female swimmers in a landscape with a diving-block, their clothes and aryballoi hanging in the trees as they swim and bathe, and by the red-figure amphora of female swimmers by the Andokides Painter.[48] Explanations for all these scenes have tended to interpret them as mythological, identifying the women as nymphs, Amazons or participants in Dionysiac cult, and I have shown in a

Figure 4.10 Chalcidian black-figure cup, Würzburg, M. von Wagner Museum 354, *c.*530 BC (drawing). After Pfuhl, fig. 164.

previous article that it does indeed make better sense to consider them in an Etruscan context, rather than as reflecting Greek reality – none of the four pots has a provenance in mainland Greece.[49] With the introduction of the fountain-house as a theme in Attic black-figure, men begin to be shown washing under fountain-spouts, and an amphora in Berlin (fig. 4.11) similarly illustrates four women knee-deep in water at a fountain, washing with their clothes hanging in the background. Other early scenes depict women washing at less elaborate fountains – a pelike by the Nikoxenos Painter in Athens depicts a naked woman with a comb washing at a single fountain-spout, and a hydria in St Petersburg a seated woman washing at a fountain.[50] Interpretation of these scenes varies according to the preoccupations of the commentator: Ginouvès and Yegül, both studying bathing in antiquity, take the scenes as realistic, suggesting that women bathed at fountains at specified times; for others, the idea of female nudity in public means that scenes must be understood either as fantasy, or as a scene of reality in which the women are 'hetairai'. Keuls goes so far as to suggest that the woman on the St Petersburg hydria is masturbating, when in fact her wet hair and clothes suspended behind her indicate that she is simply washing.[51] As noted in the previous chapter, it is not helpful to label a figure as a 'hetaira' if she is alone or with other women; the parallel with images of men washing at fountains, and the frequency with which washing scenes appear on hydriai, suggest that this is a variation on the fountain theme, erotic perhaps, but hardly depicting the women as prostitutes.

Scenes of women washing at fountains are in any case a minority: the bulk of washing scenes are found in mid and late red-figure, when the predominant form of the motif changes, placing bathers in the space of the louterion. Many scenes show athletes washing in the palaistra, signalled by the presence of a louterion (pedestalled basin) and column or herm, and, more surprisingly, women are shown at louteria too, with bathing equipment such as sponges and strigils, as on the hydria by Polygnotos in Munich (fig. 4.12).[52] Washing at a louterion at first retains its public context – a hydria by Euthymides once in Frankfurt depicts two women at a louterion next to a fountain, with a third woman

Figure 4.11 Attic black-figure neck-amphora, Berlin, Staatliche Museen F1843, 500–490 BC (drawing). After Pfuhl, fig. 295.

collecting water from the fountain to use in the basin.[53] But the identification of the space in which bathing takes place is difficult. Many scenes of young men washing at louteria include a herm or column, and have washing gear hanging in the background, leading to an identification of the setting as the palaistra, after exercise. Where women appear in similar scenes, the juxtaposition of women and the space of athletics has seemed confusing, since there is no literary evidence to support the idea that women exercised in Athens. Bérard has advanced the view that such scenes of women washing are a parallel to images of male athletes, and refer to female sporting activity: the exercise itself is not shown, but the pots dwell on the aftermath of exercise, presenting the health and beauty of the young women. The presence of Atalanta as a mythological prototype shows the possibility of female sport.[54] Others have seen the images as fantasy, with a strong sexual element. I wonder, however, whether localising such scenes to the palaistra is correct – the motif may take its inspiration from here, but some scenes have no column to suggest a palaistra setting, and many include bathing accessories such as hairbrushes, stools and attendants. We need to understand a continuity in the depictions, which centres on the role of the louterion. Lissarrague and Durand, investigating the louterion as a symbol, concluded that it has multiple meanings, according to where it appears: it can symbolise the space of ritual, of athletics, of the symposion, or of the erotic.[55] This analysis, however, concentrates on male interests where the louterion appears; if we examine images involving women, we find that there is good reason to see the louterion as a central feature of female life, not a fixture of the palaistra.

We have seen earlier that a frequent theme in the depiction of domestic work is the woman in an interior working at a louterion, washing or cooking. The louterion is a locus

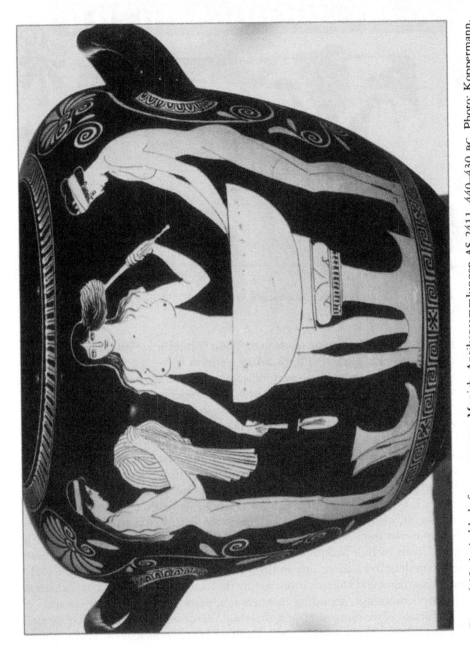

Figure 4.12 Attic black-figure stamnos, Munich, Antikensammlungen AS 2411, 440–430 BC. Photo: Koppermann, courtesy Staatliche Antikensammlungen und Glyptothek, München.

of female work: a whole series of cups shows us women at domestic tasks, often with vessels (oinochoai or buckets) to show where the water is coming from (fig. 4.3 and figs. 2.21–2). The louterion, moreover, is not confined to scenes of work, but is a feature of domestic interiors too: many pyxides with scenes of leisure include a louterion as part of the furniture, and the louterion figures as the place for some departure and conversation scenes too (fig. 5.8).[56] It is, therefore, part of the female domestic environment, and hence there is a strong continuity between working and washing at the louterion. In scenes of wedding preparations we encounter both functions: a lekanis in the Hermitage includes women making ritual cakes at a louterion, while the pyxis in Berlin (fig. 4.9) shows the bride washing at one.[57] We should not therefore assume that women at a louterion are automatically in 'masculine space', or unusually exposed: the louterion is not necessarily an indicator that a scene is outdoors. It is unnecessary to interpret strigils and sponges as 'athletic' in meaning, particularly where women are washing with servants in attendance – they are simply the paraphernalia of washing.

In later art the representation of washing gradually comes to favour indoor bathing scenes, and scenes which are more explicitly ritual, as on the pyxides we have discussed. The motif embraces new poses, where the woman (or man) squats, and water is poured from above in an echo of sculptural styles, and Aphrodite herself appears as a bather attended by erotes. New themes such as hairwashing also appear, although these reflect changes in artistic style, not real developments in bathing practice.[58] This is the central point for Sutton's argument: washing is a motif which runs and develops from black-figure to the end of red-figure, and it is wrong to isolate any particular aspect as representing reality. The reason for an insistence on bathers in the early period as hetairai is because some early red-figure cups show the private act of bathing, with a single naked female (or male) figure (fig. 4.13).[59] These scenes have been categorised as pornographic: Sutton comments that they are 'recognisable as a sort of peephole pornography, aimed at an audience of males and disreputable females'.[60] One should not exaggerate the proportions of this type of scene – the main form of the washing motif is always washing around the louterion, and there are fewer than ten examples of women with basins washing in private. It is true that two examples include phalloi or phallos-birds in the scene, but the others (like the example here) are simply nudes, and bear a close comparison with similar scenes of youths. There is here a fundamental question about the motives of both artist and viewer, which Sutton's argument fails to answer: is it possible to paint a nude which is not eroticised? On those scenes relating unequivocally to marriage, the erotic attraction of the bride (and groom) is being celebrated, and even the nude statues of Aphrodite so celebrated in the fourth century are discussed in explicitly erotic terms.[61] It is impossible to paint such a thing as a 'respectable' nude, since the viewer and his or her response can never be controlled; a naked woman, whether nymph, athlete or bride, can always be eroticised. As we saw in the previous chapter, nudity in art has different meanings in different contexts – it can be signalled as explicitly erotic, but is not so of itself. Thus seeking to characterise early washing scenes as 'pornographic' and later as 'respectable' is pointless; there was never in vase-painting the strict division between seen and unseen women which we encounter in the claims of literature, and both adornment and washing as themes cannot be forced to conform with the idea.

Figure 4.13 Attic red-figure cup, Brussels, Musées Royaux A889, 490–480 BC. Photo: ACL, courtesy Musées Royaux d'Art et d'Histoire, Brussels.

Eating and drinking

If these pots are to reveal something of the private lives of women, we might look for illustrations of women eating and drinking, since the ideology behind the gynaikonitis suggests that while the men of a household regularly dined in company in the appropriate room (andron), the women ate separately within their own apartments. On the face of it, this is an attractive idea for pots; so many images depict sympotic dining that one would naturally expect to find female dining too, and it has been asserted that we do indeed find this difference illustrated, with depictions of women eating alone in the women's quarters. The division is not, however, balanced in the way that one might expect. Only four pots seem to illustrate women eating within the house: a chous in London which shows a woman and boy eating and drinking at a table, and a pyxis, also in London, which has a domestic scene including a woman seated on a stool before a table with a skyphos and bread. Keuls uses these two pots, along with an Apulian example, to suggest that men's and women's dining are depicted as opposite poles – women alone, men in company – and that husband and wife did not share meals in the classical period.[62] The other two images of female dining, however, are a black-figure lekythos and a hydria, both of which carry similar scenes: on the lekythos (fig. 4.14) two women are seated at a table on which are pieces of meat, one holding a knife and the other a skyphos, and a third woman stands

Figure 4.14 Attic black-figure lekythos, once Kusnacht, *c*.480 BC. Photo: D. Widmer, courtesy Dr H.A. Cahn.

between them.[63] Neither of these has as explicit a setting as the previous examples, but the components of the meal (bread, meat and wine) are clearly shown. These images of dining have been associated by Pingiatoglou with a group of similar black-figure pots, all of which carry images of women seated at a table with skyphoi, baskets and meat. On four of the scenes the setting is outside, with trees or vines in the background, while on the fifth columns suggest an indoor setting, though all the participants wear crowns of branches.[64] Pingiatoglou concludes that the scenes represent ritual feasting by women at an all-female festival, and identifies the occasion as the Dionysiac feast of the Thesmophoria, where the consumption of meat was prescribed. She also identifies the Haverford lekythos (fig. 2.9), depicting two women with ladle, psykter and cup, as part of the same ritual theme. There is a strong connection between these pots and those already considered in Chapter 2, which show women seated in orchards or vineyards; women's role as actors in religious rites is one of the most important aspects of their presentation on pottery. In these scenes there is not a contrast, but rather a very close correlation with the images of the symposion: the Thesmophoria pots are about companionship, music and dining in ritual quantities, including meat and wine, and black-figure thus presents ritual eating as part of women's public role. In accordance with its concentration on the private realm, the theme dies out in red-figure, but private eating does not emerge as an important theme instead. This evidently has more to do with the preoccupations of the painters than with gender relations, since scenes of men eating outside the symposion or sacrifice are also very rare.

The two apparently domestic scenes of women eating rather than preparing food show the diners as part of a regular interior scene. Yet I am not convinced that these two examples constitute a clear opposition to masculine dining at the symposion. Keuls presents them as images of women eating alone, without ceremony or enjoyment, suggesting ideas of female deprivation, but I think in fact they reflect more positively on female experience. Ideas of female gluttony and self-indulgence are strong in comedy (with the often-repeated joke about women stealing from the store cupboard), in philosophy (it is striking that Ischomachos' perfect wife is said to have learned σωφροσύνη (self-control) as her main accomplishment) and in poetry (Semonides' negative characterisation of women includes the ass-woman, who eats all day and night rather than contributing to the oikos).[65] The idea underlying these stereotypes is of masculine disapproval of female appetite, and there is good reason to believe that within families women were systematically underfed, required to wait for their share of food until the more important family members had eaten.[66] Women eating in private can therefore be seen as positive images of plenty, just like the festival scenes where women assert control over their right to eat. Both black- and red-figure themes link in a celebration of appetite and plenty, in the same way as male ritual dining; there is no reason in the imagery to adopt the negative view advanced by Keuls. Rather than a vision of female appetite controlled by men, we see once again the power of women in ritual, as their celebration is essential to the well-being of the polis and gives them a high-level of self-determination. The main distinction in the imagery is to be found not between men eating in public and women in private, but between ritual eating (very frequently depicted, in gendered groups) and private (very infrequently shown, either for men or women).

Pastimes

What was women's alternative to work? For many, this question may barely have arisen, but later pot-painters are far more interested in women's leisure than women's work. Many scenes simply set women in an interior with fine clothes and jewellery, and show them engaged in dressing or conversation, but some illustrate particular pastimes and games. The white-ground cup by Hegesiboulos showing a woman playing with a top is well-known, but a hydria by the Washing Painter now in Poznan depicts two women playing morra at the fountain (fig. 4.15), and an onos in Amsterdam shows a group of women, one of whom balances a stick on her finger, while two others play astragaloi (knucklebones) (fig. 4.16).[67] These are part of a suite of games and activities which pot-painters illustrate as the pastimes of women. The boardgame played by Achilles and Ajax, which enters black-figure iconography early on, remains a masculine (and heroic) pursuit, but many other games, both complex and simple, are well illustrated on pottery. Some are solitary amusements, such as juggling with balls, or stick-balancing. Balls are common

Figure 4.15 Attic red-figure hydria, Poznan, National Museum MNP A746, 440–430 BC. Photo courtesy Musée Nationale de Poznan.

as children's toys (as on the black-figure hydria showing a girl playing ball at the fountain), but women juggle surprisingly often on pots, not always with balls but with fruit (apples or quinces), or with balls of wool (as on a white-ground pyxis in London).[68] The game of balancing a stick on one finger is played by a girl on a chous (fig. 1.6), but there are six other examples of women playing this game, including a lekythos in Minneapolis, on which an elaborately dressed woman looks intently at the stick she holds.[69] Other games are more sociable: morra, mentioned above, was something like Paper–Scissors–Stone, played by the Washing Painter's women, and also by two women on an egg-shaped pot (ôon) by the Eretria Painter.[70] Women play with astragaloi on several pyxides and lekythoi, and spinning tops are also fairly common.[71] More surprisingly, physical games are also shown: women play on see-saws, most famously on a column-krater fragment in Boston but also on a hydria by the Dwarf Painter (fig. 4.17) and a cup in New York. There is also one example on a bell-krater of girls playing the piggy-back game known as ephedrismos, although the presence of a satyr removes this from the everyday.[72]

On the topic of games as part of feminine experience, art and literature are at odds; literary sources represent toys as part of childhood, something which was left behind

Figure 4.16 Attic red-figure onos fragment, Amsterdam, Allard Pierson Museum 2021, c.430 BC (drawing).

Figure 4.17 Attic red-figure hydria, Madrid, Museo Arqueologico Nacional 11128, 450–440 BC. Photo courtesy Archivo Fotografico, Museo Arqueologico Nacional, Madrid.

as part of the process of transition to adulthood, through dedication to the gods. The *Anthologia Palatina* is the most often quoted source on the dedication of toys at puberty by girls, symbolising the abandonment of childhood; girls dedicate tops, balls and astragaloi:

Τιμαρέτα πρὸ γάμοιο τὰ τύμπανα, τάν τ' ἐρατεινὰν
σφαῖραν, τόν τε κόμας ῥύτορα κεκρύφαλον,
τάς τε κόρας, Λιμνᾶτι, κόρα κόρα, ὡς ἐπιεικές,
ἄνθετο, καὶ τὰ κορᾶν ἐνδύματ', Ἀρτέμιδι.

[Before her marriage Timareta dedicated her tambourine, her lovely ball, the flowing veil for her hair, and her dolls with their dresses, to Artemis of the Lake, a virgin to a virgin, as is fitting.]

On gravestones too, the iconography of childhood includes games – girls are represented with balls, astragaloi or pet birds.[73] As a consequence, studies of games in antiquity implicitly place all games as childhood activities, although they sometimes illustrate comments on children with images of adults.[74] Yet the game-players on pots are not children, but adult: why should adult women be pictured at children's games? Several explanations have been offered: Keuls suggests that there is a desire by painters to infantilise women, to show them safely cloistered with undemanding and childlike pastimes.[75] This concentrates on images like the Hegesiboulos cup, in which women are shown alone, engaged in simple and non-competitive games. But play, as we have seen, appears social in some scenes, and is not always confined to the house – the see-saw is shown outside on the Boston fragment, with a tree in the background – as are games at the fountain. Alternatively, women's games have been interpreted as a form of love oracle: Sabetai has examined the hydriai of the Washing Painter, which include several scenes of game-playing along with dance and washing, and concludes that the games depicted (swinging, morra and astragaloi) have an erotic meaning and can be seen as love oracles, played to find out when or whom a women would marry.[76] She extends this to ball-playing as well, associating the motif of juggling apples with the wedding. This idea is supported by the presence of erotes in some of these scenes: on the Washing Painter's hydria Eros flies to crown the winner, while he stands at the centre of the see-saw on the Madrid hydria, and erotes play morra among themselves on an Apulian krater in Munich. On the unusual ôon by the Eretria Painter depicting two women playing morra, Oakley interprets the two playing figures as Aphrodite and the bride's mother, watched by the bride and groom, in a dramatisation of the competition between old and new families for the bride's affection.[77]

Other games, however, do not seem so open to this interpretation. Balancing sticks or juggling with balls of wool are difficult to see as suffused with an erotic meaning, and morra, too, sets up different associations. It is interactive, a game of both chance and skill, and is played not only by women but also by others such as satyrs.[78] The morra-players on the Poznan hydria have nothing erotic about them: they sit on hydriai, and seem old to be guessing when they will marry. Swinging has a place in Athenian ritual, and cannot be considered a pure game as the others. The argument is also complicated by the fact that all the Washing Painter's small hydriai were exported (with provenances from Nola, Cumae and Camarina), and so one must assume an international meaning for these games. To assume that all games are love oracles means, additionally, that all game-players must be interpreted as unmarried, which seems unwarranted on some pyxides. Perhaps the most serious objection to this view is that an iconography of erotic magic already existed for painters: the iunx or magic wheel, used as a charm to draw a lover, appears in scenes of both marriage preparations and Aphrodite's garden. On the hydria depicting Aphrodite and Adonis (fig. 5.22) an iunx appears in the hands of Eros, while on a pyxis by the Eretria Painter the nymph Pontomedeia plays with one in a scene of bridal ritual.[79] If the intention of a painter was to show a love charm, or a casting of the future, it was not necessary to do this through a game.[80]

The theme of play also lends itself to a funerary interpretation. We are familiar with the scenes of children at play found on choes – children were accompanied to the grave by images of games with toys or pets. A similar interpretation for women at play has been advanced by Hoffmann, who devotes a chapter of his work on Sotades to a consideration of the role of play themes on pots, starting from the image of satyrs playing morra on the skyphos in Basle.[81] He has no difficulty in demonstrating depictions of morra to be funerary in purpose, citing the ôon, the Poznan pot and a funerary relief in Berlin, and he draws an extended comparison between the heroic board game of Ajax and Achilles in black-figure and the 'child's play' of morra, suggesting that it symbolises the individual surrendering to fate by abandoning him or herself to chance. The argument about morra is unnecessarily complex, since the game is a more frequent theme in Apulian and Lucanian vase-painting than Attic, and here the funerary meaning of the imagery is not in doubt.[82] But just as the claim that all games are love oracles is hard to substantiate, so is the claim that all games have a funerary meaning. Some of the examples of female play cited here plainly are funerary, such as the white-ground cup with the top player, which was found in a tomb in Athens, and the white-ground lekythoi which carry scenes of ball games. And game-playing as a theme appears rather later in terracottas: in the Hellenistic period a group of astragal-playing women becomes popular, and there are also terracottas of women playing ephedrismos. Higgins suggests that the themes were chosen largely for the interest of the poses, but most examples are from graves.[83] But while morra may be explicable in this way, balancing sticks or juggling balls has a far less obvious meaning; even if game-playing is an appropriate funerary theme, not all games need have a mystical meaning attached to them.

Figure 4.18 Attic red-figure chous, Erlangen, Universität Erlangen-Nürnberg 1321, *c.* 420 BC. Photo courtesy Institut für Klassische Archäologie und Antikensammlung, Universität Erlangen-Nürnberg.

It seems better to consider the games as a group, although the initial question, of course, is whether these images do actually form a group, or whether we are simply imposing a category on a disparate body of scenes and seeking an explanation to cover all cases. There are some differences between the games represented: some are individual pastimes, such as the top, or ball-juggling, while others are played in pairs (morra, astragaloi), groups (ball-games) or by individuals within a group (sticks). What is certain, however, is that the painters were not trying to exhibit 'real life', in the sense of parents playing with their children – women play games among themselves or alone. Female children may play with boys on choes and some black-figure pots, but only on choes, whose focus is on the child's preoccupations, do mothers and babies play – as on a chous in Erlangen on which a woman holds up her baby so that he can reach a bunch of grapes (fig. 4.18). Women's pastimes, however, are for women only. Nor is there a complete identity between women's and children's games – women, for instance, do not play with the toy carts so common on choes, nor with hoops, and other games are said to be the province of women only: Pollux 9.126 refers to πεντάλιθα, fivestones or jacks, which was played with astragaloi as a women's pastime, and the see-saw is played only by women on pots, never by children. Furthermore, although Frontisi-Ducroux interprets game-playing on pots as 'other' – the province of women, children and satyrs – in literature it is fathers who play with their children. In Aristophanes' *Clouds* we see the indulgent father remembering how his son played with carts and toy frogs made of pomegranate peel, and, according to Plutarch, the Spartan king Agesilaus is said to have played at hobby-horses with his children.[84]

Games for women, on the other hand, are not located in real life; it is interesting that Paidia (Play) takes her place among the personifications on classical pots, along with more recognisably feminine virtues such as Eukleia and Eunomia, and that playfulness personified is female rather than male.[85] In the one example where her characterisation reflects her name, Paidia is represented on a pyxis in New York as a youthful and wild-haired figure playing by herself.[86] She balances a stick on her finger, and is demonstrably younger than her peers. Women's games are thus related to feminine virtues: although literature does tend to emphasise correct roles, representing women who occupy themselves with domestic activities, we might see on the pots a sense of what women do when they are alone, translated into harmless play rather than anything threatening. This may account for the lack of women playing board games which carry an implication of literacy. Leisure is not part of the normal stereotype of the good wife – the good wife works, for women's work is never completed, therefore if one wants to express an ideal of female leisure one must appeal either to educated pastimes (music or reading), or to the evocation of carefree childhood, before the imposition of economic necessity for labour. One can note as well the pyxis depicting the astragal-player, on which one of the players has curly hair in a ponytail and seems freer and more active than the others; women viewers might read play as a liberating experience. Games, therefore, were not outside female experience, and can suggest a more carefree existence in the afterlife. The idea that a woman's work will finally be over after death is not confined to classical times.[87]

These kinds of game suggest some unexpected things about female life, and there is also a group of images which refer to more intellectual pastimes, music and poetry. Music is a theme prominent on pottery from its beginnings; as well as music at the symposium, painters show competitors in musical competitions, and music as a part of education. Women and music, however, becomes more common as a motif in classical painting with the increase in private scenes: many scenes set in interiors include women playing instruments, primarily the lyre, for each other's entertainment, as in the Washing Painter's wedding scenes where the bride often holds a harp.[88] Other images show more organised musical sessions, with larger numbers of instruments including the aulos and cithara: on a hydria in London, for instance (fig. 4.19), a group of women play lyres as others stand holding an aulos case and scrolls.[89] Considerable debate has (predictably) centred on whether playing music was 'respectable', given the appearance of female musicians with auloi and lyres (as we have seen) in sympotic contexts. Many of the classical scenes, however, identify musicians as Muses, either by name or generically: some scenes are clearly mythological, depicting Apollo or Mousaios with the Muses, but others are of the same type as 'women in an interior', and the distinction between myth and reality can be hard to perceive. Webster suggested that all women playing in 'concerts of mixed instruments' should be considered to be Muses, to avoid the connotations of entertainment, but there is no reason to assume that musical skill was considered unsuitable.[90] Just as with the status of attendants, the fact that ordinary women can become 'Muses' with the addition of an inscription demonstrates that painters were not concerned with the accurate depiction of life. The real departure in the representation of music by classical painters is the emphasis on the private – women play music for their own entertainment, not as professional musicians, and the skill has become an aspirational 'accomplishment'.

The presence of scrolls being handled and read by women (figs. 4.19, 4.20) has engendered a different debate – about literacy. This set of images (about twenty-five pots in total) has been seen as important evidence for the reality of women's lives, suggesting that the ability both to play instruments and to read was normal for elite women.[91] The existence of the scenes is the more striking because Greek literature does not support the idea that female literacy was common; fifth-century literature does not provide any secure example of a literate woman, nor is there any evidence for the teaching of reading and writing to girls. Our only evidence comes from pottery, and there is obviously a danger that the apparent testimony of the imagery will be co-opted too readily to support the idea of female literacy. The question is whether the pots can be taken as representing a milieu ordinary enough to constitute real evidence. Whatever the reservations commonly expressed about the value of art as evidence, most commentators nevertheless adopt a reading which takes the presence of furniture and children as signalling a realistic milieu, and therefore allows the claim that female literacy was normal among the elite.[92] A

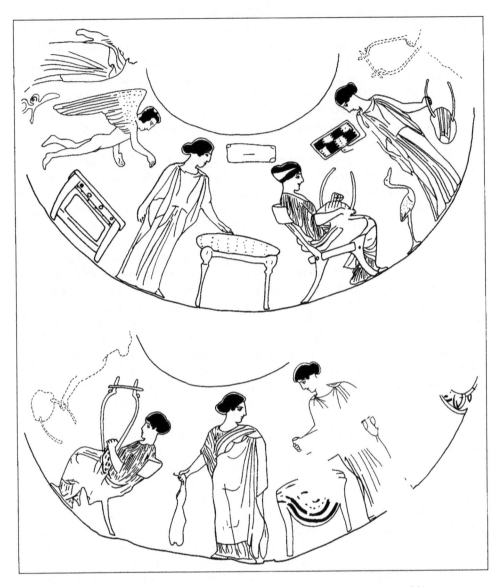

Figure 4.19 Attic red-figure hydria, London, British Museum 1921.7–10.2, *c.*440 BC
(drawing).

relevant feature, however, is the date of the images: school scenes appear in the early red-
figure period, with boys shown reciting poetry and learning from scrolls; at this period
female reading of any kind is absent. It is only in classical red-figure, from 475 BC onwards,
that images of female literacy begin to appear, at the same time as representations of the
Muses.[93] Given the nature of the literary evidence, it is not possible to argue for a real
change in the level of female literacy at this time, and the reason for the change must lie
in the nature of the iconographic theme. The frequency with which scrolls appear in
conjunction with musical instruments makes it likely that the painters' aim was to

Figure 4.20 Attic red-figure lekythos, Paris, Musée du Louvre CA 2220, 440–430 BC (drawing).

illustrate music and recitation rather than education and literacy.[94] Although it is tempting to use an example like the cup in Amsterdam with an image of a woman holding a scroll as a boy recites to show that mothers taught their sons, I do not think that the evidence of pots can be used so easily.[95] The point made above about status is important: if a female figure can be transformed into a Muse or poet by the addition of an inscription, seeking a clear distinction between myth and reality may be pointless. Literacy thus seems to function in a way removed from the everyday, as another perceived attribute of the wealthy, who have time and money for artistic pursuits. Poetry and music of this kind are a far cry from the lyre and aulos players of early red-figure: later scenes reduce women's significance, removing them from their roles in public life and ritual into a closed world of personal entertainment.

Domestic animals

A similar question about the 'realism' of domestic scenes with women surrounds the depiction of animals. When an image is of the 'garden of Aphrodite', with nymphs or women in an idealised landscape, it is not surprising that animals such as hares, birds or deer should be present, either as pets or as fauna. But animals accompany women very frequently in interior scenes too: a pyxis in Winchester (fig. 4.21), for instance, depicts women in a room, one running towards an altar, and the scene includes both a large bird perched on top of a kalathos and a hare (rather oversized) scampering along the floor.[96] It is usual to identify the animals in domestic scenes as pets, and there is no doubt that pets existed in classical Athens: the main sources for depictions of children's pets are choes and grave reliefs, and the animals kept included both Maltese dogs and hunting dogs (for young men), hares, tortoises, mice and (particularly) birds. These include quail and cocks, swans and geese, ducks and sparrow-like songbirds. On funerary monuments, young children in particular very often hold birds, either dove-like creatures which are held in the hand, or bigger birds such as ducks which are held and caressed in both hands, and similarly mothers are often shown holding out a bird to their child; pet birds were sometimes buried with their owners.[97] Our literary sources indicate that birds were often kept as pets by adults: quails and partridges, for instance, were kept as decoys, or for sport, and cocks for fighting; others mentioned are crows and parrots kept for their mimicry, or exotics such as peacocks. However, the pets in literature almost always belong to men, such as Alcibiades' quail, Demo's peafowl, or Lachydas the philosopher and his

Figure 4.21 Attic red-figure pyxis, Winchester College 29, *c*.450 BC. Photos: R. Shorter, courtesy Winchester College.

devoted goose; Lesbia's sparrow seems to be a Roman phenomenon.[98] The pet par excellence in Athens was the small white Maltese dog (fig. 4.18) (as opposed to the hunting dog), and these appear on pottery with all kinds of individuals: as well as children, men and women walk with and interact with them, as on the lekythos where a woman feeds a begging dog (fig. 2.13). Yet Maltese dogs are not regularly found in the domestic setting; there is no clear mapping between the pets of childhood and those of women.

The animals shown with women are slightly different. Birds are by far the most common, including not only songbirds and quails but swans, geese and stilt birds (cranes and herons). Examples can be seen on many of our illustrations: a swan among the women on the pyxis lid in fig. 4.5, the quail on the lekythos in fig. 4.2, and the white egret with two women on a white-ground lekythos in Athens (fig. 4.22).[99] Should we interpret these birds as simply domestic pets, tame creatures which actually inhabited the women's quarters? While caged birds are occasionally shown, or empty cages, most birds are free within the house, and indeed often take up strange positions seated on women's laps, or perched on kalathoi. On a pyxis in Athens a woman holds a swan seated on her hand at arm's length.[100] The idea of large water-birds, such as swans or cranes, loose inside the house seems unlikely. Nor are women's birds always presented realistically – some are extremely large (the quail in fig. 4.2, for instance, is huge, knee-high to the seated woman). Birds appear mostly in domestic scenes, and in some of courtship too, but not in scenes of work, which may suggest that we are in symbolic rather than realistic territory. With the appearance of hares, which were common as courting gifts between men, we must begin to wonder whether the animals are to be interpreted symbolically. Hares too were kept as pets – a white-ground lekythos in Athens, for instance, shows a young woman standing at the grave holding a hare as a female relation mourns.[101] But the hare is also the typical gift of courtship offered by the lover to the beloved, and Schnapp has demonstrated a development in the motif from a gift of a dead hare as the offering of a hunter, to the gift of a live hare as a pet.[102] The hare appears in male–female courtship as well as male–male, offered by the man to the woman. It is possible that the hare in the women's interior is the end-point of this process, and that it is as much a symbol of erotic attraction as a pet. If the same is true of birds, what, then, should we make of the phiale depicting a dance lesson (fig. 1.17) on which a small bird perches on the floor, or the hydria in the British Museum on which women playing music are accompanied by a crane at the centre of the scene (fig. 4.19), or the pyxis in Manchester on which a woman sits with a large bird perched on her lap (fig. 5.2)?[103]

There are several obvious ways in which birds may be symbolic in depictions of the domestic interior. First, just as the cock features as an icon of courtship in relations between men, so the domestic birds may be symbolic of the temper and preoccupations of women. Indeed, the reasons for keeping most birds – display and music – are the very female qualities celebrated in these scenes by painters. Second, and more important, birds had strong connections with the divine in Greek thought. Geese, for instance, were sacred to Aphrodite, as were doves, and a white-ground cup from Rhodes portrays Aphrodite riding a bird which is clearly a goose.[104] Perhaps for this reason the goose becomes a symbol of domestic harmony, as on the white-ground lekythos by the Achilles Painter (fig. 4.23), on which a wife bids farewell to her departing husband while a goose pecks at the ground between them. A loutrophoros in Boston with a scene of a wedding procession includes a goose standing on the ground, and this in turn may offer a further perspective on the cup by Douris depicting a woman feeding geese (fig. 2.27).[105] Swans were sacred to Apollo,

Figure 4.22 Attic white-ground lekythos, Athens, National Museum 1963, *c.*440 BC. Photo courtesy National Archaeological Museum, Athens.

Figure 4.23 Attic white-ground lekythos, London, British Museum D51, 440–435 BC. Photo courtesy British Museum. © The British Museum.

and also to Artemis, and a white-ground lekythos by the Pan Painter in St Petersburg shows Artemis with a swan.[106] This would account for the common motif of the swan on lekanis lids, along with women's heads, since the swan as a real pet is unlikely. The quail had a reputation in Greek bird lore as lecherous, but was also sacred to Artemis, who was supposedly born on the island of Ortygia (Quail Island) near Delos, and in some places had the cult title of Ὀρτυγία.[107]

Other aspects of bird lore may be relevant too: Aristotle makes several observations on the habits of different species: the dove mates for life, and will never seek another partner if the first dies; storks and cranes are devoted parents; while according to Aelian (admittedly late), the purple gallinule is so chaste that it will hang itself if the mistress of the house is unfaithful.[108] Whether these meanings can be extended to individual birds in particular scenes is another question. Some have tried to bring together all birds as erotic symbols, functioning as an indication of a past or future marriage, but in Attic painting the scenes are just too various to accept a single symbolic explanation.[109] In certain cases an erotic element is suggested by a bird: for example, it is common among classical pot-painters to depict nymphs or women with a small bird held on the finger, as in fig. 5.22, a hydria in Florence. One can interpret the bird as an iunx or wryneck, the magical bird used in love spells, similar in purpose to the iunx wheel that an Eros whirls above Adonis' head in the same scene.[110] The identification of an iunx opens a set of interpretative possibilities, for instance on a pointed amphoriskos by the Heimarmone Painter, depicting Helen and Paris, two women stand looking at a small bird which one holds on her finger. On the left of the scene stand Nemesis and Tyche; to the right with the bird are Heimarmone (Destiny) and an unnamed figure whom Shapiro takes to be Themis.[111] If the bird in this scene is read as an iunx, it would accord well with the image of igniting desire on the pot, as Himeros locks gaze with Paris and Peitho attends Helen.

But not all birds have such a clear-cut meaning, and the most problematic bird to interpret is the heron. A wide variety of stilt-birds are depicted in scenes with women, with varying degrees of clarity. Some are obvious herons, such as that on a cup by the Codrus Painter, on which the markings are well shown, and on a series of white-ground alabastra (fig. 4.24). On the white-ground lekythos by the Achilles Painter (fig. 4.22), the

Figure 4.24 Attic white-ground alabastron, Palermo, Mormino Collection 796, 460–450 BC. Photo courtesy Fondazione Banco di Sicilia.

white long-legged bird which accompanies two women to be an egret.[112] Others are less easy to categorise: Böhr identifies the bird on a hydria in Houston with crest and feathers as a demoiselle crane, a tameable bird, while most other commentators use the generic term 'heron'. While one might wonder about the practicality of a pet swan, the idea of a pet heron is even more problematic – herons are large, aquatic and difficult to tame, and no mention of pet herons appears in literature.[113] The one illustration which does seem to bear out the idea is a hydria in Harvard, on which three women feed two very lively herons. Herons also appear in scenes like fig. 2.2, where they interact with female figures.[114] But most herons on pots are passive, and they are not shown caged; neither, with one exception, are they shown tied up. Furthermore, although pets are very common on choes as companions of children, we find in this context birds of fowl and sparrow types, but not herons or cranes. On the other hand, if one is to claim a symbolic meaning for birds, including herons, on pots it is troublesome that the heron does not carry an obvious mythological or sacred meaning.[115] We should instead consider in more detail the ways in which herons are depicted.

If the heron can be characterised in the Greek mind as a devoted parent, a chaste creature, or a home-loving bird like the stork, this would offer a symbolism appropriate to the domestic scenes. This suggests an explanation for the heron which accompanies the women on the Houston hydria (fig. 2.2), and the musicians on the hydria in fig. 4.19. Similarly we find on a lekanis lid in Naples Aphrodite and her retinue (Harmonia, Eukleia, Eunomia, Pannychis and Klymene) appearing with kalathoi and jewel chests, plus a heron. The domestic symbolism would echo that of the goose, which replaces the heron on an otherwise very similar lid in Mainz.[116] The appearance of a stilt-bird in the scene of preparations for a visit to the tomb (fig. 4.22) can also be read as a reference to the domestic. Reading the symbolism of stilt-birds in this way finds difficulties only with a pelike by the Chicago Painter in Lecce (fig. 4.25), where a scene of Polynikes bribing Eriphyle includes a very delicate (almost flamingo-like) bird.[117] In a scene of domestic treachery the heron cannot represent domestic devotion, unless it is the devotion which is at the very moment of being undone, as Polynikes offers the necklace of Harmonia and Eriphyle stretches a hand to receive it.

Figure 4.25 Attic red-figure pelike, Lecce 570, *c.*460 BC. Photo courtesy Museo Provinciale 'Sigismundo Castromediano', Lecce.

The appearance of herons with young women on grave stelai develops this symbolism: there are only five depictions of herons on extant Attic gravestones, but they constitute an interesting group. On all five the bird appears with a female figure: two children, two maidens and a young woman.[118] The association of the heron with the female is clear. The stele of Philoumene illustrates the regular pattern (fig. 4.26): Philoumene holds a small bird in one hand, lowered towards the heron, which looks upwards. This mirrors the more usual pose of a child with a dog, where the child, male or female, holds out the small bird to a dog, which jumps to catch it. On the other four stelai, however, the iconography is different: each female figure holds a 'doll'; that is, a votive in the form of a female torso or body.[119] One figure holds the votive out to the heron; the others hold it up in two hands, and the heron stands in front of them. There is a distinct pattern to the iconography: votives are not held out to dogs, but do appear with herons. If the votives are intended to indicate successful achievement of menarche, the birds are perhaps relevant to a theme of female sexuality.

An alternative explanation for the meaning of the heron is that, with its long neck, it is phallic. The phallic aspect of other long-necked birds is often explicit in Greek myth and art: myths of rape include those of both Leda and Nemesis by Zeus in the form of a swan, and certainly the phallic aspect of both geese and swans is exploited by painters too – there are images of both youths and women riding swans with huge necks pointing straight up. The general phallic implication may partly account for the perception of ducks, geese and even wrynecks as peculiarly feminine in their appeal; one can think of Penelope in the *Odyssey* with her pet geese, which play a sexually symbolic role in the poem.[120] This would offer an alternative explanation for the Chicago Painter's pelike discussed above, and the occasional appearance of a heron or crane in erotic scenes, as on a cup once sold in Lucerne.[121] On the other hand, the discussion of the phallos-bird in the previous chapter demonstrated that phallos-birds rarely take the form of geese or swans; they are usually small bird types, and only one heron-like phallos-bird is documented. While the idea of a phallic connection is obviously present at some level, painters do not often choose to make it explicit.

The bird as companion to women thus seems to be one symbol which is truly polysemic, invoking simultaneously the domestic, the divine and the erotic. One cannot say with confidence that women never had pets, and certainly some birds can be understood as such, but pets by and large are represented as a preoccupation of childhood, and the variety of birds shown in interiors, including swans and herons, make unconvincing pets. Assigning a single meaning either to individual birds, or to animals

Figure 4.26 Attic funerary stele, Athens, National Museum Karapanos Coll. 1023, 400–375 BC (drawing).

in general, is also unsatisfactory: in some cases there is a clear symbolism, as with the quails attending Herakles' marriage, but generally there is no obvious symbolism, and the birds and animals which we find on pots are being used to express the ideology of sexual and domestic (and divine) roles.

Woman as decoration

By the end of the red-figure period, the women appearing on pyxis and lekanis lids have become a pure decorative motif, repetitive and stylised (fig. 4.27). All attempts to individualise figures have vanished, and a few iconographic types are continually reproduced. This process is represented as part of the decay of vase-painting as art, since it is such a contrast with the earlier period when every image was different. Unsurprisingly this period of vase-painting has attracted much less attention from historians, because the images are far less relevant to their concerns – the lack of variety and simple motifs do not seem to offer much evidence for fourth-century life.[122] But repetitive though the motifs may become, there are some interesting attitudes towards women implicit in the styles of decoration, especially in the growth in use of the female head as an isolated decoration. Between 450 and 375 BC, several hundred lekythoi and squat lekythoi are decorated with heads, male and female, as are askoi and lids of pyxides and lekanides.[123] It may seem unnecessary to devote space to a consideration of the choice of female heads as a decorative motif – after all, we are so used to the sight of woman as spectacle and women's faces as a suitable form of decoration that it is hard not to assume that the meaning in a Greek context was the same. But the question needs asking: why women? In classical Greece the female face was not the commodity that it is in the West today, and we cannot read heads as an uncomplicated celebration of female beauty, since that theme was surrounded by issues of visibility and privacy. It requires a rather more detailed analysis of the meaning of the motif, and the reason for its proliferation.

Although it is rarely emphasised as a theme in Attic art, the human head is a very significant motif across a range of fabrics, and different periods, from seventh-century Corinth to fourth-century Italy. The female head in particular plays a large part in the decoration of non-Athenian fabrics, in early Corinthian painting, fifth-century Boiotian, and fourth-century Apulian and Sicilian. In Corinth, both male and female outline heads

Figure 4.27 Attic red-figure lekanis lid, Reading, Ure Museum 45.10.4, *c*.350 BC. Photo courtesy Ure Museum of Greek Archaeology, University of Reading.

appear frequently on aryballoi, or the handle-plates of column-kraters. Many are given names, as on the cup with Nebris and Glyka (fig. 3.14). A seventh-century aryballos in London has a female head with an inscription, Αἰνέτα Ἐμί (I am Aineta), and a column-krater in Amsterdam a female head named Erata.[124] Some busts are added to pots in relief, as on a pyxis in San Simeon, or another in New York, on which the handles each carry a female head in relief, named as Ἰόπα, Ἱμερώι and Χαρίτα (Iopa, Himeroi and Charita).[125] In red-figure, fabrics like Boiotian turn to the head as a major decorative theme; a whole series of bell-kraters carry a female head as decoration on one side (fig. 4.28), as well as plates and lids.[126] There are suggestions that Boiotian pots exported to Spina may have influenced the Italian artists who took up the theme: certainly it is in Italian painting that the theme reaches its greatest importance. Enormous numbers of small lekythoi decorated with female heads, as well as kraters and pelikai, have been found in graves in Campania

Figure 4.28 Boiotian red-figure bell-krater, Reading, Ure Museum 35.iv.5, *c.*470 BC. Photo courtesy Ure Museum of Greek Archaeology, University of Reading.

and Apulia (fig. 4.29).[127] Other types of head feature occasionally, such as youths, satyrs and orientals, but hundreds repeat the female bust.

In contrast, the use of the head as a motif in Athenian art is often overlooked, probably because it is rarely presented as a coherent theme; there has been no overview, and instead different types of head motif have been considered separately. Yet heads play a significant role in Athenian painting too: although they are not common early on they become a feature of black-figure, with a distinct series of 'head cups' (lip and band-cups decorated with a single outline head) produced by black-figure cup painters. Many are unidentified female heads, but others include heads of Athena and other deities.[128] Later the head becomes the primary mode of decoration for certain shapes, notably among painters of cylindrical lekythoi, who decorate pots with heads of deities, particularly Athena and her owl, a common motif on coins.[129] In the fourth century, the theme finds its way onto

Figure 4.29 Sicilian bell-krater, Reinbach, Koch Collection, *c*.340 BC (drawing).

squat lekythoi and askoi as well as the lids of pyxides and lekanides: more than two hundred squat lekythoi, for instance, carry heads of different types, as well as lekythoi and askoi.

Can we find an overall meaning for the theme, given its scale and persistence? Explanations have tended to be ad hoc for each period and fabric: the named heads in Corinthian painting, for instance, are said (once more) to be portraits of hetairai because they are named. The head of Aineta on the aryballos in London, for instance, which has nine masculine names underneath the picture, is supposed to be a portrait of the prostitute for whom it was made. Similarly, it has been suggested that the figures on the pyxis in New York with relief heads are also to be understood as hetairai, but the names are equally applicable for nymphs or Nereids.[130] Other fabrics, however, present mainly the heads of identifiable deities; many are labelled with a distinctive attribute – pilos and caduceus for Hermes, bow for Artemis, crescent moon for Selene – or even by name, as on an Apulian volute-krater which depicts Aura, the breeze. A rare Athenian cup which has a female bust in the tondo has been identified by Beazley as an image of Selene.[131] But most common in all fabrics are images of women without any identifying attribute; how should we understand these? We can compare a variant in Attic art, in the theme of the anodos of a goddess: among red-figure pots (partly influenced by drama) scenes of the birth of Aphrodite, Pandora and other deities develop a type in which a giant female head appears from the earth. Similar scenes show Persephone returning from Hades.[132] If a head alone can be recognisable as a goddess, this offers support for the argument which identifies all busts, including those without obvious characteristics, as images of deities, often those of death and the underworld such as Persephone. A comparison with terracottas goes some way to uphold the idea: the female head or bust forms a significant proportion of the production of terracottas, used either as dedications or in tombs. An interesting study by Croissant has drawn attention to the stylistic similarities between terracottas and vase-painting; clearly there are regional similarities, and the two forms of art may be closer in relationship than we think.[133] The emphasis on the head as a form of decoration is thus not a reference to female beauty (and the many poorly drawn examples would make a mockery of the idea!) but to the role of the female in religion, especially the rites of death.

In this connection it is salutary to compare the modern interpretations of plastic head vases, a group of Attic pots modelled in the form of human heads.[134] These have garnered much scholarly interest in recent years, in sharp contrast to fourth-century lekanis lids. Probably this is because their intrinsic interest is much greater – they are very well made, and represent a number of interesting types, such as satyrs, gods and negroes as well as women. But it is also because the interpretations of these pots have accorded very easily with perceived Athenian attitudes towards women. Head-kantharoi and oinochoai are invariably seen as located at the symposium, and therefore are expected to reflect stereotyped male–female power relations. For instance, Reeder includes in her study of women through art two head-oinochoai in the form of women, both from *c*.500 BC, and follows modern interpretation by suggesting that they are degrading to women – the woman as servant objectified, becoming the pot itself.[135] She suggests that the oinochoai would be the subject of 'ribald remarks' at the symposion, and that the women must be understood to represent hetairai. The conviction that oinochoai always belong to the symposion overrides the fact that her examples were found in the same tomb in Vulci. The conviction that women are degraded through a portrayal in pottery also underlies Lissarrague's more sophisticated treatment of head vases, which nevertheless still places them within the symposion, as depictions of marginal figures (blacks, women and satyrs) in opposition to the white citizen symposiast.[136] Both these analyses, however, begin with an assumption that the figures depicted are low status, but this fails to account for the numbers of pots which take the form of gods, notably Dionysus and Herakles, as well as the fact that the findspots of these objects are once again Etruscan graves, not Athenian houses. Lissarrague rejects the foreign provenances of head vases as largely irrelevant, but two examples, a century apart, indicate a clear funerary theme: one is an Attic head vase found in a tomb at Spina, representing the Greek death-demon Charos, and the other a similar Etruscan kantharos which takes the form of Charun, the Etruscan god of the Underworld.[137] The fifth-century head has been dismissed as a singular 'grotesque', but the creation of explicitly funerary head-kantharoi must reflect on the meaning of similar pots placed in the same tombs. The reappraisal of other figures in a funerary context is not difficult – Dionysus with his satyrs and Herakles on the one hand are as suited to the afterlife as to the banquet, while it is now suggested that the women be identified as Aphrodite.[138] What is significant, however, is the way that the argument has been deformed by expectations about female status, and the centrality of the symposion to Athenian ideas, neglecting comparisons to other thematic patterns in Attic vase-painting. If we consider the head motif as a whole in Athenian art, and indeed across other fabrics, we see not the decline of painters' inventiveness, nor a 'degradation' of women, but a further presentation of the importance of the female principle in religion as protector of the living and (especially) the dead.

Conclusion

This chapter has presented a series of paradoxes: in classical Athenian vase-painting we find that the range of themes involving women narrows, at the same time as the treatments of individual themes become more complex; that there is a growth in popularity of female scenes as they become less realistic and informative; and that painters produced a set of images which are independent of (and very different from) the view of Athenian life we find represented in literature and on funerary monuments. Although literature presents us with the idea that marriage, household and motherhood were central to female life, pottery at this period in contrast privileges only the short space of time before marriage, and an indeterminate time immediately after – images of women with babies and children die out, as do scenes of women at work in their houses. Even representations of festivals lose their public character and come down to a domestic level with the rise in popularity of scenes of the Adonia, a private female celebration. The change in imagery is in large part a consequence of changes in the market: most of the themes of women's activity, in work, entertainment or sex, were part of the demand of Etruscan customers, and once these themes were no longer required the rather limited view of women in Athenian popular art comes to dominate the imagery. The pots therefore have less to say about the reality of female life and much more about the aspirations of both women and men, and the abstract virtues which they valued. Our difficulty in reading the images arises precisely because what happens on pots is more interesting than a simple mirroring of literary concerns. The representations of female space and female activities are complex and differ markedly from other art forms of the period, and it is these differences which will constitute the topic of our final chapter.

5

WOMEN AND MEN

So far we have considered depictions of women's lives, and the ways in which they are reflected on pots, largely in isolation, looking at women among women. We have touched on representations of women with men to a limited extent, men as sexual partners, husbands or slaves, but have by and large preserved a distinction between male and female spheres. This division is one to which the Greeks adhered too, yet one of the surprising features of later pot-painting is the number of non-mythological images depicting men and women in each other's company. There are numerous scenes of men and women 'in conversation', and images of men and women together in contexts both public and private. For example, a column-krater by the Orchard Painter in New York depicts a man and two women in conversation (fig. 5.1), a pyxis in Manchester a scene of men and women in an interior (fig. 5.2), and a cup by the Veii Painter in Tokyo shows a woman conversing with an athlete (fig. 5.23).[1]

Despite their numbers, such scenes can be difficult to 'see': Greek figure-painted pots are so numerous and various that one has to sort them into categories in order to impose any kind of systematic interpretation, and hence it is regular to divide the themes by genre – departure, symposion, komos, erotic, domestic. But difficulties can arise if these categories become rigid, and come to dominate the interpretation of scenes; that is, when the desire to fit all scenes into one or another category leads us to minimise the significance of variations in depiction (a tendency already encountered in Chapter 3, whereby all scenes of male–female interaction attract the label of prostitution). Some scenes depicting men and women together have obvious elements which allow them to be pigeon-holed – a woman holding an oinochoe and phiale, for instance, indicates a scene of departure, and one at a symposion is a hetaira – but many images fall outside these categories, depicting men and women together in a decontextualised way. For example, some alabastra carry clear scenes of courtship (a man offering gifts of game, a motif adapted from homosexual courtship), but others depict a woman holding an apple and a man leaning on a staff – not courtship in the traditional sense, but still an interaction. Some lekythoi show funerary scenes in which women and youths mourn at a tomb, but others depict youths and women seated together without a setting. And some kraters have scenes of symposia or komos, but the reverses carry images of men and women simply standing in 'conversation' scenes. The pattern becomes even more marked in South Italian vase-painting, where youths and women appear together in scenes of athletics, conversation or mourning. Such images raise two related questions of interpretation: why they fail to conform to the ideas of male–female encounters expressed in classical literature, and whether they have an intrinsic meaning.

Figure 5.1 Attic red-figure column-krater, New York, The Metropolitan Museum of Art, Harris Brisbane Dick Fund, 1934 (34.11.7), *c*.460 BC. Photo courtesy The Metropolitan Museum of Art, New York.

Recognising relationships

When men and women are depicted in each other's company, this is of course at odds with the ideas expressed in literature about the seclusion of women. As we have seen, there are two methods of understanding the Greek concept of seclusion: the 'strong' reading states that unmarried women never mixed with men, and that even when married were expected to stay indoors and would meet only their close male relatives. The 'weak' reading allows

Figure 5.2 Attic red-figure pyxis, Manchester Museum 40096, 470–460 BC. Photo courtesy The Manchester Museum, The University of Manchester.

that seclusion did not happen in practice, but that nevertheless it was an ideal to which all adhered and paid at least lip service. Attempts have been made to marry the two ideas using ideas of veiling, suggesting that women could come and go in public, while still technically considered 'secluded' because they were veiled.[2] Nevertheless, whichever reading is chosen, there is a clear disjunction between literature and the images of pottery, on which men and women mix face-to-face in public without veiling. Why should male–female relations be depicted as so open? In the early days it was accepted that vase-paintings were a representation of reality, and the freedom of male–female encounters prompted the response that most of the women involved must by definition be prostitutes.[3] This view has been shown to be unsatisfactory in many different areas, and more recently commentators have explained scenes which appear problematic to them by ascribing 'permitted' relationships to the figures involved: thus if a woman appears in a funerary scene, she should be understood to be related to the man with whom she appears; on cups women are defined as hetairai by the action of appearing with a man; if the scene is religious, we must be seeing the rare occasions on which mixing of the genders was permitted; otherwise the women must be slaves. What this effectively means is the interpretation of the imagery through the expectations generated by literature: we construct a plausible scenario around an apparently unrealistic scene to marry the evidence of the two media. Many scenes can be recuperated in this way by identifying the men as relations of the women – husbands, fathers, brothers – but there are few instances where the identifications can be definite. Vase-painters had very limited methods of signifying family relationships, as a comparison of the conventions of funerary reliefs demonstrates. Although individuals within a family were depicted in appropriate age-groups (unbearded youth/bearded man, or girl/maiden/ woman), identifying the relationships between them depends wholly on inscriptions. Without this guidance fathers, husbands and uncles are indistinguishable, as are sons and brothers, and mothers and grandmothers.[4] Relatively few stelai which depict men and women together have identifying inscriptions, and those which do are often less explicit than we would wish, recording names but not relationships. Ascription of the figures to different family roles is thus done on the basis of appearance, and some, for instance Frel, have argued that this is essentially a sterile activity since in most cases the conclusions can only be speculative.[5] The same speculative approach is even more marked in the case of pots because the scenes are much more various.

Furthermore, given that literature privileges certain female roles and ignores others, we can be led by our expectations to read pots in the way which seems most convenient to our preoccupations. For instance, the comic oinochoe in New York on which a reveller thumps at the door of a house with his staff, while a worried young woman holding a lamp stands inside, is usually interpreted as a commentary on relations between husband and wife, although nothing in the scene actively denotes the relationship between the two figures.[6] This inevitably leads to a second and more fundamental question, raised in the introduction: are we asking questions which the pots are capable of answering? Can we interrogate a scene in order to determine whether the man and woman are related, or what the context may be in which they are depicted? If we play 'guess the meaning of the scene', implicit in that is the assumption that there is a meaning to be grasped – that whenever a painter drew a man and woman he did so with a clear idea in mind of their respective roles and relationship, which we in turn can fathom. The practice of interrogation is additionally complicated by the assumptions which we make about family roles; when looking at pots it is easy to think only in terms of nuclear families and clear-cut relationships, although contemporary evidence should make us aware of the huge variety of family organisation in Athens, with concubines, children of mistresses, widows and stepchildren, none of whom are ever identified on pots. Do we fail to find these statuses shown on pots because painters adhered to a strictly idealising system, or because our ideas are not sufficiently flexible?[7] As Frel has argued for funerary reliefs, the attempt to attribute a relationship to every figure can be a vain activity; it is more profitable to focus our attention on the response of the viewer, particularly of women.

Wives and husbands

To begin at the beginning with relationships, in twenty-first-century Britain we expect the marital bond between husband and wife to be the most important relationship in an individual's life, because in the last fifty years or so the idea of companionate marriage has come to dominate Western ideas. But the idea of marriage as a primary affectionate relationship, implying friendship and commonality of interests between spouses, has been alien to most societies throughout history, including our own. One has only to envisage marriage among the middle and upper classes in Victorian Britain to recognise the scenario of large age gaps between husband and wife, marriages contracted primarily for reasons of property or social influence, and spouses who inhabited separate social circles. In classical Athens this was clearly the pattern: men's primary social relations came from their participation in public life, while women concentrated their energies into family, female friendships and religion. Greek men explicitly reject the concept of commonality of interests with a wife.[8] Saying this, however, does not entail taking an automatically bleak view of women's marital experience: there is plenty of literary evidence to suggest that couples could be close, such as the argument advanced in Isaeus that a husband would not initiate a court case if it would risk losing him his wife, and the fact that a law existed to compel a husband to divorce an adulterous wife, implying that affection might override outrage. In Xenophon's *Symposium* Sokrates comments on (among other examples of lovers) one Nikeratos, of whom it is said ἐρῶν τῆς γυναικὸς ἀντερᾶται [he is in love with his wife, and she returns his affection]; to love one's wife may have been unusual, but it was not unknown.[9] One can see here a similarity with other cultures in which arranged marriages are the norm: the expectation is that once a couple have children they will be drawn closer together in the way that Demosthenes describes:

πολὺ γὰρ μᾶλλον εἰώθασιν, ὧν ἂν ἑαυτοῖς διενεχθῶσιν ἀνὴρ καὶ γυνή, διὰ τοὺς παῖδας καταλλάττεσθαι ἢ δι' ἂν ἀδικηθῶσιν ὑφ' αὑτῶν, τοὺς κοινοὺς παῖδας πρὸς μισεῖν.

[It is much more likely that a husband and wife will be reconciled from their disagreements for the sake of their children, rather than that they should come to hate their children because of the wrongs they receive from each other.][10]

Pottery, however, is probably not the place to look for the expression of marital affection: pots present a particular and not very informative view of marriage, not unlike the modern wedding photograph which has much to say about conspicuous consumption and little about the individuality of the participants. The most frequent moment at which husband and wife are depicted is of course at the wedding itself: we see not only the bride in preparation for the wedding but also the groom, and the procession either on foot or in chariot as the bride is brought to her new home. Some commentators have tried to draw strong conclusions from pictured demonstrations of affection between bride and groom as demonstrating a romantic aspect of marriage, but such gestures are not very meaningful, since the wedding is a stylised ceremony, and visible gestures of affection such as the reciprocal gaze of the couple are a part of the stylisation.[11] Many pots make indirect reference to procreation by showing the marriage bed through an open door, but scenes of marriage emphatically stop at the threshold of the house. Furthermore, the secure identification of husband and wife in pot scenes other than wedding scenes is much more difficult, because marriage was practically the only event at which husband and wife were shown in identifiable roles. Discussions of the role of the wife in Attic society often have no illustrations beyond those of the wedding, because there are so few scenes of women as 'wife' per se.[12] Certain types of scene contain some elements of these roles, but have little to offer as evidence: departure, for instance, sometimes involves husband and wife, although mothers are in general more prominent than wives. A small number of departure scenes from myth show warriors taking leave of wives with babies (Herakles and Deianeira, and Amphiareos and Eriphyle), but only two examples of non-mythological departure repeat the theme – a white-ground lekythos in Berlin, which shows a mother holding a swaddled baby as she bids farewell to her husband, and an amphora in London which has a warrior on one side and on the other a woman holding a child.[13] These two examples contrast with the enormous number of departure scenes between fathers and sons, and even in the mythological scenes the wives are present but marginal: the role of the wife is simply to hold the baby, and the scene does not dwell on the emotion of parting between spouses, concentrating instead on the handshake between older and younger generations of men.

A second strand of imagery which seems to depict family life is the composition of man and woman in an interior with a child. Only three examples (discussed in Chapter 2) present a mother and baby with the father looking on – the hydria from Vari (fig. 1.3), the hydria in Munich showing a boy with a hoop, and the pelike in London on which a man and woman watch a crawling child – although again there is no actual indication of the relationship between the figures.[14] The man has been taken for a paidagogos rather than a parent, and certainly there is a lack of explicit emotional engagement on the man's part. More tentatively the motif of the 'man in the women's apartments' can also be read more extensively in scenes without babies: we might therefore see husbands standing while their wives spin or gesture on a selection of hydriai. A hydria in London, for example, shows a seated woman spinning, and a crowned and bearded man holding a staff.[15] But the very indeterminacy of such scenes should make us aware of the differences in ideology surrounding marriage: rather than reading weakly defined scenes in the way that best fits our expectations, we should realise the limitations of the depictions – men were not supposed to spend time at home, and hence we never see family gatherings, or an affectionate nucleus of mother, father and child.

Beyond this, what indications of husband–wife relationships can be found? There is little idea of sexual or romantic involvement on pots: Keuls discusses a Dionysiac pelike from London, arguing that we see ritual sex of satyr and maenad on one side and conjugal sex on the other, but in fact what we see is much more similar to the indeterminate setting of other sex scenes, a man and woman embracing in a field of vines: the stool with himation on it is not sufficient to create a domestic scene.[16] It is only in the funerary sphere that there is a limited expression of these emotions, both in inscriptions and in art. The white-ground lekythoi from the Achilles Painter are well known for the emotion between husband and wife which they communicate: fig. 4.23 depicts a bearded man, naked but for sword and spear, gesturing to a woman who holds out a helmet, and more famous is the lekythos in Athens on which a man stands with shield, spear and helmet, gesturing to a seated woman.[17] Yet even on these it is not always easy to identify husband and wife: there are few overt signs of closeness. Funerary reliefs offer a contrast, albeit within a culture of restraint: numbers of husbands and wives are securely identified by inscriptions, and these do make signs of affection, and also sometimes appear with their children. Pots, on the other hand, are very non-committal, and mythical scenes hardly very encouraging: the family scenes discussed above are notable for their air of menace, since the warriors leaving will of course be killed by their wives.[18]

Daughters and fathers

Father–daughter relationships are even more difficult to fathom. Images of daughters with fathers are rare on pottery, and literary evidence provides us with very mixed messages. One strand of ideas in drama appears to suggest a positive relationship as evidenced by the comments of Evadne's father in Euripides' *Supplices* on the pleasure of having daughters:

οὐδὲν ἥδιον πατρὶ
γέροντι θυγατρός· ἀρσένων δὲ μείζονες
ψυχαί, γλυκεῖαι δ' ἧσσον ἐς θωπεύματα.

177

[There is nothing sweeter than a daughter for an aged father; sons have greater spirit, but are less sweet and endearing.]

(*Supplices* 1101–3)

A similar idea is celebrated in Sophocles' *Oidipus Coloneus*, which depicts the affection between Oidipus and his daughters Antigone and Ismene.[19] The evidence of comedy, on the other hand, is contradictory: Trygaeus in *Peace* demonstrates love and concern for his three daughters, but *Wasps* includes the unpleasant image of a father exploiting his daughter's affection in a sexual way, and in *Acharnians* the Megarian sells his daughters as a response to poverty.[20] I have suggested previously that mothers retained a close bond with daughters, even after marriage, but the father's role within the family is less clear. On pottery, one of the few visible roles of the father is to preside over the period of his daughter's nubility, accepting the loss of his child, both in pursuit scenes where a father ('king') watches as his daughter is stolen by a god or hero (fig. 5.3), or in mythological scenes where a daughter is won or rescued by a hero.[21] Myths involving a father and daughter tend to centre mainly on sexual betrayal, as a young suitor wins the daughter's loyalty away from her father: for instance in the myth of Pelops' contest with Oinomaus for the hand of his daughter Hippodamia: Hippodamia fell in love with Pelops, and aided him in outwitting her father. Similarly, Ariadne assisted Theseus to defeat the Minotaur and escape from her father; Nisos was betrayed by his daughter Scylla for her love of Minos; and Medea betrayed her father for Jason.[22] Daughters suffering at the hands of their fathers before being rescued by a hero are also common in mythological scenes – Akrisios imprisoning Danae with her son in the chest, for example, or Kepheus pegging out Andromeda for the monster.[23]

There is little evidence for close relationships – most contemporary fathers speak of giving daughters away – except in the funerary sphere. Clearly a father was expected to mourn the death of a daughter, as for a son: Aeschines criticises his opponent Demosthenes because he took part in public ceremonies only seven days after the death of his daughter, before the period of mourning was complete, and characterises him as μισότεκνος, child-hating.[24] On items of pottery for funerary use, too, there is again more interaction between fathers and daughters to be found. The figure of the aged man appears sometimes on white-ground lekythoi, most often with a younger man dressed as a warrior, and this is the same poignant juxtaposition as found in departure scenes – the old father, beyond the age of fighting, watches as his son is taken from him. On two lekythoi by the Achilles Painter (fig. 5.4), however, an old man appears with a woman who is plainly the deceased, since the grave carries a kalathos and diphros, indicating that it is a woman's.[25] The ageing father mourns for his daughter. Similarly evidence from grave stelai is also more plentiful; many stelai show fathers with their adult daughters, and that relationships did last into adulthood is shown by the stelai which commemorate married daughters, shown with both father and husband (or father-in-law), such as the stele of Peisikrateia in Piraeus Museum (fig. 5.5) – Peisikrateia shakes hands with her father Euphronios (named in the inscription), and Aristodikos (presumably her husband) stands behind them.[26] There is also an intriguing black-figure cup, once in Rome, which has on its outside a departure scene, and inside an old man and a child, described by Beazley as a girl (although the gender of the figure is hard to determine).[27] If the child is female, we see here a grandfather and granddaughter, two non-combatants associated in family solidarity.

Figure 5.3 Attic red-figure pyxis, Cambridge, Fitzwilliam Museum GR 1.1933, *c.*470 BC.
Photo courtesy The Fitzwilliam Museum, University of Cambridge.

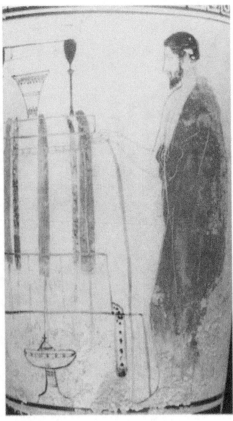

Figure 5.4 Attic white-ground lekythos, Vienna, Kunsthistorisches Museum 3746, *c.*440 BC. Photo courtesy Kunsthistorisches Museum, Vienna (neg. nos. II 33.428 and 429).

There is an interesting slant to Athenian interpretations of this relationship, in that father and daughter in states other than Athens are credited with greater closeness. Herodotus, for instance, recounts several stories involving fathers and daughters, of which the best known is the Spartan Gorgo advising her father Kleomenes; Spartan daughters play quite a large role in Athenian thought, consistent with the higher status of women there, although this is not something which is indicated in their art.[28] One also encounters daughters with prophetic powers, such as Polykrates' daughter who warns him against his final expedition, and daughters conspicuous for their bravery, such as Phaidime, daughter of Otanes, who played a role in unmasking the Persian pretender Smerdis.[29] This contrasts with Athens where the unmarried daughter is celebrated in drama primarily for her willingness to sacrifice herself for parent and city, as do Iphigeneia in Euripides' *Iphigeneia in Aulis* and Macaria in *Herakleidai.*[30] Possibly there is more evidence for father–daughter relationships in Herodotus because of his concentration on powerful families where the daughter retains her loyalty to, and place in, the family even after marriage, but it may also be an implicit recognition that such relationships were not as important at Athens – the father–daughter relationship ceased to be visible once past childhood, as the daughter moved to the family of her husband and became visible again only in death.

Figure 5.5 Funerary stele of Peisikrateia, Athens, Piraeus Museum 1625, 375–350 BC. Photo courtesy The Archaeological Museum, Piraeus.

Sisters and brothers

In contrast to this, several scholars have argued for the importance of the brother–sister relationship as a unique opportunity for affectionate relationships between the sexes in Athens. Children who grew up together often retained close relationships as adults – brothers and sisters would be more likely to be of an age, as opposed to the large gap between husband and wife, and the relationship is one of the rare examples of women and men meeting on a basis of equality.[31] There were expected standards of behaviour for siblings – a brother was required to take in a widowed sister or to provide a dowry – but many sibling relationships documented in speeches go beyond this. Both Isaeus and Demosthenes describe a sister conspiring with her brother to win a legal case, one pretending to have divorced her husband and the other deceiving her (wealthy) husband with repeated false pregnancies at her brother's suggestion.[32] After the death of a father, a woman would become dependent on her brothers for legal matters; in our sources sisters are married off by brothers a lot of the time, and in practice this would affect the quality of the kurios relationship. There is also some recognition of the affection which could exist between brother and sister: in Isaeus' *On the Estate of Apollodoros* the speaker describes the affection between a brother and his half-sister, while in Herodotus the tyrant Periander of Corinth sends his daughter to persuade his son to be reconciled with him, δοκέων μιν μάλιστα ταύτῃ ἂν πείθεσθαι [thinking that he was most likely to be persuaded by her].[33]

Affectionate relationships between brothers and sisters are strongly marked in drama (as opposed to the rivalry which marks fraternal relations): Elektra and Orestes, Antigone and Polynikes (although this is rather one-sided), and Helen with the Dioskouroi; these are not, however, myths which are regularly depicted on pottery. Orestes and Elektra are popular on Italian pots, often shown at the tomb of Agamemnon, but this is more a consequence of Italian painters' interest in dramatic productions than concern with sibling relationships.[34] Where a woman appears with two youths, as on a series of cups by the Meleager Painter, some try to see Helen and the Dioskouroi, but this is far-fetched; the Dioskouroi are more commonly depicted on their own, identified by their dress and horses.[35] The interest of drama in sibling relationships is not replicated on pottery – the only brother and sister depicted with any frequency are the divine pair Apollo and Artemis.

On the other hand, siblings in childhood are quite common on pottery: choes most often depict a single child, but some play in mixed pairs or groups, such as the girl holding out a chous to a baby boy on an example in the Louvre, or the girls and boys playing with dogs or geese on choes in St Petersburg and London.[36] Young siblings are also prominent in funerary art – the best-known example is the grave stele of Megakles from archaic Athens, which shows Megakles as a young man accompanied by his small sister. Indeed, grave reliefs have brothers and sisters of all ages in affectionate relations.[37] Fourth-century inscriptions reveal some interesting facts about the burial of sibling groups: often inscriptions record brothers and sisters buried in the same family peribolos, and the striking feature of these is that the spouses are choosing to be buried and commemorated in the family of their husband or wife, rather than their own, so that their partner can have both spouse and sister or brother around them; perhaps most surprising is that this happens with husbands as well as wives, overriding the husband's loyalty to his own family. An inscription found in the Piraeus records the burial of Euphrosyne and Eubios, children of Eunikos of the deme Aixone, together with Kallisto, daughter of Diogenes of Kothokidai; another from Sepolia commmemorates Demokleia and her brother Aristophon of Kothokidai, with Exopios of Halai, Demokleia's husband.[38] Given these links, might we see brother and sister on white-ground lekythoi too? Many lekythoi show young men and women at the tomb, one the deceased and the other a mourner, but several scenes depict young men and women without the tomb setting. On a lekythos in New York (fig. 5.6) a woman and beardless young man reach to shake hands, while on another in London a young man with petasos and staff confronts a woman; a lekythos in Athens shows a woman and a youth with a spear who gesture to each other.[39] The age of women on white-ground lekythoi can be notoriously hard to identify, but these seem to be of an age with the men, especially those standing rather than seated. Similarly we should be aware of the possibility that women in departure scenes may be sisters: a bell-krater in Syracuse carries a scene of departure with two couples, a youth in armour who takes leave of a woman and bearded man, and a younger couple, a woman with loose hair who shakes hands with a youth in ephebe garb, who may be meant for brother and sister.[40]

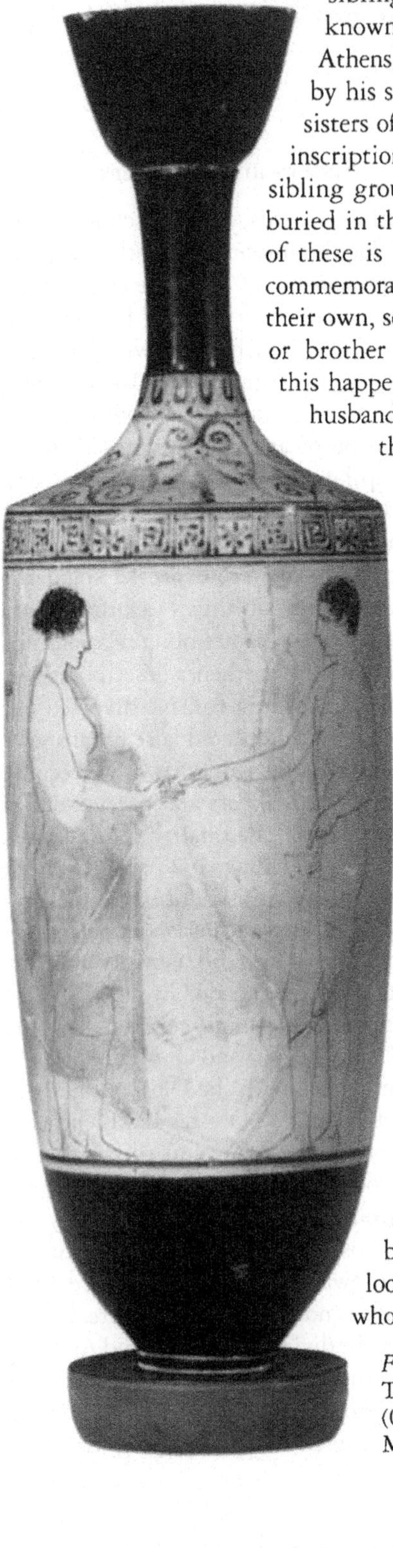

Figure 5.6 Attic white-ground lekythos, New York, The Metropolitan Museum of Art, Rogers Fund, 1908 (08.258.18), 440–430 BC. Photo courtesy The Metropolitan Museum of Art, New York.

182

What is most significant in the three areas we have examined is how much of our understanding of families is derived exclusively from funerary representations – white-ground lekythoi and stelai. This is partly because stelai carry inscriptions, and lekythoi use a comparatively simple system of depictions (ritual, farewell, visits to the tomb) with age groupings which make identification possible, but mainly because this is where the evidence is to be found; the existence of inscriptions on funerary stelai indicates a desire to identify the individuals commemorated to the passing viewer. This raises once more the question of the purpose of black- and red-figure pots. In some areas of art it is important to define roles exactly – like the plaque in the Louvre, which has a prothesis scene in which every mourner is labelled with their relationship to the dead: ἀδελφή (sister), θήθη (grandmother), θηθίς προσπατήρ (paternal aunt).[41] The contrast with black- and red-figure could not be stronger: the relations between figures seem opaque to us, because these pots are not following the same agenda. They were created with export in mind, not for use by Athenians in the same way as the funerary pots, and it is only in this area that concern for the family is acute.

Beyond the family

Relevant though family relationships are to women's experience, they go only a small part of the way to making sense of the scale and variety of male–female interaction on pottery; women and men are depicted meeting, conversing, offering each other gifts, pursuing and interacting in a host of different ways. Literary accounts of male–female interaction depict it as extremely circumscribed, which makes what we find on pottery all the more surprising. Several different approaches have been enlisted to explain this diversity. The idea that pottery depicts the seclusion of women can be supported only by selective illustration; some pots depict women in all-female groups, but just as many represent men, young or old, in domestic settings alongside women. For example, a pyxis in Manchester (fig. 5.2) depicts an interior with two seated women, two standing and two men; one of the latter is young and wears a chlamys and petasos, the other is older and holds a spear. Although all the figures look at one another, there is no gesture to make any relationship clear. Many other pyxides similarly show youths and women together, conversing or offering gifts.[42] A black-figure onos in Leiden (fig. 5.7) carries two domestic scenes: one depicts three figures standing, a man holding out a mirror, a woman and an older man with a staff; the other the same three figures seated, with a dog beneath the woman's chair.[43] The kalathos and items hanging on the wall place it in an interior, but there is little else to go on. Examples like these can be understood as representing families, but the question is whether we are right to see families in every instance: a column-krater by the Harrow Painter, for instance, on which a woman gestures with an empty distaff as a man and youth look on, is read by Keuls as a family group – husband, wife and son – but is the approach legitimate?[44] The boundary of family scenes begins to blur with the pyxis in Athens (fig. 2.25), on which women sit in a domestic scene with children and kalathoi, and a man stands to one side holding out a fruit: for those keen to find illustrations of family life he is an 'onlooking husband', but the gesture of offering fruit belongs in the motif of courtship. A pyxis in Liverpool by the Cage Painter (fig. 5.8) raises all kinds of questions about circumstances and status: on it a woman works at a laver in an interior (dressed in heavy clothes), while a youth looks on, seated at a table and holding a walking stick.[45] Is the woman a family member or a slave, and why is the youth watching

Figure 5.7 Attic black-figure onos, Leiden, Rijksmuseum van Oudheden I.1955.1.2, *c*.480 BC.
Photo courtesy Rijksmuseum van Oudheden, Leiden.

an apparently mundane task? Does the louterion place the image in a kitchen, or a less
defined space?[46] Can a scene like this, with a minimal setting and no obvious explanation
of roles, be susceptible to an interpretation of individual relationships? Reading families
in scenes is easily done when there are only domestic items in the field, when the ages of
the figures are clearly delineated, and when the genre seems to demand it, but it becomes
gradually less possible and is not the answer to every scene.

The appearance of men, especially young men, in domestic scenes, where the women
prepare their toilette while men offer presents, has been interpreted more recently as part
of a different iconography – that of marriage. As we have already seen, when women are
shown dressing (putting on girdles or jewellery, fastening sandals or headbands) these
actions are understood to be symbolic of preparation for marriage, and therefore any man
who appears in the scene is identified as the bridegroom. There are some clear examples
where this interpretation is signalled, such as the hydria in New York by the Orpheus

Figure 5.8 Attic red-figure pyxis, Liverpool Museums 49.50.7, *c.*480 BC. Photo courtesy The Board of Trustees of the National Museums and Galleries on Merseyside (Liverpool Museum).

Painter (fig. 4.8), where a young man reaches to touch the arm of a seated woman as Eros stands in front of her holding a pair of sandals, a clear nuptial motif. Similar examples are an alabastron in London on which a young man offers a necklace from a box to a woman as she fastens her girdle, and a skyphos in Palermo with a crowned and veiled woman on one side, working wool, and a youth at the door on the other.[17] The presence of a bridegroom is part of the narrative of the scene, and the figure gradually becomes a fixed component of the theme, just like Eros, expressing the purpose of the woman's actions. But the definition of a nuptial scene can be hard to establish – not every scene of a man and woman together involves a clearly nuptial iconography, and where men offer gifts (e.g. fig. 5.9), or sit and converse in the presence of others, it is less easy to be certain that the man is to be identified as a bridegroom.

It is therefore difficult to impose on all images a model of female–male interaction derived from literary sources – the scenes are too various and (often) indeterminate to support division into a few clear genres. A frequent response by scholars to scenes where the relationships are ambiguous is to argue that the ambiguity is deliberate, but this assumes precisely what it is trying to demonstrate: that painters always had a particular relationship in mind when they painted a scene. A more profitable approach is to accept the limitations of the form, recognising that not every picture represents reality, and to examine some types of interaction to see what they encompass, and what they imply about the ideas and activity of women.

Courtship

The scenes of women with men which have attracted the most discussion in recent years are those in which men offer gifts to women. Fig. 5.9 illustrates the type: on a pyxis in

Figure 5.9 Attic red-figure pyxis, Mount Holyoke College 1932 BS.II.5, *c.*450 BC (drawing).

Mount Holyoke, in a domestic interior marked by a door and a kalathos, a seated woman holds a fruit as a youth offers her another round object, and holds in his other hand what is probably a leg of meat.[48] The woman holds his gaze and gestures, wrapped in her himation. The theme of gift-giving has produced a great deal of angst among scholars, because it has seemed so difficult to match the imagery with any real-life scenario. According to our sources, women rarely mixed with men outside their family, so to what occasion could images of gift-giving refer? Is it a form of transaction? The approach in the past has been to see a simple and coherent theme which begins in black-figure as a pederastic phenomenon, where men offer youths gifts of various kinds in exchange for sexual favours. A conventional range of objects and gestures develops, and in time the theme is extended to heterosexual relations too, and the same form used to illustrate male–female erotic relations. On the analogy of male interaction, the scene is understood as a dramatisation of persuasion, with sex as its ultimate aim, and hence the women being offered gifts are deemed to be prostitutes being hired for pay.[49] The giving of any kind of gift is interpreted as erotic courtship, and the status of the woman determined by the assumed transaction. This approach, however, is too narrow to do justice to the number and types of scenes found: is male–female interaction on pottery really limited to a few stereotypical actions? Sutton, in a now classic study, divided male–female interaction into three areas (marriage, gift-giving and sex), but this (as he acknowledges) involves some very loosely drawn categories. Gift-giving is not a transparent category, and the topic recalls the initial remarks on the pitfalls of establishing genres in male–female interaction.

Gift-giving, as outlined above, is often considered exclusively as a dramatisation of persuasion, but this aspect is a limited part of a much broader concept. All kinds of gifts flowed from one person to another in Greek society, and they were an important aspect of many relationships: gifts to the gods, within the family, from parents to children, between friends and to the dead. Often language serves to obscure the gift aspect of an action: gifts to the gods are called sacrifices or dedications, and those to the dead, grave offerings, but all gifts have the establishment of a relationship between donor and recipient in common. The multiplicity of gift events finds a place on pots, including children holding out toys or pets to babies and parents offering gifts to children on choes, mourners offering lekythoi and fillets at the tomb, and scenes of sacrifice, as well as men and women offering gifts to each other. This reflects the role of pottery itself as a major part of the gift economy – pots were bought to be given to the dead or to a god at a sanctuary, as well as to the living, like the black-figure kantharos given by a husband to a wife described in the Introduction.[50] We should therefore try not to limit our understanding of gift-giving scenes: for instance,

Figure 5.10 Attic white-ground alabastron, Palermo, Mormino Collection 796, 460–450 BC.
Photo courtesy Fondazione Banco di Sicilia.

an alabastron in Palermo (fig. 5.10) carries a scene which has been interpreted as romantic:
a woman offers a cock to a youth, which is seen as a typical courting gift. Yet if we compare
this with a similar alabastron in Copenhagen (fig. 1.24), we find a woman holding a cock
with an identical gesture, but in this case her companion is a woman who holds a wreath,
and the image is read as a scene of sacrifice. The gesture is repeated by a figure of Nike on
a black-figure oinochoe, and this time she holds out the bird over an altar, faced by an Eros
holding a wreath.[51] It is plain that both the gift and the gesture can have many meanings,
and in this wide context, gift-giving between men and women needs freeing from an
assumed connotation of persuasion for sex: gifts were a means of contact and persuasion
between individuals, not always erotically charged, and to interpret every gift offered by
a man to a woman as a bribe for sex is unrealistic.[52]

The question of definitions becomes acute over both the nature of the gift, and the
gesture which defines it. Sutton defines the motif of gift-giving as one person handing an

object to another, and includes under the general heading of gifts any object held out by one person to another. The focus on gesture to indicate a gift means that one individual holding out a flower to another becomes a scene of gift-giving, but where a man and woman stand holding objects without gesturing, as on many alabastra, the scene does not qualify for inclusion. The effects of this are easily seen: according to Sutton, relatively few alabastra carry scenes of gift-giving, but very many depict a woman and man together, and the wider one's definition of gift-giving is drawn, the more alabastra will fall into the category. The inclusion of all objects in the category of gifts is similarly problematic, as shown by a cup by Douris in Paris where a man holds out a kalathos to a woman.[53] This scene is characterised by Sutton as an episode of gift-giving, but at this boundary the distinction is not easily made between actual gifts and objects which are held out or offered for practical reasons, signalling some relation between the figures but not necessarily a romantic one. The same feature obviously arises in scenes of sale or purchase, as on the oil-selling pelikai. Additionally, subsuming all objects offered under a heading of 'gifts' creates more problems: Sutton draws a distinction between gifts of value (such as perfume, ribbons or legs of meat) and 'romantic' tokens (flowers and wreaths), but the wreath or the flower are not simple concrete presents. Wreaths can be understood as low-value symbolic gifts, but their iconography establishes different expectations: crowning with a wreath by nikai or erotes is in other contexts a mark of success or skill, and there is no reason to see this meaning changing. The symbolic value of the wreath is far more important that its actual value. Gifts of meat, too, were not simple bribes with everyday necessities: meat in pot-painting (and in Greek life) was either game (in which case it is shown whole), or sacrificial, and the gift of a leg of meat was a way of involving the recipient in the sacrifice, and hence cementing ties of family or friendship.[54]

One of the main results to emerge from examining the theme of 'gift-giving' as a totality is the removal of an automatic assumption of a male-to-female power dynamic. There are many examples of women as donors – obviously they form the majority of mourners, offering gifts to the dead, but they also offer gifts to the living: on the alabastron in Palermo, as we have seen, a woman offers a cock to a youth (fig. 5.10) (and this is a strong motif from homosexual courting); a skyphos in St Petersburg (fig. 5.11) depicts a woman offering an alabastron to a youth; one might add a cup by the Euaion Painter in Oxford (fig. 5.12), since Beazley suggested that the man may just have received the apple from the woman who holds the basket.[55] On two pots, a cup by the Briseis Painter in Ruvo and a Nolan amphora in Munich, women offer legs of meat to men.[56] Therefore gift-giving does not always show the expected power dynamic; women initiate contact, or seek out an object of affection too. It is useful to compare female roles in arming scenes, where they hold out weapons or armour to the men; the gesture of offering an object has a wide application.

These variations to the idea cast new light on the narrowly defined terms of 'courtship' as male–female interaction. On the assumption that any woman offered a gift is a prostitute, many scenes have been identified as problematic, especially those which associate the imagery of courtship with that of domestic activity. The apparent anomalies have generated a whole scholarship of their own, in an attempt to explain what seems to be an impossible juxtaposition of symbols: the most famous case is an alabastron by the Pan Painter in Berlin, on which a veiled woman sits spinning as a young man offers her a purse. Our expectations about female depictions (veiling, lowered gaze, wool-work) clash with the image of the man offering money, and, for the most part, scholars have

Figure 5.11 Attic red-figure skyphos, St Petersburg, The State Hermitage Museum 4224, *c.*460 BC (side B). Photo courtesy The State Hermitage Museum, St Petersburg.

suggested that the images be seen as representing either prostitution or seduction: they cannot be in the 'respectable' world.[57] The problem derives, however, not from the pots themselves but from the perspective from which we view them. The apparent anomalies arise mainly from considering a small number of pots in isolation from the totality of gift-giving scenes, and this is a field where closer consideration of the archaeology is illuminating. It takes us back to a question posed in the introduction: are pots of different shapes with a similar 'theme' more like each other than the same shape with different themes? We find differing aspects of 'courtship' on different pots; it is rarely noted that the 'spinning hetairai' are almost all on alabastra, and the alabastron seems to be the courting shape par excellence. Apart from the much-discussed examples of women being offered gifts by youths in traditional gift-giving type, large numbers of alabastra found in Greece carry scenes of contact between men and women, and in most cases these take the form of decorous courtship with symbolic gifts such as fruit: an alabastron in Oxford, for instance (fig. 5.13), depicts a heavily draped woman holding an apple facing a youth, and this is part of a significant series. On another example in Essen we see a woman gesturing and a man leaning on a staff; the famous example in Paris (fig. 1.16) shows a young man offering a taenia to a woman who holds a wreath and lowers her gaze.[58]

Almost all alabastra have two-person compositions (one or two show two couples, or extra figures such as maids or nurses), but the range of interactions is wide: while some depict the offering of gifts, others have nuptial overtones (like the example from London discussed on p. 161), while some show confrontation or conversation, without overt gift-giving at all. There is (as always) a difficulty in defining the boundary of the theme: much

Figure 5.12 Attic red-figure cup, Oxford, Ashmolean Museum 1911.618, *c.*440 BC. Photo courtesy The Ashmolean Museum, Oxford.

male–female interaction on alabastra takes the form of gift-giving or courting, but another significant strand of depictions shows women dancing, and it is just as artificial to separate these out as a different 'theme'. Should these influence our reading of the gift scenes? The archaeological background is significant: the alabastra under discussion are funerary, and

Figure 5.13 Attic red-figure alabastron, Oxford, Ashmolean Museum 1916.6, 520–500 BC. Photo: Beazley Archive, reproduced by permission of The Ashmolean Museum, Oxford.

even those on which interactions have been seen as more commercial were found in graves – for example, the alabastron depicting two couples, one a youth offering a hare to a seated spinning woman, and the other embracing; this was found in the Athenian Kerameikos, in the grave of a twelve-year-old girl.[59] Many others in the series of gift-giving were found in Boiotia, and many are white-ground. There are in fact stronger links between the alabastra scenes and the men and women shown on white-ground lekythoi, which no one identifies as prostitution: white-ground lekythoi have quite a few scenes of men and women confronting each other, often with fruit, of a very similar kind – a lekythos in New York by the Achilles Painter, for instance, shows a seated man holding a fruit (apple or pomegranate), facing a standing woman, and another in Berlin depicts a woman seated holding a wreath with a bird on her knee, facing a man who leans on his staff.[60] Given the funerary nature of the genre, these scenes are never read as courting, but they expose the difficulty of drawing a firm boundary between themes. Alabastra clearly are a locus for the interaction of men and women, but there is more to the imagery than persuasion for sex.

Pyxides similarly adopt courtship themes, depicting men actually within the house, offering gifts. Scenes on pyxides, however, are far less often cited as problematic than those on alabastra, possibly because their setting is clearer: they are obviously placed inside the same kind of interior as scenes of domestic life. Arguments about female status have led to the suggestion that scenes of erotic courtship predominate on cups and amphorae, because they reflect male preoccupations, while marriage is the theme of pyxides and small hydriai. This is not supported by the range of scenes: it is not possible to draw a contrast between depictions of courtship on pots for male and female use. The Euiaon Painter's cup in Oxford (fig. 5.12) is a good example, depicting a young man and woman, the former holding an apple, and the latter a situla of fruit, which is a far more delicate scene than many on pyxides or alabastra. Likewise gifts of meat appear on cups and pyxides alike.[61] The presence of courtship scenes on pyxides is important, since it indicates that these themes were painted for the benefit of female users too. This offers a new perspective on the question of why women might have pots with apparently unsuitable themes in their possession, a question which has been raised many times.

The primary stumbling block in taking courtship scenes at face value has always been the difficulty of believing that courtship could ever have been a reality, whether for a teenage bride-to-be or an older woman in classical Athens. Our evidence is in fact hard to interpret: literary sources are very sure that it never happened, that citizen girls were protected even from the male gaze, and that marriages were arranged by family members without consultation. Writers suggest that funerals and festivals were the only legitimate occasions on which marriageable women might be seen.[62] We might be made suspicious about this by the emphasis on how they do things differently in Sparta, showing off their girls, even nude, as a counterpoint to the proper Athenian way.[63] Yet there is ample evidence, demographic and legal, to show that ideology did not always match reality. It has already been pointed out that the image of a girl married off by her father at fourteen once and for all cannot be right in terms of demographics. If the age disparity between husband and wife was about fifteen years, then widowhood and remarriage would have been common: in the oratorical sources there are fifty-three cases of remarriage, fairly evenly divided between men and women, at least forty-three of which produced children.[64] Nor would the father always have been present to arrange a betrothal: many died before a daughter was marriageable, and we see brothers or other family members taking the parental role. In fact in the speeches of Isaeus brothers give sisters in marriage quite often, because a father has died.[65] This may be partly due to Athens' military involvements in the period, but a father would presumably be at least forty-five when a daughter became marriageable for the first time, and could be very much older. Furthermore, we tend to have a view conditioned by Christianity that only the first marriage is important, that subsequent ones are somehow of lesser value. There is no sign that this view prevailed in Athens: each marriage was of equal value, even though after the first time the bride was no longer a virgin. Hyperides' speech *In Defence of Lycophron*, which refers to a remarriage, indicates that the ceremony was exactly the same whether the bride was fifteen or forty. The circumstances of the case are also telling: the speaker is refuting the accusation that he seduced the sister of Dioxippos before her wedding, and that he followed the actual wedding procession urging her not to consummate the marriage with her husband.[66] This implies that an adult woman might be expected to have some contact with men outside her family. So in reality, marriage was something that could happen more than once, and not all brides would be fourteen-year-olds who knew 'as little as possible'. Similarly, ideas about romantic love are hard to pin down: there are some indications that the idea was recognised – the wealthy Kallias in the mid-sixth century is said to have allowed his daughters to choose their own husbands as a mark of his wealth (demonstrating that they need not marry for money or status) – even though female preference was supposed to be irrelevant in practice; comparative evidence from modern peasant societies reveals a similar pattern, where strict matchmaking for property and status can coexist with a tradition of love songs.[67] It is also suggested that financial matters would have been irrelevant to the poor, opening the way to marriage for emotional motives.

The idea of courtship, then, was present in the abstract as a possible interaction between men and women. But to define a few images as 'official and respectable courtship' while reading the rest as seduction is unfounded, when there are in fact no indications of status or relationship beyond the act of gift-giving itself.[68] Instead we should ask what purpose these images of interaction might fulfil, especially when they appear on funerary pots used within Athens, and by women. There is no support for the idea that this is a motif concerned with commercial sex which shifts into the iconography of marriage – there is no evidence for a change in attitudes towards marriage between the appearance of red-figure painting in 530/520 BC, and the disappearance of gift-giving as a motif c.430 BC. What we should see instead is that the idea of choosing and being chosen develops in marriage imagery because it is attractive to women. Just as with the imagery of the wedding, where the iconography of pottery centres on the bride, we see a contrast with the literary view of betrothal as a transaction between two men, in a way which allows the woman an active role. A bridegroom does not simply come and announce a father's decision: he woos the bride with gifts, and there is implicit in the act the possibility that power can shift the woman's way and she may refuse. Whether or not courtship was a reality, it does not mean that women did not aspire to the condition of being courted: of being persuaded, rather than being given, and this is what the imagery invokes. The rigidity of our normal view of male–female relationships in Athens has been called into question, epecially by Cohen, in a very illuminating treatment of adultery and other non-marital relations; he emphasises the many instances of courtship of married and unmarried women which we find in the texts, particularly in comedy, which include the sending of gifts and messages.[69] The fact that women conducted relationships with men despite the severity of the consequences suggests that an emotional reward was recognised and sought, and it is this aspect which is central to the imagery. Pottery also presents images of women as active participants in relationships: they are not simply passive recipients of gifts but initiate contact too; this may relate to the comparative ages of men and women in the motif, since all are shown to be young, the men beardless. There is a similar strain in images of love in literature: when the Kinsman in *Thesmophoriazusai* describes an imaginary affair, it is said to have started in childhood, hence with a contemporary, and *Ekklesiazusai* depicts a clandestine relationship between a young man and woman.[70] If the men and women who interact on pots are both youthful too, this may all be part of the same idea of a relationship of equality between partners, where acceptance or refusal is in the power of the individual.

The use of courtship imagery in marital contexts is found in other fabrics: a late sixth-century Etruscan pot, for example, depicts a young man and woman offering each other gifts in a representation of courting, he a hind and she a hare. Similarly a seventh-century terracotta from Taranto shows Theseus and Ariadne making a gesture of courtship, and is contemporary with the well-known Cretan oinochoe on which a young man makes a gesture of supplication to a woman.[71] Although they are early, these examples demonstrate that representations of courtship were regular in those areas which formed the market for early pots; the courtship theme can be found in early Attic contexts too, on several black-figure skyphoi which depict men and women in stylised courting poses. There is, however, an interesting reluctance to credit the idea of courtship in other media; an Attic tombstone from the fifth century (fig. 5.14) has an epigram recording it as the monument of Phyrkias:

Figure 5.14 Attic funerary stele, Athens, National Museum 2062, late fifth century BC. Photo courtesy The Archaeological Museum of Piraeus.

κεῖσαι πατρὶ γόον δούς, Φυρκία· εἰ δέ τίς ἐστί / τέρψις ἐν ἡλικίαι, τήνδε θανὼν ἔλιπες. [You lie here, Phyrkias, having brought grief to your father; if there is any pleasure in the prime of life, dying, you left this behind].[72] The relief shows a young man standing (named as Phyrkias) and a seated woman named as Nikoboule. He holds a lyre and a small hare, she a bird. It was suggested by Clairmont that the figures should be interpreted, from the objects they hold and the inscription, as a betrothed couple: Phyrkias' death was so disappointing for his father because of his thwarted marriage. The idea that this was a betrothed couple, however, received little credit elsewhere, and in a subsequent publication Clairmont too moved away from this interpretation, suggesting instead that the figures must be mother and son.[73] The presence of the hare, nevertheless, suggests a courting gift; one has to wonder whether the apparent rarity of courting as a theme on funerary stelai is in fact the result of modern commentators' unwillingness to consider the idea when the relationships between figures are unclear.

Money, sex and power

Despite all this, a belief in women's desire to be courted has not solved the whole problem, since a particular difficulty has been found in recent years with the foregrounding of the purse or money-pouch in courtship. Fig. 3.15 illustrates the type of image: on the other side of the skyphos in St Petersburg a bearded man wearing a wreath faces a woman, holding out what appears to be a money bag.[74] This item has been afforded a huge importance in the interpretation of images, and two examples will make clear how the appearance of a purse supposedly alters the meaning of a scene. We have already seen several examples of white-ground lekythoi on which men and women offer each other objects; the white-ground lekythos is a specifically Attic funerary item. But a white-ground lekythos in London (fig. 5.15) depicts a man offering a purse to a woman who holds a flower; the purpose of this pot can only be funerary, but the power of the purse as symbol is such that it was suggested to me that the lekythos must have been a funerary offering for a whore. I doubt, however, that families thought about their women entirely in terms of their sexual status.[75] Similarly the black-figure onos in Leiden discussed above depicts a man and two women in what appears to be a family scene; another red-figure onos in Berlin (fig. 5.16) depicts a scene very similar in outline: a woman sits and offers an alabastron to a youth who leans on his staff, while another youth stands behind her.[76] The scene is an interior, yet the bag held by the youth facing has been enough for the scene to be interpreted as one of prostitution, showing a pimp, customer and prostitute. Does the purse completely alter the nature of the scene in which it appears? Modern opinion,

Figure 5.15 Attic white-ground lekythos, London, British Museum 1914.5–12.1, *c*.480 BC. Photo courtesy British Museum. © The British Museum.

on the whole, accepts that it does, and that whatever one makes of other gifts, money is an undeniable symbol for prostitution. Thinking on this topic has not always been as sharp as it might: if a purse in a scene of male–female interaction signals an image of prostitute and client, why should so many other scenes, also identified as images of prostitution, lack that symbol? How can it be both so strongly determinative and at the same time unnecessary?[77] We have already seen in Chapter 3 that in negotiation scenes we never see a lover who has accepted money: we are always at the point of offering. We do not even see the type of transaction as on sale pots, where customer and vendor offer purse and commodity respectively. The purse in such scenes is a statement about the relationship between the participants; it is not meant to reflect the reality of, say, negotiation with an owner for a slave. Second, we never see an explicit connection between purses and sex, such as a woman having sex and holding a purse; those who offer or receive purses are invariably fully dressed.

The purse is in fact not the dominant symbol that the argument requires it to be; we encounter purses in a multiplicity of images. An examination of the money motif is helpful to elucidate the imagery, since the purse as a symbol in the hands of an individual has more than one meaning. It is, for example, used in scenes of purchase, such as the sale of oil or wine in fig. 3.2; other images show customers with purses buying items such as pots. The purse also appears in scenes without commodities as an abstract symbol of wealth, and even hangs in the background of scenes.[78] Recent work on money, led by von Reden, has taken a broad view of pictures involving purses, and she suggests that the purse be read as an attribute of the person who holds it, rather than of the recipient: it refers to the role of money within a relationship.[79] Keuls has developed the idea of money as a symbol of male power, as on the kalpis in Heidelberg (fig. 1.19) on which a man holds (but does not offer) a purse, surrounded by three women. Rather than seeing a customer among prostitutes, Keuls is surely right to see the man as a husband

Figure 5.16 Attic red-figure onos, Berlin, Staatliche Museen F2624, 440–430 BC. Photo: Antikensammlung, Staatliche Museen zu Berlin – Preussischer Kulturbesitz.

with the wherewithal to buy whatever is needed, and in her characterisation of the purse as an 'economic phallus'.[80] Both these approaches have much to recommend them, but a close observation of the motif is still needed. The idea that purses appear only in the hands of men has assumed the status of factoid in recent years, but it is not the case. A cup in Florence, for instance (fig. 5.17), shows a woman between two youths, offering a purse to one. On the Mount Holyoke pyxis (fig. 5.9) the running woman holds what may be a purse, and on a lekythos in the Fogg collection there is a rather opaque scene of a man holding a flower and a snake standing before a fair-haired female figure who holds a purse and stands on a platform. The woman may represent a statue or a deity, but it is not a scene of sale.[81] This fact alone must move away from the idea that women can be the purchased, but not the purchaser. Second, purses are not a separate category of gift; they appear with all kinds of other gifts and symbols. On a column-krater by the Harrow Painter (fig. 5.18), which is early, a man holds a purse as he talks to a woman, yet both are attended by erotes, more usual in nuptial scenes. Purses figure throughout the whole span of black- and red-figure production; they do not disappear in the classical period.[82] A convenient distinction between hetairai at symposia who are offered money and wives in domestic scenes who are offered valueless 'romantic' gifts thus cannot be supported from the evidence – as we have seen, value is not a central part of the connotations of gifts. The money-pouch is offered in just the same way as less valuable gifts such as wreaths, or tokens such as fruit and flowers.

In scenes where a man offers a purse, the relationship between man and woman is therefore not one of simple commerce, where the woman is bound to sell: it is one of persuasion, in which the man must present himself as a suitable partner, and the woman

Figure 5.17 Attic red-figure cup, Florence 3961, *c.*450 BC. Photo courtesy Soprintendenza Archeologica di Firenze.

could potentially refuse. What is happening on pots is that the imagery of courtship with purses, far from being degrading to the female figures, can assume positive aspects. The scenes we encounter on pots are not of transactions, a simple exchange of cash for sex in the world of prostitution, but images of negotiation – is it enough? Will the woman agree? It is a scene which dramatises female power, capturing the moment at which the woman's power is greatest. This places the two examples highlighted above in a different light – if we grant that the purse may be an abstract symbol, then the Berlin onos could depict a woman being approached for courtship in the presence of her relations, a theme very appropriate to an onos (designed to aid female textile work), and one which has been tentatively suggested in connection with a fragmentary hydria in Alexandria too.[83] Equally the white-ground lekythos becomes not an object whose primary reference is prostitution but an image of a woman approached as an object of value. The contrast to be found is not between wife (not courted) and prostitute (offered money), but between the kind of woman one might court, who chooses whether or not to accept a suitor, and the kind who has no choice. Lack of personal choice characterises the porne, it is true, the common prostitute 'available to anyone who wants', but it also characterised the wife, given to a husband with no say in the matter and with no right to refuse sex. In this sense the hetaira has the right which a wife does not – to refuse. The imagery of courtship, then, places the woman in a position of power, with a would-be partner seeking to win her favour.

Other aspects of the imagery also become clearer in the context of this interpretation. Sabetai, in her discussion of marital imagery, is happy to account for the presence of men in the gynaikeon by interpreting them as bridegrooms, and emphasises that relating the presence of men to the social status of the women is mistaken.[84] In some cases, however,

Figure 5.18 Attic red-figure column-krater, Rome, Villa Giulia 1054, *c*.480 BC. Photo courtesy Soprintendenza Archeologica per l'Etruria Meridionale (neg. no. 83012).

she (possibly inadvertently) takes this further and describes men who appear with moneybags as bridegrooms as well. If we can have bride and groom with fruit, with hare and with sash, why not with money as sign of status and property? Attic comedy seems to imply that men thought that women wished for a wealthy husband (the kinsman's wish for his (imaginary) daughter in *Thesmophoriazusai* is that she find a husband who is rich and stupid), and for that reason perhaps the interests of the wife and the whore are consonant: one would wish not just for a wealthy husband but also for a generous one.[85] The presentation of wealth as an element of courtship should not surprise us, because of course it could take other forms apart from the money-pouch. The gift of valuable jewellery from man to woman is another area which has seemed problematic, with its implication of exchange. But this too relates to the role of jewellery, especially the necklace, as part of female possessions – consider Demosthenes' mother Kleoboule, who was willed by her husband to his associate Aphobos. When Aphobos received the will, he took Kleoboule's jewellery and the plate (amounting to 50 mnai in value), and then refused to marry her; when attacked for this, he claimed that they were in dispute over the jewellery. In contrast Isaeus' *On the Estate of Menekles* describes an apparently amicable divorce in which the wife was able to keep her clothes and jewellery.[86] This view of the gift of jewellery helps to explain the popularity of the story of Polynikes and Eriphyle in later red-figure (fig. 4.25): in the black-figure period the departure of Amphiareos was frequently depicted, but later the emphasis of the scene changed to a moment before the departure, as Polynikes bribes Eriphyle with the cursed necklace of Harmoneia.[87] The composition of the scene mirrors that of the bridegroom presenting a gift to the bride, and in the past the connotation was seen to be one of overt sexual corruption – a woman offered a valuable object to betray her husband – but this is a misreading. It is instead the incongruity of the scene which is notable: gifts in themselves are not bad, but the addition of names to the characters in the scene converts it from the regular gift to the poisoned context of the myth.[88]

In conclusion, then, the available images of marriage were not only images of ceremony; the period before marriage, of both courtship and preparation, features extensively on small pots for personal use such as alabastra (frequently used as grave-goods in Greece). We can identify scenes for female users which represent their personal value in marriage, as actors agreeing or disagreeing, rather than simply as passive objects of exchange. Contrary to the very negative views of literature the imagery suggests that marriage for women might be an opportunity for personal gain and independence. Of course, pots do not necessarily represent what was true, but they do offer a view of an alternative and independent ideology, and rather than trying to document a change in the attitude towards marriage through the fifth century we should instead see a separate group of motifs surrounding courtship and gifts because of the positive aspects they reflected for their users.

Pursuit

The other large-scale interaction between men and women is more antagonistic: several hundred pots carry images of men in pursuit of fleeing women, or vice versa. A typical pursuit scene depicts a woman (mortal or nymph) running from a male, god, hero or mortal. She gestures in alarm, looking back towards her pursuer (fig. 5.19).[89] There is often an older man in the scene, to whom the woman flees, and usually female companions who mirror her distress. The theme of pursuit is unusual in that it is an idea generated in the mythological realm which also takes its place in mortal settings. Most pursuits involve gods or heroes, and would normally be outside the scope of this study, but the theme is relevant here because the boundary between myth and reality is exceptionally permeable for pursuits. Most scenes depict deities with identifiable characteristics (Zeus, Poseidon, Boreas, Eos), or heroes (Theseus, Peleus), but others lose any connection with the world of myth, and depict men and women, or women alone, whose status, real or mythical, is impossible to determine. It seems obvious that such scenes are not images of 'real life', but they differ from most scenes in an interesting way. Themes like departure and marriage

Figure 5.19 Attic red-figure pyxis, The Art Institute of Chicago 92.125, *c.*440 BC. Photo: Robert Hashimoto, courtesy The Art Institute of Chicago. © 2001, The Art Institute of Chicago, all rights reserved.

Figure 5.20 Attic red-figure lekythos, Cambridge, Fitzwilliam Museum GR 28.1937, 500–480 BC (drawing).

hesitate between myth and reality because they are generalisations of real scenes – warriors did depart for war, and men and women did ride in marriage processions, so in one sense the hero is 'everyman'. But pursuit is a purely heroic event: heroes like Theseus pursued and seized women, but it is not something which was supposed to happen in Greek states. Sourvinou-Inwood is right to read such scenes as emblematic rather than generic, but it is ineffective to try to relate aspects of the iconography to reality; they are not realistic in such an obvious way.

Pursuits have received considerable attention from scholars, because they have been adopted enthusiastically by some as evidence about attitudes towards sex and woman in classical Athens; in the service of this interest they have even been categorised as images of rape.[90] But it is far from certain that the theme should be seen only in terms of sexual conquest, since the pursuit of a marriageable woman by a man is only one aspect of a wider theme. Hobden, in a study of the theme of pursuit in Greek art, has traced the idea through literary and other media, showing its use in the military and religious spheres in addition to the erotic. On pottery alone, heroes pursue their prey (Theseus and the Bull, Herakles and Nereus), warriors their opponents, and Athena the disobedient daughters of Kekrops, all with a similar iconography.[91] Furthermore, what we include under the title of 'pursuit' is an interesting question, since once one begins to investigate it is extremely difficult to establish sharp boundaries for the theme. The regular pursuit scene can be broken down into smaller symbolic elements: so, on a pelike in Stockholm Zeus pursues a woman on one side of the pot and on the other a woman flees to a man. Less complex is the common type with a pursuit on one side and a man or youth on the other. When the theme is further reduced, we find, as on a lekythos once sold in Berlin, on one side a woman fleeing and on the other a female onlooker; finally there is a series of lekythoi with only one figure, a fleeing woman (fig. 5.20).[92] Both pursuer and pursued can stand alone: so we find Eos alone on pots, or a running youth, as well as pursuing warriors and fleeing women. We also find other isolated elements such as women fleeing to a 'king' figure, without a pursuer.[93] There is considerable variation in the extent of threat attending the scene, from the violent to the gentle. Examining the provenances of individual themes reveals clear patterns: images of Eos as pursuer, for instance, appear on forty-seven examples from South Italy and Sicily, and on thirty from North Italy, as opposed to twelve found at Athens (as always, pots without provenance are the majority). Rather fewer scenes of Boreas and Oreithyia have a provenance, but he is more popular in Athens: ten examples were found there, and two in Greece, compared to eight in the south of Italy and Sicily, and thirteen in the north. Zeus in his various pursuits appears only three times in Attica, compared with twenty-two examples in southern Italy and Sicily, and nineteen in the north. Theseus, in his incarnation as ephebe, appears only seven times in Attica, on ten examples across Greece, but on twenty-two in South Italy, and twenty-one in North Italy and Etruria.[94]

With these principles in mind, what do we make of pursuit? Despite the limited uses of the theme on pots within Athens, most scholars have tried to interpret the pursuit as expressing Athenian preoccupations. Some see them as essentially male fantasy, demonstrating the self-assertion of the citizen, or hostility towards women; others have read political messages into Zeus' abduction of the nymph Aegina, or the appearance of Boreas as a pursuer after 480.[95] Individual pursuits have been singled out for interpretation; that involving Zeus and Ganymede, for instance, has been described as principally an erotic paradigm. More balanced views see pursuits as funerary, representing the deceased being carried off into death, or as a metaphor for marriage, with the pursuit and abduction of a reluctant woman taken from her family and 'tamed' in marriage. Trying to subsume all pursuits into one meaning, however, is probably mistaken: certain examples will lend themselves better to one or other interpretation. What is important to emphasise is the role of women: one has to consider whether the theme really is centred on men and their perceptions, as the above interpretations suggest, since when it is reduced to its elements the figure which can appear alone is the fleeing woman, without any pursuer.

Immortal pursuits of nymphs by gods make up the bulk of the scenes: the most common are couples such as Zeus and Aigina, Poseidon and Amymone, Boreas and Oreithyia, and the version in which female pursues male, Eos with Tithonos or Kephalos. These appear to have an unproblematically funerary meaning: as well as presenting a story from myth, the scene can be understood to represent the deceased being snatched away by a divine being, emphasising both his or her desirability and the untimely nature of the death. Other aspects of the motif lend credibility to this interpretation: as well as merely pursuing, both Eos and Zeus sometimes physically carry off their quarry, and the end of the myths, with the abductees granted eternal life, is also relevant. Such a reading is supported by the many pots with pursuit scenes which were deposited in graves, Greek and non-Greek. The Brygos tomb in Capua, for instance, contained three pots with pursuit scenes: a pair of stamnoi which both have Eos pursuing Kephalos on one side, and on the reverse a youth pursuing a woman, and Boreas pursuing Oreithyia respectively, and also a rhyton with Eos and Kephalos. Tomb III in the same place contained three hydriai and three neck-amphorae as gifts for a burial of twenty people, which included one with Boreas and Oreithyia and one with Apollo pursuing a woman, as well as Achilles killing Penthesilea.[96] Similarly a pyxis depicting Peleus' pursuit of Thetis was found in the Athenian Kerameikos in an offering ditch, while a calyx-krater in Boston with an image of Zeus pursuing a woman was found at Suessula in South Italy with cremated remains inside.[97] One or two instances of the theme appear on white-ground lekythoi – Eos and Tithonos appear on two white-ground lekythoi, and Boreas and Oreithyia on one – and the theme of Boreas and Oreithyia also appears on bronze funeral hydriai.[98] It is no coincidence that the most popular scenes by number are those depicting Boreas and Eos, since both are distinguished by their wings: Eos as the personification of the dawn and Boreas the North Wind. These figures are similar to the Etruscan spirits of the underworld, who are also winged, and comparable to the figures of Hypnos and Thanatos, also usually winged, who sometimes carry away the body of the dead in funerary scenes.[99]

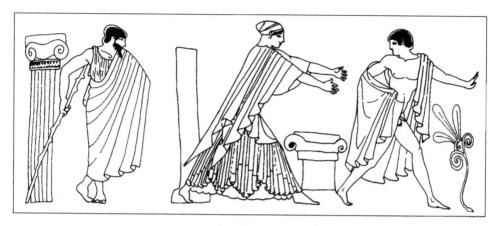

Figure 5.21 Attic red-figure rhyton, London, British Museum E796, 480–470 BC (drawing).

Other groups of pots, however, accord more easily with different interpretations: pursuits, especially that of Thetis by Peleus, are common on pyxides, and here they are usually interpreted as a 'mythological paradigm of marriage'. The pursuit and abduction of a reluctant woman is seen as a metaphor for marriage, with women taken from their family and 'tamed' in marriage. Certain aspects of the theme have been singled out in this interpretation; pursuits by heroes in ephebe garb, for instance, have been read as a commentary on Athenian rites of passage for men as well as women.[100] But it is hard to see that all pursuits can relate to ideas of marriage, given that Eos as pursuer of young men, a female iconographic equivalent to the male gods and heroes, with a male quarry, is deliberately introduced. Nor is there any clear evidence that depictions of pursuit were chosen to match the purpose of the pot: the gender of the deceased is not relevant to the theme of grave-goods, nor those used in wedding ritual.

It is where the scenes approach most closely to the everyday that they become more difficult to decipher. If an ephebe pursues a woman in an architectural setting, for instance, with column, door or chair, is there any justification for seeing a 'real' setting of a courtyard in a woman's house?[101] Likewise, what should we make of fig. 5.21, a rhyton in the British Museum by Douris? It carries a very odd scene in which a woman pursues a young man in a setting marked by a column, marker post and altar, while an older man looks on.[102] There is no indication of the identity of any of the figures. Can we read the scene as Eos and Kephalos, if Eos is without wings and Kephalos without his lyre? Most prefer to do so, because there can be no non-mythological analogue to Eos' pursuits – women cannot 'really' pursue young men. Osborne has suggested that while the figure of Eos acknowledges the existence of female desire, this desire can be shown only as winged and fantastical, because it is a shocking and dangerous concept.[103] Yet the rhyton is not alone in this depiction of a wingless female pursuer – other instances are found on three skyphoi, a stamnos and a fragmentary hydria.[104] With a number of 'wingless Eos' figures, one must wonder whether painters perceived as rigid a rule about portraying female desire as modern viewers do. This is not to say that female desire is unproblematic – there are scenes in which Eos is resisted by the youth she pursues – but female desire nevertheless spreads from the divine realm into a kind of 'no man's land' between the mythical and real worlds.[105] The depiction of active desire is also found in the scenes of Aphrodite which

Figure 5.22 Attic red-figure hydria, Florence 81948, 420–410 BC. After Pfuhl, fig. 594.

become more popular in the classical period: Aphrodite does not pursue her lovers, but she is depicted in her garden with a mortal lover, Adonis or Anchises, and there is a clear evocation of the power differential between mortal man and divine woman, as can be seen on the Meidias Painter's hydria in Florence (fig. 5.22).[106] Aphrodite sits above Adonis and clutches him possessively as Eros spins an iunx to charm him. Another Eros catches a hare at the bottom of the picture, dramatising the capture.

Similarly, what of the unnamed fleeing women who appear (especially) on lekythoi found in Greek Sicily – why depict the pursued without a pursuer? One explanation that has been offered is that the image of a fleeing woman was designed to be one of a pair, to be matched with a solo pursuer on a different pot, but the archaeology does not bear this argument out. The appearance of fleeing figures (and male as well as female are found) indicates that interpretations of pursuit as solely erotic, and indicative of violent sexual attack, are not satisfactory: if one can depict the act of fleeing, without an indication of what is being fled, it must indicate a theme with multiple possibilities. Pursuit is more than a depiction of masculine desire and female victimhood in which the roles of pursuer and pursued are fixed; those who interpret the theme as a generalised imagery of the rite of passage are closer to the truth, whether it be funerary, nuptial or initiatory. Even in those images which we have examined there is a strong case for seeing the woman at the centre of the theme, not the man and his self-aggrandisement. Being pursued can carry implications of danger and fear, but also of desirability and value, of being chosen by a god or by fate itself for one's own innate qualities, and it is this duality which gives the theme its versatility. The pursuit theme is not simply a function of gender ideology in classical Athens, and in particular does not close off routes to female power as both pursuer and pursued.

The limits of interaction: friendship?

We have examined the themes of family, courtship and pursuit, yet there still remains a group of pots unexplained, those depicting men and women in contextless scenes of 'conversation', or in public places. Many column-kraters, whatever the depiction on one side, carry on the other a generic scene of three or four draped figures, usually men with walking sticks and mantles or athletic gear, standing in a group. As a variation we find mixed scenes: two men depicted with a woman, or a man with two women, as on the Orchard Painter's column-krater in New York (fig. 5.1). Women are not uncommon in these scenes, and where they appear their pose and activity are just the same as for men: their presence seems unremarkable, and the only real difference between the genders is their clothing.[107] Sometimes the figures can be understood as related to the image on the other side of the krater – if it is a departure, for instance, the figures can be seen as relatives or onlookers – but in most cases the two sides are unrelated, and we simply appear to have a scene of men and women conversing. Later this type of scene moves from column-kraters to other shapes: a series of cups by later artists show women conversing with athletes, as on a cup by the Veii Painter in Tokyo (fig. 5.23), which depicts on one side a woman with a flower standing opposite an athlete with strigil, and similarly a cup in Florence which depicts a man and woman in conversation at a louterion.[108]

In what sense can such scenes be taken as reflections of reality? The difficulty once again lies in envisaging the real-life scenario which the pots depict, a scenario in which men and women talk together in public. Of course, the idea that unrelated men and women never

Figure 5.23 Attic red-figure cup, Tokyo, Bridgestone Museum of Art 89, *c.*450 BC. Photo courtesy Bridgestone Museum of Art, Ishibashi Foundation, Tokyo.

came into contact was in the service of class distinction: we have already considered the depictions of women working alongside men in the early period, as traders of oil and perfume, washers and artisans.[109] It was noted there that many such images appear on pelikai, and if this was a shape particularly given to celebrating the role of the banausos it is not surprising that they should show a mixed environment, similar to that of comedy, where lower-class women and men worked side by side. But images of men and women in conversation without a working context are much less frequent in the early period, and grow in popularity in classical painting. Should we see the growth in conversation scenes as a result of changing attitudes? The first thing which can be said is that we are plainly not in the real world with these images, since the one group of women with freedom to come and go among men were old women, yet they barely figure on pots, and certainly not in conversation groups. As in the cases of marriage and literacy it is not possible to trace changes in expectations about male–female relations between 500 and 430 BC in the literary sources, so the cause must be sought in the pots themselves. Some commentators are reluctant to accept any degree of realism, and argue that these 'mantle' scenes are merely stereotypical, with the presence of women an irrelevant artistic variant; such an attitude is dismissive, suggesting that such scenes occupied the 'back' of the pot and were usually turned to the wall.[110] Implicit in this, however, is the idea of display in a modern sense, of a 'front' and 'back' as in a museum cabinet, but kraters, whether in a house or a tomb, were not displayed against the wall. Furthermore, a scene may be formulaic, but it does not follow from this that it is insignificant.

It is the case that the depictions of women with youths or loosely defined athletes in later art become both more frequent and gradually more abstract: on a series of later cups, for instance, men and women stand and gesture in ill-defined landscapes, often seated on rocks.[111] Beazley suggested that the female figure who appears with athletes on many cups by the Meleager Painter may be the personification of the Phyle (Tribe), but there is no name in any scene to indicate this. Nevertheless, the suggestion highlights a significant factor; namely, that there is no analogue in myth to the conversation scene, as there is to departure, family or pursuit scenes: the figures are never named, and we are given no encouragement to see a scene which is 'happening' in the unreal world of myth. This

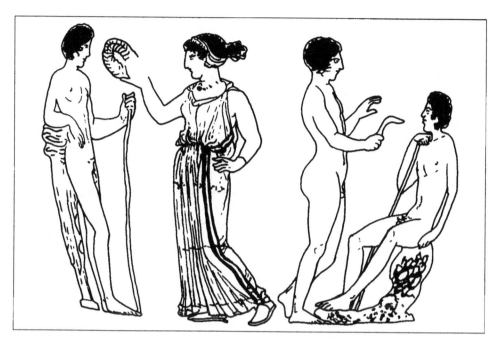

Figure 5.24 Sicilian red-figure krater, Bari 6264, *c*.380 BC (drawing).

makes them all the more difficult to interpret, as the choice is stark: real or imaginary?
The growing abstraction of the scenes finds a counterpart in South Italian painting, in
which youths and women in conversation form an extremely common theme, especially
in Lucanian art: young men, characterised by the strigils or jumping weights which they
hold as athletes, stand talking to women or receiving crowns from them. A Sicilian bell-
krater by the Dolon Painter (fig. 5.24) illustrates the type: on the left a woman holds out
a crown to an athlete who leans on a pillar, while to the right an athlete holding a strigil
converses with another young man seated on a rock.[112] Young men and women converse
at fountains or louteria, or simply in an empty field; this is not courtship in the Athenian
sense, as there is no exchange of gifts, and elements of 'palaistra' and 'departure' scenes
mingle with 'gift-giving'. The nature of these pots is not in doubt: they are clearly funerary,
as was most Italian vase-painting. Indeed many pots were made without bases, useless for
any everyday purpose but suited for deposition at a grave. The scenes of young women
and men in conversation are actually closely related to the funerary theme: many appear
in naiskos scenes, depictions of the grave monument, where they replace the family
mourners familiar in Attic art. It has been suggested that they may represent some kind
of initiatory group; certainly they do not offer a comment on relationships between men
and women.[113]

This does not, however, answer the question about the Attic conversation scenes which
appear quite early on, and show men and women in apparently public places. The
awkwardness of explaining conversation scenes means that such images are usually absent
from discussions of women in Athens, because they seem to tell us something we cannot
accept: that men and women might chat together in public. The question of categories
is, however, important here once more because there are many more scenes of conversation

between men and women than appears at first sight. The theme is not confined to kraters: some alabastra, on which women and youths confront each other without a gift or other form of contact, fall into this category, and conversation scenes are also very frequent on white-ground lekythoi. Some depictions on lekythoi show the participants with objects which make us think of particular genres, such as the helmet held by the woman on the Achilles Painter's lekythos (fig. 4.23), or the pomegranate held by the seated man on the Achilles Painter's Berlin lekythos; but others are without symbols: the lekythos in Berlin noted above has simply a seated woman holding a wreath, and a man leaning on his staff.[114] Because the shape of the lekythos signals it as a scene of mourning, we tend to assume a 'permissible' relationship between the figures, but this is a result of modern preoccupation rather than ancient indication. Athenian painters had no established forms for showing that a woman was related to, or permitted to be in the company of, a man. Ultimately, within the parameters of modern debate, the imagery cannot answer the questions that we wish to ask: we must accept the gulf between the claims of literature about female activity, and the representation of art.

This in turn draws attention to one final aspect of male–female interaction where our knowledge lapses totally: neither pottery nor literature can illuminate for us the idea of friendship between men and women. According to Athenian writers, friendship is a situation which simply cannot be: there is no reason for a woman to have contact with a man unless there is a sexual or familial link between them. Certainly there are no documented cases of an adult citizen man and woman who, though neither related nor sexually linked, were friends; but should we believe that it never happened? Our sources are quite clear that friendship was possible between non-citizen women and men; that is, between foreign women who lived in the city as metics, and Athenian men: women like Aspasia and Theodote were able to mix with men as their equals, and to join in political and philosophical debate.[115] These two were, however, hetairai by trade, and in a society where contact between unrelated women and men is meant to be regulated, implications of sexual behaviour to explain contacts between them will never be far away. For instance, in his speech *Against Aristogeiton* Demosthenes describes how Aristogeiton was assisted in his escape from jail in Athens by a woman called Zobia, a metic.[116] Demosthenes comments in passing that Zobia's help was given because she and Aristogeiton had been lovers, but his phrasing (τότε πρὸς γυναῖκά τιν' ἔρχεται Ζωβίαν ὄνομα, ᾗ ἐτύγχανεν, ὡς ἔοικε, κεχρημένος ποτέ [he went to a certain woman called Zobia, whose lover, it seems likely, he had at one time been]) shows that this is speculation – how else would a woman and man be connected? Might she have acted through friendship? In the case of citizen women, literary sources are much less forthcoming: as we have seen, there are hints that families might become friendly, including wives and husband's male friends: Demosthenes' *Against Nikostratos* relates how the speaker regularly left his affairs in the care of a friend while he was abroad, and situations like this cannot but have brought a friend into contact with a wife.[117] This is doubly true for widows: the image presented by literature is one of women totally enclosed by their family, but if a woman had no husband, the role of friends would be as important as of distant family. The fundamental difficulty in the search for evidence on pots is that it is impossible to identify an iconography for friendship on Greek pottery, either for male friendship, female (which as we have seen is very hard to disentangle from the domestic), or for friendship between the genders; whether or not it was possible, painters did not seek to illustrate it. We have no knowledge from women themselves how they related to men outside their family, whether family friends, hired labour, vendors or slaves; it is a testament to the preoccupations of pottery that male–female friendship must remain a closed book for us.

Conclusion

This last topic is an appropriate reminder that, as with the experience of concubines and of female childhood, there are areas of women's lives which pottery cannot penetrate. Although we cannot expect vase-painting to provide a key to every area of experience, what is striking about its depiction of women and men is the difference in emphasis which it offers to the literary evidence. The depiction of family relationships on pots gives little importance to the husband–wife relationship outside the funerary, and even less to other bonds such as that between sister and brother – a language of iconography never evolved to depict family ties beyond the depiction of funerary ritual. Apart from the family, pottery seems to depict far more interaction between women and men than literature implies, although the sheer range of interpretations offered for many scenes demonstrates how difficult the recognition of relationships can be, once detached from expectations generated by literature. The approach which tries to ascribe relationships to figures in each scene is unlikely to be successful, since painters do not show the interest we might expect in determining relationships so as to depict 'respectable' behaviour on the part of female figures. What is particularly surprising is the number of scenes depicting courtship in the fifth century, especially as so many of them appear on alabastra found in Greece. In direct contrast to the claims of literature that courtship behaviour was inappropriate for citizen women, the imagery seems to make a positive statement about female aspirations and choice, and to present women not as passive objects of exchange within their families but as actively choosing or rejecting a partner.

CONCLUSION

This survey has, I hope, demonstrated clearly the richness of the evidence which pottery has to offer in its depiction of women. Women form part of painters' themes at all periods and in all fabrics, and Athenian painters illustrated women with their family, working, participating in ritual, at leisure, dressing, partying, with animals, courting and trading, fulfilling a wide variety of roles in contexts both public and private. The very diversity of the material, however, has highlighted a central problem of approach in that it is not a neutral act to bring together a series of pots to illustrate an overarching theme. It is one of the paradoxes of iconographic study that the imposition of order is necessary to make sense of the profusion of images, yet any imposition of order prejudges the question of which scenes belong to a group. In studying images of women we have identified a group of scenes united by the significant factor of a female figure, but such a choice inevitably discounts other potential groupings, whether generic or thematic. The departure scene, for instance, constitutes a coherent and very well-defined theme in Attic black- and red-figure, in which a warrior takes leave of his family. A female figure is sometimes, but not always, present: does the presence of a woman in an image justify considering it in isolation from its genre? On the other hand, many scenes which include female figures have been excluded from this study: images from drama, for instance, which form a substantial group of scenes, and very many images of mythological women. The rationale for this exclusion is their lack of relevance to the everyday – can an image of Andromeda or Helen tell us anything practical about female experience? – but it highlights how difficult it would be to consider every female image.[1]

Such selectivity towards the images is inevitable, and it is worth remembering that Athenian pot-painting is in any case not a 'complete system'. In the first place, pots were only one medium for the expression of ideas by and about women; we have seen that different aspects of female life were commemorated in different forms (motherhood and sickness through votives, for example, and relationships with adult children on funerary stelai), and imagery on other media which have not survived such as wall-painting or gold and silver plate may have offered different perspectives. Furthermore, even the corpus of images with which we work is partial – we possess a very small proportion of the total images painted, and have to accept that any conclusion drawn from them cannot be definitive: when new pots can be found at any time, in the field or in museum collections, certainty is hard to attain. Most importantly, a consideration of the archaeology of figure-decorated pottery indicates that, especially where the theme of women is concerned, Attic pottery cannot be considered a homogeneous mass of evidence. It is clear that certain themes were found appropriate for pots intended for use by Athenians, with a fixed and often limited repertoire of decoration which closely reflected their use. Athenian preoccupations on pots are family and ritual (and the ritual of the family) – children at the Anthesteria, marriage on loutrophoroi and lebetes gamikoi, funerary rites and mourning on white-ground lekythoi. In contrast it is those pots which went to export markets which carry the explosive variety of decorative motifs developed in red-figure, with almost every juxtaposition of types of image – altars and symposia, chariots and wells, myth and marriage, scatology and housework.

The main question about the representation of women on pottery has always been posed in the form: why did Athenian painters choose to illustrate so varied a range of scenes from Athenian life, especially in red-figure – sacrifice, symposium, trade, sex, courting – and why did they then lose interest in these themes later on, confining themselves to abstract domestic interiors and marriage scenes? Answers to the question, as we have seen, have been framed in terms of Athenian self-definition: Athenian painters depicted what they saw around them, or what was important to them, and themes changed under the influence of political events such as the development of democracy, or as a response to the Peloponnesian War. But it is hard to demonstrate that this claim is true, since the view of the city projected by the pottery is very different from the image of the citizen and his preoccupations suggested in other sources. Certain aspects of Athenian self-definition which are made central in dramatic sources, such as agriculture, democracy and the role of the law courts, are absent from pottery: Aristophanes, for instance, makes his character Strepsiades in *Clouds* identify Athens on a map by the constant litigation that goes on there:

Μα: αὕτη δέ σοι γῆς περίοδος πάσης. ὁρᾷς;
          αἵδε μὲν Ἀθῆναι.
Στ: τί σὺ λέγεις; οὐ πείσομαι,
          ἐπεὶ δικαστὰς οὐχ ὁρῶ καθημένους.

[*Pupil*:   Look, here's a map of the whole world. Do you see? Here's Athens.
Streps.: What do you mean? How can it be Athens, when I can't see any
             jurymen sitting!]

Yet no representation of the legal process on pottery is known.[2] Agriculture is rarely seen, and the democratic assembly never. One could argue that such themes were difficult to depict, but why should we see the rhapsode and not the rhetor? Why the stand of viewers at the funeral games and not the jury?[3] Important though these aspects of civic life were in Athens, the significant fact is that they were alien to Etruscan culture in a way that images of sacrifice and symposium were not, and hence did not find their place among images for export. Scenes on pottery are therefore not a deliberate Athenian formulation about the city, but a vision dominated by the interests of the external market, and only because they were destined for sale elsewhere do we find the exuberant pictures of Athenian life – of myths, religious activities, trade and parties. They constitute a view of the city, certainly, but an outsider's view in.

In the light of this, this study has suggested that the representation of women on Attic pottery, early and late, is not quite what it seems. The female roles celebrated on pots used within Athens are precisely those rather limited ones we find emphasised in literature – women within the family, as wives, mothers and daughters. The great variety of roles which one finds in black-figure and early red-figure, in contrast, is more properly seen as a function of the export market: these images of festivals, of work, even of domestic labour, all go abroad. Indeed, the archaeology indicates that certain themes, most notably 'erotica' and housework, are of very limited applicability as evidence for life in Athens itself: painters were not representing their view of the city, or illustrating the world in which they lived, but supplying images for Etruscan graves, and this makes the imagery what it is. In some cases pottery can offer more interesting evidence for cultural contacts across the Mediterranean than for Athens itself; to characterise pursuit scenes as 'for men', for instance, when most are found in South Italian graves, is to ignore what the theme has to tell us about the real consumers of the imagery. Reading the images through the archaeology allows one to move away from the idea of 'men's' and 'women's' pots, with certain images unavailable to female users, and to consider a much greater range of users – not just the 'Athenian citizen male' but women like Melosa in Tarentum and Phanyllis in Delos.

These conclusions in turn prompt a new perspective on what has been seen as the explosion of interest in women in vase-painting from the end of the fifth and the fourth century. There is no doubt that images of women become more numerous, but, as noted above, the themes are limited and repetitive, heralding a narrowing view of female experience. Attempts have been made to link this change to a desire for escapism prompted by the Peloponnesian War, or to a growth in numbers of female consumers. But the phenomenon is better understood as a reversal: the shift towards domestic themes is a result of the changing market, as the multiplicity of thematic types vanishes with the export market, and what is left is a kind of representation closer to Athenian interests – women in inward-looking roles, with an emphasis on family, music and domestic pastimes.

Our conclusions also demonstrate the need for a more sophisticated understanding of status on pots: recent work on women has tended towards the assumption that the stereotypes of women which are detectable in literature dominate representations in art too – the idea that vase-painting represented women in two sharply defined roles (the wife and the hetaira), and that the intention of this was to reinforce cultural norms of behaviour to the extent that a purposeful interplay between the stereotypes can be detected. This is based on often circular interpretations of the images, in which certain symbols or acts are taken as representing 'respectable' or 'unrespectable' behaviour. Close examination has shown how unreliable these indicators are, and that attempts to impose the division of female figures into 'wives and hetairai' break down once the view is expanded to include both black-figure and classical red-figure. This is one instance of how the categories summoned up in literary sources simply will not map onto the imagery – female interactions with men on pots take many forms, and there is no organised system of symbolism for painters to 'explain' it since no such need was ever perceived. Some fundamental anomalies remain insoluble; for example, the treatment of female nudity, which has caused much concern to scholars attempting to interpret pots as representations of social life. Literary sources assert clearly that nudity was unacceptable for women, and indeed have been read as implying that women in Athens were regularly heavily covered and veiled, yet pottery illustrates the naked celebrant of ritual, the naked mourner and the naked bride, without apparent concern.

This study has shown that if the images on pots are not in harmony with literature, neither are they in simple counterpoint: we cannot look to pottery to fill the gaps left by classical writers, because painting was a different medium, and painters worked to a different agenda. But although we cannot use the imagery to create a complete picture of women's lives, it can nevertheless shed light on areas ignored by writers and offer new perspectives on old ones. Perhaps most of all, a study of pottery enables us to answer the question: were women important? Clearly they were, both in reality and in imagination, and for a city where women were supposed to be veiled and hidden away, this is probably the greatest paradox of all.

GLOSSARY

Note: The names of pottery shapes given below are those used by modern scholars; we do not always know the name which was used in antiquity. The figure-decorated pots we find were modelled on the types of everyday container used by the Greeks, but to say that a particular shape is designed for pouring water or holding wine does not (as I hope the text makes clear) imply that a figure-decorated pot was necessarily used for that purpose.

Adonia   A festival in honour of Adonis, beloved of Aphrodite, which was introduced into Athens by the mid-fifth century. The festival was celebrated by women only, who sang laments for Adonis and planted miniature gardens in pots, which they allowed to shrivel in the heat of the sun.

alabastron (pl. alabastra)   A small cylindrical container without a foot, designed to be suspended from a cord or strap (e.g. fig. 1.16). The name indicates that the model was a jar carved from alabaster: many pottery alabastra were made in white-ground to imitate this material.

amphora (pl. amphorae)   The standard large-bodied pot, with two vertical handles and an offset neck, modelled on the storage jar for grain, oil or wine (e.g. fig. 1.27). Many amphorae once had pattern-decorated lids, which have not survived.

Anthesteria   One of the major Athenian religious festivals, celebrated every year in the month Anthesterion over three days. The first day was the Pithoigia, the Day of Opening Casks, the second Choes, the Day of Pitchers, and the third Chytroi, the Day of Pots. Children were presented with miniature jugs (choes) at the festival.

aryballos (pl. aryballoi)   A small rounded container with a flat handle, designed to be held in the palm of the hand. Aryballoi were containers for perfume or oil, and were more frequently made in Corinth than in Attic ware.

askos (pl. askoi)   A small flat flask with a spout and a raised handle.

aulos (pl. auloi)   The Greek pipe, played by both women and men at occasions secular and sacred (e.g. fig. 1.31).

banausos   Greek term for an individual who worked for a living, signifying a lower status compared to the self-sufficient farmer-citizen.

chous (pl. choes)   see oinochoe.

epinetron (pl. epinetra)   see onos.

hydria (pl. hydriai)   A shape of decorated pot modelled on the plain water jar, having a round body, tall neck, and three handles – two horizontal for lifting and one vertical for pouring (e.g. fig. 0.1). The kalpis is a later variant, flatter in shape.

kalpis   see hydria.

kline (pl. klinai)   A couch, often shown with ornate decoration, used both by diners at banquets (symposia), and as a bed (e.g. fig. 3.23).

krater   A large open shape with a flaring mouth, based on the mixing bowl used for wine (Greeks drank their wine mixed with water, never neat). A bell-krater echoes the shape of a bell (e.g. fig. 4.28), and a column-krater has handles at the rim supported by small columns (e.g. fig. 5.1); a calyx-krater has handles at the base.

kylix (pl. kylikes)   The Greek name for the flat drinking cup with two horizontal handles and usually a high foot. Kylikes vary in size from the small (*c*.10 cm across) to the enormous (*c*.38 cm across) – the latter are often decorated in white-ground, suggesting that they were specially made for the tomb.

lebes gamikos (pl. lebetes gamikoi)   A round shape of pot with two high handles, usually made with a tall stand. The lebes gamikos, as its name indicates, was used in wedding ritual and appears in many wedding scenes.

lekanis (pl. lekanides)   A flat, lidded dish. Sometimes the main decoration is on the lid (e.g. fig. 4.27).

lekythos (pl. lekythoi)   A cylindrical pot with a narrow neck and vertical handle, used most often in funerary ritual as containers of oil or perfume (e.g. fig. 1.1). Many were made with false bottoms to economise on the amount of oil or perfume dedicated.

Lenaia   A religious festival held in January/February, in Athens and elsewhere, in honour of Dionysus as god of the winepress. At Athens it was celebrated with contests of drama, and women took part in ecstatic rites, with dancing and offerings of wine to an image of Dionysus.

loutrophoros (pl. loutrophoroi)   A tall pot used to bring water for ritual washing in the marriage ceremony; a girl carries a loutrophoros in the wedding procession illustrated in fig. 1.10. Loutrophoroi are very elongated, with long necks, bodies and feet. Many have been found in Athens, since they were often dedicated after the marriage at the Sanctuary of the Nymph on the Acropolis.

metic   From the Greek 'metoikos', a citizen of another state who settled in Athens as an alien. All metics, male and female, required an Athenian patron and paid a tax to the state each month; in return they enjoyed limited legal rights.

oinochoe (pl. oinochoai)   A general term for a jug, with a vertical handle for pouring; oinochoai vary in size, shape and design of mouth. The chous (pl. choes) is a particular type of oinochoe, with a squat body and narrow neck, used in the festival of the Anthesteria, the second day of which was called Choes. Choes were made in large and miniature sizes, the latter often buried in the graves of children (e.g. figs. 1.6 and 1.7).

onos (pl. onoi), also called epinetron (pl. epinetra)   A ceramic leg-protector used by women for the process of carding wool – drawing the fibre out to rid it of burrs and tangles (e.g. figs. 5.7 and 5.16). Onoi for everyday use had a rough surface to catch the fibre, and painted ones often use a scale pattern to suggest the rough surface.

Panathenaic amphora   An amphora given as a prize in the games at the Great Panathenaia in Athens. Panathenaic amphorae carry a standard decoration (Athena on one side, the event for which the prize was awarded on the other), and were given filled with Athenian olive oil.

pelike (pl. pelikai)   A sagging, bottom-heavy form of amphora, apparently modelled on skin containers such as wineskins (e.g. fig. 2.19).

phiale (pl. phialai)   A shallow bowl with a central indentation, which was made to be held in one hand (e.g. figs. 1.17 and 1.31). Phialai were used in ritual for pouring libations, and were often dedicated. Many silver phialai are found on the list of dedications to Athena Parthenos on the Acropolis.

phormiskos (pl. phormiskoi)   A small handleless flask with a very narrow neck and moulded base, similar in shape to a gourd or a leather pouch. Phormiskoi were used to sprinkle oil or water in funerary rites, and are very often decorated with funerary motifs.

pinax (pl. pinakes)   A terracotta plaque with painted decoration, often dedicated in sanctuaries of the gods, where they were hung on the wall (e.g. fig. 1.9).

plemochoe (pl. plemochoai)   The plemochoe (sometimes called exaleiptron) is a container with a tall foot and lid, and a pointed handle, apparently used to contain perfume. The shape is not found among extant pots, but is often illustrated in scenes with women (e.g. fig. 5.2).

psykter   An odd and relatively uncommon shape of pot, cylindrical with a swelling body, designed to float inside a larger pot and act as a wine cooler (illustrated on fig. 2.9). Opinion is divided as to whether the psykter was filled with cold water and floated in the wine, or vice versa.

pyxis (pl. pyxides)   A small round box with a lid, apparently based on wooden designs (e.g. figs. 4.9 and 5.8). Sometimes both body and lid are decorated, sometimes the lid only. Potters' marks can be seen on some, to assist the potter in matching pot and lid after firing.

rhyton (pl. rhyta)   A pottery shape based on a drinking-horn, often in the shape of an animal head; the decoration is found on the neck (e.g. fig. 5.21).

skyphos (pl. skyphoi)   A deep cup with two handles at the rim (e.g fig. 2.11).

stamnos (pl. stamnoi)   A rounded pot with a short neck and two horizontal handles. Stamnoi often show their own use in ritual, holding wine which is ladled into cups, as on fig. 1.33.

stele (pl. stelai)   The Greek name for a stone pillar or monument. Stelai were set up as grave markers (e.g. fig. 5.5), or to record honours, laws and other types of public business.

taenia   A ribbon or fillet, particularly one worn as a headband, illustrated in fig. 1.16.

Thesmophoria   A religious festival celebrated annually in Athens in honour of Demeter by women only: the festival took place over three days in the month Pyanopsion, during which the women took over the public spaces of the city, camping out on the Acropolis. They carried out rites involving sacrifice and ritual abuse to ensure the state's fertility for the coming year.

white-ground decoration   A scheme of decoration in which the clay (naturally red in colour in Attica) was covered by a white slip, and the design painted on top using a range of colours.

ABBREVIATIONS

Main sources

ABFV J. Boardman, *Athenian Black Figure Vases* (London, Thames & Hudson, 1974).

ABL C.H.E. Haspels, *Athenian Black-figured Lekythoi* (Paris, De Boccard, 1936).

ABV J.D. Beazley, *Attic Black-Figure Vase-Painters* (Oxford, Clarendon Press, 1956).

Add. T.H. Carpenter (ed.), *Beazley Addenda* (2nd edn) (Oxford, Oxford University Press, 1989).

APP J.H. Oakley, W. Coulson and O. Palagia (eds), *Athenian Potters and Painters: the conference proceedings* (Oxford, Oxbow Books, 1997).

ARFV J. Boardman, *Athenian Red Figure Vases: the archaic period* (London, Thames & Hudson, 1975).

ARV² J.D. Beazley, *Attic Red-Figure Vase-Painters* (2nd edn) (Oxford, Clarendon Press, 1963).

CAT C.W. Clairmont, *Classical Attic Tombstones* (7 vols) (Kilchberg, Akanthus, 1993).

CdI C. Bérard et al., *City of Images: iconography and society in ancient Greece* (tr. D. Lyons) (Princeton, Princeton University Press, 1989).

CP J. Boardman, *Athenian Red Figure Vases: the classical period* (London, Thames & Hudson, 1989).

CVA *Corpus Vasorum Antiquorum.*

EGVP J. Boardman, *Early Greek Vase Painting: a handbook* (London, Thames & Hudson, 1998).

EVP J.D. Beazley, *Etruscan Vase-Painting* (Oxford, Clarendon Press, 1947).

FaF F. Lissarrague, 'Femmes au figuré', in G. Duby, M. Perrot and P. Schmitt-Pantel (eds), *Histoire des Femmes en Occident*, vol. i: *L'Antiquité* (Paris, Plon, 1991), pp. 159–251.

FR A. Fürtwangler and K. Reichhold, *Griechische Vasenmalerei* i–iii (Munich, Bruckmann, 1900–23).

LGV T. Rasmussen and N. Spivey (eds), *Looking at Greek Vases* (Cambridge, Cambridge University Press, 1991).

LIMC *Lexicon Iconographicum Mythologiae Classicae* (Zürich and Munich, Artemis, 1981–).

Moon, W.G. Moon (ed.), *Ancient Greek Art and Iconography* (Madison, University
Iconography of Wisconsin Press, 1983).

Pandora	E.D. Reeder (ed.), *Pandora: women in classical Greece* (Princeton, Princeton University Press, 1995).
Para	J.D. Beazley, *Paralipomena* (Oxford, Clarendon Press, 1971).
Pfuhl	E. Pfuhl, *Malerei und Zeichnung der Griechen* (Munich, F. Bruckmann, 1923).
RE	A. von Pauly, rev. G. Wissowa et al., *Realencyclopädie der klassischen Altertumswissenschaft* (Stuttgart and Munich, Metzler/Druckenmüller, 1894–1980)
Richter/Hall	G.M.A. Richter and L.F. Hall, *Red-Figured Athenian Vases in the Metropolitan Museum of Art* (New Haven and London, Yale University Press and Oxford University Press, 1936).
RoP	E.C. Keuls, *The Reign of the Phallus: sexual politics in ancient Athens* (Berkeley, University of California Press, 1985) (2nd edn 1993).
Sutton, 'Interactions'	R.F. Sutton, Jr, 'The interactions between men and women portrayed on Attic red-figure pottery' (Diss., University of North Carolina at Chapel Hill, 1981).

Journals

AA	*Archäologischer Anzeiger*
ABSA	*Annual of the British School at Athens*
AION	*Annuali dell' Instituto orientale di Napoli*
AJA	*American Journal of Archaeology*
AK	*Antike Kunst*
AM	*Athenische Mitteilungen*
Anc. Soc.	*Ancient Society*
BCH	*Bulletin de Correspondance Hellénique*
CQ	*Classical Quarterly*
CSCA	*California Studies in Classical Antiquity*
CW	*Classical World*
G&R	*Greece and Rome*
HSCP	*Harvard Studies in Classical Philology*
JdI	*Jahrbuch des deutschen archäologischen Instituts*
JHS	*Journal of Hellenic Studies*
Mus. Helv.	*Museum Helveticum*
OJA	*Oxford Journal of Archaeology*
RA	*Revue Archéologique*
REA	*Revue des Etudes Anciennes*
ZPE	*Zeitschrift für Papyrologie und Epigraphik*

NOTES

INTRODUCTION

1 Hydria, A.D. Painter, London BM B329, *ABV* 334.1, fr. Vulci. See also figs. 2.15 and 2.16.

2 Hydria, Priam Painter, Boulogne 406, *ABV* 332.21, fr. Vulci.

3 W.G. Moon, 'The Priam Painter: some iconographic and stylistic considerations', in Moon, *Iconography* 97–118; J. Boardman, 'The sixth-century potters and painters of Athens and their public', in *LGV* 79–102.

4 Hydria, Priam Painter, London BM B32, *ABV* 333.27, fr. Vulci.

5 *ABV* nos. 334–5.1–8, *Para* 147–8.

6 Amphora, Amasis Painter, New York MM 31.10.11, *ABV* 154.57, fr. Vari. Illustrated in *ABFV* fig. 78, *CdI* fig. 123, *RoP* fig. 93a–b, *FaF* fig. 47, B.A. Sparkes, *The Red and the Black: studies in Greek pottery* (London 1996) fig. III.7, and many others.

7 A. Johnston, 'Greek vases in the marketplace', in *LGV* 203–32.

8 N.J. Spivey, 'Greek vases in Etruria', in *LGV* 131–50, pp. 149–50.

9 Sparkes, *The Red and the Black* ch. 2.

10 See E.C. Keuls, 'The *CVA*, the *LIMC* and the Beazley Archive Project: different databases for the study of Greek iconography', in E.C. Keuls, *Painter and Poet in Ancient Greece: iconography and the literary arts* (Stuttgart and Leipzig 1997) 293–312.

11 The Beazley catalogues and archive include Attic pots only: the main catalogues of other fabrics are: H.G.G. Payne, *Necrocorinthia* (Oxford 1931); D.A. Amyx, *Corinthian Vase-Painting of the Archaic Period* (Berkeley, Los Angeles and London 1988); K. Kilinski, *Boeotian Black-Figure Vase-Painting of the Archaic Period* (Mainz 1990); C.M. Stibbe, *Lakonische Vasenmaler des sechsten Jahrhunderts v. Chr.* (Amsterdam 1972); A.D. Trendall, *The Red-Figure Vases of Lucania, Campania and Sicily* (Oxford 1967); A.D. Trendall and A. Cambitoglou, *The Red-Figured Vases of Apulia* (Oxford 1978–82); J.D. Beazley, *Etruscan Vase-Painting* (Oxford 1947); N.J. Spivey, *The Micali Painter and His Followers* (Oxford 1987). The publication by John Boardman, *Early Greek Vase Painting: a handbook* (London, Thames and Hudson, 1998), is a welcome antidote to this trend, including as it does early black-figure in all fabrics.

12 This topic is debated in J. Whitley, 'Beazley as theorist', *Antiquity* 71 (1997) 40–7 and J.H. Oakley, 'Why study a Greek vase-painter? A response to Whitley . . .' *Antiquity* 72 (1998) 209ff.

13 The two are merged at *Para* 147.

14 A close examination of Beazley's lists is thought-provoking: did painters really 'specialise' in particular scenes, or is it more likely that once one fountain-scene (or departure scene or work scene) has been assigned to an artist, similarities will most easily be identified in similar types of scene?

15 Examples of this kind of approach are H. Hoffmann, *Sotades: symbols of immortality on Greek vases* (Oxford 1997); P. Schmitt-Pantel and F. Thelamon, 'Image et histoire: illustration ou document' in F. Lissarrague and F. Thelamon (eds.) *Image et Céramique Grecque: actes du colloque de Rouen, 25–6 novembre 1982* (Rouen 1983) 9–20. See the comments of J. Boardman, in 'Boy meets girl: an iconographic encounter', in *APP* 659–67, pp. 259–60.

16 V. Philippaki, *The Attic Stamnos* (Oxford 1967); D.C. Kurtz, *Athenian White Lekythoi: patterns and painters* (Oxford 1975); D. Buitron-Oliver, *Douris: a master-painter of Athenian red-figure*

vases (Mainz 1995); A. Lezzi-Hafter, *Der Eretria-Maler: Werke und Weggefährten* (Mainz 1988); M. Kilmer, *Greek Erotica on Athenian Red-Figure Vases* (London 1993); S. Pfisterer-Haas, *Darstellungen alter Frauen in der Griechischen Kunst* (Frankfurt 1989).

17 Hdt. 6.137; Thuc. 2.16; Ar. *Lys.* 327–31.

18 B. Dunkley, 'Greek fountain-buildings before 300 BC', *ABSA* 36 (1935/6) 142–204.

19 White-ground cup, Brussels A890, *ARV²* 771.1, fr. Athens.

20 M. Beard, 'Adopting an approach II', in *LGV* 12–35; the reference is to [Dem.] 59.122, often quoted out of context.

21 Kilmer, *Greek Erotica*, introduction. See further, Chapter 3, this volume.

22 Lekythos, Delos Heraion 548, *ABL* 199.1; L. Kahil, 'Autour de l'Artémis attique', *AK* 8 (1965) 20–33; 'Le cratérisque d'Artémis et le Brauronion de l'Acropole', *Hesperia* 50 (1981) 252–63; M. Lang, *The Athenian Agora vol. xxi: graffiti and dipinti* (Princeton 1976) 27–52.

23 Cup, New York MM 44.11.1, fr. Taranto, discussed in M.J. Milne, 'A prize for wool-working', *AJA* 49 (1945) 528–33; T.B.L. Webster, *Potter and Patron in Classical Athens* (London, 1972).

24 Hydria, Leningrad Painter, Milan, Torno coll. C278, *ARV²* 571.73, fr. Ruvo; calyx-krater, Nekyia Painter, New York MMA 08.258.21, *ARV²* 1086.1, n.p.

25 A. Stewart, 'Reflections', in N.B. Kampen, *Sexuality in Ancient Art* (Cambridge 1995) 136–54; Spivey, 'Greek vases in Etruria'; Beard, 'Adopting an approach II' 27; S. Lewis, 'Slaves as viewers and users of Athenian pottery', *Hephaistos* 16/17 (1998/9) 71–90.

1 BECOMING VISIBLE

1 See J. du Boulay, *Portrait of a Greek Mountain Village* (Oxford 1974) p. 131; the comments of D. Engels (*Classical Cats: the rise and fall of the sacred cat* (London 1999) p. 193 n. 29) are also instructive: 'In classicists' books on women one seldom encounters the fact that motherhood, family, childbirth and childrearing were central to the lives of nearly all women . . . the constraints on women in pre- and non-industrial societies are well known in other fields. See L.T. Ulrich, *A Midwife's Tale: the life of Martha Ballard* (New York, Vintage Books, 1990), which studies the diary of Martha Ballard, who lived in Massachusetts and Maine. Even during the early industrial era, her life centred on marriage, family, childbirth, childrearing, suffering, illness and death. Her (and other women's) main economic concerns were taking care of the household, together with carding, spinning, weaving, sewing and mending of cloth.'

2 Lekythos, Providence Painter, Oxford 1925.68, *ARV²* 641.87, fr. Gela.

3 Many of the images frequently cited in discussions of Athenian life are far from Athens in origin: several Apulian and Theran pots appear presented as Athenian evidence in discussions cited below.

4 See N.H. Demand, *Birth. Death and Motherhood in Classical Greece* (Baltimore 1994) 121–8; a Hellenistic stele in Alexandria (Demand pl. 10) shows a clearly pregnant woman.

5 Terracotta, Cyprus Museum, fr. Lapithos; see Demand, *Birth. Death and Motherhood* 89, V. Karageorghis, *The Cyprus Museum* (tr. A.H. and S. Foster Krumholz) (Nicosia 1989) 86, and S. Pingiatoglou, *Eileithyia* (Würzburg 1981) 243–4. *RoP* fig. 124 is an Attic votive of a woman giving birth.

6 For example, loutrophoros, Manner of Naples Painter, Karlsruhe Bad. Land. Mus. 69/78, *ARV²* 1102.2, *Para* 451, *Add.* 329, n.p.; loutrophoros, Pan Painter, Houston 37.10, *ARV²* 554.79, n.p. (*Pandora* no. 22); lebes gamikos, Amphitrite Painter, Paris Louvre S1671, *ARV²* 833.45, n.p. (*Cdl* fig. 13). See J.H. Oakley and R. Sinos, *The Wedding in Ancient Athens* (Madison 1993) 6–7, 15–20.

7 Demand, *Birth. Death and Motherhood* 17.

8 Ar. *Lys.* 746, *Ekkl.* 526–49, *Thesm.* 505–16.

9 See L. Beaumont, 'Born old or never young? Femininity, childhood and the goddesses of ancient Greece', in S. Blundell and M. Williamson (eds), *The Sacred and the Feminine in Ancient Greece* (London 1998) 71–95.

10 Pyxis, Athens NM 1635 (CC 1962), fr. Eretria; red-figure cup fr., coll. D. von Bothmer; see *LIMC* vol. VI 258 s.v. Leto.

11 Black-figure pinax, Berlin F1813, *ABV* 146.22, fr. Athens: see E. Fantham et al., *Women in the Classical World: image and text* (New York and Oxford 1994) fig. 1.4; children at fountain-house: hydria, A.D. Painter, Naples SA 12, *ABV* 334.3, fr. Vulci (*RoP* fig. 210); a black-figure amphora, Tarquinia Mus. Naz. 621, *ABV* 133.10, fr. Tarquinia, may show a small girl in a departure scene.

12 Hydria, Sackler Mus. 1960.342, fr. Vari; hydria, London BM E219, *ARV*² 1258.3, *Add.* 355, n.p. (*RoP* fig. 96).

13 White-ground lekythoi: Thanatos Painter, New Orleans, private coll., *ARV*² 1230.45, n.p.; Timokrates Painter, Athens 12771, *ARV*² 743.1, 1668, *Para* 521, fr. Eretria; New York 09.221.44, *ARV*² 1168.128, n.p. (*CP* fig. 268); see also London BM 1907.7–10.10, *ARV*² 1227.10, n.p.; Berlin 2443, *ARV*² 995.118, fr. Pikrodafni. See C. Sourvinou-Inwood, *Reading Greek Death to the End of the Classical Period* (Oxford 1995) 328–35.

14 Hydria, Harvard Sackler Mus. 1960.341, *ARV*² 617.13, fr. Vari (*Pandora* no. 52).

15 *RoP* 72–3, and E.C. Keuls, 'Attic vase-painting and the home textile industry', in Moon, *Iconography* 209–23, p. 216: 'girl children were conceptually non-existent'.

16 White-ground lekythos, Timokrates Painter, Athens 12771, *ARV*² 743.1, 1668, *Para* 521, fr. Eretria; red-figure lekythos, Manner of the Pistoxenos Painter, Oxford 320, *ARV*² 864.13, n.p. (*CP* fig. 70).

17 R.S.J. Garland, *The Greek Way of Life: from conception to old age* (London 1990) 81–3.

18 Hydria, Oinanthe Painter, London BM E182, *ARV*² 580.2, 1615, fr. Vulci (*Pandora* no. 67); terracotta, London BM Reg. 68.1–10.725, from Taras; stele, Paris Louvre Ma 2872 (= *CAT* 2.180). See also *RoP* fig. 120, a stele in Houston with a swaddled baby.

19 Stele of Ampharete: *IG* ii² 10650, Athens Kerameikos Museum, *CAT* 1.660, *RoP* fig. 118. See *CAT* vol. i 405 for comment on the gender of the infant. Stele of Phylonoe: *CAT* 2.780, Athens NM 3790; another stele in Leiden (1903.12.1) showing a baby handed to its mother by a nurse, demonstrates the difficulty of interpretations, since some scholars (*RoP* 139, *CAT* vol. ii 647) make the child male, while others (*Pandora* 136–7) assert that it is female.

20 We can contrast the child in the high chair on the white-ground cup, who reaches out to his mother, with the child shown alone on the red-figure chous, London BM GR 1910.6–15.4, fr. Athens (*JHS* 41 (1921) pl. 4). Swaddled baby: lekythos, Berlin F2444, *ARV*² 746.14, fr. Athens: see Chapter 5.

21 W. Burkert, *Homo Necans: the anthropology of ancient Greek sacrificial ritual and myth* (tr. P. Bing) (Berkeley 1983) 221; R. Hamilton, *Choes and Anthesteria: Athenian iconography and ritual* (Ann Arbor 1992) ch. 2 for a collection of testimonia.

22 Hamilton, *Choes and Anthesteria* p. 145 n. 68; cf. Demand, *Birth. Death and Motherhood* 7.

23 G. van Hoorn, *Choes and Anthesteria* (Leiden 1951).

24 Chous, Athens NM 1322 (CC1333) (van Hoorn cat. no. 41).

25 Chous, Munich Antikensammlung 2466 (van Hoorn cat. no. 708); chous, London BM (no no.), *JHS* 41 (1921) p. 148 fig. 14.

26 Chous, St Petersburg Hermitage P 1867.89 (ST 2259A) (van Hoorn no. 582); see Beaumont, 'Born old or never young?'

27 M. Golden, *Children and Childhood in Classical Athens* (Baltimore and London 1990) 135–6 (on sisters).

28 H. Rühfel, *Kinderleben im klassischen Athen: Bilder auf klassischen Vasen* (Mainz 1984) 45–61; A.E. Klein, *Child Life in Greek Art* (New York 1932) 28–30.

29 K. Stears, 'Dead women's society: constructing female gender in classical Athenian funerary sculpture', in N. Spencer (ed.), *Time. Tradition and Society in Greek Archaeology: bridging the 'great divide'* (London and New York 1995) 109–31, pp. 118–23.

30 Lekythos, Thanatos Painter, New Orleans, private coll., *ARV*² 1230.45, n.p.; lekythos, Harvard 59.221, *ARV*² 1232.11, fr. Attica.

31 Sappho fr. 83 and Erinna, *Distaff* (West, *ZPE* 25 (1977) 95–119).

32 Sophocles *Tereus* fr. 582.1–10; cf. *Trachiniai* 144–50.

33 Cup, New York MM 06.1021.167, *ARV*² 908.13, *Add.* 304, n.p. (Golden, *Children and Childhood* fig. 11); in the same context Golden illustrates a chous (London BM F101) which is Apulian, not Attic.

34 H.A. Shapiro, 'The iconography of mourning in Athenian art', *AJA* 95 (1991) 629–56; plaque, New York MMA 54.11.5 (*CdI* fig. 142).

35 Black-figure plaque, Dresden ZV814; J. Boardman, 'Painted funerary plaques and some remarks on prothesis', *ABSA* 50 (1955) 51–66.

36 Plaque, Sappho Painter, Paris Louvre MNB 905, *ABL* 229.58 (*ABFV* fig. 265).

37 Loutrophoros, Karlsruhe Bad. Land. Mus. 69/78, *ARV*^{2} 1102.2, *Para* 451, *Add.* 329, n.p.; volute-krater, Polygnotos, Ferrara T128, *ARV*^{2} 1052.25, 1680, fr. Spina (*RoP* fig. 312).

38 L. Kahil, 'Autour de l'Artémis attique', *AK* 8 (1965) 20–33; 'L'Artémis de Brauron: rites et mystère', *AK* 20 (1977) 86–98; 'Mythological repertoire of Brauron', in Moon, *Iconography* 231–44.

39 Frag. krater, Basel, Coll. H. Cahn, inv. HC501.

40 T. Linders, *Studies in the Treasure Records of Artemis Brauronia Found in Athens* (Stockholm 1972).

41 *LIMC* vol. II 676–7 s.v. Artemis.

42 See in general P. Brulé, *La Fille d'Athènes: le réligion des filles à Athènes à l'époque classique. Mythes, cultes et société* (Paris 1987). On Corinth, see p. 49, this volume.

43 *Anth. Pal.* VI.265.

44 Burkert, *Homo Necans* p. 241 n. 11.

45 Hydria, Pregny, coll. Rothschild, *ARV*^{2} 527.66, *Para* 383, n.p.

46 Lekythos, Brygos Painter, Paestum Mus. Naz. Arch. (no no.), *ARV*^{2} 384.212, fr. Paestum; M.C. Miller, 'The parasol: an oriental status-symbol in late archaic and classical Athens', *JHS* 112 (1992) 91–105.

47 Arrêphoroi: hydria fr., attr. Kleophon Painter, Tübingen E112, *ARV*^{2} 1147.61, *Add.* 335, n.p. (Rühfel fig. 56, Golden, *Children and Childhood* fig. 13).

48 M.R. Lefkowitz, 'The last hours of the parthenos', in *Pandora* 32–8.

49 Stears, 'Dead women's society'; C. Sourvinou-Inwood, *Studies in Girls' Transitions: aspects of the arkteia and age representation in Attic iconography* (Athens 1988) 31–66.

50 For further discussion of female hairstyles, with reference to slavery and sexual status, see Chapter 3.

51 L. Byvanck-Quarles van Ufford, 'La coiffure des jeunes dames d'Athènes au second quart du 5ième siècle av.J-C.', in H.A.G. Brijder et al. (eds), *Enthousiasmos: essays on Greek and related pottery presented to J.M. Hemelrijk* (Amsterdam 1986) 135–40.

52 An exhaustive list is not possible, but examples are: Artemis: white-ground lekythos, St Petersburg 670, *ARV*^{2} 557.121, n.p. (*Pandora* no. 90); bell-krater, Pan Painter, Boston 10.185, *ARV*^{2} 550.1, fr. Cumae; Athena: stamnos, Munich 2406, *ARV*^{2} 207.137, fr. Vulci; krater, Paris Louvre G341, *ARV*^{2} 601.22, fr. Orvieto (*CP* fig. 4) (and many other examples in van Ufford); Nereids: dinos, Achilles Painter, Würzburg K540, *ARV*^{2} 992.69, fr. Vulci; stamnos, Munich 8738, *ARV*^{2} 209.161, n.p.; Amymone: lekythos, Dresden Painter, Zurich, *ARV*^{2} 656.15, fr. Sicily (*Pandora* no. 111); Medea: hydria, Copenhagen Painter, London BM E163, *ARV*^{2} 258.26, fr. Vulci (*Pandora* no. 134).

53 Skyphos, PS Painter, private collection, *Para* 353.1, n.p. (*ARFV* fig. 205).

54 Stamnos, Copenhagen Painter, once Paris, *ARV*^{2} 257.17 (*Pandora* p. 93 fig. 2).

55 See, for example, lekythos, Timokrates Painter, Athens 1929, *ARV*^{2} 743.5, fr. Eretria (*ARFV* fig. 252).

56 Cup fr., Douris, Christchurch (NZ) AR 430, *ARV*^{2} 438.138, fr. Orvieto; cup, Douris, New York MM 23.160.54, *ARV*^{2} 441.186, n.p.

57 N. Himmelmann, *Archäologisches zum Problem der griechischen Sklaverei* (Wiesbaden 1971) 25–6.

58 Lekythos, Timokrates Painter, Athens 12771, *ARV*^{2} 743.1, 1668, fr. Eretria; lekythos, Nikon Painter, Brussels 1019A, *ARV*^{2} 652.3, fr. Eretria; krater, Orchard Painter, New York MM 07.286.74, *ARV*^{2} 523.1, *Add.* 126, n.p. (Fantham et al., *Women in the Classical World* fig. 3.23).

59 Lekythos, Bosanquet Painter, Berlin inv. 3291, *ARV*^{2} 1227.9, fr. Athens.

60 Alabastron, Glasgow Burrell collection 19.9; see also the pyxis, Eretria Painter, London BM E774, *ARV*^{2} 1250.32, *Para* 469, *Add.* 354, fr. Athens.

61 Alabastron, Paris, Bib. Nat. 508, *ARV*^{2} 1610, n.p.

62 S. Lewis, 'Slaves as viewers and users of Athenian pottery', *Hephaistos* 16/17 (1998/9) 71–90; Rühfel, *Kinderleben* 72.

63 Ar. *Thesm.* 1177–98; Xen. *Symp.* 2.1–2, 8, 11, 15.

64 Rühfel, *Kinderleben* 41–5; M.-H. Delavaud-Roux, *Les Danses armées en Grèce antique* (Aix-en-Provence 1993) 131–2; S.H. Lonsdale, *Dance and Ritual Play in Greek Religion* (Baltimore 1993) 9.

65 Phiale, Phiale Painter, Boston 97.371, *ARV²* 1023.146, fr. nr. Sunium.

66 Hydria, Polygnotos, Naples 3232, *ARV²* 1032.61, fr. Nola.

67 Early Apulian bell-krater, Berlin (Ost), (Rühfel, *Kinderleben* fig. 22); see also hydria, Washing Painter, London BM E203, *ARV²* 1131.164, fr. Nola and column-krater, Pig Painter, Lecce 572, *ARV²* 564.21, fr. Rugge. For terracottas see M.-H. Delavaud-Roux, *Les danses pacifiques en Grèce antique* (Aix-en-Provence 1994).

68 Training for Roman girls: *CIL* VI 9213 (gold-weaver, aged nine years), VI 10127 (actress, aged twelve years), VI 10131 (dancer, aged nine years); Xen. *Oik.* 7.41, Aeschin. 1.97.

69 *Hesperia* 28 (1959) 208–38 (4th cent. BC).

70 See further, Chapter 5.

71 Ar. *Thesm.* 289–91; *Ach.* 247ff.; *Peace* 111ff.; *Clouds* 60–74.

72 Dem. 39 and 40; Isae. 6.19–21; Dem. 47.55. See V.J. Hunter, *Policing Athens: social control in the Attic lawsuits, 420–320 BC* (Princeton 1994) ch. 1.

73 Kalpis, Nausicaa Painter, Heidelberg Universität 64.5, n.p.

74 See Oakley and Sinos, *The Wedding*, for a study of the iconography of the wedding.

75 *IG* i³ 1295 bis: Euthylla mourns Biote, her 'hetaira'; also Ar. *Lys.* 701 and *Ekkl.* 528.

76 Pyxis, Painter of Orvieto 191A, Sydney Nicholson Museum 53.06, *ARV²* 939.32, *Add.* 149, fr. Greece.

77 L.H. Petersen, 'Divided consciousness and female companionship: reconstructing female subjectivity in Greek vases', *Arethusa* 30 (1997) 35–74.

78 Isae. 2 (two sisters), 5 (Dicaeogenes has four married sisters), 6 (Philoktemon has two daughters and three sons); see Golden, *Children and Childhood* 135–6.

79 Lys. 3.6, Xen. *Mem.* 2.7.3.

80 Petersen, 'Divided consciousness'; *RoP* 85–6; M. Kilmer, *Greek Erotica on Attic Red-Figure Vases* (London 1993) 27–8.

81 Plate, Thera Museum (Petersen, 'Divided consciousness' fig. 13); pelike, Truro Painter, Taranto 4803 (*RoP* fig. 81); cup, Apollodoros, Tarquinia, *Para* 333.9bis, fr. Tarquinia (*RoP* fig. 151); cup fr., Douris, Leipzig T550, *ARV²* 438.139, n.p. (D. Buitron-Oliver, *Douris: a master-painter of Athenian red-figure vases* (Mainz 1995) p. 37 and cat. no. 183).

82 Arist. *EE* 1241b 7–9; also *NE* 1166a 8, 1168a 23, Xen. *Oik.* 7.24, *Mem.* 1.4.7, 2.2.5, Lycurg. *Leoc.* 101.

83 Lekythos, Phiale Painter, Athens 19355, from Anavyssos, *ARV²* 1022.139bis.

84 Hydria, Berlin F2395, from Attica (*FaF* fig. 27). See *FaF* p. 203, and L. Bonfante, 'Nursing mothers in classical antiquity', in A.O. Koloski-Ostrow and C.L. Lyons (eds), *Naked Truths: women, sexuality and gender in classical art and archaeology* (London/New York 1997), 174–96.

85 Neck-amphora, Kleophrades Painter, Munich J411, *ARV²* 182.4, *Add.* 186, fr. Vulci. For a collection of examples, see F. Lissarrague, *L'Autre Guerrier: archers, peltastes, cavaliers dans l'imagerie attique* (Paris and Rome 1990) ch. 3, and 'The world of the warrior', in *CdI* 38–51.

86 Armour: lekythos, Providence Painter, London E572, fr. Gela (spear and helmet), *ARV²* 641.82; lekythos, Providence Painter Palermo V676, *ARV²* 641.83, fr. Gela (corselet); lekythos, Palermo MN 277, fr. Gela?; lekythos, Achilles Painter, London D51, *ARV²* 1000.201, fr. Marion. See Lissarrague, *L'Autre Guerrier* 43–7.

87 Lissarrague, *L'Autre Guerrier* 66 and 90 for gesture of awe.

88 Stamnos, Kleophon Painter, St Petersburg ST 1428, *ARV²* 1143.3, n.p. (*Pandora* no. 18); also stamnos, Kleophon Painter, Munich 2415, *ARV²* 1143.2, fr. Vulci (*CP* fig. 172).

89 Neck-amphora, Niobid Painter, Oxford 280, *ARV²* 604.56, fr. Nola.

90 Lissarrague, *L'Autre Guerrier* 43–4, 89–91.

91 Ar. *Lys.* 651, 590; *Ekkl.* 232–3; Plut. *Mor.* 241D (and in general 241A–242B).

92 For Amphiareos see *LIMC* vol. i pp. 691–713, and H.A. Shapiro, *Myth into Art: poet and painter in classical Greece* (London and New York 1994) 90.

93 N. Loraux, *Mothers in Mourning* (tr. C. Pache) (Ithaca 1998) 9–28; *RoP* 147–8.

94 Ôon, Athens, Stathatou coll. 332, from nr. Athens, *ARV*² 1257.2, *Para* 470; see commentary in Oakley and Sinos, *The Wedding* p. 134 n. 53.

95 Demand, *Birth, Death and Motherhood* 4, 15–17.

96 Hdt. 1.61.2; Andok.1.124–5.

97 C. Sourvinou-Inwood, 'Male and female, public and private, ancient and modern', in *Pandora* 111–20.

98 N. Spivey, 'Greek vases in Etruria', in *LGV* 142–50, esp. 148.

99 Lekythos, Providence Painter, Tübingen 7319 (O.Z.119), *ARV*² 642.110, fr. Greece; lekythos, Bowdoin Painter, Würzburg H4978, *ARV*² 686.204, fr. Spata (*CP* 58); cup, Painter of London E80, Louvre G477, *ARV*² 815.2, n.p.

100 Cup, Villa Giulia Painter, Oxford 1973.1, n.p. (*JHS* 94 (1974) pls. 17–18); dish, Dish Painter, Copenhagen Nat. Mus. 6, *ARV*² 787.3, fr. Nola.

101 Cup, Triptolemos Painter, Tarquinia Mus. Arch. RC 1918, fr. Tarquinia, *ARV*² 366.88 (*CdI* fig. 33); see F. Lissarrague, 'Un rituel du vin: la libation', in O. Murray and M. Tecuşan (eds), *In Vino Veritas* (London 1995) 126–44, p. 134 n. 32 for other examples.

102 Cup, Paris Louvre G477, *ARV*² 815.2, *Add.* 292 (women); cup, Bordeaux Painter, Sotheby's (NY) (domestic); cup, Villa Giulia Painter, New York MM 1979.11.15, n.p. (Eos and Tithonos).

103 Athletes: cup, Boot Painter, Paris Louvre S1329, *ARV*² 822.15, n.p.; school scene: cup, Athens NM 12462, *ARV*² 959.2, n.p.; symposium: cup, London BM E100, *ARV*² 834.1, fr. Vulci.

104 Cup, Amphitrite Painter, Berlin F2299, *Para* 422, fr. Vulci (see Lissarrague, 'Un rituel du vin').

105 Cup, London BM E100, *ARV*² 834.1, fr. Vulci (symposium); cup, New York MM GR596, *ARV*² 834.2, fr. Capua (courting); cup, Berkeley, Robert L. Howie Mus. 8.923, *ARV*² 810.22, fr. near Falerii (courting); cup, manner of Antiphon Painter, Basel Market, *ARV*² 1646F, *Para* 362 (men and youths).

106 Cup, Makron, Toledo 72.55 (*Pandora* no. 38).

107 M. Beard, 'Adopting an approach II', in *LGV* 28–30; *Pandora* 187.

108 Alabastron, Copenhagen inv. 3830, *ARV*² 723.1, fr. Attica.

109 Argive krater, Argos C26611; R. Hägg, 'A scene of funerary cult from Argos', in Hägg (ed.), *The Iconography of Greek Cult in the Archaic and Classical Periods* [Kernos Suppl. 1] (Athens-Liège 1992) 169–76.

110 Column-krater, Orchard Painter, Naples 3369, *ARV*² 523.9, n.p.; krater, Boreas Painter, Bologna 206, *ARV*² 537.12, fr. Bologna.

111 Terracottas: R. Higgins, *Greek Terracottas* (London 1967) 78, and F.T. van Straten, *Hiera Kala: images of animal sacrifice in archaic and classical Greece* (Brill 1995) 56–7; votive reliefs: van Straten, *Hiera Kala* sect. 2.2.3.

112 Klazomenian amphora, Berlin inv. 4530; see Delavaud-Roux, *Les danses pacifiques* 100–11; Alcman 1.39–101, Sappho fr. 47.

113 Black-figure amphora, Painter of Berlin 1686, Berlin 1686 *ABV* 296.4, fr. Vulci; black-figure hydria, Nikoxenos Painter, once Rome Market, *ABV* 393.20, n.p.

114 *APF* 4549. See D.M. Lewis, 'Notes on Attic inscriptions II', *ABSA* (1955) 1–36, pp. 1–12; Sourvinou-Inwood, 'Male and female' 114–16; Thuc. 2.2.1 and 4.133.

115 See *CdI* 112, and J. Neils (ed.) *Goddess and Polis: the Panathenaic festival in ancient Athens* (Hanover, N.H. 1992).

116 Pelike, Pan Painter, Newcastle Shefton Museum, *ARV*² 1659, *Para* 386; see also Higgins, *Greek Terracottas* 77.

117 Corinthian jug, London BM 1865.7–20.20; see I. Jucker, 'Frauenfest in Korinth', *Antike Kunst* 6 (1963) 47–61.

118 C. Sheffer, 'Boeotian festival scenes: competition, consumption and cult in archaic black-figure', in Hägg, *Iconography of Greek Cult*, 117–41.

119 Phiale, Boston 65.908, n.p.

120 Lekythos, Athens 1695, *ARV*² 1204.2, n.p. (*RoP* fig. 295); black-figure band-cup, London BM 1906.12–15.1, *ABV* 90.7, fr. Camiros (*JHS* 66 (1946) pls. 2–3).

121 Squat lekythos, Berlin 3248, *ARV²* 1482.5, fr. Apollonia; Ar. *Lys.* 389 and Henderson note ad loc.

122 Stamnos, Villa Giulia Painter, Oxford V523, *ARV²* 621.41, *Add.* 270, fr. Gela; see F. Frontisi-Ducroux, *Le Dieu-masque: une figure du Dionysos d'Athènes* (Paris 1991) ch. 4. The claim in *CdI* (p. 124) with reference to a stamnos in the Villa Giulia (983, *ARV²* 621.33, fr. Falerii) that the painter was envisaging the women as waiting on a nearby banquet which he did not depict is groundless. (J.-L. Durand, F. Frontisi-Ducroux and F. Lissarrague, 'Wine: human and divine', in *CdI* 121–9.)

123 Cup, Makron, Berlin F2290, *ARV²* 462.48, fr. Vulci.

124 *RoP* 375.

125 Skyphos, Penelope Painter, Berlin 2589, fr. Chiusi, *ARV²* 1301.7.

126 Most obviously in Euripides' *Bacchae*.

127 See S. McNally, 'The maenad in early Greek art', in J. Peradotto and J.P. Sullivan, *Women in the Ancient World. The Arethusa papers* (Albany 1984), and R. Osborne, 'Desiring women on Athenian pottery', in N.B. Kampen (ed.), *Sexuality in Ancient Art* (Cambridge 1996) 65–80.

128 Adonia: Thrace: squat lekythos, Berlin 3248, *ARV²* 1482.5, fr. Apollonia; squat lekythos, St Petersburg 928, *ARV²* 1482.6; Cyrenaica: hydria, London BM E241, *ARV²* 1482.1; Naucratis: lekythos, London BM E721; Ruvo: squat lekythos, Karlsruhe 278 (*CdI* fig. 131); Attica: hydria, Athens 1179, *ARV²* 1312.3; lekanis, unknown; squat lekythos, Paris Louvre MNB 2109, *ARV²* 1175.7; lekythos, Athens Akropolis 6471, *ARV²* 1175.11; Greece: lebes, Paris Louvre CA1679, *ARV²* 1179.3.

129 Loutrophoros, Painter of Bologna 228, Athens NM 1170, *ARV²* 512.13, *Para* 382, fr. Pikrodafni.

130 Lekythos, Painter of the Yale Lekythos, Naples H3353, *ARV²* 659.54, 676.7, fr. Nocera de' Pagani; hydria fr., Athens Akr. 1009, *ARV²* 215.13, fr. Athens; lekythos, London BM GR 1922.10–18.1, *ARV²* 332.1, fr. Sicily (S. Pfisterer-Haas, *Darstellungen alter Frauen in der Griechischen Kunst* (Frankfurt 1989) fig. 137); kalpis, Pan Painter, Hamburg private coll.: see *LIMC* vol. iv 481, s.v. Hekale.

131 Skyphos, Pistoxenos Painter, Schwerin Mus., *ARV²* 862.30, fr. Cervetri; skyphos, Penelope Painter, Chiusi 1831, *ARV²* 1300.2, fr. Chiusi. See Pfisterer-Haas, *Darstellungen*.

132 Amphora, Paris Louvre G46, *ARV²* 220.3, n.p. (Lissarrague, *L'Autre Guerrier* p. 64 fig. 34).

133 Pfisterer-Haas, *Darstellungen* p. 8 and n. 28.

134 Stele of Ampharete: see n. 19.

135 Graiai: Hes. *Theog.* 270–3, Pherekydes *FGrH* 3 F11, *LIMC* vol. iv 362–4; Moirai: *LIMC* vol. vi 636–48; black-figure volute-krater, Florence 4209, *ABV* 76.1, 682, fr. Chiusi (François Vase).

136 Dem. 55.23–4, 47.55.

137 J. Bremmer, 'The old women of ancient Greece', in J. Blok and P. Mason (eds), *Sexual Asymmetry: studies in ancient society* (Amsterdam 1987) 191–215, pp. 198–9.

138 Ar. *Ekkl.* 877–end; Plut. *Kimon* 14. Old age for men is also characterised by physical deformity on the pelike depicting Herakles and Geras, Villa Giulia 48238, *ARV²* 284.1, fr. Cervetri.

139 Plut. *Thes.* 9 on the sow; see *LIMC* vol. vi 139–42, s.v. Krommyo.

140 Terracotta, Paris Louvre MNB 1003; Pfisterer-Haas, *Darstellungen* 55–64 and Higgins, *Greek Terracottas* 103.

141 See P. Wolters and G. Bruns, *Das Kabirenheiligtum bei Theben* vol. i (Berlin 1940) 95–128, and K. Braun, *Bemalte Keramik und Glas aus dem Kabirenheiligtum bei Theben* (Berlin 1981) 1–74.

142 Bremmer, 'Old women' 203.

143 Lys. 1.6–7, 15, Dem. 37.45 and 59.22; see V.J. Hunter, 'The Athenian widow and her kin', *Journal of Family History* 14 (1989) 291–311.

144 K. Stears, 'Death becomes her: gender and Athenian death-ritual', in S. Blundell and M. Williamson (eds), *The Sacred and the Feminine in Ancient Greece* (London 1998) 113–27, 123.

2 DOMESTIC LABOUR

1 Cup, Steiglitz Painter, Florence 3918, *ARV*² 827.7, n.p.; cup, Douris, Berlin 2289, *ARV*² 435.95, fr. Vulci; pyxis, Painter of Philadelphia 2449, New York MM 06.1117, *ARV*² 815.3, *Add.* 292, fr. Athens (see fig. 2.3); skyphos, Phiale Painter, Palermo Mormino coll. 788 (*Pandora* p. 72 fig. 20).

2 J. Boardman, 'The sixth-century potters and painters of Athens and their public', in *LGV* 79–102, pp. 97–8.

3 Xen. *Oik.* 7.24, 7.37; the importance of women in caring for the sick is also indicated at [Dem.] 59.56.

4 See C. Davidson, *A Woman's Work is Never Done: a history of housework in the British Isles 1650–1950* (London 1982).

5 J. Hartley, *Understanding News* (London 1982) ch. 5.

6 Sisyphus, also condemned to eternal labour, has a more neutral task, although there is also the figure of Oknos (another painter's theme) who makes a rope which is immediately eaten by his ass. E.C. Keuls, 'The ass in the cult of Dionysus as a symbol of toil and suffering', *in Painter and Poet in Ancient Greece: iconography and the literary arts* (Stuttgart and Leipzig 1997) 41–70, sees the task of the Danaidai as a rite of passage for initiates, and a symbol of the unending toil of the non-initiated (49–58).

7 *Inscr. Creticae* 4.72 ii. 45–54; see S.B. Pomeroy, *Xenophon's Oeconomicus: a social and historical commentary* (Oxford 1994), 61–4.

8 Stamnos, Copenhagen Painter, once Paris, *ARV*² 257.17, fr. Vulci (*Pandora* p. 93 fig. 2); pyxis, Louvre CA 587, *ARV*² 1094.104, fr. Greece. Another possible explanation relates this to the display of evidence of the bride's virginity, but there is no unambiguous depiction of such a practice in Greek art.

9 Hydria, Rhodes 13261, *ARV*² 571.82, fr. Camiros (E. C. Keuls, 'Attic vase-painting and the home textile industry', in Moon, *Iconography* 209–23, p. 227 fig. 14.37); hydria, Painter of the Yale Oinochoe, Houston 80.95 (see P.J. Holliday, 'Red-figure hydria: a theme in Greek vase-painting', *Bulletin of the Museum of Fine Arts, Houston* 8.3 (1984) 2–7).

10 Xen. *Oik.* 7.35; Erinna *Distaff* 23–4, see M.L. West, 'Erinna', *ZPE* 25 (1977) 95–119; the role of lanipendes is also found in Roman imperial occupations (S. Treggiari, 'Jobs for women', *AJAH* 1 (1976) 76–104, pp. 83–4).

11 See n. 1; cup, New York MM 44.11.1, fr. Taranto (M.J. Milne, 'A prize for wool-working', *AJA* 49 (1945) 528–33).

12 P.E. Benbow, 'Epinetra' (Harvard diss. 1975): summary at *HSCP* 80 (1976) 290–1.

13 Hydria, Group of Polygnotos, Harvard Sackler Museum 1960.342, fr. Vari; skyphos, Penelope Painter, Chiusi 1831, *ARV*² 1300.2, fr. Chiusi.

14 Livy 1.57.8–11.

15 Keuls, 'Attic vase-painting' 219 and n. 8.

16 Skyphos, Malibu Getty Museum 85.AE.304, n.p.

17 Hes. *WD* 373–4, 704, *Th.* 594ff.; Semonides 7.24, 45–6, 55; see L.S. Sussman, 'Workers and drones: labor, idleness and gender definition in Hesiod's beehive', *Arethusa* 11 (1978) 27–41.

18 Euboulus (fr. 65) wrote a play entitled Μυλῶθρις [Milleress]; see R. Brock, 'The labour of women in classical Athens', *CQ* 44 (1994) 336–46.

19 B.A. Sparkes, 'The Greek kitchen: addenda', *JHS* 85 (1965) 162–3, p. 163.

20 Ar. *Lys.* 643, and Schol.

21 Cup, Makron, Laon 37.1055, *ARV*² 812.59 bis, n.p.; lekythos, Athens 1912 (CC1648), *ARV*² 747.25, fr. Athens.

22 R. Osborne, 'Economy and trade', in *Cambridge Ancient History: plates to vols IV and V* (Cambridge 1994) 92: 'Finds of grinding stones in domestic contexts, notably at Olynthus, suggest that many households ground their own grain and produced their own bread.'

23 Cup, Berlin 1966.21, n.p.

24 Terracottas: Lausanne, Marion Schuster collection; London BM 234; London BM 233. See B.A. Sparkes, 'The Greek kitchen', *JHS* 82 (1962) 121–37.

25 Amphora, St Petersburg 2065, *ABV* 309.95, n.p.; frr., Eleusis Arch. Mus., fr. Eleusis; cf.

Pausan. 5.18.2; cup frr., Onesimos, New York D. von Bothmer coll. 27592, *Para* 360.93 quater, n.p.

26 Death of Orpheus: hydria, Paris, Petit Palais 319, *ARV*² 1112.4, fr. Nola; hydria, Würzburg 534, *ARV*² 1123.7, fr. Athens; pelike, Myson, Munich 8762, *ARV*² 1638.2 bis, n.p. (*RoP* fig. 327); stamnos, Rome Basseggio 0.2122, *ARV*² 215.12, n.p. Andromache: cup, Onesimos, Malibu Getty Museum 83.AE.362, *Add.* 404; column-krater, Tyszkiewicz Painter, Rome Villa Giulia 3578, *ARV*² 290.2, 1642, fr. Falerii; cup, Brygos Painter, Paris Louvre G152, *ARV*² 369.1, fr. Vulci. See H.-G. Buchholz, 'Morsersymbolik', *Acta Praehistorica et Archaeologica* 7/8 (1976/77) 249–70, and *RoP* 379.

27 Lekythos, Vienna Kunsthistorisches Museum inv. 4.1921; cup, Brygos Painter, Florence PD425, *ARV*² 376.84, *Para* 366, n.p.; cup, Akestorides Painter, Paris Louvre G476, *ARV*² 782 (B.A. Sparkes, 'Not cooking but baking', *G&R* 28 (1981) 172–8); lekanis, St Petersburg St.1791, *ARV*² 1476.3, fr. Kerch (J.H. Oakley and R.H. Sinos, *The Wedding in Ancient Athens* (Madison 1993) fig. 44); lekythos, Haverford College, *ARV*² 557.116, 1659, n.p.

28 Lekythos, Athens NM Serpieri Coll. 121.

29 Skyphos, Athens, Canellopoulos inv. 384, see J.-J. Maffré, 'Collection Paul Canellopoulos VIII: vases béotiens', *BCH* 99 (1975) 409–520, pp. 467–76. On the name Kodomê, toaster of grain, see Pollux 1.246, 6.64, 7.181.

30 Krater, Louvre E632 (D.A. Amyx, *Corinthian Vase-Painting of the Archaic Period* vol. ii (Berkeley 1988) 233–4, pl. 102 1b); dinos, Boston 13.205 (J. Boardman, *Early Greek Vase Painting: a handbook* (London 1998) fig. 492). On flute music, cf. Plut. *Mor.* 157e: L.A. Moritz, *Grain-mills and Flour in Classical Antiquity* (Oxford 1958) 31.

31 Grinding or pounding grain: see note 19; also NY MM 56.43; kneading dough: Athens NM 4044; Boston MFA 01.7783; cooking: Boston MFA 01.7788; cakes and loaves to oven: Brussels, Musées Royaux inv. 2164B; Athens NM 4756; watching cakes: Berlin SM 31.644; Louvre MNB 812; bakery scenes: Athens NM 4431 and 5773. See Sparkes, 'Greek kitchen' and 'Greek kitchen add.'.

32 R. Higgins, *Greek Terracottas* (London 1967) 77, and *Tanagra and the Figurines* (London 1986) 84–8.

33 Cup, Makron, Paris Louvre CP 10918, *ARV*² 467.130, *Para* 378, n.p.

34 Stand, Toledo Museum of Art 1958.69B, *Para* 168. Cf. cup by Onesimos (see n. 25) on which a youth and a woman pound grain together.

35 See R. Osborne, 'Women and sacrifice in classical Greece', *CQ* 43 (1993) 392–405; A. Dalby, 'Food and sexuality in classical Greece', in *Food, Culture and History* 1 (1993) 165–90. Pherekrates fr. 70 claims that one never finds a female butcher or fishmonger, although as comic evidence this is not strong.

36 Legs of meat as gifts: pyxis, Veii Painter, Mt Holyoke 1932 BS.II.5, *ARV*² 906.109, n.p.; pelike, Naples 81614, *ARV*² 778. Woman feeds dog: lekythos, Providence Painter, Rome Accademia dei Lincei 2478, *ARV*² 642, n.p.

37 Medea and daughters of Pelias: lekythos, Beldam Painter, Erlangen University I429, *ABL* 267.19, n.p.; also Athens NM 599, *ABL* 268.56, n.p. (*ABFV* fig. 278); Athens NM E1556, *ABL* 269.57, n.p.; Athens NM 12805, *ABL* 269.58; neck-amphora, London BM B221, *ABV* 321.4; stamnos, Hephaisteon Painter, Berlin F2188, *ABV* 297.1, fr. Vulci (Sparkes, 'Greek kitchen add.' pl. 31). See H. Meyer, *Medeia und den Peliaden: eine attische Novelle und ihre Entstehung* (Rome 1980), and M. Schmidt, 'Medea at work', in G.R. Tsetskhladze et al. (eds), *Periplous: papers on classical art and archaeology presented to Sir John Boardman* (London 2000) 263–70. Circe, e.g. lekythos, Taranto Mus. Naz. 20324, *ABL* 199; pelike, Ethiop Painter, Dresden 323, *ARV*² 665.4, n.p.; cup, Boston MFA 99.519, *ABV* 69; calyx-krater, Persephone Painter, New York MM 41.83, *ARV*² 1012.3, fr. near Taranto. See M. Schmidt, 'Sorceresses', in *Pandora* 57–62.

38 There is obviously a spectrum of washing scenes, from women working to women and youths depicted naked at a laver. Here I am interested in washing as a domestic chore; I will return to erotic washing scenes in Chapter 4.

39 Hydria, Naples SA 12, *ABV* 334.3, fr. Vulci. See B. Dunkley, 'Greek fountain-buildings before 300 BC', *ABSA* 36 (1935/6) 142–204; L. Hannestad, 'Slaves and the fountain-house theme', in H.A.G. Brijder (ed.), *Ancient Greek and Related Pottery* (Amsterdam 1984) 252–5;

W.G. Moon, 'The Priam Painter: some iconographic and stylistic considerations', in Moon, *Iconography* 97–118. Gods as onlookers: London BM B332, *ABV* 333.27.

40 For example, hydria, Würzburg L304, *ABV* 678, fr. Vulci, and hydria, Antimenes Painter, Vatican 426, *ABV* 266.2, fr. Vulci; hydria, Florence 3792.

41 I. Manfrini-Aragno, 'Femmes à la fontaine: réalité et imaginaire', in C. Bron and E. Kassapoglou (eds), *L'image en jeu: de l'antiquité à Paul Klee* (Yens-sur-Morges 1992).

42 Moon 'The Priam Painter' 109–10; E. Diehl, *Die Hydria: Formgeschichte und Verwendung in Kult des Altertums* (Mainz 1964) 182ff.; Hannestad, 'Slaves' 255.

43 N.J. Spivey, 'Greek vases in Etruria', in *LGV* 131–50, pp. 142–8.

44 Cup, Brygos Painter, Milan Mus. Arch. 266, *ARV²* 379.145, n.p.; see G. Richter, 'The woman at the well in Milan', *RA* (1935) 200–5; M. Philippaert, 'Deux vases attiques inédits', *RA* (1933), 154–62.

45 Cup, Brygos Painter, Florence 76103, *ARV²* 379.142, fr. Chiusi; cup, Brygos Painter, Vienna Univ. 502, *ARV²* 377.109, fr. Orvieto; pelike, Pan Painter, St Petersburg (B. Follmann, *Der Panmaler* (Bonn 1968) cat. no. (d) and pl. 1.2).

46 Pelike, Pan Painter, Madrid 11201, *ARV²* 554.86, n.p.; pelike, Pan Painter, Paris Louvre G547, *ARV²* 555.89, n.p.; cup, Douris, Vatican Astarita 760, *ARV²* 444.249, n.p. (S. Lewis, 'Shifting images: Athenian women in Etruria', in K. Lomas and T. Cornell (eds), *Gender and Ethnicity in Ancient Italy* (London 1997) fig. 18).

47 Cup frr., Brygos Painter, Leipzig T530, *ARV²* 377.102, fr. Orvieto; cup, Paris, Bib. Nat. 652, *ARV²* 377.103, n.p.

48 Cup, Douris, New York 1986.322.1; cup, Douris, Boston 97.369, *ARV²* 444.248, fr. Falerii; cup, Tarquinia RC1116, *ARV²* 445.250, fr. Tarquinia; cup fr., Brygos Painter, Adria Museo Civico BC70, *ARV²* 389.21 bis, fr. Adria; cup, Frankfurt B405, *ARV²* 396.12, *Add.* 230, n.p.; cup, Painter of the Yale Lekythos, London E90, *ARV²* 662.96, *Para* 1664, fr. Nola; cup, Copenhagen Thorvaldsen's Museum 115, *ARV²* 455.2, *Add.* 243, fr. Vulci.

49 F. Lissarrague and J.-L. Durand, 'Un lieu d'image: l'espace du loutérion', *Hephaistos* 2 (1980) 89–106.

50 Cup, Eucharides Painter, Munich 2679, *ARV²* 231.85, n.p.

51 Cup, Euergides Painter, Boston 10.214, *ARV²* 94.103, fr. Tarquinia.

52 Pyxis, Aison, Boston MFA 04.18, *ARV²* 1177.48, fr. Athens; neck-amphora, Nausicaa Painter, Munich 2332, *ARV²* 1107.2, fr. Vulci.

53 A.D. Ure, 'Boeotian vases with women's heads', *AJA* 57 (1953) 245–9, p. 246, pl. 66.2 and pl. 67.5 (Louvre CA 1341).

54 Cup, Onesimos, Brussels A889, *ARV²* 329.130, fr. Chiusi.

55 M. Robertson, 'Two pelikai by the Pan Painter', *Greek Vases from the J. Paul Getty Museum* 3 (1986) 71–90.

56 Xen. *Oik.* 7.35–6, 7.41, 10.10; Dem. 47.56; Lys. 1.16; comedy: Ar. *Lys.* 18, *Thesm.* 279ff.

57 S. Lewis, 'Slaves as viewers and users of Athenian pottery', *Hephaistos* 16/17 (1998/9) 71–90.

58 A. Ashmead, 'Bread and soup for dinner: a lekythos by the Pan Painter at Haverford College', in J.-P. Descoedres (ed.), *Eumousia: ceramic and iconographic studies in honour of A. Cambitoglou* (Sydney 1990) 95–103.

59 Hydria, Aigisthos Painter, Paris Louvre CA 2587, *ARV²* 506.29, n.p. K. Zimmermann, 'Tätowierte Thrakerinnen auf griechischen Vasenbildern', *JdI* 95 (1980) 163–96.

60 See Ashmead, 'Bread', and also G. Davies, 'The language of gesture in Greek art: gender and status on grave stelai', *Apollo* 140, no. 389 (1994) 6–11, for the suggestion that close relationships between citizen women and their servants are indicated in funerary art.

61 M. Golden, *Children and Childhood in Classical Athens* (Baltimore and London 1990) 82–99. See also H. Rühfel, *Kinderleben im klassischen Athen: Bilder auf klassischen vasen* (Mainz 1984).

62 Choes: see R. Hamilton, *Choes and Anthesteria: Athenian iconography and ritual* (Ann Arbor 1992) ch. 3; G. van Hoorn, *Choes and Anthesteria* (Leiden 1951). Toddlers on pots: pyxis, Leningrad Painter, Athens NM TE1623, *Para* 391, fr. Athens; pyxis, Manchester University 40096, *ARV²* 931.1, n.p.

63 Pyxis, Dallas Mus. of Art 1968.28.A (*RoP* fig. 97); hydria, Munich SL476, *ARV²* 1083.2, n.p. (*RoP* fig. 219); cup, once Berlin 4282, *ARV²* 644.134, n.p. (*RoP* fig. 98).

64 *CAT* vol. i 292–3; examples of parent/child affection are *CAT* 1.610, 1.630, 1.660, 1.690, 1.700, 1.714, 1.715, 1.763, 1.771, 1.786, 1.867, 2.650, 2.780, 2.851, 2.871; see K.E. Stears, 'Dead women's society: constructing female gender in classical Athenian funerary sculpture', in N. Spencer (ed.), *Time, Tradition and Society in Greek Archaeology: bridging the 'great divide'* (London and New York, 1995) 109–31; also K.E. Stears, 'Women and the family in the funerary ritual and art of classical Athens', Diss. London 1993.

65 See n. 61.

66 Cup, Sabouroff Painter, Amsterdam Allard Pierson Museum 8210, *ARV²* 838.27, n.p. (Golden, *Children and Childhood* fig. 10).

67 S.G. Cole, 'The social function of rituals of maturation: the Koureion and the Arkteia', *ZPE* 55 (1984) 233–44, p. 239 and n. 32.

68 Terracotta, Boston MFA 01.7788; plaque, Acropolis Museum 2525.

69 A. Giddens, *Beyond Left and Right: the future of radical politics* (Cambridge 1994) 161; S. Coontz and P. Henderson (eds), *Women's Work, Men's Property: the origins of gender and class* (London 1985) 77–81.

70 J. du Boulay, *Portrait of a Greek Mountain Village* (Oxford 1974) 131.

71 D. Cohen, *Law, Sexuality and Society: the enforcement of morals in classical Athens* (Cambridge 1991) 162–6.

72 Ploughing scenes: cup, Louvre F77 (*JHS* 34 (1914) p. 251 fig. 1); amphora, New York private coll. (J. Boardman, *The Oxford History of Classical Art* (Oxford 1993) p. 72, fig. 67); lebes, Eleusis 1231 (*RA* 25 (1946) p. 213 fig. 1); bell-krater, Hephaistos Painter, Harvard Sackler Museum 60.345, *ARV²* 1115.30, *Para* 453, fr. Vari; cup, London BM 1906.12–15.1, *ABV* 90.7, fr. Camiros; cup, Berlin F1806, *ABV* 223.66, *Para* 104, fr. Vulci. Herding animals: kyathos, Paris Louvre F69, *ABV* 349, fr. Vulci; cup, Dokimasia Painter, Bologna Museo Civico 366, *ARV²* 412.9, fr. Bologna.

73 Lekythos, Naples H3353, *ARV²* 659.54, 676.7, fr. Nocera de' Pagani (see p. 54); cup, Douris, Berlin Pergamonmuseum F2306; chous, Athens 1654 (Golden, *Children and Childhood* fig. 7).

74 Pelike, Hasselmann Painter, London BM E819, *ARV²* 1137.25, fr. Nola; see J.J. Winkler, *The Constraints of Desire: the anthropology of sex and gender in ancient Greece* (London 1990) 206.

75 Fruit-trees: Haimon Group: Braunschweig AT 700 (331493), *ABV* 554.400, fr. Eretria (fig. 2.31); Zurich 2488; Hannover 1966.32; Baltimore 48.245, *ABV* 554.401; Madrid 10960 bis, *ABV* 554.402, fr. Greece; San Simeon 12600.2, *ABV* 568.641, *Para* 271; Delphi 4719, *Para* 281, fr. Delphi; Ferrara T199, *Para* 285, fr. Spina. Kalinderu Group: London Mkt 6327; Athens Agora Mus. P24522, *ABV* 702.2 bis, fr. Athens. Other black-figure scenes: Palermo 684; Braunschweig P2; Metaponto 133528; Munich J142, *ABV* 334.6, 677, 694, fr. Vulci; Munich J540, *ABV* 604.68, fr. Vulci; Oxford 1954.116, *ABV* 710.188 bis. Red-figure scenes: Tübingen 5704; Chiusi 18004; San Simeon 9936, *ARV²* 503.21, *Add.* 251; New York MM 07.286.74, *ARV²* 523.1 (E. Fantham et al., *Women in the Classical World: image and text* (New York and Oxford 1994, fig. 3.23); Munich 8737, *ARV²* 578.67; Adolphseck 39, *ARV²* 582.19; Compiègne 1090, *ARV²* 922.1, *Add.* 305, fr. Vulci (*Cdl* fig. 129); Boston 95.26, *ARV²* 1317.2, fr. Greece; London E697, *ARV²* 1324.45, *Add.* 364, fr. Athens; Luzern Mkt 275568, *ARV²* 1694.11 bis; skyphos, private coll., *Para* 353.1.

76 H. Fracchia, 'The San Simeon fruit-pickers', *California Studies in Classical Antiquity* 5 (1972) 103–11; Fantham et al., *Women in the Classical World* 109 (the pot on which a woman stands on the trunk of a tree, Munich 1702A (Moon, 'The Priam Painter' fig. 7.10) is by no means as strenuous as Fantham implies); *Cdl* 93–4.

77 C. Sheffer, 'Workshop and trade patterns in Athenian black-figure', in J. Christiansen and T. Melander (eds), *Proceedings of the 3rd Symposium on Ancient Greek and Related Pottery* (Copenhagen 1988) 536–46.

78 Homer *Od.* 8.112–124, 24.220–7, 336–44.

79 Pyxis, London BM E773, *ARV²* 805.89, fr. Athens; cup, Euaion Painter, Oxford 1911.618, *ARV²* 795.104, fr. Cervetri; cup, Florence 76103 (see n. 45); column-krater frr., Leningrad Painter, Boston MFA 10.191A, *ARV²* 569.49, *Add.* 261, n.p.

80 Brock, 'The labour of women' 342–4.

81 Bell-krater, Harvard Fogg Museum 60.345, *ARV²* 1115.30, *Para* 453; Siana cup, London BM 1906.12–15.1, *ABV* 90.7, fr. Camiros; see *LIMC* s.v. Bouzyges.

82 On the plaques at Locri, C. Sourvinou-Inwood, 'Persephone and Aphrodite at Locri', *JHS* 98 (1978) 101–21.

83 Tyrrhenian amphora, Castellani Painter, St Petersburg B1403, *ABV* 98.34, *Para* 37, *Add.* 26.

84 Hydria, Meidias Painter, New York MM 25.2.11, *ARV²* 1313.11, fr. Athens.

85 H.A. Shapiro, *Art and Cult under the Tyrants in Athens* (Mainz 1989) 81–3.

86 Keuls, 'Attic vase-painting' 212; *RoP* 253.

87 M. Beard, 'Adopting an approach II', in *LGV* 12–35, pp. 29–30.

88 B.A. Sparkes, *The Red and the Black: studies in Greek pottery* (London 1996) 77–8 and fig. 3.10.

89 *ARV²* 377–9; provenances: Orvieto (377.102, 109); Vulci (377.114); Chiusi (379.142).

90 L. Bonfante, 'Iconografie delle madri: Etruria e Italia antica', in A. Rallo (ed.), *Le Donne in Etruria* (Studia Archeologica 52) (Rome 1989) 85–106.

91 One might ask whether the shape or the theme was more important; it is true that cups dominated the export trade to Etruria, but the early red-figure painters expanded their themes over a very diverse range of subjects, many of which seem designed solely for the export market.

92 Spivey, 'Greek vases' 144–9; H. Hoffmann, 'Why did the Greeks need imagery? An anthropological approach to the study of Greek vase-painting', *Hephaistos* 9 (1988) 143–62.

93 S. Steingräber (tr. D. and F.R. Ridgway), *Etruscan Painting: catalogue raisonné of Etruscan wall paintings* (New York 1986): no. 32 pl. 3, no. 123 pls. 342–3; see *LGV* figs. 54–5.

94 J. Boardman, 'The phallos-bird in archaic and classical Greek art', *RA* (1992), 227–42, p. 239.

95 M. Kilmer, *Greek Erotica on Attic Red-Figure Vases* (London 1993) 195.

96 Steingräber, *Etruscan Painting* no. 119, pl. 156; see also N.J. Spivey, *The Micali Painter and His Followers* (Oxford 1987) 8.

3 WORKING WOMEN

1 Ar. *Wasps* 496–9, 1388–1408, *Lys.* 456–8, *Thesm.* 444–58; R. Brock, 'The labour of women in classical Athens', *CQ* 44 (1994) 336–46.

2 Hydria, Leningrad Painter, Milan Torno Coll. C278, *ARV²* 571.73, fr. Ruvo (*ARFV* fig. 323); see M.S. Venit, 'The Caputi hydria and working women in classical Athens', *CW* 81.4 (1988) 265–72.

3 *IG* III.iii.69: Καταδῶ [Δι]ονύσιον τὸν κρανοποιὸν καὶ τὴν γυναῖκα αὐτοῦ Ἀρτεμείν τὴν χρυσωτρίαν καὶ τὴν [ο]ἰ – κ]ίαν αὐτῶν καὶ τὴν [ἐ]ργα-σίαν καὶ τὰ [ἔργ]α καὶ τὸν βί[ο]ν αὐτῶ[ν καὶ] Κάλλιπ-[πον . . .] (I curse Dionysus the helmet-maker and his wife Artemeis the gilder, and their household and workshop and business and their livelihood, and Kallippos . . .).

4 Sale of oil: red-figure amphora, Paris, private collection, *ARV²* 604.51, *Add.* 267, fr. Vulci; black-figure lekythos, Boston MFA 99.526, *ABL* 209.81; black-figure pelike, Tarquinia RC 1063; black-figure pelike, Florence 15585; black-figure pelike, Vatican 413 (*ABFV* fig. 212); red-figure pelike, Agrigento 34; red-figure pelike, Adolphseck 42, *ARV²* 285.1, n.p.; sale of amphorae: white-ground lekythos, Athens NA57a 2360, *Para* 216, fr. Athens. See H.A. Shapiro 'Correlating shape and subject: the case of the archaic pelike', in *APP* 259–67.

5 Pelike, Manner of Altamura Painter, Berne 12227, *ARV²* 596.1, *Para* 265, n.p.

6 Pelike, Nikoxenos Painter, Paris Louvre F376, *ABV* 393.16, n.p.; also black-figure pelike, Mykonos 302994, *ABV* 396.25, from Delos; red-figure pelike, Paris Market, *ARV²* 1162.18, n.p.

7 Ar. *Wasps* 1388–1408.

8 N.B. Kampen, *Image and Status: Roman working women in Ostia* (Berlin 1981).

9 Pelike, Pan Painter, Madrid L157, *ARV²* 554.86, n.p.; J.D. Beazley, *The Pan Painter* (Mainz 1974) 13, Sutton, 'Interactions' 293, M. Meyer, 'Männer mit Geld: zu einem rotfigurigen Vase mit "Alltagszene"', *JdI* 103 (1988) 87–125, p. 103 n. 79, B. Follmann, *Der Panmaler* (Bonn 1968) 67.

10 *IG* I² 473, *IG* II² 2934.

11 Black-figure skyphos frr., Athens NM 1.1271, *ABL* 253.12, fr. Athens, Acropolis.

12 Cup, Makron, London BM E61, *ARV²* 468.145, fr. Vulci.

13 Ar. *Thesm.* 457–8: some have suggested that this is sexualised because of the link with the symposium, but this overinterprets a contextual joke.

14 Pelike, Hephaistos Painter, Rhodes 12887, *ARV²* 1116.40, fr. Camiros (*RoP* fig. 241).

15 Column-krater, Pig Painter, Taranto 0.6436, *ARV²* 563.11, fr. Cavallino.

16 J. Davidson, *Courtesans and Fishcakes: the consuming passions of ancient Athens* (London 1997) 81–2; A. Stewart, *Art, Desire and the Body in Ancient Greece* (Cambridge 1997) 165; J.G. Landels, *Music in Ancient Greece and Rome* (London and New York 1998) 7.

17 Men. *Peri.* 337ff.; Ar. *Wasps.* 1345–6.

18 Plato *Rep.* 455e, *Symp.* 176e; Xen. *Symp.* 9.

19 M. West, *Ancient Greek Music* (Oxford 1992) ch. 1 'Music in Greek life'; Xen. *Hell.* 2.2.3 and Plut. *Lys.* 15.5; Davidson *Courtesans and Fishcakes* 82.

20 N. Roberts, *Whores in History: prostitution in Western society* (London 1993).

21 Dinos fr., Kleophrades Painter, Copenhagen NM 13365, *ARV²* 185.32, n.p. (*ARFV* fig. 131.2); cup, Brygos Painter, Würzburg 479, *ARV²* 372.32, *Para* 366, fr. Vulci; also cup, Brygos Painter, London BM E71, *ARV²* 372.29, fr. Vulci, and cup, Brygos Painter, Berlin Antikensammlungen F2309, *ARV²* 373.46, fr. Capua. See F. Frontisi-Ducroux and F. Lissarrague, 'From ambiguity to ambivalence', in J. Halperin et al. (eds), *Before Sexuality: the construction of erotic experience in the ancient Greek world* (Princeton 1990) 211–56, pp. 222–3.

22 Cup, Foundry Painter, Cambridge Corpus Christi, *ARV²* 402.12, n.p. (*ARFV* fig. 265); belly-amphora, Kleophrades Painter, Würzburg 507, *ARV²* 181.1, fr. Vulci (*ARFV* fig. 129.2); cup, Brygos Painter, Würzburg 479, *ARV²* 372.32, fr. Vulci (*RoP* fig. 152).

23 See Shapiro, 'Correlating shape and subject'.

24 D. Williams, 'Women on Athenian vases: problems of interpretation', in A. Cameron and A. Kuhrt (eds), *Images of Women in Antiquity* (London 1993) 92–106; D. Ogden, *Polygamy, Prostitutes and Death* (London 1999) 217.

25 White-ground lekythos, Harvard, Sackler Museum Schimmel coll., inv. no. 1991.28; *Pandora* no. 46, pp. 211–12.

26 Lekythos, Achilles Painter, London BM D51, *ARV²* 1000.201, fr. Marion.

27 See M. Beard and J. Henderson, 'With this body I thee worship: sacred prostitution in antiquity', *Gender and History* 9.3 (1997) 480–503.

28 Roberts, *Whores in History*, esp. ch. 16.

29 [Dem.] 59.122.

30 [Dem.] 59.53, 56, 71.

31 Isae. 3.13–15.

32 [Dem.] 59.85–7, Aeschin. 1.183.

33 [Dem.] 59.31–2; Phaedo: D.L. 2.105; Antiphon 1.14.

34 C. Patterson, 'The case against Neaira and the public ideology of the Athenian family', in A.L. Boegehold and A.C. Scafuro (eds), *Athenian Identity and Civic Ideology* (Baltimore 1994) 199–216; compare the Hellenistic epigram *Anth. Pal.* 208, which records a dedication by three 'freeborn hetairai' who all later married.

35 Theodote: Xen. *Mem.* 3.11; Aspasia: Plut. *Per.* 24; see M.M. Henry, *Prisoner of History: Aspasia of Miletus and her biographical tradition* (New York and Oxford 1995).

36 L. Kurke, *Coins, Bodies, Games and Gold: the politics of meaning in archaic Greece* (Princeton 1999) ch. 5.

37 Philemon fr. 3 K–A (= Athen. *Deipn.* 569e); see Williams, 'Women on Athenian vases', and L. Bonfante, 'Nudity as costume in classical art', *AJA* 93 (1989) 543–70.

38 Pyxis, Berlin inv. 3403, *ARV²* 1319.1, fr. Greece; see R.F. Sutton, 'Female bathers on Attic pottery' (abstract), *AJA* 95 (1991) 318, and pyxis, New York MM 1972.118.148 (no *ARV²*) (A. Richlin (ed.), *Pornography and Representation in Greece and Rome* (New York and Oxford 1992) p. 25 fig. 1.9); kalpis, Kleophrades Painter, Naples Mus. Naz. 2422, *ARV²* 189.74, fr. Nola (*ARFV* fig. 135).

39 White-ground lekythos, Baltimore, Johns Hopkins University 41.133 (no *ARV²*); white-ground lekythos, Copenhagen NM 8015 (no *ARV²*), CVA Copenhagen 4 pl. 173.2. A naked slave appears on the red-figure pelike, Washing Painter, New York Mkt, *ARV²* 1140.11, n.p. For a discussion of the Brauronia see Chapter 1, pp. 25–6.

40 Plut. *Mor.* 178 C–D; Theophr. *Char.* 11.2 (*Bdelurias*). See R. Osborne, 'Men without clothes: heroic nakedness and Greek art', *Gender and History* 9.3 (1997) 504–28.

41 L. Llewellyn-Jones, 'Women and veiling in the ancient Greek world', (Ph.D. thesis, University of Wales Cardiff 2000).

42 Cup, Agora Chaireas Painter, Athens Agora Mus. P24102, *ARV²* 176.1, fr. Athens Agora; cf. white-ground cup, Hesiod Painter, Berlin inv. 3408, *ARV²* 774, fr. Athens. See H.-P. Isler, 'Eine Schäle aus Iaitas: neues zum Werk des Malers der Agora-Chaireas-Schalen', *Antike Kunst* 41 (1998) 3–16.

43 Hydria, Washing Painter, Copenhagen NM Chr. VIII 520, *ARV²* 1131.161, fr. Nola.

44 Williams, 'Women on Athenian vases': 'Here we see a madam seated on a klismos teaching a young hetaera, naked but for an amulet round her thigh, to spin wool' (p. 96); Beard, 'Adopting an approach II' in *LGV*: 'perhaps it is simply a slightly eccentric version of everyday life – everyday life in the brothel' (p. 30); Davidson, *Courtesans and Fishcakes*: 'a seated woman apparently instructing a naked prostitute to spin wool' (p. 88).

45 Pelike, Paris Louvre G549, *ARV²* 1128.106, fr. Nola (?) (*CP* fig. 208); pelike, Havana, *ARV²* 1128.107; pelike, Paris Louvre G550, *ARV²* 1129.108; pelike, Basel Mkt, *ARV²* 1129.108 bis; hydria, London BM E202, *ARV²* 1131.155, fr. Nola; hydria, Oxford 296, *ARV²* 1131.156; hydria, Vienna 836, *ARV²* 1131.157; hydria, Paris Louvre G557, *ARV²* 1131.158; hydria, Winchester 89, *ARV²* 1131.159; hydria, London BM E207, *ARV²* 1131.160, fr. Nola; squat lekythos, London BM E651, *ARV²* 1132.193. [No provenance unless stated.]

46 V. Sabetai, 'The Washing Painter' (Diss., University of Cincinnati, 1993).

47 This volume pp. 27–8.

48 Cup, Antiphon Painter, Florence (no no.), *ARV²* 339.54, fr. Chiusi (M. Kilmer, *Greek Erotica on Attic Red-Figure Vases* (London 1993) fig. R489).

49 Cup, Triptolemos Painter, Tarquinia Mus. Naz, *ARV²* 367.93, fr. Tarquinia; cup, Triptolemos Painter, Tarquinia Mus. Naz, *ARV²* 367.94, fr. Tarquinia.

50 I. Peschel, *Die Hetäre bei Symposium und Komos in der attisch-rotfigurigen Vasenmalerei des 6–4 Jahrh. v. Chr.* (Frankfurt 1987) 358–9.

51 See R. Hamilton, *Choes and Anthesteria: Athenian iconography and ritual* (Ann Arbor 1992) 98–9; R. Kotansky, 'Incantations and prayers for salvation on inscribed Greek amulets', in C.A. Faraone and D. Obbink (eds), *Magika Hiera: ancient Greek magic and religion* (New York and Oxford 1991) 107–37, pp. 107–10.

52 Contraception: Pliny *NH* 29.27.85, Aetius 16.17: see J.M. Riddle, *Contraception and Abortion from the Ancient World to the Renaissance* (Cambridge, Mass. and London 1992) 96–7; Plut. *Perikles* 38.2.

53 Hydria, London BM B333, *ABV* 677.3, fr. Vulci; hydria, A.D. Painter, Munich 1712A, *ABV* 334.6, fr. Vulci; lid fr., Athens NM Acrop. Coll. 1.2644 (no *ARV²*), fr. Acropolis (Graef and Langlotz vol. i pl. 112); stamnos, Smikros, Brussels A717, *ARV²* 20.1, n.p.

54 D. Schaps, 'The woman least mentioned', *CQ* 27 (1977) 323–30; see now C. Sourvinou-Inwood, 'Male and female, public and private, ancient and modern', in *Pandora* 111–20, p. 118 on named dedicants and priestesses.

55 Cup, Athens NM 992; *RoP* 155.

56 Hydria, Naples 3232, *ARV²* 1032.61, fr. Nola (*RoP* fig. 84).

57 H.A. Shapiro, *Personifications in Greek Art* (Zurich 1993).

58 Athen. 13.583, 596.

59 R. Schneider, *RE* VIII (1913) s.v. Hetairai.

60 Ogden, *Polygamy* 251. One pot offered as clinching evidence by Williams and Davidson is the cup by the Ambrosios Painter (Munich private, H.R. Immerwahr, 'An inscribed cup by the Ambrosios Painter', *Antike Kunst* 27 (1984) 10–13 with pls. 2–3), depicting men and women preparing for a symposion. All are named, the men as Kallias, Aristonymus and possibly Lichas, the women as Rhodo[. . .], Antiphane, Aphrodisia and [. . .]obole. Davidson interprets this as a complete name, Obole (Penny), signifying a prostitute with a commercial name, but Immerwahr reads it either as the final component of a longer name such as Aristobole, or as an address, 'o Boule', comparing another cup (Athens 1666, *ARV²*1567.13, *Add.* 196), which has the inscription 'o Dori'.

61 Williams, 'Women on Athenian vases' (Iope); also M.J. Milne, 'Three names on a Corinthian

jar', *AJA* 46 (1942) 216–22; this attitude can be taken to extremes, as demonstrated by the discussion of whether Melosa is a prostitute's name (in M.J. Milne, 'A prize for wool-working', *AJA* 49 (1945) 528–33). Lyda: F. Canciani and G. Neumann, 'Lydos, der Sklave', *Antike Kunst* 21 (1978) 17–22.

62 White-ground lekythos, Germany, private coll. (Beazley Archive Database no. 19742); black-figure phormiskos, Athens Kerameikos 691, *ABV* 678, *Add.* 70 (H. Brijder (ed.), *Ancient Greek and Related Pottery* (Amsterdam 1984) p. 322 fig. 5).

63 A. Kossatz, 'Satyr- und Mänadennamen auf Vasenbildern', *Greek Vases in the Getty Museum* 5 (1991) 131–99. Kleophonis: bell-krater, Polygnotos Group, Agrigento 1, *ARV²* 1055.64, fr. Agrigento; Kallisto: cup, Brygos Painter, London E68, *ARV²* 371.24, fr. Vulci.

64 Skyphos, Penthesilea Painter, St Petersburg Hermitage 4224, *ARV²* 889.166, *Para* 516, n.p.; cup, Munich private, Wedding Painter, *ARV²* 923.29, n.p. (*RoP* fig. 162).

65 Davidson, *Courtesans and Fishcakes* 95.

66 Oinochoe, Berlin Painter, San Antonio 86.134.59, *Para* 345.184 ter, *Add.* 196; Nolan amphora, Providence Painter, Harvard Sackler Museum 1972.45, *ARV²* 638.43, *Add.* 273, n.p., both discussed by Reeder, *Pandora* nos. 36 and 37, pp. 181–3.

67 J. Bažant, 'Les Vases athéniens et les réformes démocratiques', in C. Bérard et al. (eds), *Images et Société en Grèce ancienne: l'iconographie comme méthode d'analyse* (Lausanne 1987) 33–40, p. 37 reaches the same conclusion. For similar conclusions on slaves, see S. Lewis, 'Slaves as viewers and users of Athenian pottery', *Hephaistos* 16/17 (1998/9) 71–90.

68 Antiphon 1.14, Dem.23.53; Isae. 3.39. Much debate still surrounds the status of concubines: see R. Sealey, 'On lawful concubinage in Athens', *CA* 3 (1984) 111–33; C. Patterson, 'Those Athenian bastards', *CA* 9 (1990) 39–73; and D. Ogden, *Greek Bastardy* (Oxford 1996) 158–9.

69 *RoP* ch. 10 is without illustrations on the topic, as is C. Reinsburg, *Ehe, Hetärentum und Knabenliebe im antiken Griechenland* (Munich 1989).

70 Beard, 'Adopting an approach II' 26–30.

71 For example, *RoP* 223, and Stewart, *Art* 26.

72 Plato *Symp.*; Athen. 2.37b–e; [Dem.] 59.33; Xen. *Symp.* 9.7.

73 A. Schafer, *Unterhaltung beim griechischen Symposion: Darbietungen, Spiele und Wettkämpfe von homerischer bis in spätklassische Zeit* (Mainz 1997) ch. 5; T. Sini, 'A symposium scene on an Attic fourth-century calyx-krater in St. Petersburg', in O. Palagia (ed.), *Greek Offerings: essays on Greek art in honour of John Boardman* (Oxford 1997) 159–65.

74 Cup, Hegesiboulos Painter, NY MM 07.286.47, *ARV²* 175, n.p.

75 Stamnos, Brussels A717 (see n. 53).

76 Cup, Tarquinia Painter, Basel Kä 415, *ARV²* 868.45, *Para* 426.

77 Psykter, Euphronios, St Petersburg B644, *ARV²* 16.15, *Para* 509, fr. Cervetri; hydria, Phintias, Munich 2421, *ARV²* 23.7, fr. Vulci; cup, Oltos, Madrid 11267, *ARV²* 58.53, fr. Vulci; cup, Curtius Painter, Basel M&M Dec. 1977 Sonderliste R, fig. 57 (*RoP* fig. 140); cup, New York MM 56.171.61, *ARV²* 50.192, *Para* 325, n.p. See Peschel, *Die Hetäre* 70–4.

78 Cup, Copenhagen Thorvaldsen's Museum H616, *ARV²* 393.36, n.p.; also cup, Proto-Panaitian Group, Munich 2636, *ARV²* 317.16, fr. Vulci; plate, Harvard Fogg Art Museum 1960.350, *ARV²* 456.2, fr. Vari; cup fr., Tübingen 1583, *ARV²* 332.34, n.p.; cup, Onesimos, Heidelberg 55 + Florence 10B 106, *ARV²* 326.91, n.p.

79 E. Csapo and M.C. Miller, 'The "Kottabos-Toast" and an inscribed red-figure cup', *Hesperia* 60 (1991) 367–82, p. 380; Kurke, *Coins, Bodies* 204–5.

80 Philemon fr. 3 K–A, Euboulos fr. 82 K–A, Xenarchus fr. 4 K–A (all at Athen. 13.568–9).

81 That the form existed is demonstrated by the common theme of the Judgement of Paris. Keuls (*RoP* 158) comments 'We have no Greek picture of such a line-up, nor any scene that can securely be located inside a brothel or pimp's establishment.'

82 Cup, Euaion Painter, Berlin Schloss Charlottenburg 31426, *ARV²* 795.100, *Add.* 142, n.p.; hydria, Harrow Painter, Maplewood, Noble Coll., *ARV²* 276.70, fr. Vulci: see Aeschin. 1.74 (with N. Fisher *Aeschines: Against Timarchos* (Oxford 2000) ad loc.) and Meyer, 'Männer mit Geld'; cup, Makron, Paris Louvre G143, *ARV²* 469.148, fr. Vulci; cup, Ambrosios Painter, Munich private (see Immerwahr, 'An inscribed cup' with pls. 2–3).

83 Davidson, *Courtesans and Fishcakes*, caption to Euaion cup; Sutton 'Interactions' 294; Williams, 'Women on Athenian vases' 97 (on the Harrow Painter's hydria).

84 Bell-krater, Dinos Painter, London BM F65, *ARV²* 1154.35, fr. Capua (*CP* fig. 182); hydria, Leningrad Painter, Chicago 1911.456, *ARV²* 572.88, n.p. (*RoP* fig. 175).

85 J.R. Clarke, *Looking at Lovemaking: constructions of sexuality in Roman art, 100 BC–AD 250* (Berkeley 1998).

86 On Tyrrhenian amphorae see T.H. Carpenter, 'On the dating of the Tyrrhenian Group', *OJA* 2 (1983) 279–93, and 'The Tyrrhenian Group: problems of provenance', *OJA* 3 (1984) 45–56.

87 Cup, Rhodes Arch. Mus., fr. Ano Achaia; see A. Lemos, 'Athenian black-figure: Rhodes revisited', in *APP* 457–68, and A. Dierichs, *Erotik in der Kunst Griechenlands* (Mainz 1993) 50–5.

88 Stewart, *Art*, describes the scenes as 'statements of homosociality – projections of male bonding onto the sexual landscape' (p. 161), which discounts the female figures altogether.

89 Kilmer, in his now standard treatment *Greek Erotica*, lists about 500 pots in his 'List of Vases', although he discusses only about 200. His list (not catalogue) includes some pots which carry only 'erotic inscriptions' (p. 237), and many others whose definition as 'erotica' is dubious: the Fall of Troy (R321), Herakles and Busiris (R699), running maenad (R763), sacrifice at a Herm (R692.1), white-ground lekythoi (R887, R890, R894).

90 *CdI* 89–90, *RoP* 165.

91 Black-figure: pyxis, Bologna PU239, fr. Athens; cup fr., Athens Agora Mus. P26645, fr. Agora; cup fr., Athens Agora Mus. P4222, fr. Agora; two cup frs., Athens Akrop. Coll. 1.1913 and 1.1772, fr. Akropolis (B. Graef and E. Langlotz, *Die antiken Vasen von der Akropolis zu Athen* (Berlin 1925–33) pls. 83 and 86); four Little Master cups, Athens Akrop. Coll. 1.1639, 1.1669, 1.1684, 1.1685 (*APP* p. 463 figs. 8.1–4); red-figure: plaque fr., Athens Akr. J4 (*ARFV* fig. 18); plate fr., Athens Akr. 2.17, *ARV²* 175.35, fr. Akropolis; lebes frr., Athens, Vlasto coll., *ARV²* 552.28; askos, Athens Kerameikos Coll. 1063, fr. Kerameikos (Kilmer, *Greek Erotica* fig. R1184); cup fr., Athens Kerameikos Coll., *Add.* 214, *Para* 358; cup fr., Athens Akrop. 802, *ARV²* 242.76.

92 U. Knigge, 'Kerameikos: Tätigkeitsbericht 1978', *AA* (1980) 256–65, and Knigge, *The Athenian Kerameikos: history, monuments, excavations* (Athens 1991) 88–94; H. Lind, 'Ein Hetärenhaus am heiligen Tor?', *Mus. Helv.* 45 (1988) 158–69.

93 See R.D. de Puma, 'Eos and Memnon on Etruscan mirrors', in de Puma and J.P. Small (eds) *Murlo and the Etruscans* (Madison 1994) 186–7; L. Bonfante (ed.), *Etruscan Life and Afterlife: a handbook of Etruscan studies* (Warminster 1986) 240.

94 S. Steingräber, *Etruscan Painting: catalogue raisonné of Etruscan wall paintings* (tr. D. and F.R. Ridgeway) (New York 1986) no. 120 pls. 159–60.

95 R.R. Holloway, 'The bulls in the "Tomb of the Bulls" at Tarquinia', *AJA* 90 (1986) 447–52.

96 Cup, Antiphon Painter, Malibu Getty Museum 86.AE.285, *Para* 360.74 ter, fr. Turkey.

97 F. Lissarrague, *Un flot d'images: une esthétique du banquet grec* (Paris 1987) ch. 2.

98 Cup fr., Douris, Christchurch (NZ), Canterbury Museum AR 430 (currently on loan to the James Logie Memorial Collection at the University of Canterbury, inv.CML 6), *ARV²* 438.138, fr. Orvieto. On questions of status, see Kilmer, *Greek Erotica* 159–67.

99 *RoP* 212.

100 Plut. *Solon* 20.3; Ar. *Lys.* 845–951.

101 Cup, Douris, Boston MFA 1970.223, *ARV²* 444.241, n.p. (*ARFV* fig. 297); cup, Makron, Louvre G143 (see n. 82).

102 Cup, Gales Painter, New Haven 163, *ARV²* 36.a, fr. Vulci.

103 For example, oinochoe, Shuvalov Painter, Berlin F2414, *ARV²* 1208.41, *Para* 463, fr. Locri (*RoP* fig. 173; p. 190 describes as 'prostitute and customer').

104 Cup, Kiss Painter, Berlin 2269, *ARV²* 177.1, fr. Chiusi (*RoP* fig. 174); also cup fr., New York 07.286.50, *ARV²* 177.2, fr. Arezzo. Such affection is interesting in the context of modern prostitution, where kissing is considered far too intimate a gesture to be permitted to a client.

105 Cup, Foundry Painter, Milan A8037, *Para* 370.33 ter, fr. Cervetri; cup, Pedieus Painter, Louvre G13, *ARV²* 86.a, n.p.; cup, Brygos Painter, Florence 3912, *ARV²* 372.31, n.p.; kantharos, Nikosthenes Painter, Boston 95.61, *ARV²* 132, fr. Vulci; cup, Thalia Painter, Berlin 3251, *ARV²* 113.7, *Para* 332, fr. Vulci.

106 Kilmer, *Greek Erotica* 56–8, Keuls, *RoP* 176, Kurke, *Coins, Bodies* 208. Because the group is so small, it is unrepresentative, yet is given an undue prominence in illustrations; for this reason I have chosen not to illustrate it. See comments in the Introduction, pp. 4–5.

107 Kilmer, *Greek Erotica*, in the captions to his fig. 156.1 and fig. 518 describes the tondo scene as a prelude to the outside, but this is unfounded. A recent exception is Kurke, *Coins, Bodies* 211–12.

108 Cup, Phintias, Malibu Getty Museum 80.AE.31, *ARV²* 1620.12; cup, Basel Market 1977 (*RoP* fig. 148); cf. skyphos, Malibu Getty Mus. 85.AE.304.

109 Mockery of the unfit: Ar. *Frogs* 1089–98, *Clouds* 1010–19.

110 Cup, Pheidippos, London BM E6, *ARV²* 166.11, fr. Vulci (*ARFV* fig. 80); black-figure oinochoe, Kleisophos, Athens NM 1045, *ABV* 186, fr. Athens (*Hephaistos* 16/17 (1998/9 p. 79 fig. 6).

111 Black-figure lekythos, Beldam Painter, Athens NM 1129, *ABL* 266.1, fr. Eretria (*ABFV* fig. 277); Ar. *Lys.* 517–21, *Wasps* 448–51, 1292–6.

112 Tomba del Fustigazione: Steingräber, *Etruscan Painting* no. 67.

113 See E. Knauer, 'Οὐ γὰρ ἦν ἁμίς: a chous by the Oionokles Painter', *Greek Vases in the J. Paul Getty Museum* 2 (1985) 91–100.

114 Ar. *Ekkl.* 311ff., *Thesm.* 628–33, Athen. 10.444b, Plut. *Mor.* 232F; see L. Stone, *The Family, Sex and Marriage in England 1500–1800* (London 1977) 159–60.

115 Hydria, Paris Louvre G51, *ARV²* 32.1, n.p.; cup, Berlin 3757, *ARV²* 404.11, fr. Orvieto (*RoP* fig. 149); see Kilmer, *Greek Erotica* 109.

116 Tomb of the Jugglers: Steingräber, *Etruscan Painting* no. 70 pl. 92.

117 J. Boardman, 'The phallos-bird in archaic and classical Greek art', *RA* (1992) 227–42; Kilmer, *Greek Erotica* 193–7.

118 Pelike fr., Athens Agora P27396 (Kilmer, *Greek Erotica* no. 416); amphora, Flying Angel Painter, Paris Petit Palais 307, *ARV²* 279.2, fr. Capua (*ARFV* fig. 176).

119 Column-krater, Pan Painter, Berlin 3206, *ARV²* 551.10, fr. Etruria (*ARFV* fig. 342).

120 Cup fr., Athens NM Akropolis Coll. 802, *ARV²* 242.76, fr. Akropolis.

121 Tomba del Topolino: Steingräber, *Etruscan Painting* no. 119 pl. 156.

4 THE WOMEN'S ROOM

1 S.B. Pomeroy, *Goddesses, Whores, Wives and Slaves* (New York 1975) 79, a view echoed by Keuls, *RoP* 97: 'locked away in the dark recesses of closed-in homes'.

2 Hydria, Chrysis Painter, New York MM 06.1021.185, *ARV²* 1158.5, fr. Suessula.

3 Lekythos, Bowdoin Painter, New York MM 06.1021.90, *ARV²* 682.102, n.p.

4 R. Sutton, 'Pornography and persuasion on Attic pottery', in A. Richlin (ed.), *Pornography and Representation in Greece and Rome* (New York and Oxford 1992) 1–33, p. 33; Boardman *CP* 219; L. Burn, *The Meidias Painter* (Oxford 1987) 84–5.

5 The topic of relationships between husband and wife is treated in detail in the next chapter.

6 J. Bažant, 'Les Vases athéniens et les réformes démocratiques', in C. Bérard et al. (eds), *Images et société en Grèce ancienne: l'iconographie comme méthode d'analyse* (Lausanne 1987) 32ff.

7 J. Boardman, 'The Athenian pottery trade', *Expedition* (Summer 1979) 33–9.

8 F. Lissarrague, 'Voyages d'images: iconographie et aires culturelles', *REA* 89 (1987) 261–9.

9 F. Lissarrague, 'Intrusions au gynécée', in P. Veyne, F. Lissarrague and F. Frontisi-Ducroux, *Les Mystères du Gynécée* (Paris 1998) 155–98, p. 160; Boardman *CP* 239.

10 S.R. Roberts, *The Attic Pyxis* (Chicago 1978) 3.

11 Pyxis, Athens Kerameikos coll. 1008, *ARV²* 806.92, *Add.* 291, fr. Kerameikos, and pyxis, Athens Kerameikos coll., both illustrated in U. Knigge, *The Athenian Kerameikos: history, monuments, excavations* (Athens 1991) figs. 103 and 39.

12 S.I. Rotroff and J.H. Oakley, *Debris from a Public Dining Place in the Athenian Agora* (*Hesperia* Supplement 25) (Princeton 1992) 12.

13 Lebes gamikos, Marsyas Painter, St Petersburg 15592, *ARV²* 1475.1, *Para* 495, *Add.* 381, fr. Kerch (J.H. Oakley and R. Sinos, *The Wedding in Ancient Athens* (Madison 1993) p. 40 and fig. 125).

14 Hes. *WD* 699–705; Semonides fr. 7 ll.57–70; Ar. *Clouds* 46–55; Xen. *Mem.* 2.7.

15 J.H. Oakley, 'Nuptial nuances: wedding images in non-wedding scenes of myth', in *Pandora* 63–73.

16 L. Llewellyn-Jones, 'Women and veiling in the ancient Greek world', Ph.D. thesis, University of Wales Cardiff 2000.

17 S. Walker, 'Women and housing in classical Greece', in A. Cameron and A. Kuhrt (eds), *Images of Women in Antiquity* (London 1983) 81–91; *RoP* 108–9.

18 D. Cohen, *Law, Society and Sexuality: the enforcement of morals in classical Athens* (Cambridge 1991); L.C. Nevett, *House and Society in the Ancient Greek World* (Cambridge 1999).

19 Nevett, *House and Society* 68–74; storage: 67.

20 C. Bérard and J.-L. Durand, 'Entering the imagery', in *CdI* 30–5.

21 *RoP* 108–9, *Pandora* 205, 209; in contrast Bérard and Durand, 'Entering' 31–3 bring out the ambiguity of the door as a symbol, and Bérard *CdI* 102 has some pertinent comments on the double door as a symbol of wealth.

22 Onos, Eretria Painter, Athens 1629, *ARV²* 1250.34, fr. Eretria.

23 Cup, Paris Louvre G332, *ARV²* 396.16, *Add.* 230, n.p.; pyxis, London E773, *ARV²* 805.89, fr. Athens.

24 For example, M. Beard, 'Adopting an approach II', in *LGV* 12–35, pp. 23–6.

25 White-ground lekythos, Achilles Painter, Vienna 3746, *ARV²* 998.164, *Add.* 313, fr. Cape Zoster. The funerary meaning of the kalathos is much stronger in Apulian vase-painting – see H. Cassimatis, 'Propros sur le calathos dans la céramique italiote', in J.-P. Descoedres (ed.), *Eumousia: ceramic and iconographic studies in honour of A. Cambitoglou* (Sydney 1990) 195–201.

26 Ar. *Thesm.* 797; also *Peace* 979–85, *Ekkl.* 877ff.; Lys 1.8; cf. Plut. *Mor.* 232C.

27 Cohen, *Law, Sexuality and Society*.

28 For example, lebes gamikos, Washing Painter, New York MM 16.73, *ARV²* 1126.6, n.p. (*CP* fig. 207); lebes gamikos, Washing Painter, New York MM 07.286.35, *ARV²* 1126.1, fr. Greece.

29 Pyxis, Toronto 919.5.31, *ARV²* 1328.96, fr. Athens; compare lekanis lid, Mainz 118, *ARV²* 1327.87, n.p. (Burn, *Meidias Painter* pl. 21).

30 Ar. *Thesm.* 279–93, *Ach.* 271–6, *Peace* 1138–9, 1146.

31 Lys 1.8; [Dem.] 59.46; Theoc. *Id.* 2.1, 19, 94ff. and 15.66–70; also Theophr. *Char.* 22.10.

32 Pyxis, Eretria Painter, London BM E774, *ARV²* 1250.32, fr. Athens.

33 N. Himmelmann, *Archäologisches zum Problem der griechischen Sklaverei* (Wiesbaden 1971) 36–7.

34 Loutrophoros, Painter of Bologna 228, Athens NM CC1167, *ARV²* 512.13, *Add.* 123, fr. Pikrodafni.

35 K. Zimmermann, 'Tatöwierte Thrakerinnen auf griechischen Vasenbildern', *JdI* 95 (1980) 163–96.

36 G. Davies, 'The language of gesture in Greek art: gender and status on grave stelai', *Apollo* 140 no. 389 (1994) 6–11.

37 Ar. *Thesm.* 340–2; Lys. 1.18; Ovid *Am.* 1.14.17–18, *Ars Am.* 3.239–40, Juvenal 6.475–7, 487–93, Martial 2.66.

38 Skyphos, Malibu Getty Museum 85.AE.304, n. p.: see p. 65–6.

39 Lekythos, Manner of the Alkimachos Painter, Syracuse 21972, *ARV²* 535.2, fr. Gela; cup, Douris, Paris Louvre S1350, *ARV²* 432.60, n.p.

40 Pyxis lid, Chalki Group, London E778, *ARV²* 1503.2, fr. Athens.

41 Hydria, Orpheus Painter, New York 17.230.15, *ARV²* 1104.16, n.p.; pyxis, Berlin 3403, *ARV²* 1319.1, fr. Greece; pyxis, New York 1972.118.148; also oinochoe, Rome Accademia dei Lincei inv. 2772, *ARV²* 1206.10, n.p. (*JHS* 72 pl. 8.1).

42 Volute-krater, Oxford V525, *ARV²* 1562.4 (*JHS* 21 (1941) pl. 1); see C. Calame, *The Poetics of Eros in Ancient Greece* (tr. J. Lloyd) (Princeton 1999) ch. 4.

43 V. Sabetai, 'Aspects of nuptial and genre imagery in fifth-century Athens: issues of interpretation and methodology', in *APP* 319–35.

44 J. Reilly, 'Many brides: "mistress and maid" on Athenian lekythoi', *Hesperia* 58 (1989) 411–44.

45 R.F. Sutton, Jr., 'Female bathers on Attic pottery' (abstract), *AJA* 95 (1991) 318.

46 The Francis–Vickers chronology suggested down-dating Attic figure-decorated pots by about sixty years. This was refuted by R.M. Cook ('The Francis–Vickers chronology', *JHS*

109 (1989) 164–70), but it is interesting that in this case it would create a closer continuity between ceramic art and sculpture.

47 Cup, Hunt Painter, fr. Samos, in M. Pipili, *Laconian Iconography of the Sixth Century BC* (Oxford 1987), no. 95 (fig. 51); cup, Phineus Painter, Würzburg 354, fr. Rhegium.

48 Amphora, Priam Painter, Rome Villa Giulia 2609, *Para* 146.8 ter, fr. Cervetri; amphora, Andokides Painter, Louvre F203, *ARV²* 4.13, n.p.

49 See Pipili, *Laconian Iconography*, and S. Lewis, 'Shifting images: Athenian women in Etruria', in K. Lomas and T. Cornell (eds), *Gender and Ethnicity in Ancient Italy* (London 1997) 141–54.

50 Neck-amphora, Edinburgh Painter, Berlin F1843, *ABV* 478; pelike, Nikoxenos Painter, Athens 1425, *ARV²* 223.6, fr. Aegina; hydria, St Petersburg ST1612, *ARV²* 34.16, *Add.* 157, n.p. (*RoP* fig. 215).

51 F.K. Yegül, *Baths and Bathing in Classical Antiquity* (New York 1992) 17–21; R. Ginouvès, *Balaneutiké: recherches sur le bain dans l'antiquité grecque* (Paris 1962) 220–4; *RoP* 239–40.

52 Stamnos, Polygnotos Group, Munich AS 2411, *ARV²* 1051.18, fr. Vulci.

53 Hydria, Euthymides, once Frankfurt, *ARV²* 28.13, n.p.

54 C. Bérard, 'L'Impossible Femme athlète', *AION* VIII (1986) 195–202.

55 F. Lissarrague and J.-L. Durand, 'Un lieu d'image: l'espace du loutérion', *Hephaistos* 2 (1980) 89–106.

56 Pyxis, Paris Louvre CA 1857, n.p. (*CdI* fig. 141); pyxis, Drouot Group, Berlin F2518, fr. Euboia; pyxis, Bowdoin College 30.3, *ARV²* 1223, *Add.* 350; conversation: cup, Florence 935121, fr. Populonia (*Boll. dell' Arte* 50 figs. 47–9); pelike fr., Syriskos Painter, Oxford (no no.), *ARV²* 262.31, n.p.; pyxis, Cage Painter, Liverpool 49.50.7, *ARV²* 348, n.p.

57 Lekanis, Eleusinian Painter, St Petersburg ST1791, *ARV²* 1476.3, *Para* 496, *Add.* 381, fr. Kerch (Oakley and Sinos, *Wedding* fig. 44); pyxis, Berlin 3403, *ARV²* 1319.1, fr. Greece.

58 Lekanis, Marsyas Painter, St Petersburg ST1858, *ARV²* 1475.7, fr. Kerch (*CP* fig. 391); pelike, Athens 1472 (CC1856), *ARV²* 1477.1, n.p.; see Ginouvès, *Balaneutiké* 168–9, and also the Boiotian skyphos with a hairwashing scene (fig. 2.24, this volume).

59 Cup, Onesimos, Brussels Mus. Royaux A889, *ARV²* 329.130, fr. Chiusi.

60 Sutton, 'Pornography and persuasion' 22.

61 Pliny *NH* 36.21–2.

62 Chous, London 1910.6–15.3; pyxis, Briseis Painter, London E769, *ARV²* 410.63, *Add.* 115, fr. Athens (Keuls, *RoP* p. 212 and figs. 186 and 187). Keuls also uses an Apulian bell-krater depicting a scene from drama as a reflection of domestic life, captioning it 'husband and wife snacking together', but it is hardly legitimate to describe actors as demonstrating 'everyday life'.

63 Lekythos, Sappho Painter, once Kusnacht, *Para* 247, 252; hydria, Luzern Mkt (*AM* 109 (1994) pl. 16.2).

64 S. Pingiatoglou, 'Rituelle Frauengelage auf schwarzfigurigen attischen Vasen', *AM* 109 (1994) 39–51; amphora, Munich 1538, *ABV* 395.3, *Add.* 103, fr. Vulci; hydria, Leagros Group, Rome Villa Giulia 50466, *ABV* 366.75, n.p.; column-krater, Agrigento 134, *ABV* 377.235, fr. Agrigento; lekythos, Leagros Group, Athens NM 12951, *ABV* 380.287, n.p. Also black-figure fr., Athens, NM Akropolis coll. 1.2260, fr. Akropolis; lekythos frr., Adria Museo Civico A2054, fr. Adria.

65 Xen. *Oik.* 7.6, Semonides fr. 7 lines 43–7.

66 Xen. *Lak. Pol.* 1.3; compare J.K. Campbell, *Honour, Family and Patronage: a study of institutions and moral values in a Greek mountain community* (Oxford 1964) 151.

67 Cup, Hegesiboulos, Brussels Mus. Royaux A891, *ARV²* 771.2, fr. Athens (*CP* fig. 108, *RoP* fig. 88); hydria, Washing Painter, Poznan Nat. Mus. MNP A746 (previously Warsaw 142293), *ARV²* 1130.150, *Add.* 333, fr. Nola; onos fr., Eretria P, Amsterdam AP 2021, *ARV²* 1251.35, *Add.* 354, n.p.

68 White-ground pyxis, Painter of London D12, Toledo Mus. of Art, *Para* 434.94 bis, n.p. (*CP* fig. 91); lekythos, Rome Accademia dei Lincei inv. no. 2756, *ARV²* 733.63, n.p. (*JHS* 72 pl. 8.2); lekythos Munich SL 475, *ARV²* 1365.2, n.p. (*RoP* fig. 89).

69 Stick-balancing: chous, Athens NM 1322 (CC1333) (van Hoorn cat. 41); pyxis, New York MM 09.221.40, *ARV²* 1328.99, *Add.* 364, n.p.; lekythos, Minneapolis Inst. of Arts 57.41.1,

ARV^2 1326.74, n.p.; pyxis, Athens 1242, ARV^2 1360.5, *Add.* 370, n.p.; onos fr. (see n. 67); pelike, Shuvalov Painter, Naples RC117, ARV^2 1209.57, *Add.* 346, fr. Cumae; squat lekythos, Nicosia Cyprus Museum C760, n.p.

70 Ôon, Eretria Painter, Athens Stathatou coll. 332, ARV^2 1257.2, *Para* 470, fr. near Athens.

71 Astragaloi: pyxis NY 06.1021.119; hydria, Washing Painter, London BM E205, ARV^2 1132.175, fr. Nola; lekythos, Naples H3123, ARV^2 671.12, fr. Nola; onos fr. (see n. 67); skyphos frr. Athens Acropolis 512a, ARV^2 806.2, fr. Athens. See L. Deubner, 'Zum Astragalspiel', in Deubner, *Kleine Schriften zur klassischen Altertumskunde* (Königstein 1982) 342–7.

Tops: cup, Hegesiboulos (see n. 67); lekythos, Providence Painter, Athens NM 15876, ARV^2 643.119, n.p.; white-ground lekythos, Sabouroff Painter, Athens M. Vlasto coll., ARV^2 845.163, fr. Athens; cup, Painter of London E777, Ferrara T991A, ARV^2 941.33, fr. Spina; squat lekythos, New York MM GR538, *AJA* 11 (1907) p. 421 fig. 4; lekythos, Bosanquet Painter, Boston Herrmann coll., *APP* p. 246, figs. 11–14.

72 See-saw: bell-krater fr., Athens Agora Mus. P20157; column-krater frs., Leningrad Painter, Boston MFA 10.191, ARV^2 569.49, *Add.* 261, n.p.; hydria, Dwarf Painter, Madrid 11128, ARV^2 1011.17, fr. Apulia; hydria, Painter of Athens 1454, Athens 1178, ARV^2 1179.5, fr. Attica; cup, Codrus Painter, New York, Love coll., ARV^2 1271.38 bis, *Para* 472, n.p. Youths play see-saw on cup, Euergides Painter, Rome Villa Giulia (no no.), *Para* 330, fr. Vulci.

Ephedrismos: bell-krater, Munich 2396, ARV^2 1468.139, fr. Sicily (*CP* fig. 413). Many other images of ephedrismos exist, but all others involve youths or satyrs.

73 *Anth Pal.* VI 280 and 276 (girl described as λιπαστραγάλη); K. Stears, 'Dead women's society: constructing female gender in classical Athenian funerary sculpture' in N. Spencer (ed.), *Time, Tradition and Society in Greek Archaeology: bridging the great divide* (London and New York 1995), 109–31, pp. 118–23.

74 A.E. Klein, *Child Life in Greek Art* (New York 1932); J.-M. André, *Jouer dans l'antiquité (Exposition)* (Paris, Réunion des musées nationaux, 1991).

75 *RoP* 104.

76 V. Sabetai, 'The Washing Painter' (Diss., University of Cincinnati 1993); see also H. Hoffmann, *Sotades: symbols of immortality on Greek vases* (Oxford 1996) 142.

77 Oakley and Sinos, *Wedding* p. 134 n. 53; erotes: Apulian volute-krater, Munich 3268, *RVAp.* 16.51 (André, *Jouer dans l'antiquité* ill. 74).

78 Cup-skyphos, Basle, coll. Cahn HC431 (Lissarrague, 'Intrusions' fig. 39).

79 Hydria, Meidias Painter, Florence 81948, ARV^2 1312.1, fr. Populonia; pyxis, Eretria Painter, London E774, ARV^2 1250.32, fr. Athens; see E. Böhr, 'A rare bird on Greek vases: the wryneck', in *APP* 109–23. 116–20.

80 See A.D. Ure, 'Boeotian vases with women's heads', *AJA* 57 (1953) 245–9 for the suggestion that several Boiotian bell-kraters on which a woman leans over a louterion with cupped hands, may represent a form of hydromancy.

81 Hoffmann, *Sotades* ch. 13; see also E. Vermeule, *Aspects of Death in Early Greek Art and Poetry* (Berkeley and London 1979) 80–2.

82 H. Cahn, 'Morra: drei Silene beim knobeln', in H. Froning et al. (eds), *Kotinos: Festschrift für E. Simon* (Mainz 1992) 214–17.

83 Terracottas: Boston 01.7798–9t, 03.897t, Paris Louvre 128. See R. Higgins, *Tanagra and the Figurines* (London 1986) 143–4 and figs. 175 and 176; note also Pausan. 10.30.1, which describes the fifth-century wall-painting in the Lesche of the Knidians at Delphi, depicting the daughters of Pandareos playing with astragaloi in the Underworld.

84 Lissarrague, 'Intrusions' 193; Ar. *Clouds* 877–81; Plut. *Mor.* 213E, *Ages.* 25.

85 H.A. Shapiro, *Personifications in Greek Art* (Zurich 1993) 180–5: Shapiro makes a connection with erotic play, but this is not borne out by the imagery: in all but one case there is little to distinguish Paidia from other nymphs – she holds jewellery or stands in attendance, and is simply one of the canonical names for Aphrodite's followers. On a squat lekythos in Munich (J234, fr. Vulci, Shapiro figs. 73 and 140) a nymph named Paidia swings Himeros (desire), which does link love and play more closely, but on the whole there is nothing to render play among women erotic.

86 Pyxis, New York MM 09.221.40, *ARV*² 1328.99, *Para* 479, n.p.

87 One is reminded of the anonymous *Epitaph to a Tired Housewife*, which ends: 'Don't mourn for me now, don't mourn for me never,/I'm going to do nothing for ever and ever.'

88 See M. West, *Ancient Greek Music* (Oxford 1992) ch. 1, and W.D. Anderson, *Music and Musicians in Ancient Greece* (Ithaca and London 1994) ch. 5; for music in wedding scenes, see n. 28 above).

89 Hydria, Polygnotos Group, London BM 1921.7–10.2, *ARV*² 1060.138, *Add.* 323, n.p.

90 T.B.L. Webster, *Potter and Patron in Classical Athens* (London 1972) 242.

91 Lekythos, Klügmann Painter, Paris Louvre CA 2220, *ARV*² 1199.25, n.p.; H.R. Immerwahr, 'Book rolls on Attic vases', in C. Henderson, Jr. (ed.), *Classical, Medieval and Renaissance Studies in Honor of Berthold Louis Ullmann* (Rome 1964) i, 17–48, and 'More book rolls on Attic vases', *Antike Kunst* 16 (1973) 143–7.

92 S.G. Cole, 'Could Greek women read and write?', in H.P. Foley (ed.), *Reflections of Women in Antiquity* (New York 1981) 219–45.

93 Scenes of youths with scrolls begin in the period 500–450 (five examples), are most numerous between 475 and 425 (six), and disappear in 450–400 (two); images of women and Muses with scrolls do not appear until 475–25 (nine), and are most numerous in 450–400 (eleven).

94 *Pandora* 209.

95 Cup, Sabouroff Painter, Amsterdam Allard Pierson 8210, *ARV*² 838.27 (M. Golden, *Children and Childhood in Classical Athens* (Baltimore and London 1990) fig. 10).

96 Pyxis, Winchester Coll. 29, fr. Athens.

97 *CAT* vol. i p. 139; e.g. white-ground lekythos, Athens NM CC1814, *ARV*² 1168.133, fr. Eretria, and squat lekythos, Meidias Painter, London 1895.10–29.2, *ARV*² 1326.66, fr. Athens. Birds buried with owners: A. Breuckner and E. Pernice, 'Ein attischer Friedhof', *AM* 18 (1893) 73–191, p. 175.

98 Plut. *Alc.* 10, Athen. 397c, Aelian *Hist. Anim.* 7.41 and 5.29; see J. Pollard, *Birds in Greek Life and Myth* (London 1977) ch. 15.

99 Lekythos, see n. 3; pyxis lid, see n. 29; white-ground lekythos, Achilles Painter, Athens NM 1963, *ARV*² 995.122, 1677, *Para* 438, fr. Eretria.

100 Pyxis, Painter of London D12, Athens M. Vlasto coll., *ARV*² 963.87, *Para* 434, n.p.

101 White-ground lekythos, Athens 19355, *ARV*² 1022.139 bis, fr. Anavyssos (*CP* fig. 267); also white-ground lekythos, Athens NM CC1679, *ARV*² 1239.56, fr. Eretria; white-ground lekythos, Vienna, Oest Mus. 1086 (A. Fairbanks, *Athenian Lekythoi* (New York 1907) p. 85 no. 9).

102 A. Schnapp, 'Eros the Hunter', in *CdI* 71–87.

103 See also: pyxis lid, Philadelphia Univ. MS 5462 (*CP* fig. 400); pyxis, Dallas, private coll. (*RoP* fig. 94).

104 Cup, Pistoxenos Painter, London D2, *ARV*² 862.22, fr. Camiros (*CP* fig. 67).

105 White-ground lekythos, Achilles Painter, London D51, *ARV*² 1000.201, fr. Marion; loutrophoros, Boston MFA Bartlett coll. inv. 03.802 (*Pandora* no. 24).

106 Lekythos, Pan Painter, St Petersburg inv. B2363, B670, *ARV*² 557.121, 1659, *Para* 513, *Add.* 259 (*Pandora* no. 90).

107 *Hom. Hymn Ap.* 14–16, Ar. *Birds* 870, Soph. *Trach.* 213; see L.R. Farnell, *Cults of the Greek States* vol. ii (Oxford 1896) 443–4.

108 Aristotle *HA* 612 B 32, 616; Aelian *Hist. Anim.* 3.42.

109 For example, C. Celle, 'La Femme et l'oiseau dans la céramique grecque', *Pallas* 42 (1995) 113–28.

110 Böhr, 'A rare bird'.

111 Amphoriskos, Heimarmone Painter, Berlin inv. 30036, *ARV*² 1173.1, fr. Greece: see Shapiro, *Personifications* 192–5 and figs. 151–4.

112 Cup, Codros Painter, Cambridge Fitzwilliam Mus. GR 2–1977 (L. Burn, 'A heron on the left', in J. Christiansen and T. Melander (eds) *Proceedings of the 3rd Symposium on Ancient Greek and Related Pottery* (Copenhagen 1988) 99–105 says that this heron is stuffed); alabastron, Palermo Mormino Coll. 796, no *ARV*²; alabastron, Pasiades Painter, London B668, *ARV*² 98.1, fr. Marion; alabastron, Pasiades Painter, Athens NM15002, *ARV*² 98.2, fr. Delphi.

113 In fact the contention that herons were domestic pets, and that pots are presenting scenes of reality, traces back to Beazley who suggested that 'the real reason for the appearance of the heron and similar birds (on gems) is that they were domestic pets, cherished by the engraver's patrons, and admired and studied by the engraver' (Beazley, in E.P. Warren, *The Lewes House Collection of Ancient Gems* (Oxford 1920) 59–60). This comment has been reproduced by many writers since, but on examination the scenes are not as straightforward as described. On the gem discussed, a half-naked woman reclines, and strokes the bill of a heron (or crane) which seems to walk on the end of her couch; in the field above is a large ant. On other gems cited by Beazley the women with herons are naked, and he describes a third gem, in Oxford, as a woman 'engaged with' a bird of the same sort.

114 Hydria, Painter of the Yale Oinochoe, Houston 80.96 (fig. 2.2); feeding herons: hydria, Harvard Fogg Art Museum 60.340, *ARV²* 503.22, fr. Vari? See P.J. Holliday, 'Red-figure hydria: a theme in Greek vase-painting', *Bulletin of the Museum of Fine Arts, Houston* 8.3 (1984) 2–7.

115 Its only appearance in myth is in the Hellenistic *Mythographiae* of Antoninus Liberalis (7.7), in a story recounting the metamorphosis of Anthos and his family, including his brother Erodios, who is transformed at the end of the tale into a heron (ἐρῳδιός). While this myth may reach back into the fourth century, it does not illuminate herons on pottery: Erodios is a peripheral figure in the tale.

116 Lekanis lid, Meidias Painter, Naples Stg 316, *ARV²* 1327.85, *Add.* 364, fr. Egnazia (Shapiro, *Personifications* fig. 26); lekanis lid (see n. 29).

117 Pelike, Chicago Painter, Lecce 570, *ARV²* 629.23, fr. Rugge.

118 Stele of Philoumene: Athens Nat. Mus. Karapanos coll. 1023 (*CAT* 0.783); others: Athens Nat. Mus. 2775 (*CAT* 0.918), Piraeus Museum 1703 (*CAT* 1.247), Athens Nat. Mus. Apothiki coll. 363 (*CAT* 1.263), Malibu, J.P. Getty Museum 82.AA.135 (*CAT* 1.311).

119 See J. Reilly, 'Naked and limbless: learning about the feminine body in ancient Athens', in A.O. Koloski-Ostrow and C.L. Lyons (eds), *Naked Truths: women, sexuality and gender in classical art and archaeology* (London 1997) 154–73. The same gesture is repeated with a large goose on *CAT* 0.869a.

120 For example, cup, Akestorides Painter, Basel Mkt, *Para* 417 (*ARFV* fig. 368); Hom. *Od.* 19.536ff.

121 Cup, Epidromos Painter, Lucerne Mkt, *ARV²* 118.14, 1577, n.p.

122 Lekanis lid, Reading Ure Museum 45.10.4, *ARV²* 1501.1. See, for example, M. Robertson, *The Art of Vase-painting in Classical Athens* (Cambridge 1992) 267–74, and D. von Bothmer, 'Observations on the subject matter of South Italian vases', *Arts in Virginia* 23.3 (1983) 28–41: 'reduced even further, to mere female heads' (p. 41).

123 These include more than two hundred squat lekythoi, about sixty cylindrical lekythoi and thirty-six askoi, as well as lekanis and pyxis lids.

124 D.A. Amyx, *Corinthian Vase-Painting of the Archaic Period* (Berkeley, Los Angeles and London 1988) vol. ii 542 and pls. 63, 76 and 93; round aryballos, London BM 65.12.13.1; column-krater, Amsterdam Allard Pierson 2031.

125 Pyxis, San Simeon 5620, Amyx, *Corinthian Vase-Painting* cat. p. 224 and pl. 93; pyxis, New York MM CP-54, fr. Corinth.

126 Bell-krater, Reading Ure Museum 35.iv.5; Ure, 'Boeotian vases'; N.H. Demand, *Thebes in the Fifth Century: Heracles resurgent* (London and Boston 1982) 119–20.

127 Bell-krater, Ascoli Satriano Painter, Reinbach, Koch coll. (A.D. Trendall and A. Cambitoglou, *The Red-Figured Vases of Apulia* [=*RVAp*] (Oxford 1978–82) ii 719, 22.865); A.D. Trendall, *Red-Figured Vases of Apulia* (Oxford 1978–82) ii 646–9.

128 J.D. Beazley, 'Little Master Cups', *JHS* 52 (1932) 167–204, pp. 174–5 for a list of 'head cups'; see *ABFV* figs. 115, 121.

129 D.C. Kurtz, *Athenian White Lekythoi: patterns and painters* (Oxford 1975) 109; *ABL* 82.

130 Amyx, *Corinthian Vase-Painting* 554–5; F. Lorber, *Inschriften auf Korinthischen Vasen: archaologisch-epigraphische untersuchungen zur Korinthischen Vasenmalerei im 7 und 6 jh. v. chr.* (Berlin 1979) 28–30; M.J. Milne, 'Three names on a Corinthian jar', *AJA* 46 (1942) 216–22.

131 Apulian volute-krater, Iliupersis Painter, London BM F227, Trendall and Cambitoglou,

RVAp i 193.5 (*LIMC* vol. iii 52, fig. Aurai 2); cup, Elpinikos Painter, Bonn 63, *ARV²* 119.1, *Add.* 86, fr. Orvieto; see J.D. Beazley, Review of *Corpus Vasorum Antiquorum Deutschland I* = *Bonn, Akademisches Kunstmuseum* 1, by A. Griefenhagen, *JHS* 59 (1939) 150–1.

132 For example, hydria, Herakles Painter, Brussels Mus. Royaux R286, *ARV²* 1472.4, fr. Capua (*CP* fig. 377); see C. Bérard, *Anodoi: essai sur l'imagerie des passages chthoniens* (Rome 1974).

133 F. Croissant, *Les Protomes féminines archaïques: recherches sur les représentations du visage dans la plastique grecque de 550 à 480 av. J-C* (Paris 1983).

134 For an overview of plastic heads, J.D. Beazley, 'Charinos', *JHS* 49 (1929) 38–78.

135 *Pandora* 212–15.

136 F. Lissarrague, 'Identity and otherness: the case of Attic head-vases and plastic vases', *Source* 15 (1995) 4–9 figs. 1–2.

137 Head kantharos, Ferrara 20401, *ARV²* 766.5, fr. Spina; Etruscan head-kantharos, Munich NI 1728, *EVP* 188–9. See H. Hoffmann, 'Charos, Charon, Charun', *OJA* 3 (1984) 65–9.

138 See *LIMC* vol. ii, s.v. Aphrodite VII.

5 WOMEN AND MEN

1 Column-krater, Orchard Painter, New York MM 34.11.7, *ARV²* 524.28, *Add.* 254, n.p.; pyxis, Manchester University 40096, *ARV²* 931.2, n.p.; cup, Veii Painter, Tokyo Bridge-stone Museum 89, n.p.

2 For example, D. Cohen, *Law, Society and Sexuality: the enforcement of morals in classical Athens* (Cambridge 1991) ch. 6; L. Llewellyn-Jones, 'Women and veiling in ancient Greece', Ph.D. thesis, University of Wales Cardiff 2000.

3 D. Williams, 'Women on Athenian vases: problems of interpretation', in A. Cameron and A. Kuhrt (eds), *Images of Women in Antiquity* (London 1993) 92–106.

4 *CAT* Introductory volume section 1D (19–29).

5 J. Frel, 'Études sur les stèles funéraires attiques du 5ième et du 4ième s. av. n. é. I', *Listy Filologicke* 88 (1965) 13–21, p. 20: 'Il vaut mieux ne pas insister sur les relations familiales entre les personnages représentés et sur la distinction entre les défunts et les survivants; des discussions pareilles s'avèrent stériles.'

6 Chous, New York MM 37.11.19, no *ARV²*, n.p. (*RoP* fig. 48 and p. 67).

7 As previously noted, the chapter on concubines in E.C. Keul's *The Reign of the Phallus: sexual politics in ancient Athens* (Berkeley [1985] 1993) contains no illustrations, as there are no recognised images of this female status.

8 Xen. *Oik.* 3.12.

9 Isae. 10.19; [Dem.] 59.87; Xen. *Symp.* 8.3.

10 Dem. 39.23; cf. Lys. 1.6.

11 R.F. Sutton, Jr, 'Pornography and persuasion on Attic pottery', in A. Richlin (ed.), *Pornography and Representation in Greece and Rome* (New York and Oxford 1992) 1–33, pp. 26–7 and 34; compare the artificiality (and conventional form) of the required gesture of affection in modern weddings: 'you may kiss the bride'.

12 C. Reinsburg, *Ehe, Hetärentum und Knabenliebe im antiken Griechenland* (Munich 1989) ch. 1 considers the role of the wife, but its illustrations are either wedding scenes or funerary reliefs and white-ground lekythoi. Identifying the wife at any other moment of her life is difficult.

13 White-ground lekythos, Berlin F2444, *ARV²* 746.14, fr. Athens (*FaF* fig. 26); amphora, London BM E282, *ARV²* 538.39, fr. Vulci (*JHS* 9 pl. 3). See N. Massar, 'Images de la famille sur les vases attiques à figures rouges de l'époque classique', *Annales d'Histoire de l'Art et d'Archéologie* 17 (1995), 27–38. R.F. Sutton 'The interactions between men and women portrayed on Attic red-figure pottery' (Diss., University of North Carolina at Chapel Hill, 1981) adds a stamnos sold in London depicting a woman and boy with a warrior (*ARV²* 1121.19, fr. Camarina (*LIMC* I pl. 568)), but this is usually taken to be Amphiareos and his family.

14 Hydria, Harvard Sackler Museum (fig. 1.3, this volume); hydria, Munich SL 476, *ARV²* 1083.2, n.p. (*RoP* fig. 219); pelike, London BM E396, *ARV²* 1134.6, fr. Camiros.

15 Hydria, London BM E215, *ARV²* 1082.1, fr. Nola (*RoP* fig. 111, and M. Beard, 'Adopting an approach II', in *LGV* fig. 4).
16 Pelike, Acheloos Painter, London BM W40, *ABV* 384.20 (*RoP* figs. 319, 320 and p. 375).
17 White-ground lekythos, Achilles Painter, London D51, *ARV²* 1000.201, 1677, *Add.* 313, fr. Marion; lekythos, Achilles Painter, Athens NM 1818, *ARV²* 998.161, fr. Eretria.
18 Massar, 'Images' 38.
19 Soph. *OC* 1251–63; see also Eur. *Suppl.* 1101–3, *IA* 1220–30.
20 Ar. *Peace* 110–49, *Wasps* 605–9, *Ach.* 731–43.
21 Pyxis, Cambridge Fitzwilliam Museum GR 1.1933, *ARV²* 451.32, *Para* 521, *Add.* 242, fr. Greece.
22 Hippodamia: Apollodorus *Epitome* 2.4–7, Apollonius Rhodius, *Argonautika* i.752ff., Pausan. 5.17.7, 8.14.4–10; Ariadne: Plut. *Thes.* 19; Scylla: Hyginus *Fab.* 198, Virgil *Ciris*, Apoll. 3.15.8; Medea: Apollonius Rhodius, *Argonautika* 3.616–743.
23 See *LIMC* Akrisios (I 449–52), Kepheus (VI 6–10).
24 Aeschines, *Against Ctesiphon* 77–8.
25 White-ground lekythos, Vienna 3746; lekythos, Amiens 3057.172.33; see J.H. Oakley, *The Achilles Painter* (Mainz 1997) 67.
26 Stele of Peisikrateia: Athens, Piraeus Museum 1625, *CAT* 3.382a.
27 Cup, Rome Mkt: M. Vickers and A.A. Barrett, 'The Oxford Brygos cup reconsidered', *JHS* 98 (1978) 17–24, pl. 2b. (Old man seated with staff, child holds bird in both hands.)
28 Hdt. 5.49–51; Plut. *Mor.* 240D–E.
29 Hdt. 3.124, 68–9.
30 Eur. *Hkld.* 500–34, *IA* 1368–1401; see M. Lefkowitz, 'The last hours of the parthenos', in *Pandora* 32–8.
31 P. Walcot, 'Romantic love and true love: Greek attitudes to marriage', *Anc. Soc.* 18 (1987) 5–33; M. Golden, *Children and Childhood in Classical Athens* (Baltimore and London 1990) 121–35.
32 Lys. 19.33, Isae.2.3–5; Isae. 8.36; Dem. 30.25–7, 34. See Golden, *Children and Childhood* 129–30.
33 Isae. 7.14, Hdt. 3.53.
34 See *LIMC* III 709–19 (Electra I) and D. Knoepfler, *Les Imagiers de l'Orestie: mille ans d'art antique autour d'un mythe grec* (Kilchberg 1993).
35 Cup, Meleager Painter, Würzburg 493, *ARV²* 1414.90, fr. near Naples; cup, Meleager Painter, S. Agata de' Goti, *ARV²* 1412.55, n.p. See *LIMC* III 567–93 (Dioscuroi): no images of the Dioskouroi as adults with Helen exist.
36 Chous, Louvre L73 MNB 3061; chous, St Petersburg Hermitage 14444; chous, London BM (no no.), *JHS* 41 (1921) p. 148 fig. 14, from Eretria.
37 Stele, New York MM 11.185 (G.M.A. Richter, *The Archaic Gravestones of Attica* (London 1961, Bristol 1988) no. 37; Golden, *Children and Childhood* fig. 17); see Golden 125–8 and note the stele Athens NM 877 (*CAT* 0.910), on which Nikandros and his sister shake hands like adults.
38 *IG* ii² 6476, *IG* ii² 5479; S.C. Humphreys, *The Family, Women and Death: comparative studies* (London and Boston, Mass. 1983) 112.
39 Lekythos, New York MM 08.258.18, *ARV²* 998.180, *Para* 438, fr. Eretria; lekythos, London BM D55, *ARV²* 1000.94, fr. Eretria; lekythos, Athens NM 19353, *Para* 439.204 bis, fr. Anavyssos. Oakley, *Achilles Painter* 65–6.
40 Bell-krater, Syracuse 30747, Dinos Painter, *ARV²* 1153.17, *Add.* 336, fr. Camarina (*Pandora* fig. 20).
41 Black-figure plaque, Paris, Louvre MNB 905, *ABL* 229.58 (*ARFV* fig. 265).
42 Pyxis, Manchester University 40096, *ARV²* 931.2, n.p.; pyxis, Boston 93.108; pyxis, Phiale Painter, Athens 1588, *ARV²* 1023.144, fr. Attica; pyxis, Würzburg 542, *ARV²* 1296.3, *Add.* 352, fr. Boiotia.
43 Onos, Diosphos Painter, Leiden, I.1955.1.2.
44 Column-krater, Harrow Painter, Baltimore Walters Art Gallery 48.70, *ARV²* 278.1, n.p.; *RoP* p. 262 and fig. 243.
45 Pyxis, Cage Painter, Liverpool 49.50.7, *ARV²* 348, n.p.

46 A similar type of scene on an oinochoe in Russia, where a man and woman work at a laver, and an armed youth looks on, has been interpreted as ritual (the preparation for a funerary feast), but the mundane atmosphere of the Liverpool pyxis argues against this: oinochoe, Ferrara 2504, *ARV²* 1324.42, fr. Spina; W. Burkert and H. Hoffmann, 'La cuisine des morts: zu einem Vasenbild aus Spina und verwandten Darstellungen', *Hephaistos* 2 (1980) 107–11.

47 Hydria, Orpheus Painter, New York MM 17.230.15, *ARV²* 1104.16, n.p.; alabastron, London BM E719, *ARV²* 1560, fr. Elateia (V. Sabetai, 'Aspects of nuptial and genre imagery in fifth-century Athens: issues of interpretation and methodology', in *APP* 319–35, fig. 4a–b); skyphos, Phiale Painter, Palermo Mormino inv. 788 (*Pandora* p. 72 fig. 20).

48 Pyxis, Veii Painter, Hadley (MA), Mt. Holyoke College 1932 BS.II.5, *ARV²* 906.109, *Add.* 303, n.p.

49 H.A. Shapiro, 'Courtship scenes in Attic vase-painting', *AJA* 85 (1981) 133–43; Sutton, 'Pornography and persuasion' 19.

50 Black-figure kantharos, Paris Louvre, once coll. O. Rayet, *IG* vii 3467. I am indebted to Robin Osborne for a discussion of the ideas in this section.

51 White-ground alabastron, Painter of Copenhagen 3830, Palermo Mormino coll. 796, no *ARV²*; white-ground alabastron, Copenhagen 3830 (name vase), *ARV²* 723.1, fr. Attica; black-figure oinochoe, Ferrara 203, *Para* 283, fr. Spina.

52 It is notable that commentators have no difficulty in adopting this view with homosexual scenes because male courtship is seen to exist within a circumscribed ideology where all participants are citizens, so few questions are raised about status and the nature of the gift. Although there is plenty of evidence for slaves and prostitution in the homosexual milieu, the imagery is not interpreted in the same way.

53 Cup, Douris, Louvre G276, *ARV²* 428.11, n.p.

54 R.G. Osborne, 'Women and sacrifice in classical Greece', *CQ* 43 (1993) 392–405; Theophr. (*Char.*) uses the distribution of sacrificial meat as an indicator of character: 2.2, 4 (the mean man sells the meat from his sacrifice) and 9.2 (the shameless man salts the meat instead of distributing it).

55 Alabastron (see n. 51); skyphos, Penthesilea Painter, St Petersburg Hermitage 4224, *ARV²* 889.166, *Para* 516; cup, Euaion Painter, Oxford Ashmolean Museum 1911.618, *ARV²* 795.104, fr. Cervetri.

56 Cup, Briseis Painter, Ruvo, Jatta 1539, *ARV²* 408.33, fr. Ruvo; Nolan amphora, Munich 2341, *ARV²* 668.30, n.p.; on the pelike, Naples 81614, *ARV²* 778, a woman holds a leg of meat.

57 Alabastron, Pan Painter, Berlin F2254, *ARV²* 557.123, *Para* 387, fr. Pikrodafni (*RoP* fig. 238; J. Davidson, *Courtesans and Fishcakes: the consuming passions of classical Athens* (London 1997) fig. 7; S. von Reden, *Exchange in Ancient Greece* (London 1995) fig. 7c–d; M. Meyer 'Männer mit Geld: zu einem rotfigurigen Vase mit "Alltagszene"', *JdI* 103 (1988) fig. 23); on the 'spinning hetaira' debate see most recently Davidson, *Courtesans and Fishcakes* 86–90. The topic does seem over the years to have been subject to some competition in worldliness among scholars, who have been eager to make comparisons with contemporary 'red-light' districts.

58 Alabastron, Oxford Ashmolean Museum 1916.6, *ARV²* 100.23, fr. Boiotia; alabastron, Manner of Euergides Painter, Essen Folkwang Museum, *ARV²* 100.13, n.p.; alabastron, Paris, Bib. Nat. 508, *ARV²* 1610.

59 Alabastron, Athens Akropolis Museum 2713, *Para* 331, *Add.* 172, fr. Athens (*CdI* fig. 112); see U. Knigge, *Kerameikos IX: der Südhügel* (Berlin 1976) 90–1 and pl. 19.6–7. M. Kilmer in *Greek Erotica on Attic Red-Figure Vases* (London 1993) 81–9, argues that the alabastron is a peculiarly erotic shape, given its phallic form, and suggests that as an oil container it should be considered an essential adjunct to sex, but this again results from concentration on too small a sample of scenes: alabastra are frequent in depictions of sex and washing, but also in domestic interiors and wedding scenes.

60 Lekythos, Achilles Painter, NY MM 07.286.42; white-ground lekythos, Berlin Pergamonmuseum F2252, *ARV²* 263.54, fr. Athens.

61 See nn. 48 and 56.

62 Lys. 1.8, Ar. *Ach.* 253–8.

63 Plut. *Mor.* 232C.

64 R.S.J. Garland, *The Greek Way of Life: from conception to old age* (London 1990) p. 339, reflecting W.E. Thompson, 'Athenian marriage patterns: remarriage', *CSCA* 5 (1972) 211–24.

65 Isae. 2.3–4 and 8, 3.4, 5.26, 7.9, 10.25.

66 Hyperides 1 (*In Defence of Lycophron*) fr. 4b.

67 Hdt. 6.122 and *APF* 256–7; Walcot, 'Romantic love'.

68 Sutton, 'Interactions' p. 281 considers and rejects the idea that some gift-giving couples might be cousins.

69 Cohen, *Law, Society and Sexuality* 164–6; Lys. 1.8–9, Ar. *Thesm.* 339–46, *Ekkl.* 610.

70 Ar. *Thesm.* 479–80; *Ekkl.* 938ff. Walcot, in 'Romantic love', suggests that the affair in *Ekkl.* may be a realistic representation of the practice among the poorer class.

71 Etruscan amphora (?) (N.J. Spivey and S. Stoddart, *Etruscan Italy* (London 1990) fig. 98); terracotta, private coll., fr. Taranto (*LIMC* III p. 1061 no. 106); oinochoe, Heraklion Museum Afrati L60, fr. Crete (*EGVP* fig. 269). Both the latter illustrated in K. Schefold, *Myth and Legend in Early Greek Art* (London 1966), pls. 27a–b.

72 Stele of Phyrkias: Athens NM 2062 (*CAT* 2.183), *SEG* 32.288.

73 C.W Clairmont, *Gravestone and Epigram: Greek memorials from the archaic and classical period* (Mainz 1970) 104 (with some unease): 'The interpretation of the figures which we propose may come as a surprise, but it seems to us that there is little choice'; rejected in *CAT* vol. ii 120.

74 Skyphos, Penthesilea Painter, St Petersburg Hermitage 4224, *ARV²* 889.166, *Para* 516.

75 White-ground lekythos, London BM 1914.5–12.1, *ARV²* 283.1, n.p.; the suggestion was made by a colleague, showing how deep assumptions can run. A similar theme dominates A.F. Stewart, *Art, Desire and the Body in Ancient Greece* (Cambridge 1997) 177–9, on the interpretation of a Corinthian mirror.

76 Onos, Leiden I.1955.1.2; onos, Berlin F2624, *ARV²* 1225.1, fr. Athens.

77 For example, Keuls, *RoP* 180: '[The purse] establishes . . . the fact that the man is paying for his sex, but this communication is in truth superfluous'; Reeder, *Pandora* 182: 'the purse need not be present'.

78 Sale of wine: also pelike, Paris Mkt, *ARV²* 1162.18 (youth with purse); von Reden, *Exchange* 202, 210–11 (with figs.) and Meyer, 'Männer mit Geld' 112–16. Other purses hang in the background on the cup, Splanchnopt Painter, Newcastle Shefton Museum, *ARV²* 892.10 bis, n.p. and pyxis, Berlin F2517, *ARV²* 917.205, *Para* 430, fr. Attica.

79 von Reden, *Exchange* 206–9.

80 *RoP* 262–4 (kalpis, Heidelberg University 64.5).

81 Cup, Splanchnopt Painter, Florence 3961, *ARV²* 892.20, n.p.; lekythos, Harvard Fogg Museum 2236 (*CVA* USA fasc. 8 pl. 17); pyxis (see n. 48).

82 Column-krater, Harrow Painter, Rome Villa Giulia 1054, *ARV²* 275.50, fr. Falerii; the latest examples are found on a series of hydriai by the classical Hephaistos Painter, e.g. hydria, Syracuse 18426, *ARV²* 1116.38, fr. Camarina (von Reden, *Exchange* fig. 7b (incorrect reference) and Meyer, 'Männer mit Geld' fig. 16); hydria, Rhodes 12887, *ARV²* 1116.40, fr. Camiros (*RoP* fig. 241); hydria, Havana, 155, *ARV²* 116.46; hydria, Szczecin Museum, *ARV²* 1116.47.

83 Hydria fr., Alexandria 23446, *ARV²* 587.56, fr. Egypt (?) (Sutton, 'Interactions' no. G72).

84 Sabetai, 'Aspects'.

85 Ar. *Thesm.* 289–90.

86 Dem. 41.27, 45.28, 59.46, Isae. 2.9, Lys. 12.19; see V.J. Hunter, *Policing Athens: social control in the Attic lawsuits, 420–320 BC* (Princeton 1994) 27–8, and D. Schaps, *Economic Rights of Women in Ancient Greece* (Edinburgh 1979) 9–12.

87 Pelike, Chicago Painter, Lecce 570, *ARV²* 629.23, fr. Ruvo.

88 On the theme, see F. Lissarrague, 'Women, boxes, containers', in *Pandora* 91–101, p. 93.

89 Pyxis, Euaion Painter, Chicago 92.125, *ARV²* 798.147, n.p.; see F. Frontisi-Ducroux, 'Le sexe du regard', in P. Veyne, F. Lissarrague and F. Frontisi-Ducroux, *Les Mystères du Gynécée* (Paris 1998) 199–276, pp. 211–12 on direction of gaze in pursuits.

90 S. Kaempf-Dimitriadou, *Die Liebe der Götter in der attischen Kunst des 5 Jahrhunderts v. Chr.* (*AK*-Beiheft 11) (Bern 1979); A. Stewart, 'Rape?', in *Pandora* 74–90; C. Sourvinou-Inwood, 'A series of erotic pursuits', *JHS* 107 (1987) 131–53.

91 F. Hobden, Ph.D. thesis (in progress), University of St Andrews (private communication); H.A. Shapiro, 'The cult of heroines: Kekrops' daughters', *Pandora* 39–48, pp. 44–6.

92 Pelike, Stockholm A24, ARV^2 990.48, *Add.* 311, n.p.; neck-amphora, Madrid 11753, n.p.; lekythos, Berlin Mkt, ARV^2 1001.1, n.p.; lekythos, Berlin Painter, Cambridge Fitzwilliam GR28.1937, ARV^2 211.205, fr. Agrigento (fig. 5.20); lekythos, Basel Mkt, ARV^2 645.2, n.p.; lekythos, Syracuse 21870, ARV^2 998.85, fr. Gela; lekythos, Copenhagen NM 5625, ARV^2 1003.18, fr. Keratea; lekythos, Athens NM 1294, ARV^2 1003.17, fr. Eretria. All examples except fig. 5.20 by the Achilles Painter: see Oakley, *Achilles Painter* 39.

93 For example, pyxis, Cambridge Fitzwilliam Museum GR 1933.1, ARV^2 451.32, *Para* 521, fr. Greece.

94 All figures derived from the Beazley Archive Database. Complete accuracy in statistics is hard to achieve, because (i) many pots carry more than one pursuit scene, and (ii) not all are described clearly enough to be detectable in a computer search.

95 Stewart, 'Rape?', and K. Arafat, 'State of the art – art of the state: sexual violence and politics in late archaic and early classical vase painting', in S. Deacy and K.F. Pierce (eds), *Rape in Antiquity* (London 1997) 97–121.

96 D. Williams, 'The Brygos Tomb reassembled . . .', *AJA* 96 (1992) 617–36. Stamnos, Deepdene Painter, NY MM 18.74.1, ARV^2 498.2; stamnos, Deepdene Painter, Karlsruhe 211, ARV^2 498.5; rhyton, Tarquinia Painter, London BM E787, ARV^2 870.89; hydria, Niobid Painter, Basel 1906.296, ARV^2 606.67; hydria, Coghill Painter, London BM E170, ARV^2 1042.2; neck-amphora, London BM E280, ARV^2 1030.35. (All from Capua, obviously!)

97 Pyxis, Athens Kerameikos Mus. 1008 (U. Knigge, *The Athenian Kerameikos: history, monuments, excavations* (Athens 1991) 109, fig. 103); calyx-krater, Boston 03.817, ARV^2 991.59, fr. Suessula (Oakley, *Achilles Painter* 125).

98 Lekythos, Athens NM CC1062, ARV^2 715.188, *ABL* 178, fr. Eretria; lekythos, Aischines Painter, Paris Mkt, ARV^2 715.189; lekythos, Aischines Painter, Basel Mkt, *Para* 409.189 bis, *Add.* 282 (*CP* fig. 61). G. Richter, 'A fourth-century bronze hydria in New York', *AJA* 50 (1946) 361–7, and also T.B.L. Webster, *Potter and Patron in Classical Athens* (London 1972) 287–8 on pursuit scenes in burials on Delos.

99 S. Steingräber, *Etruscan Painting: catalogue raisonné of Etruscan wall paintings* [tr. D. and F.R. Ridgway] (New York 1986) 59. This seems a more credible reason for the introduction of Boreas than a celebration of the role of the wind in the battle of Artemision; see Arafat, 'State of the art' 109–10.

100 Sourvinou-Inwood, 'A series of erotic pursuits'.

101 Ibid. 141–4.

102 Rhyton, Douris, London BM E796, ARV^2 445.258, *Add.* 241, fr. Capua.

103 R. Osborne, 'Desiring women on Athenian pottery', in N.B. Kampen (ed.), *Sexuality in Ancient Art* (Cambridge 1996) 65–80, p. 68.

104 Skyphos, Lewis Painter, Cambridge Corpus Christi College T520b2, ARV^2 973.15, fr. Capua; skyphos, Lewis Painter, Florence 4228, ARV^2 975.35, *Add.* 151, n.p.; skyphos, Lewis Painter, Matera Mus. Ridola 11957; on the skyphoi see Kaempf-Dimitriadov 194–6. Stamnos, Baltimore Walters Art Gallery 48.2034, ARV^2 509, 1657 (V. Philippaki, *The Attic Stamnos* (Oxford 1967) pl. 30); hydria fr., Syracuse Painter, Cambridge M. Robinson Coll., ARV^2 520.41, fr. Greece.

105 F. Frontisi-Ducroux, 'Eros, desire and the gaze', in N.B. Kampen (ed.), *Sexuality in Ancient Art* (Cambridge 1996) 81–100, p. 83.

106 Hydria, Meidias Painter, Florence 81948, ARV^2 1312.1, fr. Populonia.

107 Column-krater, Orchard Painter, New York MM 34.11.7, ARV^2 524.28, *Add.* 254, n.p.; see Sutton, 'Interactions' 52.

108 Cup, Veii Painter, Tokyo Bridgestone Museum 89; cup, Florence 935121 (*Boll. Dell' Arte* 50 figs. 47–9).

109 See Chapter 3, pp. 91–3.

110 Sutton, 'Interactions' 52–3.

111 *ARV*² 1412–14 for the series of cups: comment s.v. 1412.56.

112 Bell-krater, Dolon Painter, Bari 6264 (A.D. Trendall, *The Red-Figured Vases of Lucania, Campania and Sicily: second supplement* (London 1973) 102.535, *Suppl.* 3, p. 57 no. D9).

113 M. Schmidt, 'Some remarks on the subjects of South Italian vases', in M.E. Mayo (ed.), *The Art of South Italy: vases from Magna Graecia* (Richmond 1982) 23–36.

114 White-ground lekythos, Berlin Pergamonmuseum F2252, *ARV*² 263.54, fr. Athens.

115 Aspasia: Plut. *Per.* 24.3–4; Theodote: Xen. *Mem.* 3.11.

116 Dem. 25.56–7.

117 Dem. 53.4–5, Lys. 32.11; see Cohen, *Law, Society and Sexuality* 84–9.

CONCLUSION

1 I have not included a discussion of scenes of women in myth, since many excellent studies have already examined the role of Amazons, maenads and other mythological figures in Greek thinking about women.

2 Ar. *Clouds* 206–8; cf. *Birds* 39–41.

3 The stand of spectators at games is frequent in black-figure: dinos fr., Sophilos, Athens 15499, *ABV* 39.16, fr. Pharsalos (*ABFV* fig. 26; tyrrhenian amphora, Castellani Painter, Florence 3773, *ABV* 95.8, *Para.* 34, fr. Tarquinia; cf. Corinthian column-krater, Vatican Astarita 565, *LIMC* vol. VI.2 p. 238.). It is also found in Etruscan art, in the Tomb of the Biga at Cervetri (Steingräber, Etruscan Painting no. 47, O.J. Brendel, *Etruscan Art* (Harmondsworth 1978) pp. 266–8 and fig. 181).

BIBLIOGRAPHY

Amyx, D.A., *Corinthian Vase-Painting of the Archaic Period* vol. ii (Berkeley, Los Angeles and London, University of California Press, 1988).

Anderson, W.D., *Music and Musicians in Ancient Greece* (Ithaca and London, Cornell University Press, 1994).

André, J.-M., *Jouer dans l'antiquité (Exposition)* (Paris, Réunion des musées nationaux, 1991).

Arafat, K., 'State of the art – art of the state: sexual violence and politics in late archaic and early classical vasepainting', in S. Deacy and K.F. Pierce (eds), *Rape in Antiquity* (London, Duckworth, 1997) 97–121.

Ashmead, A., 'Bread and soup for dinner: a lekythos by the Pan Painter at Haverford College', in J.-P. Descoedres (ed.), *Eumousia: ceramic and iconographic studies in honour of A. Cambitoglou* (Sydney, Meditarch, 1990) 95–103.

Bažant, J., 'Les Vases athéniens et les réformes démocratiques', in C. Bérard et al. (eds), *Images et société en Grèce ancienne: l'iconographie comme méthode d'analyse* (Lausanne, University of Lausanne, 1987) 33–40.

Beard, M., 'Adopting an approach II', in T. Rasmussen and N. Spivey (eds), *Looking at Greek Vases* (Cambridge, Cambridge University Press, 1991) 12–35.

Beard, M. and Henderson, J., 'With this body I thee worship: sacred prostitution in antiquity', *Gender and History* 9.3 (1997) 480–503.

Beaumont, L., 'Born old or never young? Femininity, childhood and the goddesses of ancient Greece', in S. Blundell and M. Williamson (eds), *The Sacred and the Feminine in Ancient Greece* (London, Routledge, 1998) 71–95.

Beazley, J.D., 'Charinos', *JHS* 49 (1929) 38–78.

—— 'Little Master cups', *JHS* 52 (1932) 167–204.

—— Review of *Corpus Vasorum Antiquorum Deutschland I = Bonn, Akademisches Kunstmuseum 1*, by A. Griefenhagen, *JHS* 59 (1939) 150–1.

—— *Etruscan Vase-Painting* (Oxford, Clarendon Press, 1947).

—— *Attic Black-Figure Vase-Painters* (Oxford, Clarendon Press, 1956).

—— *Attic Red-Figure Vase-Painters* (2nd edn) (Oxford, Clarendon Press, 1963).

—— *Paralipomena* (Oxford, Clarendon Press, 1971).

—— *The Pan Painter* (Mainz, P. von Zabern, 1974).

Benbow, P.E., 'Epinetra' (Harvard diss. 1975) (summary in *HSCP* 80 (1976) 290–1).

Bérard, C., *Anodoi: essai sur l'imagerie des passages chthoniens* (Rome, Institut suisse de Rome, 1974).

—— 'L'Impossible Femme athlète', *AION* VIII (1986) 195–202.

—— 'The order of women', in C. Bérard et al., *City of Images: iconography and society in ancient Greece* (tr. D. Lyons) (Princeton, Princeton University Press, 1989) 88–107.

Bérard, C. and Durand, J.-L., 'Entering the imagery', in C. Bérard et al., *City of Images: iconography and society in ancient Greece* (tr. D. Lyons) (Princeton, Princeton University Press, 1989) 30–5.

Bérard, C. et al., *City of Images: iconography and society in ancient Greece* (tr. D. Lyons) (Princeton, Princeton University Press, 1989).

Boardman, J., 'Painted funerary plaques and some remarks on prothesis', *BSA* 50 (1955) 51–66.

—— *Athenian Black Figure Vases* (London, Thames & Hudson, 1974).

—— *Athenian Red Figure Vases: the archaic period* (London, Thames & Hudson, 1975).

—— 'The Athenian pottery trade', *Expedition* (Summer 1979) 33–9.

—— *Athenian Red Figure Vases: the classical period* (London, Thames & Hudson, 1989).

—— 'The sixth-century potters and painters of Athens and their public', in T. Rasmussen and N. Spivey (eds), *Looking at Greek Vases* (Cambridge, Cambridge University Press, 1991) 79–102.

—— 'The phallos-bird in archaic and classical Greek art', *RA* (1992), 227–42.

—— *The Oxford History of Classical Art* (Oxford, Oxford University Press, 1993).

—— 'Boy meets girl: an iconographic encounter', in J.H. Oakley, W. Coulson and O. Palagia (eds), *Athenian Potters and Painters: the conference proceedings* (Oxford, Oxbow Books, 1997) 259–67.

—— *Early Greek Vase Painting: a handbook* (London, Thames & Hudson, 1998).

Böhr, E., 'A rare bird on Greek vases: the wryneck', in J.H. Oakley, W. Coulson and O. Palagia (eds), *Athenian Potters and Painters: the conference proceedings* (Oxford, Oxbow Books, 1997) 109–23.

Bonfante, L. (ed.), *Etruscan Life and Afterlife: a handbook of Etruscan studies* (Warminster, Aris and Philips, 1986).

—— 'Iconografie delle madri: Etruria e Italia antica', in A. Rallo (ed.), *Le Donne in Etruria* (Studia Archeologica 52) (Rome, L'Erma di Bretschneider, 1989) 85–106.

—— 'Nudity as costume in classical art', *AJA* 93 (1989) 543–70.

—— 'Nursing mothers in classical antiquity', in A.O. Koloski-Ostrow and C.L. Lyons (eds), *Naked Truths: women, sexuality and gender in classical art and archaeology* (London and New York, Routledge, 1997), 174–96.

Braun, K., *Bemalte Keramik und Glas aus dem Kabirenheiligtum bei Theben* (Berlin, W. de Gruyter and Co., 1981).

Bremmer, J., 'The old women of ancient Greece', in J. Blok and P. Mason (eds), *Sexual Asymmetry: studies in ancient society* (Amsterdam, Gieben, 1987) 191–215.

Brendel, O.J., *Etruscan Art* (Harmondsworth, Penguin, 1978).

Breuckner, A. and Pernice, E., 'Ein attischer Friedhof', *AM* 18 (1893) 73–191.

Brijder, H.A.G. (ed.), *Ancient Greek and Related Pottery* (Amsterdam, Allard Pierson Museum, 1984).

Brock, R., 'The labour of women in classical Athens', *CQ* 44 (1994) 336–46.

Brulé, P., *La Fille d'Athènes: le réligion des filles à Athènes à l'époque classique. Mythes, cultes et société* (Paris: Les Belles Lettres 1987).

Buchholz, H.-G., 'Morsersymbolik', *Acta Praehistorica et Archaeologica* 7/8 (1976/77) 249–70.

Buitron-Oliver, D., *Douris: a master-painter of Athenian red-figure vases* (Mainz, P. von Zabern, 1995).

Burkert, W., *Homo Necans: the anthropology of ancient Greek sacrificial ritual and myth* (tr. P. Bing) (Berkeley, University of California Press, 1983).

Burkert, W. and Hoffmann, H., 'La Cuisine des morts: zu einem Vasenbild aus Spina und verwandten Darstellungen', *Hephaistos* 2 (1980) 107–11.

Burn, L., *The Meidias Painter* (Oxford, Clarendon Press, 1987).

—— 'A heron on the left', in J. Christiansen and T. Melander (eds), *Proceedings of the 3rd Symposium on Ancient Greek and Related Pottery* (Copenhagen, Nationalmuseet: Ny Carlsberg Glyptothek: Thorvaldsens Museum, 1988) 99–105.

Byvanck-Quarles van Ufford, L., 'La coiffure des jeunes dames d'Athènes au second quart du 5ième siècle av. J-C.', in H.A.G. Brijder et al. (eds), *Enthousiasmos: essays on Greek and related pottery presented to J.M. Hemelrijk* (Amsterdam, Allard Pierson Museum, 1986) 135–40.

Cahn, H., 'Morra: drei Silene beim knobeln', in H. Froning, T. Hölscher and H. Mielsch (eds), *Kotinos: Festschrift für E. Simon* (Mainz, P. von Zabern, 1992) 214–17.

Calame, C., *The Poetics of Eros in Ancient Greece* (tr. J. Lloyd) (Princeton, Princeton University Press, 1999).

Campbell, J.K., *Honour, Family and Patronage: a study of institutions and moral values in a Greek mountain community* (Oxford, Clarendon Press, 1964).

Canciani, F. and Neumann, G., 'Lydos, der Sklave', *AK* 21 (1978) 17–22.

Carpenter, T.H., 'On the dating of the Tyrrhenian Group', *OJA* 2 (1983) 279–93.

—— 'The Tyrrhenian Group: problems of provenance', *OJA* 3 (1984) 45–56.

—— (ed.), *Beazley Addenda* (2nd edn) (Oxford, Oxford University Press, 1989).

Cassimatis, H., 'Propros sur le calathos dans la céramique italiote', in J.-P. Descoedres (ed.), *Eumousia: ceramic and iconographic studies in honour of A. Cambitoglou* (Sydney, Meditarch, 1990) 195–201.

Celle, C., 'La Femme et l'oiseau dans la céramique grecque', *Pallas* 42 (1995) 113–28.

Clairmont, C.W., *Gravestone and Epigram: Greek memorials from the archaic and classical period* (Mainz, P. von Zabern, 1970).

—— *Classical Attic Tombstones* (7 vols) (Kilchberg, Akanthus, 1993).

Clarke, J.R., *Looking at Lovemaking: constructions of sexuality in Roman art, 100 BC–AD 250* (Berkeley, University of California Press, 1998).

Cohen, D., *Law, Society and Sexuality: the enforcement of morals in classical Athens* (Cambridge, Cambridge University Press, 1991).

Cole, S.G., 'Could Greek women read and write?', in H.P. Foley (ed.), *Reflections of Women in Antiquity* (New York, Gordon & Breach, 1981) 219–45.

—— 'The social function of rituals of maturation: the Koureion and the Arkteia', *ZPE* 55 (1984) 233–44.

Cook, R.M., 'The Francis–Vickers chronology', *JHS* 109 (1989) 164–70.

Coontz, S. and Henderson, P. (eds), *Women's Work, Men's Property: the origins of gender and class* (London, Verso, 1985).

Croissant, F., *Les Protomes féminines archaïques: recherches sur les représentations du visage dans la plastique grecque de 550 à 480 av. J-C* (Paris, De Boccard, 1983).

Csapo, E. and Miller, M.C., 'The "Kottabos-Toast" and an inscribed red-figure cup', *Hesperia* 60 (1991) 367–82.

Dalby, A., 'Food and sexuality in classical Greece', *Food, Culture and History* 1 (1993) 165–90.

Davidson, C., *A Woman's Work is Never Done: a history of housework in the British Isles 1650–1950* (London, Chatto & Windus, 1982).

Davidson, J., *Courtesans and Fishcakes: the consuming passions of classical Athens* (London, Harper-Collins, 1997).

Davies, G., 'The language of gesture in Greek art: gender and status on grave stelai', *Apollo* 140, no. 389 (1994) 6–11.

Davies, J.K., *Athenian Propertied Families, 600–300 BC* (Oxford, Clarendon Press, 1971).

De Puma, R.D., 'Eos and Memnon on Etruscan mirrors', in R.D. de Puma and J.P. Small (eds), *Murlo and the Etruscans* (Madison, University of Wisconsin Press, 1994).

Delavaud-Roux, M.-H., *Les Danses armées en Grèce antique* (Aix-en-Provence, Université de Provence, 1993).

—— *Les Danses pacifiques en Grèce antique* (Aix-en-Provence, Université de Provence, 1994).

Demand, N.H., *Thebes in the Fifth Century: Heracles resurgent* (London and Boston, Routledge and Kegan Paul, 1982).

—— *Birth, Death and Motherhood in Classical Greece* (Baltimore, Johns Hopkins University Press, 1994).

Deubner, L., 'Zum Astragalspiel', in L. Deubner, *Kleine Schriften zur klassischen Altertumskunde* (Königstein, Hain, 1982) 342–7.

Diehl, E., *Die Hydria: Formgeschichte und Verwendung in Kult des Altertums* (Mainz, P. von Zabern, 1964).

Dierichs, A., *Erotik in der Kunst Griechenlands* (Mainz, P. von Zabern, 1993).

Dikaios, P., *A Guide to the Cyprus Museum* (Nicosia, Cyprus Government Printing Office, 1947).

Du Boulay, J., *Portrait of a Greek Mountain Village* (Oxford, Clarendon Press, 1974).

Dunkley, B., 'Greek fountain-buildings before 300 BC', *ABSA* 36 (1935/6) 142–204.

Durand, J.-L., Frontisi-Ducroux, F. and Lissarrague, F., 'Wine: human and divine', in C. Bérard et al., *City of Images: iconography and society in ancient Greece* (tr. D. Lyons) (Princeton, Princeton University Press, 1989) 121–9.

Engels, D., *Classical Cats: the rise and fall of the sacred cat* (London and New York, Routledge, 1999).

Fairbanks, A., *Athenian Lekythoi* (New York, Macmillan, 1907).

Fantham, E. et al., *Women in the Classical World: image and text* (New York and Oxford, Oxford University Press, 1994).

Farnell, L.R., *Cults of the Greek States* vol. ii (Oxford, Clarendon Press, 1896).

Fisher, N., *Aeschines: Against Timarchos* (Oxford, Clarendon Press, 2000).

Follmann, B., *Der Panmaler* (Bonn, Bouvier, 1968).

Fracchia, H., 'The San Simeon fruit-pickers', *California Studies in Classical Antiquity* 5 (1972) 103–11.

Frel, J., 'Études sur les stèles funéraires attiques du 5ième et du 4ième s. av. n. é. I', *Listy Filologicke* 88 (1965) 13–21.

Frontisi-Ducroux, F., *Le Dieu-masque: une figure du Dionysos d'Athènes* (Paris, Éditions la Découverte Rome, 1991).

—— 'Eros, desire and the gaze', in N.B. Kampen (ed.), *Sexuality in Ancient Art* (Cambridge, Cambridge University Press, 1996) 81–100.

—— 'Le sexe du regard', in P. Veyne, F. Lissarrague and F. Frontisi-Ducroux, *Les Mystères du Gynécée* (Paris, Gallimard, 1998), 199–276.

Frontisi-Ducroux, F. and Lissarrague, F., 'From ambiguity to ambivalence', in D.M. Halperin, J.J. Winkler and F.I. Zeitlin (eds), *Before Sexuality: the construction of erotic experience in the ancient Greek world* (Princeton, Princeton University Press, 1990) 211–56.

Garland, R.S.J., *The Greek Way of Life: from conception to old age* (London, Duckworth, 1990).

Giddens, A., *Beyond Left and Right: the future of radical politics* (Cambridge, Polity Press, 1994).

Ginouvès, R., *Balaneutiké: recherches sur le bain dans l'antiquité grecque* (Paris, De Boccard, 1962).

Golden, M., *Children and Childhood in Classical Athens* (Baltimore and London, Johns Hopkins University Press, 1990).

Graef, B. and Langlotz, E., *Die antiken Vasen von der Akropolis zu Athen* (Berlin, de Gruyter, 1925–33).

Hägg, R., 'A scene of funerary cult from Argos', in R. Hägg (ed.), *The Iconography of Greek Cult in the Archaic and Classical Periods* [Kernos Suppl. 1] (Athens and Liège, Centre d'étude de la religion Grecque antique, 1992), 169–76.

Hamilton, R., *Choes and Anthesteria: Athenian iconography and ritual* (Ann Arbor, University of Michigan Press, 1992).

Hannestad, L., 'Slaves and the fountain-house theme', in H.A.G. Brijder (ed.), *Ancient Greek and Related Pottery* (Amsterdam, Allard Pierson Museum, 1984) 252–5.

Hartley, J., *Understanding News* (London, Routledge, 1982).

Haspels, C.H.E., *Athenian Black-Figured Lekythoi* (Paris, De Boccard, 1936).

Henderson, J., Aristophanes *Lysistrata* (Oxford, Clarendon Press, 1987).

Henry, M.M., *Prisoner of History: Aspasia of Miletus and her biographical tradition* (New York and Oxford, Oxford University Press, 1995).

Higgins, R., *Greek Terracottas* (London, Methuen, 1967).

—— *Tanagra and the Figurines* (London, Trefoil Books, 1986).

Himmelmann, N., *Archäologisches zum Problem der griechischen Sklaverei* (Wiesbaden, Verlag der Akademie der Wissenschaften und der Literatur Mainz, 1971).

Hoffmann, H., 'Charos, Charon, Charun', *OJA* 3 (1984) 65–9.

—— 'Why did the Greeks need imagery? An anthropological approach to the study of Greek vase-painting', *Hephaistos* 9 (1988) 143–62.

—— *Sotades: symbols of immortality on Greek vases* (Oxford, Clarendon Press, 1997).

Holliday, P.J., 'Red-figure hydria: a theme in Greek vase-painting', *Bulletin of the Museum of Fine Arts, Houston* 8.3 (1984) 2–7.

Holloway, R.R., 'The bulls in the "Tomb of the Bulls" at Tarquinia', *AJA* 90 (1986) 447–52.

Humphreys, S.C., *The Family, Women and Death: comparative studies* (London and Boston, Mass., Routledge & Kegan Paul, 1983).

Hunter, V.J., 'The Athenian widow and her kin', *Journal of Family History* 14 (1989) 291–311.

—— *Policing Athens: social control in the Attic lawsuits, 420–320 BC* (Princeton, Princeton University Press, 1994).

Immerwahr, H.R., 'Book rolls on Attic vases', in C. Henderson, Jr (ed.), *Classical, Medieval and Renaissance Studies in Honor of Berthold Louis Ullmann* vol. i (Rome, Ed. Di Storia e Letteratura, 1964) 17–48.

—— 'More book rolls on Attic vases', *Antike Kunst* 16 (1973) 143–7.

—— 'An inscribed cup by the Ambrosios Painter', *Antike Kunst* 27 (1984) 10–13.

Isler, H.-P., 'Eine Schäle aus Iaitas: neues zum Werk des Malers der Agora-Chaireas-Schalen', *Antike Kunst* 41 (1998) 3–16.

Johnston, A., 'Greek vases in the marketplace', in T. Rasmussen and N. Spivey (eds), *Looking at Greek Vases* (Cambridge, Cambridge University Press, 1991) 203–32.

Jucker, I., 'Frauenfest in Korinth', *Antike Kunst* 6 (1963) 47–61.

Kaempf-Dimitriadou, S., *Die Liebe der Götter in der attischen Kunst des 5 Jahrhunderts v. Chr.* (AK-Beiheft 11) (Bern, Francke, 1979).

Kahil, L., 'Autour de l'Artémis attique', *Antike Kunst* 8 (1965) 20–33.

—— 'L'Artémis de Brauron: rites et mystère', *Antike Kunst* 20 (1977) 86–98.

—— 'Le Cratérisque d'Artémis et le Brauronion de l'Acropole', *Hesperia* 50 (1981) 252–63.

—— 'Mythological repertoire of Brauron', in W.G. Moon (ed.), *Ancient Greek Art and Iconography* (Madison, University of Wisconsin Press, 1983) 231–44.

Kampen, N.B., *Image and Status: Roman working women in Ostia* (Berlin, Mann, 1981).

Karageorghis, V., *The Cyprus Museum* (tr. A.H. and S. Foster Krumholz) (Nicosia, C. Epiphaniou Publications, 1989).

Keuls, E.C., 'Attic vase-painting and the home textile industry', in W.G. Moon (ed.), *Ancient Greek Art and Iconography* (Madison, University of Wisconsin Press, 1983) 209–23.

—— *The Reign of the Phallus: sexual politics in ancient Athens* (Berkeley, University of California Press, 1985) (2nd edn 1993).

—— *Painter and Poet in Ancient Greece: iconography and the literary arts* (Stuttgart and Leipzig, Teubner, 1997).

—— 'The *CVA*, the *LIMC* and the Beazley Archive Project: different databases for the study of Greek iconography', in E.C. Keuls, *Painter and Poet in Ancient Greece: iconography and the literary arts* (Stuttgart and Leipzig, Teubner, 1997) 293–312.

—— 'The ass in the cult of Dionysus as a symbol of toil and suffering', in E.C. Keuls, *Painter and Poet in Ancient Greece: iconography and the literary arts* (Stuttgart and Leipzig, Teubner, 1997) 41–70.

Kilinski, K., *Boeotian Black-Figure Vase-Painting of the Archaic Period* (Mainz, P. von Zabern, 1990).

Kilmer, M., *Greek Erotica on Attic Red-Figure Vases* (London, Duckworth, 1993).

Klein, A.E., *Child Life in Greek Art* (New York, Colombia University Press, 1932).

Knauer, E., 'Οὐ γάφ ἦ ἁμίς: a chous by the Oionokles Painter', *Greek Vases in the J. Paul Getty Museum* 2 (1985) 91–100.

Knigge, U., *Kerameikos IX: der Südhügel* (Berlin, W. de Gruyter & Co., 1976).

—— 'Kerameikos: Tätigkeitsbericht 1978', *AA* (1980) 256–65.

—— *The Athenian Kerameikos: history, monuments, excavations* (Athens, Krene, 1991).

Knoepfler, D., *Les Imagiers de l'Orestie: mille ans d'art antique autour d'un mythe grec* (Kilchberg, Akanthus, 1993).

Kossatz, A., 'Satyr- und Mänadennamen auf Vasenbildern', *Greek Vases in the Getty Museum* 5 (1991) 131–99.

Kotansky, R., 'Incantations and prayers for salvation on inscribed Greek amulets', in C.A. Faraone and D. Obbink (eds), *Magika Hiera: ancient Greek magic and religion* (New York and Oxford, Oxford University Press 1991) 107–37.

Kurke, L., *Coins, Bodies, Games and Gold: the politics of meaning in archaic Greece* (Princeton, Princeton University Press, 1999).

Kurtz, D.C., *Athenian White Lekythoi: patterns and painters* (Oxford, Clarendon Press, 1975).

Landels, J.G., *Music in Ancient Greece and Rome* (London and New York, Routledge, 1998).

Lang, M., *The Athenian Agora vol. xxi: graffiti and dipinti* (Princeton, American School of Classical Studies at Athens, 1976).

Lefkowitz, M.R., 'The last hours of the parthenos', in E.D. Reeder (ed.), *Pandora: women in classical Greece* (Princeton, Princeton University Press, 1995) 32–8.

Lemos, A., 'Athenian black-figure: Rhodes revisited', in J.H. Oakley, W. Coulson and O. Palagia (eds), *Athenian Potters and Painters: the conference proceedings* (Oxford, Oxbow, 1997) 457–68.

Lewis, D.M., 'Notes on Attic inscriptions II', *BSA* (1955) 1–36.

Lewis, S., 'Shifting images: Athenian women in Etruria', in K. Lomas and T. Cornell (eds), *Gender and Ethnicity in Ancient Italy* (London, Accordia, 1997) 141–54.

—— 'Slaves as viewers and users of Athenian pottery', *Hephaistos* 16/17 (1998/9) 71–90.

Lexicon Iconographicum Mythologiae Classicae (Zürich and Munich, Artemis, 1981–).

Lezzi-Hafter, A., *Der Eretria-Maler: Werke und Weggefahrten* (Mainz, P. von Zabern, 1988).

Lind, H., 'Ein Hetärenhaus am heiligen Tor?', *Mus. Helv.* 45 (1988) 158–69.

Linders, T., *Studies in the Treasure Records of Artemis Brauronia Found in Athens* (Stockholm, Svenska Institutet i Athen, 1972).

Lissarrague, F., *Un flot d'images: une esthétique du banquet grec* (Paris, Adam Biro, 1987).

—— 'Voyages d'images: iconographie et aires culturelles', *REA* 89 (1987) 261–9.

—— 'The world of the warrior', in C. Bérard et al., *City of Images: iconography and society in ancient Greece* (tr. D. Lyons) (Princeton, Princeton University Press, 1989) 38–51.

—— *L'Autre Guerrier: archers, peltastes, cavaliers dans l'imagerie attique* (Paris and Rome, Éditions La Découverte, 1990).

—— 'Femmes au figuré', in G. Duby, M. Perrot and P. Schmitt-Pantel (eds), *Histoire des Femmes en Occident* vol. I (*L'Antiquité*) (Paris, Plon, 1991) 159–251.

—— 'Identity and otherness: the case of Attic head-vases and plastic vases', *Source* 15 (1995) 4–9.

—— 'Un rituel du vin: la libation', in O. Murray and M. Tecuşan (eds), *In Vino Veritas* (London, British School at Rome, 1995) 126–44.

—— 'Women, boxes, containers', in E.D. Reeder (ed.), *Pandora: women in classical Greece* (Princeton, Princeton University Press, 1995) 91–101.

—— 'Intrusions au gynécée', in P. Veyne, F. Lissarrague and F. Frontisi-Ducroux, *Les Mystères du Gynécée* (Paris, Gallimard, 1998) 155–98.

Lissarrague, F. and Durand, J.-L., 'Un lieu d'image: l'espace du loutérion', *Hephaistos* 2 (1980) 89–106.

Llewellyn-Jones, L., 'Women and veiling in the Ancient Greek world', Ph.D. thesis, University of Wales Cardiff 2000.

Lonsdale, S.H., *Dance and Ritual Play in Greek Religion* (Baltimore, Johns Hopkins University Press, 1993).

Loraux, N., *Mothers in Mourning* (tr. C. Pache) (Ithaca, Cornell University Press, 1998).

Lorber, F., *Inschriften auf Korinthischen Vasen: archaologisch-epigraphische untersuchungen zur Korinthischen Vasenmalerei im 7 und 6 jh v. chr.* (Berlin, Gebr. Mann Verlag, 1979).

McNally, S., 'The maenad in early Greek art', in J. Peradotto and J.P. Sullivan, *Women in the Ancient World. The Arethusa papers* (Albany, SUNY Press, 1984).

Maffré, J.-J., 'Collection Paul Canellopoulos VIII: vases béotiens', *BCH* 99 (1975) 409–520.

Manfrini-Aragno, I., 'Femmes à la fontaine: réalité et imaginaire', in C. Bron and E. Kassapoglou (eds), *L'Image en jeu: de l'antiquité à Paul Klee* (Yens-Sur-Morges, Institut d'archéologie et d'histoire ancienne, Université de Lausanne, 1992).

Massar, N., 'Images de la famille sur les vases attiques à figures rouges de l'époque classique', *Annales d'Histoire de l'Art et d'Archéologie* 17 (1995), 27–38.

Meyer, H., *Medeia und den Peliaden: eine attische Novelle und ihre Entstehung* (Rome, G. Bretschnieder, 1980).

Meyer, M., 'Männer mit Geld: zu einem rotfigurigen Vase mit "Alltagszene"', *JdI* 103 (1988) 87–125.

Miller, M.C., 'The parasol: an oriental status-symbol in late archaic and classical Athens', *JHS* 112 (1992) 91–105.

Milne, M.J., 'Three names on a Corinthian jar', *AJA* 46 (1942) 216–22.

—— 'A prize for wool-working', *AJA* 49 (1945) 528–33.

Moon, W.G., 'The Priam Painter: some iconographic and stylistic considerations', in W.G. Moon (ed.), *Ancient Greek Art and Iconography* (Madison, University of Wisconsin Press, 1983) 97–118.

Moritz, L.A., *Grain-mills and Flour in Classical Antiquity* (Oxford, Clarendon Press, 1958).

Neils, J. (ed.), *Goddess and Polis: the Panathenaic festival in ancient Athens* (Hanover, N.H., Princeton University Press, 1992).

Nevett, L.C., *House and Society in the Ancient Greek World* (Cambridge, Cambridge University Press, 1999).

Oakley, J.H., 'Nuptial nuances: wedding images in non-wedding scenes of myth', in E.D. Reeder (ed.), *Pandora: women in classical Greece* (Princeton, Princeton University Press, 1995) 63–73.

—— *The Achilles Painter* (Mainz, P. von Zabern, 1997).

—— 'Why study a Greek vase-painter? A response to Whitley...', *Antiquity* 72 (1998) 209–13.

Oakley, J.H. and Sinos, R., *The Wedding in Ancient Athens* (Madison, University of Wisconsin Press, 1993).

Oakley, J.H., Coulson, W. and Palagia, O. (eds), *Athenian Potters and Painters: the conference proceedings* (Oxford, Oxbow Books, 1997).

Ogden, D., *Greek Bastardy* (Oxford, Oxford University Press, 1996).

—— *Polygamy. Prostitutes and Death* (London, Duckworth with Classical Press of Wales, 1999).

Osborne, R., 'Women and sacrifice in classical Greece', *CQ* 43 (1993) 392–405.

—— 'Economy and trade', in *Cambridge Ancient History: plates to vols IV and V* (Cambridge, Cambridge University Press, 1994).

—— 'Desiring women on Athenian pottery' in N.B. Kampen (ed.), *Sexuality in Ancient Art* (Cambridge, Cambridge University Press, 1996) 65–80.

—— 'Men without clothes: heroic nakedness and Greek art', *Gender and History* 9.3 (1997) 504–28.

Patterson, C., 'Those Athenian bastards', *Classical Antiquity* 9 (1990) 39–73.

—— 'The case against Neaira and the public ideology of the Athenian family', in A.L. Boegehold and A.C. Scafuro (eds), *Athenian Identity and Civic Ideology* (Baltimore, Johns Hopkins University Press, 1994) 199–216.

Payne, H.G.G., *Necrocorinthia: a study of Corinthian art in the archaic period* (Oxford, Clarendon Press, 1931).

Peschel, I., *Die Hetäre bei Symposium und Komos in der attisch-rotfigurigen Vasenmalerei des 6–4 Jahrh. v. Chr.* (Frankfurt, Peter Lang, 1987).

Petersen, L.H., 'Divided consciousness and female companionship: reconstructing female subjectivity in Greek vases', *Arethusa* 30 (1997) 35–74.

Pfisterer-Haas, S., *Darstellungen alter Frauen in der Griechischen Kunst* (Frankfurt, Peter Lang, 1989).

Philippaert, M., 'Deux vases attiques inédits', *RA* 1 (1933) 154–62.

Philippaki, V., *The Attic Stamnos* (Oxford, Clarendon Press, 1967).

Pingiatoglou, S., *Eileithyia* (Würzburg, Könighausen and Neumann, 1981).

—— 'Rituelle Frauengelage auf schwarzfigurigen attischen Vasen', *AM* 109 (1994) 39–51.

Pipili, M., *Laconian Iconography of the Sixth Century BC* (Oxford, Oxford University Committee for Archaeology, 1987).

Pollard, J.J., *Birds in Greek Life and Myth* (London, Thames & Hudson, 1977).

Pomeroy, S.B., *Goddesses, Whores, Wives and Slaves* (New York, Schocken Books, 1975).

—— *Xenophon's Oeconomicus: a social and historical commentary* (Oxford, Clarendon Press, 1994).

Reeder, E.D. (ed.), *Pandora: women in classical Greece* (Princeton, Princeton University Press, 1995).

Reilly, J., 'Many brides: "mistress and maid" on Athenian lekythoi', *Hesperia* 58 (1989) 411–44.

—— 'Naked and limbless: learning about the feminine body in ancient Athens', in A.O. Koloski-Ostrow and C.L. Lyons (eds), *Naked Truths: women, sexuality and gender in classical art and archaeology* (London, Routledge, 1997) 154–73.

Reinsburg, C., *Ehe, Hetärentum und Knabenliebe im antiken Griechenland* (Munich, Beck, 1989).

Richter, G., 'The woman at the well in Milan', *RA* 3 (1935) 200–5.

—— 'A fourth-century bronze hydria in New York', *AJA* 50 (1946) 361–7.

Richter, G.M.A., *The Archaic Gravestones of Attica* (London, Phaidon Press, 1961; repr. Bristol, Bristol Classical Press, 1988).

—— *Attic Red-Figured Vases: a survey* (New Haven, Yale University Press, 1958).

Riddle, J.M., *Contraception and Abortion from the Ancient World to the Renaissance* (Cambridge, Mass. and London, Harvard University Press, 1992).

Roberts, N., *Whores in History: prostitution in Western society* (London, HarperCollins, 1993).

Roberts, S.R., *The Attic Pyxis* (Chicago, Ares Publishers, 1978).

Robertson, M., 'Two pelikai by the Pan Painter', *Greek Vases from the J. Paul Getty Museum* 3 (1986) 71–90.

—— *The Art of Vase-painting in Classical Athens* (Cambridge, Cambridge University Press, 1992).

Rotroff, S.I. and Oakley, J.H., *Debris from a Public Dining Place in the Athenian Agora* (*Hesperia* Supplement 25) (Princeton, N.J., American School of Classical Studies at Athens, 1992).

Rühfel, H., *Kinderleben im klassischen Athen: Bilder auf klassischen Vasen* (Mainz, P. von Zabern, 1984).

Sabetai, V., 'The Washing Painter' (Diss., University of Cincinnati, 1993).

—— 'Aspects of nuptial and genre imagery in fifth-century Athens: issues of interpretation and methodology', in J.H. Oakley, W. Coulson and O. Palagia (eds), *Athenian Potters and Painters: the conference proceedings* (Oxford, Oxbow Books, 1997) 319–35.

Schäfer, A., *Unterhaltung beim griechischen Symposion: Darbietungen, Spiele und Wettkämpfe von homerischer bis in spätklassische Zeit* (Mainz, P. von Zabern, 1997).

Schaps, D., 'The woman least mentioned', *CQ* 27 (1977) 323–30.

—— *Economic Rights of Women in Ancient Greece* (Edinburgh, Edinburgh University Press, 1979).

Schefold, K., *Myth and Legend in Early Greek Art* (London, Thames & Hudson, 1966).

Schmidt, M., 'Some remarks on the subjects of South Italian vases', in M.E. Mayo (ed.), *The Art of South Italy: vases from Magna Graecia* (Richmond, Virginia Museum of Fine Arts, 1982) 23–36.

—— 'Sorceresses', in E.D. Reeder (ed.), *Pandora: women in classical Greece* (Princeton, Princeton University Press, 1995) 57–62.

—— 'Medea at work', in G.R. Tsetskhladze, A.J.N.W. Prag and A.M. Snodgrass (eds), *Periplous: papers on classical art and archaeology presented to Sir John Boardman* (London, Thames & Hudson, 2000) 263–70.

Schmitt-Pantel, P. and Thelamon, F., 'Image et histoire: illustration ou document', in F. Lissarrague and F. Thelamon (eds), *Image et Céramique Grecque: actes du colloque de Rouen, 25–6 novembre 1982* (Rouen, Université de Rouen, 1983) 9–20.

Schnapp, A., 'Eros the Hunter', in C. Bérard et al., *City of Images: iconography and society in ancient Greece* (tr. D. Lyons) (Princeton, Princeton University Press, 1989) 71–87.

Sealey, R., 'On lawful concubinage in Athens', *Classical Antiquity* 3 (1984) 111–33.

Shapiro, H.A., 'Courtship scenes in Attic vase-painting', *AJA* 85 (1981) 133–43.

—— *Art and Cult under the Tyrants in Athens* (Mainz, P. von Zabern, 1989).

—— 'The iconography of mourning in Athenian art', *AJA* 95 (1991) 629–56.

—— *Personifications in Greek Art* (Zurich, Akanthus, 1993).

—— *Myth into Art: poet and painter in classical Greece* (London and New York, Routledge, 1994).

—— 'The cult of heroines: Kekrops' daughters', in E.D. Reeder (ed.), *Pandora: women in classical Greece* (Princeton, Princeton University Press, 1995) 39–48.

—— 'Correlating shape and subject: the case of the archaic pelike' in J.H. Oakley, W. Coulson and O. Palagia (eds), *Athenian Potters and Painters: the conference proceedings* (Oxford, Oxbow, 1997) 259–67.

Sheffer, C., 'Workshop and trade patterns in Athenian black-figure', in J. Christiansen and T. Melander (eds), *Proceedings of the 3rd Symposium on Ancient Greek and Related Pottery* (Copenhagen, Nationalmuseet: Ny Carlsberg Glyptothek: Thorvaldsens Museum, 1988) 536–46.

—— 'Boeotian festival scenes: competition, consumption and cult in archaic black-figure', in R. Hägg (ed.), *The Iconography of Greek Cult in the Archaic and Classical Periods* [Kernos Suppl.1] (Athens and Liège, Centre d'étude de la religion Grecque antique, 1992) 117–41.

Sini, T., 'A symposium scene on an Attic fourth-century calyx-krater in St. Petersburg', in O. Palagia (ed.), *Greek Offerings: essays on Greek art in honour of John Boardman* (Oxford, Oxbow Books, 1997) 159–65.

Sourvinou-Inwood, C., 'Persephone and Aphrodite at Locri', *JHS* 98 (1978) 101–21.

—— 'A series of erotic pursuits', *JHS* 107 (1987) 131–53.

—— *Studies in Girls' Transitions: aspects of the arkteia and age representation in Attic iconography* (Athens, Kardanitsa, 1988).

—— 'Male and female, public and private, ancient and modern', in E.D. Reeder (ed.), *Pandora: women in classical Greece* (Princeton, Princeton University Press, 1995) 111–20.

—— *Reading Greek Death to the End of the Classical Period* (Oxford, Clarendon Press, 1995).

Sparkes, B.A., 'The Greek kitchen', *JHS* 82 (1962) 121–37.

—— 'The Greek kitchen: addenda', *JHS* 85 (1965) 162–3.

—— 'Not cooking but baking', *G&R* 28 (1981) 172–8.

—— *The Red and the Black: studies in Greek pottery* (London, Routledge, 1996).

Spivey, N.J., *The Micali Painter and His Followers* (Oxford, Clarendon Press, 1987).

—— 'Greek vases in Etruria', in T. Rasmussen and N. Spivey (eds), *Looking at Greek Vases* (Cambridge, Cambridge University Press, 1991) 131–50.

Spivey, N.J. and Stoddart, S., *Etruscan Italy* (London, Batsford, 1990).

Stears, K.E., 'Women and the family in the funerary ritual and art of classical Athens' (Diss., London, 1993).

—— 'Dead women's society: constructing female gender in classical Athenian funerary sculpture' in N. Spencer (ed.), *Time, Tradition and Society in Greek Archaeology: bridging the 'great divide'* (London and New York, Routledge, 1995), 109–31.

—— 'Death becomes her: gender and Athenian death-ritual', in S. Blundell and M. Williamson (eds), *The Sacred and the Feminine in Ancient Greece* (London, Routledge, 1998) 113–27.

Steingräber, S., *Etruscan Painting: catalogue raisonné of Etruscan wall paintings* [tr. D. and F.R. Ridgway] (New York, Harcourt Brace Jovanovich, 1986).

Stewart, A., 'Rape?, in E.D. Reeder (ed.), *Pandora: women in classical Greece* (Princeton, Princeton University Press, 1995) 74–90.

—— 'Reflections', in N.B. Kampen (ed.), *Sexuality in Ancient Art* (Cambridge, Cambridge University Press, 1996) 136–54.

—— *Art, Desire and the Body in Ancient Greece* (Cambridge, Cambridge University Press, 1997).

Stibbe, C.M., *Lakonische Vasenmaler des sechsten Jahrhunderts v. Chr.* (Amsterdam and London, North-Holland Publishing Co., 1972).

Stone, L., *The Family, Sex and Marriage in England 1500–1800* (London, Weidenfeld & Nicolson, 1977).

Sussman, L.S., 'Workers and drones: labor, idleness and gender definition in Hesiod's beehive', *Arethusa* 11 (1978) 27–41.

Sutton, Jr, R.F., 'The interactions between men and women portrayed on Attic red-figure pottery' (Diss., University of North Carolina at Chapel Hill, 1981).

—— 'Female bathers on Attic pottery' (abstract), *AJA* 95 (1991) 318.

—— 'Pornography and persuasion on Attic pottery', in A. Richlin (ed.), *Pornography and Representation in Greece and Rome* (New York and Oxford, Oxford University Press, 1992) 1–33.

Thompson, W.E., 'Athenian marriage patterns: remarriage', *Cal. Stud. Class. Ant.* 5 (1972) 211–24.

Treggiari, S., 'Jobs for women', *AJAH* 1 (1976) 76–104.

Trendall, A.D., *The Red-Figured Vases of Lucania, Campania and Sicily* (Oxford, Clarendon Press, 1967).

—— *The Red-Figured Vases of Lucania, Campania and Sicily: second supplement* (London, University of London Institute of Classical Studies, 1973).

Trendall, A.D. and Cambitoglou, A., *The Red-Figured Vases of Apulia* (Oxford, Clarendon Press, 1978–82).

Ulrich, L.T., *A Midwife's Tale: the life of Martha Ballard* (New York, Vintage Books, 1990).

Ure, A.D., 'Boeotian vases with women's heads', *AJA* 57 (1953) 245–9.

van Hoorn, G., *Choes and Anthesteria* (Leiden, Brill, 1951).

van Straten, F.T., *Hiera Kala: images of animal sacrifice in archaic and classical Greece* (Brill, Leiden, 1995).

Venit, M.S., 'The Caputi hydria and working women in classical Athens', *CW* 81.4 (1988) 265–72.

Vermeule, E., *Aspects of Death in Early Greek Art and Poetry* (Berkeley and London, University of California Press, 1979).

Veyne, P., Lissarrague, F. and Frontisi-Ducroux, F., *Les Mystères du Gynécée* (Paris, Gallimard, 1998).

Vickers, M. and Barrett, A.A., 'The Oxford Brygos cup reconsidered', *JHS* 98 (1978) 17–24.

von Bothmer, D., 'Observations on the subject matter of South Italian vases', *Arts in Virginia* 23.3 (1983) 28–41.

von Reden, S., *Exchange in Ancient Greece* (London, Duckworth, 1995).

Walcot, P., 'Romantic love and true love: Greek attitudes to marriage' *Anc. Soc.* 18 (1987) 5–33.

Walker, S., 'Women and housing in classical Greece', in A. Cameron and A. Kuhrt (eds), *Images of Women in Antiquity* (London, Croom Helm, 1983) 81–91.

Warren, E.P., *The Lewes House Collection of Ancient Gems* (Oxford, Clarendon Press, 1920).

Webster, T.B.L., *Potter and Patron in Classical Athens* (London, Methuen, 1972).

West, M.L., 'Erinna', *ZPE* 25 (1977) 95–119.

—— *Ancient Greek Music* (Oxford, Oxford University Press, 1992).

Whitley, J., 'Beazley as theorist', *Antiquity* 71 (1997) 40–7.

Williams, D., 'The Brygos Tomb reassembled . . .', *AJA* 96 (1992) 617–36.

—— 'Women on Athenian vases: problems of interpretation', in A. Cameron and A. Kuhrt (eds), *Images of Women in Antiquity* (London, Routledge, 1993) 92–106.

Winkler, J.J., *The Constraints of Desire: the anthropology of sex and gender in ancient Greece* (London, Routledge, 1990).

Wolters, P. and Bruns, G., *Das Kabirenheiligtum bei Theben* vol. i (Berlin, W. de Gruyter, 1940).

Yegül, F.K., *Baths and Bathing in Classical Antiquity* (New York, Architectural History Foundation Cambridge, Mass., MIT Press, 1992).

Zimmermann, K., 'Tätowierte Thrakerinnen auf Griechischen Vasenbildern', *Jdl* 95 (1980) 163–96.

INDEX

Note: Painters of Attic vases are indexed only in those cases where aspects of their style or theme are discussed.

Lightning Source UK Ltd.
Milton Keynes UK
UKOW07f0510040717
304626UK00009B/137/P

9 780415 232357